Integrating Governance and Corporate Social Responsibility in Employee Share Ownership

Zyed Achour
University of Carthage, Tunisia

IGI Global
Scientific Publishing
Publishing Tomorrow's Research Today

Vice President of Editorial	Melissa Wagner
Managing Editor of Acquisitions	Mikaela Felty
Managing Editor of Book Development	Jocelynn Hessler
Production Manager	Mike Brehm
Cover Design	Phillip Shickler

Published in the United States of America by
IGI Global Scientific Publishing
701 East Chocolate Avenue
Hershey, PA, 17033, USA
Tel: 717-533-8845
Fax: 717-533-8661
E-mail: cust@igi-global.com
Website: https://www.igi-global.com

Library of Congress Cataloging-in-Publication Data

Names: Achour, Zyed, 1966- editor.
Title: Integrating governance and corporate social responsibility in employee share ownership / edited by Zyed Achour.
Description: Hershey, PA : IGI Global, [2025] | Includes bibliographical references and index. | Summary: "This book aims to explore the multiple dimensions of employee ownership by conducting an in-depth exploration of its various facets, with a particular focus on its integration with corporate governance and corporate social responsibility"-- Provided by publisher.
Identifiers: LCCN 2024052901 (print) | LCCN 2024052902 (ebook) | ISBN 9798369370315 (hardcover) | ISBN 9798369370322 (paperback) | ISBN 9798369370339 (ebook)
Subjects: LCSH: Employee ownership. | Corporate governance. | Social responsibility of business.
Classification: LCC HD5650 .I57528 2025 (print) | LCC HD5650 (ebook) | DDC 658.3/225--dc23/eng/20241220
LC record available at https://lccn.loc.gov/2024052901
LC ebook record available at https://lccn.loc.gov/2024052902
ISBN:979-8-3693-7031-5
eISBN:979-8-3693-7033-9

British Cataloguing in Publication Data
A Cataloguing in Publication record for this book is available from the British Library.

Table of Contents

Detailed Table of Contents

on Indian publicly listed companies, highlighting their role in driving growth, financial performance, and transparency.

This chapter asks a foundational question: How and to what extent do employee shareowners benefit from holding an equity stake in their companies? Using the U.S. General Social Survey (GSS) it examines outcomes such as income, wealth, employment stability, fringe benefits, and retirement security. Additionally, it explores how likely employee shareowners are to participate in company-sponsored training, problem-solving teams, and decision-making processes. This chapter offers an update to previous studies that used GSS data. It embeds the findings within discussions of employment precarity and economic inequality, providing a framework for understanding how workplace arrangements are connected to democratic theory. To contextualize the results, the outcomes for employee shareowners are compared to those of traditional workers and union members. The chapter finds that employee share ownership offers benefits that surpass those of traditional workers and are comparable to, or greater than, those provided by union membership.

Over the past three decades, employee share ownership has gained traction in both industrialized and emerging economies, drawing interest from academics, policymakers, and practitioners (Dondi, 1992). This phenomenon has sparked significant interest across academic circles and among policymakers and business practitioners (Kuvaas, 2003; Pendleton et al., 1998).This chapter explores the synergies between Employee Share Ownership (ESO), corporate governance, and Corporate Social Responsibility (CSR), demonstrating how ESO can drive organizational performance and long-term value creation. By integrating agency theory and evidence-based research, it presents best practices for implementing ESO, analyzing its effects on employee engagement, financial performance, and sustainability while addressing potential challenges in stakeholder alignment.

Employee ownership represents a strategic approach that aligns the interests of employees with those of the organization through direct or indirect ownership stakes. This ownership can manifest in various forms, including employee stock ownership plans (ESOPs), stock options, and worker cooperatives, each offering unique benefits and implications for both employees and the organization. The fundamental idea behind employee ownership is to foster a deeper sense of commitment and responsibility among employees, leveraging their stake in the company's success to drive higher productivity, innovation, and job satisfaction. An ESOP is a prevalent model where employees are granted shares of the company, typically through a trust fund, which holds the shares on behalf of employees until they retire or leave the company. ESOPs can serve as both an employee benefit and a financial strategy for companies, providing a mechanism for business owners to sell their stake while retaining employee engagement and continuity.

This research develops a framework to assess the environmental and social benefits of employee ownership models. By reviewing literature, we identify factors that contribute to positive sustainability outcomes and examine supporting evidence. Our goal is to inform policymakers, business managers, and scholars seeking to advance sustainable and equitable business practices. Additionally, we will explore the potential challenges and limitations associated with employee ownership models, such as financial risks and governance issues. Our findings will provide practical recommendations for businesses and policymakers interested in implementing or enhancing employee ownership programs.

An Employee Stock Ownership Plan (ESOP) is a strategic welfare extended to the employees in a company in the form of sharing the profits and progress of a company. The managerial personnel who have decided to go for ESOP strategy have to decide about the centre for power of control in day-to-day business operations. Thus, corporate decision making is made crucial when ESOP is decided to be followed to strengthen the ownership of an enterprise. The main challenge in issuing ESOP is the dilution in the management. This chapter deals with the corporate social responsibility, corporate governance and tax implications associated with ESOP.

In France, over the years, employees have acquired an increasingly significant stake in the capital of their companies, often to the point of becoming a key shareholder group. French legislation has made it compulsory for employee shareholders to be represented on the board of directors once they collectively hold more than 3% of the capital. This chapter examines the effects of significant employee share ownership and the resulting board representation on the overall performance of the corporate governance system. The empirical results show that significant employee share ownership has positive effects on corporate governance. The results also show that employee shareholding representation on the board of directors has negative effects in terms of governance. These results suggest a number of recommendations that could help companies in their choice of ownership structure, and that could enlighten regulators about good governance practices.

From agency theory perspective, employee ownership is a decisive factor in reducing agency problem and it can improve firms' performance. In recent years many countries

Foreword

How can businesses redefine their governance models to address pressing economic inequalities while fostering innovation and sustainability? Employee share ownership offers a powerful answer, transcending its financial roots to become a paradigm of organizational transformation. In a world marked by unprecedented economic, social, and environmental challenges, this work, coordinated by Dr. Zyed Achour from the University of Carthage, invites us to fundamentally rethink the relationship between labor and capital.

The strength of this book lies in its remarkable geographical and intellectual diversity. Contributions come from an international panel of researchers and practitioners, spanning multiple continents. This plural approach provides a nuanced and comprehensive understanding of employee share ownership, highlighting its potential to transform organizations across different cultural and economic contexts.

Integrating Governance and Corporate Social Responsibility in Employee Share Ownership demonstrates how this model addresses crucial challenges: reducing economic inequalities, enhancing corporate social responsibility, and promoting more participative and democratic governance. The chapters explore the economic, social, and governance dimensions of this innovative concept, examining questions such as: How can employee share ownership align employee interests with those of the organization? How can it foster engagement, innovation, and long-term performance? And how does it contribute to a more ethical and sustainable vision of business?

By integrating these multiple perspectives, the book demonstrates that employee share ownership is not a one-size-fits-all solution but an adaptable and powerful framework. It offers a promising path to building more resilient, inclusive, and socially responsible organizations, capable of addressing the complex challenges of our time.

This book is more than an academic work. It provides an innovative reflection on corporate governance, placing employees at the heart of strategy and value creation.

Nicolas Aubert

Graduate School of Management, Aix-Marseille University, France & Institute for the Study of Employee Ownership and Profit Sharing, Rutgers University, USA

Preface

What if the future of business lay in the hands of its employees?

In a world of rapid transformation, where businesses face unprecedented economic, social, and environmental challenges, employee ownership emerges as a groundbreaking approach that redefines organizational dynamics. Far more than a mechanism for financial participation, it is a profound shift towards shared capitalism, integrating governance mechanisms and corporate social responsibility (CSR). This model seeks to bridge economic performance, social engagement, and environmental stewardship by empowering employees as active stakeholders in shaping their organization's strategic decisions and CSR initiatives. By combining ownership rights with governance participation, it provides a powerful framework for building sustainable and accountable businesses.

Integrating Governance and Corporate Social Responsibility in Employee Share Ownership explores this transformative model through 12 chapters, offering a comprehensive and multidimensional analysis. The strength of the volume lies in its international diversity, bringing together researchers and practitioners from across the globe. Contributors span diverse regions, including North America, Latin America, North Africa, and India, each offering unique perspectives on employee ownership, corporate governance, and social responsibility. Within Europe, France emerges as a focal point, with its well-established employee ownership models providing valuable insights into successful governance and CSR practices. This rich tapestry of backgrounds and expertise enables a nuanced examination of how employee ownership can be effectively integrated across different legal and cultural contexts, demonstrating its universal potential to create more sustainable, accountable, and inclusive organizations.

This book goes beyond theoretical discourse. It presents empirical evidence demonstrating how employee share ownership addresses the interconnected challenges of economic inequality, social responsibility, and environmental sustainability. It reveals the capacity of shared capitalism to foster inclusive, responsible, and adaptive business models that align employee interests with broader organizational and societal goals. For instance, case studies highlight how specific organizations have successfully integrated employee ownership with CSR, leading to tangible improvements in both financial performance and social impact.

Integrating Governance and Corporate Social Responsibility in Employee Share Ownership caters to a wide audience. Researchers will uncover robust theoretical frameworks bridging multiple disciplines. Practitioners will find actionable strategies for implementing innovative ownership models. Policymakers will gain insights into crafting legislative frameworks that promote more equitable economic structures. These combined perspectives underscore the versatility and transformative potential of employee ownership as a model for modern business.

The chapters collectively demonstrate that employee share ownership transcends its financial roots, offering a holistic approach to value creation that redefines the relationship between labor and capital. By fostering participatory governance and shared decision-making, it paves the way for more democratic, sustainable, and high-performance organizations. As businesses navigate increasingly complex economic and social landscapes, this model presents a viable and compelling pathway to inclusive growth and long-term resilience.

Let us now delve into the rich insights and perspectives presented in the chapters that follow and explore how this model can inspire the future of business ownership.

ORGANIZATION OF THE BOOK

Chapter 1: Towards a New Paradigm of Ownership: Employee Share Ownership as a Tool for Governance and CSR

This chapter examines the intricate relationship between ESO, corporate governance, and CSR in modern business environments. Drawing on recent theoretical developments and empirical evidence, it demonstrates how ESO can serve as a catalyst for transforming traditional corporate structures while addressing contemporary challenges of stakeholder management and sustainable business practices. The analysis explores five key theoretical perspectives—agency, stakeholder, human capital, economic democracy, and psychological ownership. The chapter reveals how ESO can enhance corporate governance by improving monitoring mechanisms and aligning stakeholder interests while simultaneously strengthening CSR practices through increased employee engagement and long-term orientation. Despite identifying several implementation challenges, including risk management and capital access issues, ESO represents a promising model for creating more equitable, sustainable, and successful business organizations, particularly when integrated with effective governance mechanisms and CSR initiatives.

Chapter 2: Aligning Corporate Governance with Employee Share Ownership for Value Creation

This chapter explores the integration of CSR and ESO as strategic levers for sustainable organizational success. Governance, by ensuring transparency and accountability, plays a key role in managing stakeholder interests. Employee share ownership programs align employee and shareholder interests, fostering motivation and long-term commitment. CSR strengthens corporate reputation by addressing social and environmental challenges. Drawing on case studies of Indian companies such as Tata Group and HDFC Bank, the chapter highlights how these combined elements drive growth, financial performance, and organizational resilience. An integrated approach promotes an ethical, innovative, and long-term-oriented corporate culture, essential for meeting stakeholder expectations in a complex and evolving economic environment.

Chapter 3: Exploring the Benefits of Employee Share Ownership

This study explores how ESO can serve as an effective institutional arrangement to address rising economic inequality and employment precarity in the United States. Drawing on data from the U.S. General Social Survey, this chapter provides a comprehensive comparison between employee-owners and union members across various economic and workplace outcomes. The analysis demonstrates that employee ownership offers benefits comparable to or exceeding those of union membership, including enhanced income, wealth accumulation, employment stability, and workplace participation. What makes this chapter particularly relevant is its examination of employee ownership as a politically viable alternative, enjoying bipartisan support unlike many other policy proposals aimed at reducing economic inequality. The chapter begins by establishing the theoretical framework connecting workplace arrangements to democratic theory, then presents empirical findings on the benefits of employee ownership, and concludes by discussing policy implications and recent legislative initiatives at various governmental levels. This analysis contributes to broader discussions about workplace democracy and economic inequality by highlighting an often-overlooked but promising approach to improving workers' economic security and participation.

Chapter 4: Synergizing Employee Share Ownership with Corporate Governance and CSR: Pathways to Enhanced Organizational Performance and Sustainable Value Creation

This chapter examines the transformative potential of integrating ESO, corporate governance, and CSR to enhance organizational performance and promote sustainable value creation. It underscores how ESO fosters employee engagement and alignment with corporate goals, while CSR initiatives drive ethical and social accountability, forming a robust foundation for long-term growth. Drawing from comprehensive research and theoretical frameworks, the chapter illuminates the synergies between these elements, highlighting their collective ability to balance economic performance with social and environmental priorities. By offering actionable insights into the practical integration of ESO, governance frameworks, and CSR, this work serves as a vital resource for organizations seeking to navigate the evolving landscape of stakeholder capitalism, emphasizing sustainability and inclusive growth as essential components of modern corporate strategy.

Chapter 5: Influence of Employee Ownership on Environmental and Social Sustainability

The chapter explores the impact of employee ownership, particularly through models like Employee Stock Ownership Plans (ESOPs), on governance, CSR, and business sustainability. By aligning employee interests with organizational goals, these models enhance engagement, motivation, and innovation. The chapter also examines how employee ownership contributes to environmental and social sustainability by promoting responsible practices such as waste reduction, adoption of renewable energy, and social inclusion. Highlighting the benefits, challenges, and implications of various ownership models, it showcases their potential to transform businesses into responsible and sustainable entities while improving organizational performance and community impact.

Chapter 6: A Framework for Assessing the Environmental and Social Benefits of Employee Ownership

This chapter examines the development of a robust framework for assessing the environmental and social benefits of employee ownership. It synthesizes existing literature to identify the key elements within employee ownership models that contribute to sustainability outcomes, including energy efficiency, waste management, and community engagement. By applying theories such as stakeholder and agency theory, the chapter connects employee involvement with improved governance and long-term environmental stewardship. Furthermore, it addresses the challenges of data collection and proposes metrics aligned with global sustainability standards, offering insights for policymakers and practitioners aiming to enhance corporate social responsibility through employee ownership.

Chapter 7: Employee Stock Ownership: Demystifying Corporate Social Responsibility and Taxation in India

This chapter explores the integration of corporate governance and CSR within employee stock ownership plans (ESOPs). Initially developed by Louis Kelso in 1956, ESOPs aim to align the interests of employees with those of shareholders while rewarding employees for their contributions to a company's success. The study examines the legal and tax frameworks surrounding ESOPs in India, their role in motivating and retaining talent, and boosting productivity. It also highlights the importance of transparent governance and social responsibility to maximize the benefits of ESOPs. By integrating these principles, companies foster employee engagement and long-term goal achievement, strengthening their competitive advantage.

Chapter 8: Significant Employee Share Ownership and Corporate Governance: Evidence from French Firms

This study delves into the intricate dynamics between significant employee share ownership and corporate governance, focusing on its impact within the unique French context. As France leads Europe in employee shareholder representation, the findings are particularly compelling, shedding light on the nuanced interplay between ownership structures, governance practices, and performance. By analyzing a robust dataset from listed French firms over a decade, the study uncovers pivotal insights into how significant employee shareholding can enhance governance performance while also revealing challenges, such as potential managerial entrenchment. The research emphasizes the importance of thresholds, showing that ownership above certain levels leads to more participative and effective governance frameworks. As employee ownership continues to shape debates on corporate governance worldwide, this chapter not only contributes to academic discourse but also provides actionable insights for policymakers, practitioners, and organizations striving for sustainable and equitable governance models.

Chapter 9: Comparing Employee Ownership Models in Iran and Western Economies: Bridging Perspectives

This chapter provides a comparative analysis of employee ownership models across various countries, with a particular focus on the differences between Iran's Preferred Shares scheme and Western approaches, such as ESOPs in the U.S., PEEs in France, SLs in Spain, and EOTs in the UK. It highlights how employee ownership can mitigate agency problems, improve corporate performance, and enhance social responsibility. Employing a systematic literature review (SLR) alongside an analysis of Iran's constitutional and trade laws, the chapter synthesizes findings from academic studies, legal frameworks, and interviews with policymakers. This methodological rigor ensures a comprehensive evaluation of employee ownership's effectiveness, drawing practical insights for refining governance mechanisms and advocating for a more robust legal framework in Iran to promote inclusive and sustainable corporate practices.

Chapter 10: Does Employee Share Ownership Enhance the Financial Performance of Moroccan Companies Listed on the Casablanca Stock Exchange?

This study investigates the impact of ESO on the financial performance of Moroccan companies listed on the Casablanca Stock Exchange, employing a rigorous empirical methodology. The analysis is based on panel data collected from annual reports and financial statements over the period 2017–2023, using the Estimated Generalized Least Squares (EGLS) method. Two key financial indicators, Return on Equity (ROE) and Return on Assets (ROA), are examined to assess the relationship between ESO adoption and company performance. By comparing firms that implement ESO plans with those that do not, the study provides valuable insights into how this practice can influence profitability and organizational dynamics. The chapter highlights the nuances of ESO's effectiveness in an emerging market context, offering a methodological framework for future research and practical guidance for decision-makers seeking to leverage employee ownership as a driver of sustainable growth.

Chapter 11: The Impact of Employee Share Ownership on Corporate Governance and Performance: A Psychological Mediation Analysis

This chapter delves into the intricate relationship between ESO and organizational outcomes. By examining the mediating role of psychological factors such as perceived ownership, job satisfaction, and engagement, this study sheds light on how ESO fosters participatory governance and enhances organizational performance. Based on a comprehensive analysis involving Tunisian employees, the study highlights the transformative potential of ESO in aligning employee and organizational interests. This contribution not only enriches the understanding of ESO's influence on corporate dynamics but also offers actionable insights for implementing governance strategies that prioritize employee engagement and shared decision-making.

Chapter 12: Challenges and Opportunities for Sharing the Ownership in Peru

This chapter explores the challenges and opportunities associated with implementing employee ownership mechanisms in the Peruvian context, within an emerging economy facing certain institutional obstacles. The study builds on the idea of shared capitalism and talks about the structural, cultural, and institutional problems that make it hard for these ideas to become mainstream. These problems include a lack of trust among stakeholders, weak institutions, and the long-standing effects of centralized and hierarchical corporate governance. At the same time, the analysis identifies opportunities, particularly in the role of family businesses, multinational corporations, and social enterprises, which could act as pioneers in integrating these mechanisms into their management models. Through an in-depth examination of local institutional dynamics, the chapter calls for rethinking collaboration between businesses, government, and civil society to foster a more inclusive and sustainable economic environment.

In conclusion, *Integrating Governance and Corporate Social Responsibility in Employee Share Ownership* presents a comprehensive and forward-thinking vision for reshaping corporate governance. By combining rigorous theoretical foundations, practical organizational insights, and diverse regional perspectives, it offers a roadmap for embedding social responsibility into business practices and fostering more inclusive ownership models. This book challenges conventional labor relations and governance structures, encouraging readers to envision businesses as engines of equity, sustainability, and innovation. We invite you to engage with the ideas presented in these chapters and join the ongoing effort to redefine business ownership for a more inclusive and resilient future.

Zyed Achour
University of Carthage, Tunisia

Acknowledgment

The editor extends sincere thanks to all contributors to this project, particularly the authors and reviewers. The IGI Global team's professional support and guidance throughout the publication process have been invaluable.

A special acknowledgment to **Professor Nicolas Aubert** from *Aix-Marseille University Graduate School of Management, Faculty Fellow and Mentor, Institute for the Study of Employee Ownership and Profit Sharing, Rutgers University,* who kindly agreed to sign the foreword of this volume.

Profound gratitude is expressed to the distinguished members of the editorial advisory board:

Dr. **Wajdi Ben Rejeb**, *University of Lincoln, UK*

Dr. **Mark J. Kaswan**, *University of Texas Rio Grande Valley, USA*

Dr. **Zakeya Sanad**, *Ahlia University, Kingdom of Bahrain*

Their meticulous contributions were crucial in enhancing the quality, consistency, and presentation of the chapters, ensuring the highest standard of scholarly review.

A special tribute to Professor **Abdelwahed Omri**, *Head of the GEF2A Laboratory, University of Tunis*.

Heartfelt thanks to all.

Zyed Achour

Chapter 1
Towards a New Paradigm of Ownership:
Employee Share Ownership as a Tool for Governance and CSR

Zyed Achour
https://orcid.org/0000-0002-1578-9062
University of Carthage, Tunisia

Mark Kaswan
https://orcid.org/0000-0001-8092-2360
University of Texas Rio Grande Valley, USA

Wajdi Ben Rejeb
https://orcid.org/0000-0002-9454-0280
University of Lincoln, UK

ABSTRACT

Employee Share Ownership (ESO) is emerging as a model redefining corporate ownership and labor relations, within the broader context of "shared capitalism." Despite growing research, gaps remain in understanding its relationship with corporate governance and Corporate Social Responsibility (CSR). This chapter explores how ESO aligns employee interests with organizational goals, enhances governance, and fosters sustainable business models. It examines the theoretical foundations of ESO, its impact on governance, and its role in promoting CSR, addressing both benefits and challenges. The chapter also considers how ESO re-defines capitalism and property rights, pushing towards more inclusive economic models. Finally, it discusses the integration of ESO with governance and CSR, and future research directions, highlighting its potential to create more equitable and

DOI: 10.4018/979-8-3693-7031-5.ch001

responsible organizations.

INTRODUCTION

In an ever-evolving economic landscape in which factors other than firm financial performance have begun to take on increasing importance, employee share ownership (ESO) is emerging as a promising model, redefining traditional notions of corporate ownership and labor relations. This phenomenon is part of the broader concept of "shared capitalism," which encompasses various forms of employee participation in company ownership and profits. Recent statistics attest to the growing importance of employee share ownership on a global scale:

- In the United States, according to the National Center for Employee Ownership (2021), over 25 million employees participate in employee share ownership plans in various forms, and total contributions to ESOP accounts exceeded $101 billion.[1]
- In Europe, the European Federation of Employee Share Ownership (2021) reports that over 7 million employees own shares in their companies, with a total value exceeding 400 billion Euros.[2]
- In Japan, about 90% of publicly listed companies offer employee share ownership plans (Tokyo Stock Exchange, 2020).[3]
- In emerging countries, employee share ownership is gaining ground, with for example over 12 million participants in India (ESOP Association India, 2020)[4].

These figures illustrate the scale of the phenomenon and its potential to transform the global economic landscape, justifying the proliferation of academic research, both empirical and theoretical, in this area. However, despite the growing body of research on Employee Share Ownership (ESO), there remains a significant gap in our understanding of how ESO interacts with and influences corporate governance and Corporate Social Responsibility (CSR) practices. While studies have examined these elements separately, there is a lack of comprehensive research that integrates all three aspects - ESO, governance, and CSR - and explores their synergies and potential conflicts. This gap is particularly pronounced in the context of fundamental management theories, which have not been sufficiently leveraged to understand this new paradigm of shared ownership.

These theories originated in Western contexts, where economic conditions, cultural values, conceptions of the corporation, and organizational design emphasize competition, the primacy of shareholders' interests, and individualism. These principles often conflict with the core tenets of shared ownership, which emphasize collective responsibility and collaboration. Additionally, although the agency theory emerged over fifty years ago, it continues to dominate academic research on corporate governance. This theory has been criticized for prioritizing the relationship between shareholders and management, reducing the complexity of human relationships and motivation factors, and often neglecting the role of employees as stakeholders (Ghoshal, 2005; Huse, 2003; Panda and Leepa, 2017).

This chapter aims to address these gaps by providing a comprehensive analysis of the interplay between ESO, corporate governance, and CSR. By doing so, we seek to contribute to both the theoretical understanding of these concepts and their practical application in modern business environments.

Understanding this interplay is crucial as it intersects with the broader concept of shared capitalism, which emphasizes the significant role of employees as stakeholders in the company's success. Indeed, the concept of "shared capitalism" (Blasi et al., 2006; Freeman et al., 2010) goes beyond mere financial participation. It represents a vision where employees are considered essential stakeholders, sharing not only in the benefits but also in the responsibilities and decision-making power within the company. This approach is based on the idea that aligning interests between employees and the company can lead to increased performance, better governance, and enhanced social responsibility.

This chapter explores how employee share ownership, as a key component of shared capitalism, can serve as a powerful tool for integrating principles of good governance and corporate social responsibility (CSR), while rethinking the classic paradigm of capitalist ownership. We aim to demonstrate how employee share ownership can serve as catalysts for a more equitable, responsible, and sustainable business model, paving the way for a new ownership paradigm for the 21st century. By the same token, however, it must be recognized that shared capitalism is not a panacea, for reasons we will make clear throughout.

The remainder of the chapter is organized as follows: Section 1 discusses the implications of ESO for capitalism and property rights. Section 2 explores the theoretical foundations of employee share ownership and shared capitalism. Section 3 examines the impact of ESO on corporate governance. Section 3 investigates the role of ESO in promoting Corporate Social Responsibility. Section 4 addresses the challenges and opportunities presented by the integration of ESO with governance and CSR practices. Finally, Section 5 concludes the chapter by synthesizing key findings, discussing theoretical and managerial implications, and suggesting directions for future research in this field. Through this structure, we aim to provide a comprehensive analysis of the complex interplay between ESO, corporate governance, and CSR in the modern business landscape.

1. CAPITALISM AND PROPERTY RIGHTS IN THE CONTEXT OF EMPLOYEE SHARE OWNERSHIP

The rise of Employee Share Ownership (ESO) has prompted a re-examination of traditional notions of capitalism and property rights, reshaping these fundamental concepts in the modern business landscape.

The concept of property rights is fundamental in modern economic systems, allowing individuals and businesses to own, use, and transfer assets. In a standard limited liability company, shareholders have three ownership rights: to control, to profits and to capital gains (Mygind and Poulsen, 2021).

However, this traditional view of ownership is often criticized for contributing to economic inequality. In this context, employee ownership emerges as an innovative solution, redefining property rights to include workers in the ownership structure of companies. By enabling employees to become co-owners, this model promotes a more equitable distribution of wealth generated by businesses while enhancing workers' engagement and accountability towards their companies.

There are various forms and degrees of employee ownership, ranging from partial ownership with small minority positions to full ownership. These variations are based on employees' access to the three owner rights.

Arguments for employee ownership to ensure a fairer economic system have been put forward for a long time, dating at least as far back as John Stuart Mill's *Principles of Political Economy* (1909), in which he says that the "probable future of the laboring classes" will inevitably include workers owning the means of production. Before him, William Thompson (1824) argued that workers should be recognized as having an inherent right to the produce of their labor—not the people who provide capital (see Kaswan, 2014).

Alperovitz (2011) includes employee ownership as a key element of what he refers to as "community wealth building," which seeks to create an economy where businesses are firmly rooted in the communities where they operate. When workers own their company, he argues, they are more likely to retain wealth in their community and use their assets to benefit the community. In addition to addressing the problems of inequality that have already been mentioned, worker-owners are also much less likely to engage in offshoring or engage in a "race to the bottom" in pursuit of profit.

Sarkar, in his 2024 book "Common Good Capitalism: A New Economic Model for Growth to Benefit Business and Society", emphasizes that employee ownership is essential for transforming capitalism into a fairer system. This model advocates for significant employee stakes in companies, which not only provides financial incentives but also gives workers a voice in decision-making processes. Such an approach fosters an inclusive capitalism where property rights are extended to serve the common good. By integrating workers into the decision-making framework and sharing profits, employee ownership creates a synergy between property rights and collective well-being, paving the way for a more just and sustainable economic future.

Bryson et al. (2019) found that broad-based ESO schemes can lead to more equitable wealth distribution and contribute to inclusive economic growth, supporting the concept of "shared capitalism". Ferreras (2021) proposed the idea of "democratic firm ownership," arguing that ESO represents a shift towards a more participatory model of corporate ownership, challenging traditional views of property rights. Noteworthy is that Ferreras, (2022), in pointing out the shortcomings of the ESOP model in the U.S., argues for a "decoupling" of the question of worker participation in governance from the question of the ownership of property.

Stout (2019) positioned ESO as a practical implementation of stakeholder capitalism, arguing that it aligns with stakeholder principles by giving employees a direct stake in the company's success. Thomas et al. (2021) explored how ESO contributes to "asset-based egalitarianism," emphasizing the importance of widespread asset ownership for reducing economic inequality. De Angelis (2021) drew parallels between ESO and the concept of the commons, viewing it as a form of "commoning" within corporate structures.

Yermack (2020) examined how blockchain technology could facilitate more decentralized forms of corporate ownership, including expansive ESO schemes. Wolff (2021) argued that broad-based ESO schemes represent a step towards economic democracy, challenging traditional capitalist power structures within corporations. Carberry and Meyers (2022) explored how ESO might shape the future of work, particularly in the context of increasing automation and the gig economy.

These studies highlight how ESO is challenging and reshaping traditional concepts of capitalism and property rights. They demonstrate that ESO has the potential to contribute to a more inclusive, democratic, and equitable economic system. In essence, employee share ownership emerges as a transformative force in modern capitalism, fostering a more participatory and egalitarian approach to ownership and wealth distribution. This evolution in the concept of property rights and corporate ownership paves the way for a new economic paradigm that balances profitability with social equity and democratic principles in the workplace.

2. THEORETICAL PERSPECTIVES ON EMPLOYEE SHARE OWNERSHIP

Employee share ownership (ESO) is grounded in several economic and social theories that challenge traditional models of corporate ownership and management. These theories provide a multifaceted framework for understanding the complex dynamics of ESO and its potential impacts on corporate governance and corporate social responsibility (CSR). In this section, we review five key theoretical perspectives that have significantly contributed to our understanding of ESO: Agency Theory, Stakeholder Theory, Human Capital Theory, Economic Democracy Theory, and Psychological Ownership Theory. Recent research has deepened these theoretical foundations, offering new insights into the potential of ESO in modern business contexts.

First, agency theory, developed by Meckling and Jensen (1976), posits that corporate managers may act in their own interest to the detriment of shareholders, creating a conflict of interest. The introduction of employees as shareholders changes this governance dynamic and can lead to two potential scenarios regarding the impact on the classic principal-agent conflict. In one scenario, power could shift in favor of outside shareholders through two main mechanisms. First, employees, due to their daily proximity to management, gain better visibility into managerial performance and decisions, which they can communicate to other shareholders, allowing shareholders to exercise more effective control over managers. Second, employee-shareholders, exposed to undiversified risk by investing both their human and financial capital in the company, are strongly incentivized to closely monitor management's actions, a task that is more costly for outside shareholders. According to Cha (2014), these two channels -improved information and increased monitoring incentives- align employee interests with those of external shareholders, reducing managerial entrenchment and excessive compensation. However, there is also the possibility that employees might align themselves with management against shareholders, either out of fear for their jobs or in exchange for benefits, or simply because their greater proximity to management will lead them to adopt management's perspective. From an agency theory perspective, managers can strategically use ESOPs as part of an entrenchment strategy to enhance their reputation and gain external attention (O'Boyle et al., 2016), dilute shareholder influence, create a friendly shareholder base, and shield themselves from hostile takeovers (Park and Song, 1995). By distributing ownership among employees, managers can gain their loyalty and make hostile takeovers more challenging, as potential acquirers would face greater difficulty gaining control of the company. This unique position of employees, both as workers and capital holders, gives them a crucial but complex role in the dynamics of corporate governance. It should be noted, however, that just because they are owners does not mean that employees are given a role in governance. As Kaswan (2022) shows, ESOP regulations in the U.S. do not require that employees have meaningful voice in their company's governance and, in fact, their views may be overridden by a trustee who must use their judgment to determine what is in the best interests of the employees.

Recent studies have deepened our understanding of how ESO addresses agency problems. For instance, Aubert et al. (2017) explored the impact of ESO on agency costs, highlighting that ESO can reduce these costs by enhancing transparency and communication within organizations. Their research indicates that when employees have ownership stakes in the company, they are more likely to align their interests with those of shareholders, thereby mitigating the typical conflicts that arise between management and owners. Indeed, ESO gives employees a vested interest in their firms' long-term health, which fosters accountability, reduces managerial myopia, and encourages employees to support decisions that benefit both them and external shareholders. This increased transparency fosters a sense of ownership and accountability among employees, aligning their interests more closely with those of the organization. The findings of Cardoni and Poulain-Rehmet (2023), based on a study of 10 French companies with employee shareholder representation in governance bodies, are more ambiguous. They find that the dual nature of the "profit sharing and power sharing" role appears to influence disciplinary, partnership, cognitive, and behavioral levels. However, the authors emphasize the complexity of this phenomenon, noting that the presence of a director representing employee shareholders could generate tensions and dynamics of managerial entrenchment because of the risk differentials between employees and traditional shareholders. With respect to corporate social responsibility, Kong et al. (2024) provide evidence that ESOPs enhance communication between management and employees, which reduces information asymmetry and leads to more sustainable corporate practices.

Stakeholder theory is an alternate approach that broadens the agency theory perspective by considering the impact of ESO on a wider range of stakeholders. This shift in focus provides a more comprehensive understanding of how ESO can influence not only internal organizational dynamics but also the company's relationships with external stakeholders. Stakeholder theory, as proposed by Freeman (1984), has evolved significantly, particularly in its application to ESO. Recent work by Crane et al. (2019) explored how ESO can serve as an effective mechanism for balancing the interests of various stakeholders, particularly in the context of CSR. Their research demonstrates that employee-owners often exhibit a heightened awareness of broader stakeholder concerns, leading to more socially responsible decision-making. As ESo makes employees more invested in the firm's long-term performance and reputation, they are likely to push for initiatives that balance financial performance with other performance dimensions, benefiting both the business and its broader network of stakeholders. Blasi (2016) shows how ESOPs can create mutual gains for employees, shareholders, and other stakeholders by increasing productivity, profitability, and employee wealth. The findings suggest that ESOPs can promote a stakeholder-oriented approach when implemented effectively. This alignment can create a more holistic approach to corporate governance, where the wellbeing of employees, customers, and communities is considered alongside shareholder returns. Furthermore, this enhanced stakeholder engagement can lead to improved reputation, customer loyalty, and long-term sustainability. In a report on a large-scale qualitative and quantitative study of low and moderate-income workers in ESOPs, Boguslaw and Schur (2019) show that the improved financial conditions of the employees extended significant benefits for their families and their communities by giving the workers higher wages, greater financial stability, and the ability to build a nest-egg for retirement. Third, Human Capital Theory, originally developed by Becker (1964), has been significantly extended in the context of ESO. Recent work by Blasi et al. (2018) has applied this theory to the knowledge economy era, emphasizing how ESO can be a powerful tool for attracting, retaining, and motivating talent in knowledge-intensive industries. Kurtulus and Kruse (2017) provided empirical evidence supporting the positive relationship between ESO and human capital investment. Building on this foundation, Kim and Patel (2017) brought a cross-cultural perspective to the discussion, showing how the impact of ESO on human capital development can vary across cultural contexts. More recently, Bao et al. (2020) examined how ESO interacts with other high-performance work practices to enhance employee engagement and organizational performance, further demonstrating the role of ESO in cultivating and leveraging human capital within modern organizations.

Fourth, Economic Democracy Theory, originally conceptualized by Dahl (1985), has seen significant developments in recent years, particularly in relation to ESO. Expanding on a theme first articulated by William Thompson in the early 19th century (see Kaswan, 2014), economic democracy is based on the idea that workers have an inherent right to the produce of their labor. As argued by Ellerman (1992), workers' right to a role in the governance of their firm based on the labor they contribute to it is stronger than that of the owners of capital. Ferreras (2017) proposed the concept of "economic bicameralism," envisioning a corporate governance structure where employee-shareholders would have a chamber of representation equal to that of traditional shareholders. Building on these concepts, Mayer (2020) introduced the idea of the "purpose-driven corporation," which proposes a model where ESO plays a central role in aligning corporate objectives with societal goals. This approach integrates elements of economic democracy with broader corporate purposes. Edmans (2020) further explored how this alignment can lead to long-term value creation, demonstrating how ESO can serve as a practical mechanism for implementing more democratic and socially responsible forms of corporate governance.

Finally, Psychological Ownership Theory, building on Pierce and Jussila's (2011) seminal work, has been further explored and expanded in recent studies. This theory posits that individuals can develop feelings of ownership towards non-physical entities, such as organizations or jobs. In the context of ESO, Olckers and Du Plessis

(2020) examined how psychological ownership mediates the relationship between ESO and organizational commitment in different cultural contexts, highlighting the importance of cultural factors in shaping ownership perceptions. Complementing this research, Brown et al. (2019) investigated the role of psychological ownership in fostering innovative behaviors among employee-owners, finding a strong positive correlation. Furthermore, Liu et al. (2021) explored how psychological ownership interacts with formal ownership structures to influence employee attitudes and behaviors, revealing complex interactions between legal and psychological forms of ownership. These studies collectively demonstrate the critical role of psychological factors in realizing the full potential of ESO programs and underscore the importance of cultivating a sense of ownership beyond mere financial participation.

These five theoretical perspectives provide a rich and diverse foundation for understanding the multifaceted nature of employee share ownership. Each theory offers unique insights into how ESO can influence organizational behavior, decision-making processes, and stakeholder relationships. Collectively, they underscore the potential of ESO as a powerful tool for enhancing corporate governance and promoting corporate social responsibility. As we move forward in this chapter, these theoretical underpinnings will inform our analysis of how ESO can be effectively implemented as a mechanism for governance and CSR in modern corporations. Table 1 provides an overview of the main theoretical perspectives on employee ownership.

Table 1. Theoretical perspectives of employee share ownership

Theory	Pros (+)	Cons (-)
Agency Theory	Interest alignment Reduced agency cost Long term decision making	Risk differentials Potential for managerial entrenchment
Stakeholder Theory	Balanced interests Holistic governance Stakeholder engagement	Prioritization of employee interests over other stakeholders Convoluted decision making
Human Capital Theory	Talent retention Knowledge economy Employee development	Risk aversion among employees Free riding problems
Economic Democracy Theory	Economic bicameralism Worker self-direction Purpose-driven corporation	Increased governance and decision making complexities Tension between democratic participation and efficiency
Psychological Ownership Theory	Organizational commitment Innovative behavior Cultural Context	Overconfidence and resistance to change

(Source: Authors)

3. CORPORATE GOVERNANCE AND EMPLOYEE SHARE OWNERSHIP

The intersection of employee share ownership (ESO) and corporate governance has garnered growing interest in recent years, fundamentally reshaping governance structures and practices. The growth of ESO, where employees hold a significant or total share of a company's stock, carries with it the potential for significant changes in modern corporate governance, as even non-ESO companies may feel pressure to offer employees some role in governance in order to more effectively compete with ESOs for top employees. It must be recognized, however, that while this model offers substantial benefits, it also presents unique challenges that shape how companies are managed.

As was shown in the discussion of agency theory, one of the primary advantages of ESO is its ability to align the interests of employees with those of the company. As shareholders, employees are directly motivated to contribute to the company's success, as their financial well-being is tied to its performance. This alignment may foster a more cohesive corporate culture, where employees are driven to work collaboratively toward shared goals. For instance, the John Lewis Partnership in the UK has demonstrated that ESO can lead to higher job satisfaction, improved talent retention, and stronger loyalty to the company (Taylor; 1992).

Moreover, ESO can enhance job stability, as employee-owners are often inclined to support decisions that ensure the long-term sustainability of the business, even during economic downturns. This can result in fewer layoffs and greater job security, contributing to a more stable work environment (Mygind, and Poulsen; 2021). However, this assumes that employees are given meaningful opportunities to have input into decisions that affect them.

Recent research has further explored how ESO enhances shareholder democracy by giving employees a voice in corporate affairs. Abdelhamid (2021) found that companies with significant employee ownership tend to have more robust internal control mechanisms and improved information flow between management and employees. Gregorič and Poulsen (2020) observed that employee board representation increases board diversity and enriches decision-making by bringing unique perspectives that consider broader stakeholder interests. Blasi and Kruse (2019) argued that ESO can mitigate short-termism in corporate governance by aligning employee interests with long-term success, encouraging investment in sustainable practices.

Additionally, studies by Kurtulus and Kruse (2018) showed that companies with ESO exhibited greater resilience during economic downturns, while Landau et al. (2020) noted that broad-based ESO often leads to more equitable compensation structures; including lower CEO-to-worker pay ratios. Boubaker and Nguyen (2021) linked ESO to reduced information asymmetry and greater corporate transparency through more comprehensive and frequent disclosures.

Stout and Blair (2021) positioned ESO as a practical application of stakeholder governance theory, suggesting it represents a shift toward a more inclusive model that balances the interests of multiple stakeholders. Fatemi et al. (2018) found that firms with substantial employee ownership tend to exhibit stronger CSR practices, indicating that ESO can align governance with broader societal responsibilities.

These studies collectively highlight the multifaceted impact of ESO on corporate governance, illustrating its potential as a tool for enhancing governance practices, aligning stakeholder interests, and promoting sustainable, responsible business models. This demonstrates the potential for ESO as a powerful catalyst for transforming corporate governance, fostering a more democratic, transparent, and long-term oriented approach. This synergy between ESO and corporate governance sets the stage for a new management paradigm that reconciles the interests of employees, shareholders, and society at large.

However, this model is not without its challenges. Mainstream economic thinking suggests that employee ownership will lead to underinvestment, as employee owners may be reluctant to invest in expensive or long-term projects if it means reducing their immediate income. The research on this is mixed. For example, some industrial cooperatives in Italy have struggled to raise funds for major investments, limiting their ability to innovate or grow (Ammirato, 2018). However, Adwan and Ahamed (2024) show that ownership by non-executive employees can lead to greater investment efficiency—in other words, companies are more likely to avoid both over- and underinvesting.

Another challenge is the potential volatility of compensation. While having a stable job might be advantageous, employee-owned businesses may see larger salary and bonus fluctuations than traditional ones, particularly in the event of unsatisfactory financial performance. This can create financial insecurity for employees, even as it increases the stability of their employment (Kurtulus & Kruse, 2017).

Finally, in industries that require high capital investments, employee-owned businesses may be at a disadvantage relative to their competitors. Difficulty raising capital for major investments can limit their ability to grow and remain competitive, especially in sectors such as manufacturing or technology. However, the Mondragon cooperatives, which include their own financial institution, are a clear exception. As Arando, et al. (2010) show, their levels of investment are higher than for investor-owned firms in Spain, and their levels of investment were "much less sensitive to the business cycle."

The biggest challenge for employee ownership (ESO) in relation to corporate governance lies in the limited opportunities for employees to actively participate in the governance of their organizations. The balance between labor and capital is managed differently across countries, leading to diverse configurations regarding the interplay between ESO and employees' roles in corporate governance.

Countries with strong labor traditions, such as Germany and the Nordic nations, focus more on collaboration between labor and capital than on ownership. In these countries, governance structures emphasize employee participation through legal or institutional frameworks like codetermination in Germany or collective bargaining in the Nordic nations. These systems are designed to give employees a significant role in decision-making without the need for widespread employee share ownership (Kang and Moon, 2012). This approach has resulted in a lower tendency to use ESO as a tool to align employees' interests with capital owners, since employee governance influence is already embedded in the corporate structure through other mechanisms.

In contrast, countries like the United States and the United Kingdom primarily focus on ESO as a financial incentive to align the interests of employees with shareholders. However, ESO in these countries does not typically grant employees a substantial role in governance. In the U.S., ESOPs are popular, but their structure often leaves employees with little say in the company's strategic decisions (Kaswan; 2022).

In the U.S. ESOPs are organized as benefit trusts, and employees technically have shares in the trust, which owns all of or a share of the company and is managed by a trustee. The trustee is usually selected by the board of directors, not the employees, which often take on the role of trustee themselves. Federal law requires that employees be able to vote on major strategic decisions, such as acquisitions or the sale of the company, but their vote may be overridden by the trustee if, in their fiduciary capacity, they believe that the decision of the employees is not, in fact, in their best interests. As Kaswan (2022) argues, in such ESOPs the employees only are owners in a technical sense—they own a share of the company—but they lack any meaningful role in governance.

France offers a more balanced model that integrates ESO with employee participation in governance. In French companies, when employee ownership surpasses a threshold of 3%, the company is legally required to offer employee representation on the board of directors (Hollandts and Aubert, 2011). This framework ensures that employee shareholders have both financial incentives and a voice in corporate decision-making, aligning labor and capital interests more effectively. France's model reflects a blended approach, where ESO serves not only as a financial mechanism but also as a way to formally include employees in the governance of their organizations.

In conclusion, employee ownership offers interesting prospects for corporate governance, by strengthening employee engagement and aligning their interests with those of the company. Where employees are given a role in governance their impact can be quite positive, but not all employee-owned companies provide them with that opportunity.

4. CORPORATE SOCIAL RESPONSIBILITY AND EMPLOYEE SHARE OWNERSHIP

The intersection between employee ownership (ESO) and corporate social responsibility (CSR) has attracted considerable attention in recent years. Research has explored how ESO influences and enhances CSR practices and outcomes, revealing a complex and multifaceted relationship that offers both opportunities and challenges for organizations (Rehman et al., 2022; Onkila & Sarna, 2022). Drawing on the empirical literature, we first provide a comprehensive overview of the key mechanisms through which ESO impacts CSR. In a second section, we provide a nuanced perspective on the relationship between employee ownership and corporate social responsibility.

Key Mechanisms of Employee Share Ownership's Influence on Corporate Social Responsibility

First, employee-owners tend to be more engaged in and supportive of their company's CSR efforts, leading to more effective implementation of CSR strategies (Achour, 2024). The alignment of interests between employees and the company fosters a sense of shared responsibility for the organization's social and environmental impact. Moreover, the long-term perspective often associated with employee ownership can drive more sustainable decision-making. Sun and Liu (2023) demonstrated this in their study of ESO plans in China, which were associated with improved corporate environmental performance through enhanced productivity and green technology adoption.

Second, several studies support the idea that broad-based ESO strengthens a company's ties to its local community and enhances its ethical practices (Blasi & Kruse, 2019). Companies with ESO are often more involved in community development initiatives, reflecting the employees' personal investment in both the company and the community where they live and work. Research on Employee Stock Ownership Plans (ESOPs) and worker cooperatives also shows how employee ownership promotes transparency and ethical conduct within organizations (Novkovic & Webb, 2014; Brolis, 2018). McCarthy et al. (2010) found that companies with substantial employee ownership tend to have stronger ethical cultures and are less likely to engage in corporate misconduct. The Moral DNA of Employee-Owned Companies study (Steare et al., 2015) further explored the impact of employee ownership on ethical standards and behavior within companies. The findings suggest that shared ownership fosters a culture of collective responsibility, thereby reinforcing ethical behaviors among employees.

Third, ESO can have a positive impact on labor rights and working conditions. Poutsma et al. (2020) suggested that companies with ESO schemes tend to have better working conditions and stronger protections for labor rights. This improvement can be seen as a natural outcome of employees "having a voice" in company decisions and a share in its profits.

Another important aspect of CSR influenced by ESO is diversity and inclusion. Kruse et al. (2019) found that companies with broad-based ESO tend to have more diverse workforces and are more likely to implement effective inclusion policies. This could be due to the more democratic nature of decision-making in employee-owned companies.

Similarly, the influence of ESO can extend beyond the confines of the organization. Mao et al. (2021) discovered that companies with significant employee ownership are more likely to implement and enforce responsible supply chain practices.

Finally, in terms of overall Environmental, Social, and Governance (ESG) performance, Barzuza et al. (2020) found that companies with substantial employee ownership tend to have better ESG scores and are more likely to prioritize long-term sustainability over short-term gains.

The influence of employee share ownership on corporate social responsibility operates through multiple interconnected mechanisms. From enhancing employee engagement and fostering a long-term perspective to strengthening ethical practices and community ties, ESO has the potential to significantly impact various aspects of CSR. As organizations increasingly recognize the importance of both ESO and CSR, understanding these mechanisms can provide valuable insights for integrating these two important aspects of modern business practice.

Challenges and Complexities: A Nuanced Perspective on ESO and CSR

While the potential benefits of ESO for Corporate Social Responsibility (CSR) are significant, this relationship faces several challenges and complexities. First, the financial interests of employee-owners may sometimes conflict with broader CSR goals, particularly in the short term (Kruse, 2016). Indeed, when employees prioritize their immediate financial benefits, it can undermine the company's commitment to sustainable and ethical practices in the long term. Therefore, in situations where the pressure to make short-term profits is high, decisions made may not be aligned with CSR values, illustrating this tension between personal interests and professional obligations. Furthermore, measuring ESO's impact on CSR performance remains difficult, requiring more sophisticated methodologies and robust metrics (Blasi et al., 2013). The relationship between ESO and CSR can vary significantly across different national and cultural contexts, with some countries more amenable to integration than others (Poutsma et al., 2012). Looking forward, the integration of ESO and CSR is likely to be influenced by emerging trends such as stakeholder capitalism (Freeman et al., 2020), ESG metrics (Eccles et al., 2014), and the UN Sustainable Development Goals (Schönherr et al., 2017). Finally, the future integration of ESO and CSR will be shaped by several emerging trends and regulatory developments. The shift to stakeholder capitalism (Freeman et al., 2020) aligns well with ESO principles and could facilitate deeper integration with CSR practices, as suggested by Boiral et al. (2021) in highlighting the importance of stakeholder engagement strategies. The growing importance of ESG metrics in investment decisions (Eccles et al., 2014) is pushing companies to improve their CSR performance, with ESO-practicing companies potentially better positioned to excel in ESG ratings (Bauer et al., 2023). Aligning corporate strategies with the UN Sustainable Development Goals (Schönherr et al., 2017) highlights synergies between ESO and CSR, with ESO contributing to SDGs 8 and 10. The evolving regulatory landscape plays a crucial role, with initiatives such as mandatory CSR reporting in many jurisdictions (Gatti et al., 2019), tax incentives for ESO potentially linked to CSR performance (Poutsma & Ligthart, 2017), and the proposed EU Directive on corporate sustainability due diligence (European Commission, 2022). Technological advances, such as blockchain, could improve transparency and accountability in ESO and CSR practices (Veldhuizen, 2022), while the post-pandemic recovery increases the focus on resilient and sustainable business models, with ESO combined with strong CSR practices seen as a strategy to build more resilient organizations (Kramer, 2020). These trends suggest a growing convergence between ESO and CSR practices, paving the way for more integrated approaches in the future, although realizing this potential requires proactive efforts from companies, policymakers, and researchers to address the challenges and take advantage of the opportunities presented by this integration.

5. CHALLENGES AND OPPORTUNITIES IN INTEGRATING EMPLOYEE SHARE OWNERSHIP, GOVERNANCE, AND CSR

The integration of Employee Share Ownership with governance structures and CSR initiatives presents both challenges and opportunities. Recent studies have examined the balance between diverse stakeholder interests, including potential conflicts between employee and shareholder roles (Pendleton and Robinson, 2020). The implementation of effective governance structures incorporating employee-owners has been explored, highlighting the importance of tailoring these structures to specific organizational contexts (Hyman, 2021). Ellerman, et al. (2022) have developed a model for a European ESOP that is being piloted in Slovenia, that specifically includes democratic governance rights for employees.

Long-term financial sustainability remains a challenge, requiring a balance between ESO and the need for external capital. Innovative financing models have been proposed to support ESO while ensuring access to capital (Kruse and Blasi, 2019). Potential inequalities within ESO schemes have also been studied, leading to recommendations for more equitable designs (Carberry, 2022).

Aligning ESO with broader CSR goals has been researched, emphasizing the importance of clear communication and coherence between ESO and other CSR initiatives (Harjoto et al., 2021). The complex legal and regulatory landscape surrounding ESO has been analyzed, resulting in policy recommendations to create more supportive environments (Lampel et al., 2020).

Studies have examined how ESO can help combat short-termism in corporate decision-making, while addressing potential challenges such as risk aversion (Edmans, 2020). The impact of technological advancements on ESO implementation and management has also been investigated, exploring how emerging technologies can solve some administrative challenges and create new opportunities for more dynamic and inclusive ownership structures (Welbourne and Schlachter, 2022).

This brief overview of some recent studies highlights the complex interplay between ESO, governance, and CSR. While challenges exist, they also point to numerous opportunities for creating more inclusive, responsible, and sustainable business models. The successful integration of these elements requires careful consideration of organizational context, stakeholder interests, and evolving legal and technological landscapes.

Moving forward, realizing the full potential of ESO will require addressing these challenges through innovative policy approaches, organizational designs, and ongoing research. By acknowledging and working to overcome these obstacles, we can work towards a more balanced and realistic implementation of ESO that lives up to its transformative promise while navigating the complexities of modern corporate environments.

It is important to note, however, that the application and impact of ESO vary considerably across national contexts. For example, while ESOPs are widespread in the United States, worker cooperatives are more common in Spain and Italy. These differences are influenced by the legal frameworks, cultural traditions, and economic structures of each country. Future research should focus on comparative studies to better understand how different national contexts shape the effectiveness and implementation of ESO schemes.

6. CONCLUSION: THE FUTURE OF EMPLOYEE SHARE OWNERSHIP IN CORPORATE GOVERNANCE AND CSR

In this essay, we have attempted to show how employee share ownership (ESO) intersects corporate governance, corporate social responsibility, and evolving ideas about the shape and character of capitalism. ESO has the potential to reshape corporate structures by aligning employee-company interests, implementing stakeholder theory, enhancing CSR practices, and challenging traditional capitalist models (Aubert et al., 2017; Stout, 2019; Culpepper, 2021; Bryson et al., 2019). Moreover, ESO can serve as an effective governance mechanism against managerial entrenchment by strengthening internal monitoring and aligning long-term interests of all stakeholders (Aubert et al., 2014). However, this mostly exists as potential - while it has made important inroads in the U.S. and elsewhere, ESO still has not achieved wide acceptance, and faces implementation challenges in balancing stakeholder interests and maintaining financial flexibility (Pendleton and Robinson, 2020).

The future of ESO will undoubtedly be shaped by technological advances. Blockchain, for example, could revolutionize the management and distribution of employee shares, providing greater transparency and efficiency. Artificial intelligence could optimize decision-making in employee-owned companies, while automation could redefine the very nature of work and ownership. Digital platforms, meanwhile, could facilitate new forms of distributed ownership. These technological developments raise new questions about the nature of ownership, governance, and employee participation in the digital economy.

Key areas for future research and practical consideration include:

1. Long-term impact studies on corporate performance, employee well-being, and societal outcomes
2. Cross-cultural comparisons across different regulatory environments
3. Integration with emerging technologies
4. ESO adaptation for non-traditional work arrangements
5. ESO's role in broader economic and social transformations
6. Impact of ESO on managerial entrenchment and corporate control mechanisms.

In conclusion, ESO represents a powerful tool for reimagining relationships between corporations, employees, and society. Its integration with effective governance and CSR initiatives can create more equitable, sustainable, and successful business models. Realizing this potential requires continued innovation, careful navigation of challenges, and balancing stakeholder interests. It is important to recognize that ESO and CSR are not magic bullets that will solve all of the world's problems (Panwar, Vidal, & Holtmaat, 2024).

The future of ESO extends beyond wealth sharing to reshaping corporate structures, redefining work, and contributing to inclusive and sustainable capitalism. By empowering employees as shareholders, ESO also provides a natural counterbalance to managerial entrenchment, fostering more balanced and accountable corporate governance structures. As researchers and practitioners, we must continue exploring and refining these models to meet the evolving needs of businesses, workers, and society at large.

REFERENCES

Abdelhamid, A. B. (2021). *Corporate governance and employee ownership: evidence from France* (Doctoral dissertation, Université Clermont Auvergne).

Achour, Z. (2024). Impact of employee stock ownership on firm financial performance: Does corporate social responsibility matter? *International Journal of Management and Enterprise Development*, 23(2), 155–170. DOI: 10.1504/IJMED.2024.139275

Adwan, S., & Ahamed, M. M. (2024). Employee ownership and corporate investment efficiency in Europe. *Review of Quantitative Finance and Accounting*. Advance online publication. DOI: 10.1007/s11156-024-01300-5

Alperovitz, G. (2011). *America Beyond Capitalism: Reclaiming Our Wealth, Our Liberty, & Our Democracy* (2nd ed.). Democracy Collaborative Press.

Ammirato, P. (2018). *The growth of italian cooperatives: innovation, resilience and social responsibility*. Routledge. DOI: 10.4324/9781315158785

Arando, S., Gago, M., Kato, T., Jones, D., & Freundlich, F. (2010). Assessing Mondragon: Stability & Managed Change in the Face of Globalization. William Davidson Institute Working Paper No. 1003, Available at *SSRN*: https://ssrn.com/abstract=1726449 or http://dx.doi.org/DOI: 10.2139/ssrn.1726449

Aubert, N., Garnotel, G., Lapied, A., & Rousseau, P. (2014). Employee ownership: A theoretical and empirical investigation of management entrenchment vs. reward management. *Economic Modelling*, 40, 423–434. DOI: 10.1016/j.econmod.2013.12.011

Aubert, N., Kern, A., & Hollandts, X. (2017). Employee stock ownership and the cost of capital. *Research in International Business and Finance*, 41, 67–78. DOI: 10.1016/j.ribaf.2017.04.007

Bao, Y., Li, C., & Zhao, H. (2020). Servant leadership and employee ownership behavior: A moderated mediation model. *International Journal of Human Resource Management*, 31(17), 2155–2183.

Barzuza, M., Curtis, Q., & Webber, D. H. (2020). Shareholder Value(s): Index Fund ESG Activism and the New Millennial Corporate Governance. *Southern California Law Review*, 93(6), 1243–1322.

Bauer, R., Derwall, J., & Tissen, C. (2023). Private shareholder engagements on material ESG issues. *Financial Analysts Journal*, 79(4), 64–95. DOI: 10.1080/0015198X.2023.2220648

Becker, G. S. (1964). *Human capital theory*.

Blasi, J., Freeman, R., & Kruse, D. (2016). Do broad-based employee ownership, profit sharing and stock options help the best firms do even better? *British Journal of Industrial Relations*, 54(1), 55–82. DOI: 10.1111/bjir.12135

Blasi, J., Kruse, D., & Freeman, R. B. (2006). Shared capitalism at work: Impacts and policy options. In *America at work: Choices and challenges* (pp. 275–295). Palgrave Macmillan US. DOI: 10.1057/9781403983596_16

Blasi, J. R. (2016). *Employee ownership through ESOPs: Implications for the public corporation*. Elsevier.

Blasi, J. R., Freeman, R. B., & Kruse, D. L. (2018). Evidence and perspectives on broad-based employee stock ownership and profit sharing. *Journal of Participation and Employee Ownership*, 1(1), 38–60. DOI: 10.1108/JPEO-02-2018-0001

Blasi, J. R., & Kruse, D. L. (2019). *Building the Assets of Low and Moderate Income Workers and their Families: The Role of Employee Ownership*. Institute for the Study of Employee Ownership and Profit Sharing, Rutgers University.

Boguslaw, J., & Schur, L. (2019). Building the Assets of Low and Moderate Income Workers and their Families: The Role of Employee Ownership. Institute for the Study of Employee Ownership and Profit Sharing, Rutgers University School of Management and Labor Relations. https://smlr.rutgers.edu/sites/default/files/Documents/Centers/Institute_Employee_Ownership/rutgerskelloggreport_april2019.pdf

Boiral, O., Heras-Saizarbitoria, I., & Testa, F. (2021). Improving CSR performance through employee participation and engagement. *Journal of Business Ethics*, 170(2), 325–346.

Boubaker, S., & Nguyen, P. (2021). Does employee stock ownership mitigate information asymmetry? Evidence from Australia. *Pacific-Basin Finance Journal*, 66, 101508.

Brolis, O. (2018). Do social enterprises attract workers who are more pro-socially motivated than their counterparts in for-profit organizations to perform low-skilled jobs? *International Journal of Human Resource Management*, 29(20), 2861–2879. DOI: 10.1080/09585192.2017.1328611

Brown, R., McQuaid, R., Raeside, R., Dutton, M., Egdell, V., & Canduela, J. (2019). Buying into capitalism? Employee ownership in a disconnected era. *British Journal of Industrial Relations*, 57(1), 62–85. DOI: 10.1111/bjir.12309

Bryson, A., Clark, A. E., Freeman, R. B., & Green, C. P. (2019). Share capitalism and worker wellbeing. *Labour Economics*, 61, 101754. PMID: 28725118

Carberry, E. J. (2021). *Employee ownership and shared capitalism: New directions in research*. Cornell University Press.

Carberry, E. J. (2022). Making Sense of Employee Ownership: A Typology of Broad-Based Employee Stock Ownership Plans. *Industrial & Labor Relations Review*, 75(5), 1172–1204.

Carberry, E. J., & Meyers, J. S. (2022). Employee Ownership and the Future of Work. In The Cambridge Handbook of the Changing Nature of Work (pp. 415-432). Cambridge University Press.

Cardoni, H., & Poulain-Rehm, T. (2023). The impact of employee shareholding on corporate governance: The employee shareholder director in France. *The Journal of Management and Governance*, 27(4), 1073–1114. DOI: 10.1007/s10997-022-09634-9

Cha, T. (2014). *Two Essays on Corporate Policy and Corporate Governance*. The George Washington University.

Crane, A., Matten, D., Glozer, S., & Spence, L. J. (2019). *Business ethics: Managing corporate citizenship and sustainability in the age of globalization*. Oxford University Press. DOI: 10.1093/hebz/9780198810070.001.0001

Culpepper, P. D. (2021). Quiet politics in tumultuous times: Business power, populism, and democracy. *Politics & Society*, 49(1), 133–143. DOI: 10.1177/0032329220985725

Dahl, R. (1985). *A preface to economic democracy*. Polity. DOI: 10.1525/9780520341166

De Angelis, M. (2021). *The Commons: Social Sharing for a Sustainable Future*. Zed Books Ltd.

Eccles, R. G., Ioannou, I., & Serafeim, G. (2014). The impact of corporate sustainability on organizational processes and performance. *Management Science*, 60(11), 2835–2857. DOI: 10.1287/mnsc.2014.1984

Edmans, A. (2020). *Grow the Pie: How Great Companies Deliver Both Purpose and Profit*. Cambridge University Press. DOI: 10.1017/9781108860093

Ellerman, D. (1992). *Property and Contract in Economics: The Case for Economic Democracy*. Basil Blackwell.

Ellerman, D., Gonza, T., & Berkopec, G. (2022). European Employee Stock Ownership Plan (ESOP): The main structural features and pilot implementation in Slovenia. *SN Business & Economics*, 2(186), 186. DOI: 10.1007/s43546-022-00363-7

Fatemi, A., Glaum, M., & Kaiser, S. (2018). ESG performance and firm value: The moderating role of disclosure. *Global Finance Journal*, 38, 45–64. DOI: 10.1016/j.gfj.2017.03.001

Ferreras, I. (2017). *Firms as Political Entities: Saving Democracy through Economic Bicameralism*. Cambridge University Press. DOI: 10.1017/9781108235495

Ferreras, I. (2021). *Democratizing Firms: A Cornerstone of Shared and Sustainable Prosperity*. University of Chicago Press Economics Books.

Ferreras, I. (2022). From the Politically Impossible to the Politically Inevitable: Taking Action. In *Democratize Work: The Case for Reorganizing the Economy*. University of Chicago Press. DOI: 10.7208/chicago/9780226819631.001.0001

Freeman, R. B., Blasi, J. R., & Kruse, D. L. (2010). Introduction to" Shared Capitalism at Work: Employee Ownership, Profit and Gain Sharing, and Broad-based Stock Options". In *Shared capitalism at work: Employee ownership, profit and gain sharing, and broad-based stock options* (pp. 1-37). University of Chicago Press.

Freeman, R. E. (1984). *Stakeholder management: a strategic approach*. Pitman.

Freeman, R. E. (1984). *Stakeholder management: a strategic approach*. Pitman.

Gatti, L., Seele, P., & Rademacher, L. (2019). Grey zone in – greenwash out. A review of greenwashing research and implications for the voluntary-mandatory transition of CSR. *International Journal of Corporate Social Responsibility*, 4(1), 1–15. DOI: 10.1186/s40991-019-0044-9

Ghoshal, S. (2005). Bad management theories are destroying good management practices. *Academy of Management Learning & Education*, 4(1), 75–91. DOI: 10.5465/amle.2005.16132558

Gregorič, A., & Poulsen, T. (2020). The power of non-controlling stakes: Minority ownership and board representation. *Journal of Corporate Finance*, 64, 101660.

Harjoto, M., Laksmana, I., & Lee, R. (2021). Employee ownership and corporate social responsibility. *Business Ethics (Oxford, England)*, 30(3), 383–397.

Hollandts, X., & Aubert, N. (2011). La représentation obligatoire des actionnaires salariés au conseil d'administration: un état des lieux. *Gestion 2000, 28*(6), 15-26.

Huse, M. (2003). Renewing management and governance: New paradigms of governance? *The Journal of Management and Governance*, 7(3), 211–221. DOI: 10.1023/A:1025004111314

Hyman, J. (2021). *Employee Voice and Participation: Contested Past, Troubled Present, Uncertain Future*. Routledge.

Jensen, M. C., & Meckling, W. H. (2019). Theory of the firm: Managerial behavior, agency costs and ownership structure. In *Corporate governance* (pp. 77–132). Gower.

Kang, N., & Moon, J. (2012). Institutional complementarity between corporate governance and corporate social responsibility: A comparative institutional analysis of three capitalisms. *Socio-economic Review*, 10(1), 85–108. DOI: 10.1093/ser/mwr025

Kaswan, M. (2014). *Happiness, Democracy, and the Cooperative Movement: The Radical Utilitarianism of William Thompson*. State University of New York Press.

Kaswan, M. (2022). Property, ownership and employee ownership: Employee control in ESOPs. *Journal of Participation and Employee Ownership*, 5(1), 14–31. DOI: 10.1108/JPEO-11-2020-0028

Kim, K. Y., & Patel, P. C. (2017). Employee ownership and firm performance: A variance decomposition analysis of European firms. *Journal of Business Research*, 70, 248–254. DOI: 10.1016/j.jbusres.2016.08.014

Kong, D., Liu, J., Wang, Y., & Zhu, L. (2024). Employee stock ownership plans and corporate environmental engagement. *Journal of Business Ethics*, 189(1), 177–199. DOI: 10.1007/s10551-023-05334-y

Kramer, M. R. (2020). Coronavirus is putting corporate social responsibility to the test. *Harvard Business Review*, 1–13.

Kruse, D. L., & Blasi, J. R. (2019). Employee Ownership and Employee Stock Options in the US. In *Sharing in the Company* (pp. 257–292). Oxford University Press.

Kruse, D. L., Blasi, J. R., & Freeman, R. B. (2019). Broad-based employee stock ownership and profit sharing: History, evidence, and policy implications. *Journal of Participation and Employee Ownership*, 2(1), 38–61.

Kurtulus, F. A., & Kruse, D. L. (2017). *How Did Employee Ownership Firms Weather the Last Two Recessions?: Employee Ownership, Employment Stability, and Firm Survival: 1999-2011*. W.E. Upjohn Institute.

Kurtulus, F. A., & Kruse, D. L. (2018). An empirical analysis of the relationship between employee ownership and employment stability in the US: 1999–2011. *British Journal of Industrial Relations*, 56(2), 245–291. DOI: 10.1111/bjir.12254

Lampel, J., Bhalla, A., & Jha, P. K. (2020). Reimagining Employee Ownership for the Digital Age. *International Review of Entrepreneurship*, 18(4), 473–490.

Landau, I., Mitchell, R., O'Connell, A., & Ramsay, I. (2020). Employee Share Ownership Schemes in Australia: A Survey of Key Issues and Themes. *Melbourne University Law Review*, 43(3), 1001–1041.

Liu, Y., Qu, Z., Meng, Z., & Kou, Y. (2022). Environmentally responsible behavior of residents in tourist destinations: The mediating role of psychological ownership. *Journal of Sustainable Tourism*, 30(4), 807–823. DOI: 10.1080/09669582.2021.1891238

Mao, Z., Zhang, S., & Li, X. (2021). Corporate social responsibility, employee stock ownership and sustainable supply chain management. *International Journal of Production Economics*, 235, 108078.

Mayer, C. (2020). The Future of the Corporation and the Economics of Purpose. *Journal of Management Studies*, 58(3), 887–901. DOI: 10.1111/joms.12660

McCarthy, D., Reeves, E., & Turner, T. (2010). Can employee share-ownership improve employee attitudes and behaviour? *Employee Relations*, 32(4), 382–395. DOI: 10.1108/01425451011051604

Meckling, W. H., & Jensen, M. C. (1976). *Theory of the Firm*. Managerial Behavior, Agency Costs and Ownership Structure.

Mill, J. S. (1909). *Principles of Political Economy* (revised ed.). Longman's, Green & Co.

Muslim, A. I., & Setiawan, D. (2024). *View of institutional ownership and value relevance in Indonesia: the nexus of accounting conservatism*. Rajagiri Management Journal.

Mygind, N., & Poulsen, T. (2021). Employee ownership–pros and cons–a review. *Journal of Participation and Employee Ownership*, 4(2), 136–173. DOI: 10.1108/JPEO-08-2021-0003

Novkovic, S., & Webb, T. (2014). *Co-operatives in a post-growth era: Creating co-operative economics*. Zed Books Ltd. DOI: 10.5040/9781350219380

O'Boyle, E.H., Patel, P.C. and Gonzalez-Mulé, E. (2016) 'Employee ownership and firm performance: a meta-analysis'.Human Resource Management Journal 26: 4, 425–448doi: DOI: 10.1111/1748-8583.12115bs_bs_banner

Olckers, C., & Du Plessis, Y. (2020). Psychological ownership as a requisite for talent retention: The voice of highly skilled employees. *SA Journal of Industrial Psychology*, 38(2), 995–1003.

Onkila, T., & Sarna, B. (2022). A systematic literature review on employee ownership and corporate sustainability. *Sustainability*, 14(1), 41.

Panda, B., & Leepsa, N. M. (2017). Agency theory: Review of theory and evidence on problems and perspectives. *Indian journal of corporate governance, 10*(1), 74-95.

Panwar, R., Vidal, N., & Holtmaat, E. A. (2024). From Neoliberal to Hybrid Corporate Social Responsibility. In *Sustainable Capitalism: Essential Work for the Anthropocene* (pp. 189–198). University of Utah Press. DOI: 10.2307/jj.19255101.16

Park, S., & Song, M. H. (1995). Employee stock ownership plans, firm performance, and monitoring by outside blockholders. *Financial Management*, 24(4), 52–65. DOI: 10.2307/3665950

Pendleton, A., & Robinson, A. (2020). Employee ownership in Britain: Size, character and distribution. *Journal of Participation and Employee Ownership*, 3(1), 24–44.

Pierce, J. L., & Jussila, I. (2011). *Psychological ownership and the organizational context: Theory, research evidence, and application*. Edward Elgar Publishing. DOI: 10.4337/9780857934451

Poutsma, E., & Ligthart, P. E. (2017). Labor-management cooperation, employee ownership, and job stability in the European context. In *Advances in the Economic Analysis of Participatory & Labor-Managed Firms* (pp. 57–84). Emerald Publishing Limited.

Rehman, Z. U., Khan, M. K., Ullah, N., Alam, S., Ullah, R., & Irshad, M. (2022). Corporate social responsibility and employee ownership: A systematic literature review. *Sustainability*, 14(14), 8793.

Sarkar, A. (2024). *Common Good Capitalism: A new economic model for growth to benefit business and society*. Right Book Press.

Schönherr, N., Findler, F., & Martinuzzi, A. (2017). Exploring the interface of CSR and the Sustainable Development Goals. *Transnational Corporations*, 24(3), 33–47. DOI: 10.18356/cfb5b8b6-en

Steare, R., Stampoulidis, P., Lewis, P. N., & Woodman, P. (Sept 2015) The moraldna of employee-ownedcompanies. Available at https://www.eagatrust.com/wp-content/uploads/2017/01/The-MoralDNA-of-Employee-Owned-Companies.pdf

Stout, L. A. (2019). Stakeholder Governance and Employee Ownership. The Cambridge Handbook of Stakeholder Theory, 359-374.

Stout, L. A. (2020). The Troubling Question of Corporate Purpose. Accounting, Economics, and Law. *Convivium*, 10(3), 20200021.

Stout, L. A., & Blair, M. M. (2021). The Stakeholder Governance Model and Other Lessons from the Public Benefit Corporation Experiment. The Cambridge Handbook of Corporate Law, Corporate Governance and Sustainability, 307-321.

Sun, H., & Liu, C. (2023). Employee stock ownership plans and corporate environmental performance: Evidence from China. *International Journal of Environmental Research and Public Health*, 20(2), 1467. DOI: 10.3390/ijerph20021467 PMID: 36674233

Taylor, S. (1992). Competitive Success through Participation: The John Lewis Partnership. In Bradley, K. (Ed.), *Human Resource Management* (pp. 133–140). Routledge.

Thomas, H., Ornstein, J., & Woersdoerfer, M. (2021). The role of employee ownership in an era of economic insecurity. *Journal of Participation and Employee Ownership*, 4(1), 26–48.

Thompson, W. (1824). *Inquiry into the Principles for the Distribution of Wealth Most Conducive to Human Happiness*. Burt Franklin (1968 ed.)

Veldhuizen, M. (2022). Blockchain for corporate sustainability: Opportunities and challenges. *Business Strategy and the Environment*, 31(3), 698–713.

Welbourne, T. M., & Schlachter, S. (2022). Transforming Employee Share Ownership with Blockchain: Opportunities and Challenges. *Journal of Participation and Employee Ownership*, 5(1), 1–23.

Wolff, R. D. (2021). *The Sickness is the System: When Capitalism Fails to Save Us from Pandemics or Itself.* Democracy at Work.

Yermack, D. (2020). Corporate Governance and Blockchains. *Review of Finance*, 21(1), 7–31.

Zhang, Y. (2023). Employee Stock Ownership Plans and Corporate Innovation. *Academic Journal of Management and Social Sciences*, 2(1), 54–59. DOI: 10.54097/ajmss.v2i1.5950

Chapter 2
Aligning Corporate Governance With Employee Share Ownership for Value Creation

Pulle Thirupathi
https://orcid.org/0009-0001-1159-8322
Sharda University, India

Vishal Jain
https://orcid.org/0000-0003-1126-7424
Sharda University, India

ABSTRACT

Corporate governance, employee share ownership, and corporate social responsibility (CSR) are crucial for corporate success and enhancing shareholder value. Governance elements like management integrity, board structure, and audit quality significantly impact performance and reputation. Employee Share Ownership programs improve productivity, retention, and organizational culture. CSR initiatives address societal and environmental challenges, enhancing reputation and customer loyalty. This chapter explores the influence of governance, employee share ownership, and CSR on Indian publicly listed companies, highlighting their role in driving growth, financial performance, and transparency.

DOI: 10.4018/979-8-3693-7031-5.ch002

1. INTRODUCTION

1.1 Definition of Corporate Governance (CG)

Corporate Governance are the mechanisms, processes, and relations in a corporation structuring, directing, controlling it to operate as an effective entity with managing interests among shareholders, management, staff, customers, suppliers, financiers, government, and community. Such a firm is said to operate appropriately if it is in tune with the stipulated rules, regulations, and ethical measures in its field of work and societal demands.

Corporate governance essentially is not about compliance but about making sure that companies are viable, competitive, and aligned to the broader responsibilities of society. It talks about how decisions should be taken, how performance should be measured, and how strategic goals should be set and pursued. Companies with the strongest corporate governance are best placed to attract investments, better manage risks, and build sustainable businesses. Proper governance keeps an organization's integrity and reputation in check, but it also improves the ability to deliver sustainable long-term value.

This chapter will explore the principles of corporate governance, the role of employee share ownership as a tool for alignment, and their integration for sustainable corporate success.

1.2 Role of Corporate Governance in Corporate Success and Sustainability

The role that Corporate Governance plays in steering corporate success and sustainability can never be underestimated. There is a foundation of sound governance that will surely deliver financial performance while assuring the organization meets the legal and ethical responsibilities required of it. It operates based on the principles of transparency, accountability, responsibility, and fairness and supports businesses in navigating through such complex webs of stakeholder relationships.

1.2.1 Ensuring Accountability

Accountability will be the bedrock of CG, so the management of a firm is answerable to the board of directors, and the board is responsible to the shareholders. An accountability mechanism decreases the possibilities of managerial self-interests by making decisions more inclined toward the greater good of the organization and the shareholders.

1.2.2 Promoting Transparency

Information disclosure in the decision-making process brings trust between the company and its stakeholders. The openness for scrutiny of financial statements, strategic decisions, and practices in risk management ensures that fraud and mismanagement are prevented. Transparent practices build markets' trust, thereby attracting investors and retaining customers.

1.2.3 Fostering Ethical Behavior

The stronger companies emphasize more the ethical conduct and CSR of the concerned organizations in the corporate governance frameworks. Ethical behavior is synonymous with sustainable success because it avoids reputation damage and sustains the social license to operate for companies.

1.2.4 Risk Management and Long-term Strategy

This way, the strategy can easily be aligned with their risk appetite while navigating through uncertainty in market fluctuations or regulatory changes, hence being resilient and sustainably growing. A key component of effective CG is strong risk management. Engaged boards in understanding and managing risks are better placed to ensure that the companies they represent stay viable in the long run (Gostu et al., 2024).

In the light of such factors, attention to such areas has made CG an enabler of short-term profitability and long-term sustainability. Companies like Google, Apple, and Unilever have used superior governance structures to develop sustainable business models. This approach points to the fact that sound governance is an important bedrock for corporate success over time.

1.3 Importance of Employee Share Ownership as a CG Tool

Employee Share Ownership is fast becoming one of the most sought-after tools to be implemented in the enhancement of corporate governance. Here, the employees are rewarded through the ownership stakes in the firm; normally through ESOPs or stock options. ESO would align the interests of the employees with those of the shareholders since everyone working toward a common goal of accomplishment of the firm (Huang, 2019).

1.3.1 Aligning Interests

One of the significant issues in corporate governance is the agency problem because the interests of managers need not mirror those of the shareholders. ESO reduces this threat since employees become stakeholders of the organization. When employees have their financial interests in the performance of a company, they have a tendency to exhibit the behaviors and make decisions, which tend to align with strategic goals of an organization.

1.3.2 Promoting Engagement and Motivation

Employees who are also company shareholders tend to have strong levels of engagement and motivation with productivity. They benefit from the success of the company compared to other employees. Companies will therefore enjoy the fruits of motivated employees working towards common goals. Research studies have portrayed that companies with significant levels of employee ownership perform better on productivity and profitability (Bao et al., 2024).

1.3.3 Enhancing Transparency and Accountability

ESO also gives space for an openness of the organization. Owner employees want to know how the firm is doing concerning its financial strength and direction. This will then result in information openness where the management and the other members of staff are going to have to aim at the placement of mutual trust. In this light, ESO acts as a form through which highly internal regulation and communication is going to be achieved.

1.3.4 Long-term Focus and Stability

This would encourage long term orientation in decisions taken. External shareholders are much more concerned about short term profitability and returns while employe owners are much more interested in the long-term health and stability of an organization. This would therefore facilitate the interest of an organization in sustainable practices rather than just fast gains on the balance sheet, in keeping with the tenets of corporate governance (Bao et al., 2024; Gostu et al., 2024; Z. Liu & Huang, 2019).

1.4 Integrating Corporate Governance and Employee Share Ownership for Sustainable Success

Corporate governance and employee share ownership will, therefore, bring in a virtue cycle that promotes sustainable corporate success. While CG focuses on creating a structure accountable, transparent, and equitable, ESO ensures that the employees feel that they own it and become increasingly aligned towards long-term goals. Two, therefore, foster a rich framework in creating a resilient company adapted to change while at the same time ensuring its risks remain well managed, with stakeholders assured.

Building upon the foundational principles of corporate governance and the integration of employee share ownership, the following sections explore the role of transparency, accountability, and fairness, alongside the practical implications of employee shareholding as a driver for sustainable corporate success.

2. WHAT IS CORPORATE GOVERNANCE?

Corporate governance would relate to the system of rules, practices, and processes by which the company is directed and controlled. This provides the guideline according to which a business ought to be operated: how transparently, in ethics, and with greater responsibility for its diverse array of stakeholders, such as owners, management, the labor force, customers, or citizens. This is very imperative toward trust building, stimulation for growth, and eventually achieving sustainability.

2.1 Core Principles of Corporate Governance

The corporate governance principles would allow the companies to be managed and operate in such a way as to ensure accountability, fairness, and transparency. Governance frameworks are primarily built from these principles to enable stakeholder trust with companies.

2.1.1 Transparency

Transparency refers to real-time, accurate information about a company's performance, operations, and decision-making processes, enabling shareholders and stakeholders to receive timely and relevant data useful for assessing organizational performance. The mechanisms of transparency include financial disclosures, annual general meetings, and quarterly reports mandated by regulations. This approach reduces information asymmetry between management and owners, enhances shareholder confidence by eliminating manipulative practices, and contributes to maintaining the integrity of capital markets.

2.1.2 Accountability

Accountability in corporate governance centers on the board of directors, which serves as the core of strategic oversight and ensures management activities adhere to legal and ethical standards. Companies demonstrate accountability to shareholders through mechanisms like voting rights, board elections, and resolution proposals at Annual General Meetings. To maintain organizational responsiveness and transparency, companies implement critical policies such as audit committees, internal audits, and whistleblower mechanisms that protect shareholder interests and organizational integrity (Alhydary et al., 2024a).

2.1.3 Responsibility

Corporate responsibility extends beyond legal compliance to encompass broader societal, environmental, and ethical obligations. Most firms implement Corporate Social Responsibility (CSR) programs that benefit society and nature, enhancing their public reputation and stakeholder relationships. With increasing climate change concerns, companies are now more accountable for their environmental footprint, embracing sustainable practices such as reducing carbon emissions and ensuring source legitimacy. Responsible governance also emphasizes employee well-being through fair treatment, workplace diversity, creating safe environments, and maintaining ethical leadership that complies with anti-corruption laws (Chen et al., 2024a; Xiao, 2024).

2.1.4 Fairness

Fairness in corporate governance ensures equitable treatment of shareholders, protecting both minority and majority shareholders' rights by providing equal legal protection and access to essential information. The principle of fairness extends beyond shareholders to encompass broader stakeholder interests, including employees, suppliers, and customers, with companies recognizing that fair treatment builds stronger long-term relationships and enhances organizational reputation. To address potential conflicts of interest, corporate governance establishes robust mechanisms such as disclosure of related party transactions and independent directors' review of potentially contentious decisions (Alhydary et al., 2024b; Y. Liu et al., 2024).

2.2 Role of Employee Share Ownership in Enhancing Governance

Employee Share Ownership (ESO) is an effective governance tool that promotes shared responsibility, aligning employee and shareholder interests to support organizational goals.

2.2.1 Reducing Agency Conflicts

- **Aligning Interests**: ESO aligns workers' interests with those of shareholders, thus encouraging managerial decisions that increase shareholder values and reduce agency costs because of managerial decision-making actions.

2.2.2 Encouraging Long-term Decision-making

- **Employee Commitment**: Employee Commitment Employees who are stakeholders of the company show a strong commitment to long-term goals: they support strategically vital projects for viability and are thus not motivated by short-term returns.

2.2.3 Enhancing Transparency and Communication

- **Access to Information**: Shareholders being part of the employees would help them gain further insight in the company's procedures, make it more transparent, and equally informed. Transparency motivates mutual trust and teamwork(Kotlar & Milutinovic, 2018).

2.2.4 Promoting Ethical Culture

- **Alignment with Values**: More personally related worker relationship towards ESO and the company's mission: These can lead to more ethical governance practices in pursuit of long-term success

3. PRINCIPLES OF CORPORATE GOVERNANCE

3.1 The OECD Principles of Corporate Governance

These are the principles of effective corporate governance that the Organization for Economic Co-operation and Development (OECD) could establish to promote transparency and accountability:

- **Effective Corporate Governance Framework:** This should also align to the legal, regulatory, and institutional context. It will be one that provides a business environment supportive of sustainable economic growth.
- **Rights of Shareholders and Key Ownership Functions:** shareholders must have defined rights which include the right to decide company matters through voting; such as board appointments or any other significant corporate change.
- **Institutional Investors and Intermediaries:** Active involvement of institutional investors and intermediaries would be an improvement in corporate governance through better communication and cooperation between companies and their investors (Al-Gamrh et al., 2024; Squillace, 2022).
- **Role of Stakeholders in Corporate Governance:** Determination of the different interests that must be identified and fulfilled in creating long-term value for the corporation.
- **Disclosure and Transparency:** The companies should provide material information in a timely and proper manner so that stakeholders may make better decisions and trust the companies.
- **Responsibilities of the Board:** The board of directors is responsible for the ultimate governance. They have to supervise the management practices, ensure the compliance with the laws, and maintain the ethical standards of the company.

3.2 Rights of Shareholders & Equitable Treatment

Shareholder rights are fundamental to a fair and effective governance system. Key elements include:

- **Voting Rights:** Shareholders should have voting rights on issues like board elections, mergers, and other significant corporate actions. This participative approach ensures that their voices are heard in the company decisions.
- **Access to Information:** Access to Information includes timely relevant information, such as financial reports and operational updates, so shareholders

can see how the company is actually performing and exercise their rights effectively.

- **Equitable Treatment:** There should be fair treatment of all shareholders, especially the minority and disadvantaged shareholders. Companies must protect their rights and ensure that all have equal access to information and decision-making processes.

3.3 Role of Stakeholders in Corporate Governance

Incorporating the interests of diverse stakeholders enhances corporate governance by:

- **Broadening Governance Focus:** Companies cannot be governed only for shareholders but have to stretch out their concern to an extended spectrum of stakeholders. Employee, customer, supplier, and community involvement promote an integrated approach toward governance.
- **Building Strong Relationships:** Proactive management of stakeholder concerns builds trust and loyalty, which may improve corporate reputation and resilience in adverse times. This approach is inclusive and improves stakeholder engagement and long-term sustainability.

3.4 Disclosure, Transparency, and Responsibilities of the Board

Transparency and accountability are vital components of effective governance:

- **Accurate Reporting Mechanisms:** The companies should have disclosure practices that are continuous and comprehensive, covering financial performance, governance policies, as well as risk management strategies to avoid misinformation and build up investor confidence.
- **Board Accountability:** This will include setting the strategic direction and stewarding shareholder value and that management performs in accordance with legal and ethical requirements for such managerial performance (Chen et al., 2024b; Z. Liu & Huang, 2019).

3.5 Importance of Ethics and Compliance in Governance

Ethical practices form the cornerstone of corporate governance:

- **Upholding Integrity:** It maintains a sense of integrity and accountability. Organizations in which ethics is placed above everything else gain more the trust of stakeholders, giving them a higher reputation and viability over a long term.
- **Establishing Compliance Frameworks:** The process creates a good compliance program in order to reduce the risk and abide by the laws and regulations by providing well-developed mechanisms with training, monitoring, and reporting systems (Bao et al., 2024; Huang, 2019).

3.6 Connection to Employee Ownership for Long-term Success

Employee Share Ownership (ESO) plays a crucial role in reinforcing governance principles:

- **Aligning Interests with Shareholders:** ESO aligns the interest of employees and shareholders, thus bridging the gap between the two. The more an employee owns a share of the company, the more he would be interested in its performance.
- **Fostering a Culture of Engagement:** Ownership culture makes the people become active contributors to the governance process and, thus, stimulates transparency and collaboration, which leads to better decisions and sustainable business.
- **Promoting Ethical Behavior:** ESO lets the employee take pride in the work that he is doing and responsibility towards the company's value orientation, which binds the employee to bring more excellence into the corporate culture for sustainable success.

4. TYPES OF CORPORATE GOVERNANCE MODELS

Corporate governance models are also significantly different from country to country, depending upon the cultural, economic, and legal framework of the respective country. The insight of these models would be valuable to understand how companies are managed and controlled worldwide. The ensuing discussion will describe the Anglo-American, German, and Japanese corporate governance models as compared to the Indian model of corporate governance (Panda, 2024; Subramaniam et al., 2024).

4.1 Anglo-American Model

The **Anglo-American model** of corporate governance, illustrated in Figure 1, is predominantly practiced in countries such as the United States and the United Kingdom. It is characterized by a **shareholder-centric approach**, which prioritizes shareholders' interests as the primary organizational objective.

- **Shareholder-Centric Approach:** The most common objective of governance in this approach is to maximize value in shareholders. Companies are sources through which the profit-generating tools for the shareholders. Such is the expectation, due to the return from investing in them in form of distribution and capital gains. This focus is most on short-term as managers make efforts to satisfy current shareholders by coming up with performance in short-run finance(Alhydary et al., 2024a; Zhong et al., 2024).
- **Board Structure:** The Anglo-American model of the board of directors is unitary consisting of executive directors and independent directors. These directors sit on the board to independently look after the company as these are not directly involved with the day-to-day operation of the firm. However, the chairman often remains quite powerful, and recently the role of the chairman is separated from the role of the CEO for increased responsibility.
- **Market Orientation:** Here, market mechanisms drive the governance structure with performance metrics measured with respect to stock prices that signal a company's success. Transparency and regular financial reporting would be very important as the basis of investment decisions.
- **Regulatory Framework:** The United States has provided a set of regulations from Sarbanes-Oxley Act to safeguard the interests of the investors and ensure responsibility on the part of the corporation. SEC and many more regulatory authorities facilitate companies to perform within the bounds of legality and notify the shareholders of the events.

Figure 1. Anglo-American model representation

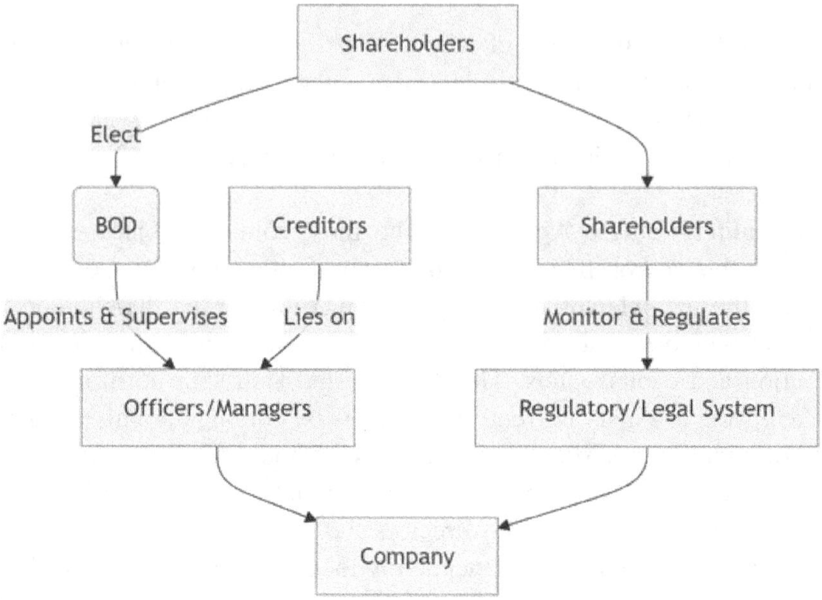

4.2 German Model

The **German model** of corporate governance is distinct from its Anglo-American counterpart, primarily due to its **dual-board system** and stakeholder emphasis, as illustrated in Figure 2. This model reflects Germany's economic structure and social values (Reddy et al., 2024a, 2024b).

- **Dual-Board System:** The second most typical characteristic of the German model is the distinction between the management board and the supervisory board. The former takes care of the company's business affairs, and the latter checks the functioning of the former. These boards have members represented from shareholder, employees, and sometimes from other stakeholders too, creating the balance of governance in this model.
- **Stakeholder Emphasis:** The German model focuses, in particular, on the interest of the stakeholders such as employees, customers, and suppliers, in addition to the remaining community. This is a kind of stakeholder-focused approach through which it indicates that companies have social obligations other than profit maximization. Thus, the companies should follow practices which benefit stakeholders, not merely the owners or shareholders.

- **Codetermination:** The German model also has an important feature, which is codetermination. Employees must be consulted in the making of decisions within a firm. Many firms have employee representatives on their supervisory boards, and this guarantees that employees' interests are taken into account when the strategic decision is made. This provides for an environment of mutual respect and collaboration between the management and employees.
- **Long-Term Focus:** German firms' strategic planning typically operates on a long-term basis. In this respect, here sustainability and stability take more prominence over short-term profits. This makes business activities very standardized, more oriented to quality and innovation, and responses to market dynamics even sharper.

Figure 2. German model representation

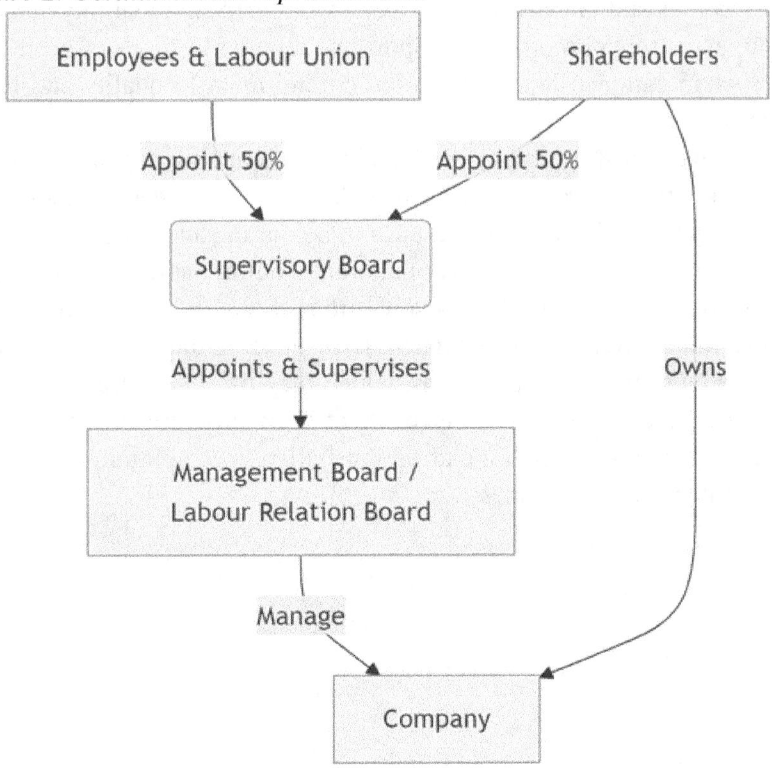

4.3 Japanese Model

The **Japanese model** of corporate governance, depicted in Figure 3, represents a unique approach characterized by its strong emphasis on long-term relationships, consensual decision-making, and intricate corporate networks (Aoki et al., 2023; Yoshimori, 2024)

- **Long-Term Relationships:** Japanese corporate governance is based on a long-term relationship with diverse parties involved, such as employees, suppliers, and customers. For instance, the companies keep tight relationships with their suppliers so they may be used for loyalty and cooperation in order to obtain better efficiency and innovation.
- **Keiretsu System:** A notable feature of the Japanese model is the keiretsu system, where groups of companies form alliances with one another, often sharing resources and information. These networks enhance stability and collaboration, as member companies support one another in times of need. The keiretsu system can also lead to a shared commitment to quality and long-term success.
- **Consensus Decision-Making:** Decisions in governance at Japanese companies are usually made through consensus, which seeks to create harmony and mutual responsibility. This creates a sense of belonging and encourages more ideas from employees, leading to a collaborative culture at the corporate level. The disadvantage of this is that it sometimes slows up decision-making.
- **Corporate Social Responsibility (CSR):** In general, Japanese firms have paid much attention to CSR programs, which they mostly portray as a long-term strategy by companies. The investment in community relations, environmental sustainability, and social welfare all reflect commitment to the value-creation of all stakeholders.

Figure 3. Japanese model representation

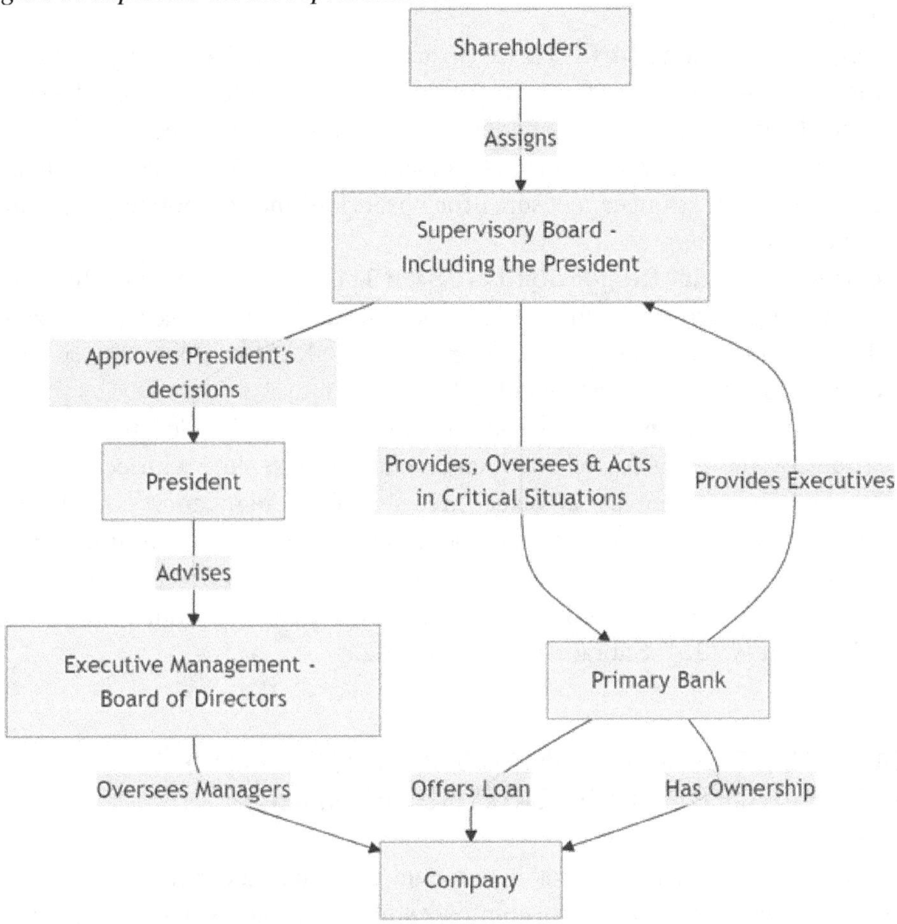

4.4 Comparison with the Indian Corporate Governance Model

The **Indian corporate governance model** is evolving, influenced by its diverse economic landscape and cultural context. It incorporates elements from both Anglo-American and German models, reflecting a hybrid approach.

- **Hybrid Approach:** India's corporate governance model is a hybrid that unites the shareholder-centric angle as in the Anglo-American Model with the stakeholder considerations incorporated in the German Model, thus allowing for a comprehensive approach toward governance in order to consider all possible aspects of groups of stakeholders comprising employees, customers, etc.

- **Regulatory Framework:** There is the Securities and Exchange Board of India (SEBI) to be used as a regulatory enforcer. Recent efforts have enhanced regulations on transparency, accountability, and protection of minority interest. New provisions in the Companies Act of 2013 made it significantly altered with stronger measures for observing finer corporate governance principles in India.
- **Corporate Social Responsibility (CSR):** This is a component of the Indian corporate governance framework. Under this act, there are some companies that set aside a percentage of their profits for CSR. This is one form of social concern and business sustainability.
- **Challenges and Opportunities:** The Indian model has led to very good strides by the practices of governance but still is replete with certain challenges. The challenges involved are, therefore, regulatory compliances, transparency, and accountability among others which makes it difficult; but, corporate governance standards and the demand for ethics provide the opportunities of improvement and innovation in such governance frameworks (Gostu et al., 2024; Subramaniam et al., 2024).

5. EMPLOYEE SHARE OWNERSHIP: A MECHANISM FOR ENHANCED CORPORATE GOVERNANCE

Employee share ownership has become an essential mechanism in corporate governance, aligning the interests of employees and shareholders. This section examines employee share ownership plans, their types, role in governance improvement, company benefits, and case studies (Raman et al., 2024).

5.1 Definition and Types of Employee Share Ownership Plans (ESOPs)

Employee share ownership plans (ESOPs) provide employees with an equity share, offering them ownership and involvement in company success. These plans foster engagement, motivation, and performance by aligning employee and shareholder interests.

Types of Employee Share Ownership Plans include:

- *Employee Stock Ownership Plans (ESOPs):*

ESOPs enable employees to purchase ownership in the company through company contributions of stock or cash. Employees benefit when the stock appreciates and, therefore, tend to be more committed for long-term periods and feel a shared ownership interest.

-Stock Options:

These available options are issued so that the employees get a chance to buy shares at a given price within a specified period, encouraging them to enhance the value of the company's stock. Stock options help companies attract and retain key talent whose interests are aligned with shareholder goals (Bao et al., 2024; Yi & Zhang, 2021).

-Profit-Sharing Plans:

Profit sharing distributes a share of the profits of the firm to employees, either in cash or in shares. Linking the financial rewards directly with company performance motivates the employees to contribute toward growth and fosters the spirit of teamwork and success shared together.

-Restricted Stock Units (RSUs):

RSUs are shares issued as incentives, which vest over time. Employees must stay with the company to gain full ownership, reinforcing long-term commitment and reducing turnover, while ensuring vested interest in the company's future.

Phantom Stock Plans:

Phantom stocks give some of the economic benefits of share ownership without giving up actual shares. Cash bonus payments directly related to stock value help employees work for greater company profitability without diluting existing shareholder equity (Sun et al., 2024).

5.2 The Role of ESOPs in Increasing Transparency and Reducing Agency Conflicts

ESOPs enhance transparency and mitigate agency conflicts, benefiting both employees and shareholders.

- Alignment of Interests:

By aligning employee financial interests with company performance, ESOPs motivate employees to act in ways that prioritize long-term value creation over short-term gains, reducing agency costs in the principal-agent relationship.

- Enhanced Transparency:

Employee shareholding increases openness in matters of company performance, strategic decisions, and financial health. This openness begets trust that will make employees feel informed and empowered to the possible conflict (Hu et al., 2019; Y. Liu et al., 2024; Reddy et al., 2024a; Smits & Van Hillegersberg, 2018).

-Encouragement of Long-Term Thinking:

ESOPs encourage employees to focus on sustainable growth rather than short-term rewards, supporting the company's long-term success and stability.

-Mitigating Agency Risks:

When employees hold shares, they are more invested in responsible corporate behavior, reducing conflicts between management and shareholders.

- Employee Engagement in Governance:

Employee ownership promotes active participation in governance, fosters a sense of belonging and responsibility toward the company, and therefore enhances corporate decision-making and innovative solutions.

5.3 Benefits for Companies

Implementing employee share ownership plans offers several advantages, including enhanced productivity, better alignment of interests, and a positive corporate culture.

- Enhanced Productivity:

People with equity in the company tend to work harder, since they want to see the prosperity of their company. Greater productivity translates to efficiency and innovation, thus boosting the bottom line of the company.

- Improved Alignment of Interests:

Aligning employee and shareholder interests promotes teamwork, helping companies reach strategic goals with a unified, focused workforce.

- Reduced Turnover:

Lower turnover is another benefit of ESOPs, as employees feel more invested in the company's success. Reduced recruitment and training costs lead to a stable workforce, preserving organizational knowledge and continuity.

- Attracting Talent:

In ESOP firms, ownership by the employee causes attraction for potential employees with job satisfaction and chances of getting gain. This is source of attraction for top employees while decreasing the recruitment cost (Roztocki & Weistroffer, 2007; Solaiman et al., 2024; Wang & Wang, 2024).

- Positive Corporate Culture:

Employee ownership is all about a culture of trust, cooperation, and good morale. It makes employees feel better and improves the image of the company as a perfect workplace and business companion.

6. INTRODUCTION TO STRATEGIC CORPORATE SUCCESS

Sustainable corporate success is the triad of sound governance, employee engagement, and CSR. These have created a need to balance short-term profit generation with long-term resilience because of the currents of rising economic uncertainty, shifting consumer expectations, and increased concern for business's social impact. A strategic framework that brings together governance with employee ownership emerges in this context for organizational resilience and stakeholder value.

6.1 The Interconnection Between Governance and Employee Ownership

6.1.1 Enhancing Accountability and Responsibility

ESO develops a culture of accountability since the employees' and shareholders' interests are aligned. Self-accountability comes across because employees who own shares feel responsible for company performance and, therefore, promote transparency, ethical behavior, and wise decision making.

6.1.2 Strengthening Stakeholder Relationships

Good governance considers stakeholders beyond shareholders, including customers, suppliers, and communities. ESO bridges employee interests with those of stakeholders, fostering stronger relationships and enhancing corporate reputation.

6.1.3 Fostering Innovation and Long-term Thinking

ESO encourages its employees to have a vested interest in the long-term success of the company, which fuels innovation and commitment to sustainable business practices that support long-term growth.

6.2 Governance Frameworks Supporting Employee Ownership

6.2.1 Designing Effective Governance Structures

For ESO to contribute effectively, companies must have governance structures empowering employees through board representation, committees, and open communication.

6.2.2 Ensuring Transparency and Fairness

Transparency builds trust, and fairness in decision-making ensures employees feel valued. ESO promotes inclusivity in corporate decisions, enhancing employee commitment to governance initiatives.

6.3 Integrating CSR for Sustainable Success

CSR strengthens sustainable corporate success by embedding ethical, social, and environmental responsibilities into governance. Companies that integrate CSR into their strategies create positive societal and environmental impacts, aligning corporate goals with broader societal values.

6.4 Technology's Role in Governance and ESO

6.4.1 Digital Tools for Governance

Digital tools enhance governance by facilitating real-time reporting, employee feedback, and collaborative communication, strengthening transparency and engagement.

6.4.2 Enabling ESO through Digital Innovations

Technological advancements streamline ESO management through the use of blockchain, which attains transparency and makes equity distribution easier while optimizing experiences for employee ownership.

6.5 Challenges in Integrating ESO with Governance Models

Company challenges are traditional governance structures where leadership might not want to involve employees, or even regulatory complexities dealing with securities laws. These must be overcome through balance between employee ownership and corporate management.

6.6 ESO as a Pathway to Long-term Success

Integrating governance and ESO enables a culture of shared accountability, ethical practices, and long-term value creation. Companies that embrace this strategic approach are better prepared to navigate complex markets, drive innovation, and achieve enduring success.

7. RELATED WORK

Table 1. Comprehensive literature review, focus areas, techniques and methods used, and proposed future work by researchers

Paper Title	Reference	Authors	Publication Year	Focus Area	Techniques/Methods Used	Proposed Future Work
Artificial Intelligence-based Analysis of Change in Public Finance between US and International Markets	IEEE - IC2PCT 2024	Kapil Panda	2024	Public Finance	LSTM Neural Networks	Scalability to various national economies. Easy for real-time outputs. Growing interpretability. Collaborating with policy decision support systems
Risk Navigation in Finance: A Deep Dive into Silicon Valley Bank and Credit Suisse Strategies	Gostu, H., Parmar, M., Naik, T., & Jagtap, N.	Hrishikumar Gostu, Manish Parmar, Tanvi Naik, Nalini Jagtap	2024	Financial Risk Management	Risk Management Practice analysis, Impact analyses of the collapse of SVB in global markets. Assessments of risk-forecasting methodologies, Case study analyses of postcrisis situations and the present case: the SVB episode.	Insights for policymakers around the world and finance institutions about how to enhance sound risk management practices that prevent systemic risk, thus offering more strength to global stability in financial systems.
Social Media Analytic-based Corporate Credit Rating Forecasting	Chen, Y. J., Hong, L. H., & Chen, Y. C.	Yuh-Jen Chen, Ling-Han Hong, Yu-Chen Chen	2024	Corporate Credit Rating Forecasting	Social media big data analysis, K-Nearest Neighbor (KNN) model, accuracy comparison with traditional financial indicators	Further exploration of unstructured non-financial data (e.g., corporate public opinion) for credit rating prediction, testing additional predictive models on social media data.

continued on following page

Table 1. Continued

Paper Title	Reference	Authors	Publication Year	Focus Area	Techniques/Methods Used	Proposed Future Work
Corporate ICT Governance of Indonesian State-Owned Companies: Governance Structure and Decision Making Archetype	Lubis, F. S., Praditha, V. S., Lubis, M., Fakhrurroja, H., Safitra, M. F., & Lubis, A. R.	Fahdi Saidi Lubis, Villy Satria Praditha, Muharman Lubis, Hanif Fakhrurroja, Muhammad Fakhrul Safitra, Arif Ridho Lubis	2023	ICT Governance in SOEs	COBIT 2019 framework, IT master planning, framework organization, IT investment management, RACI method, risk mitigation, internal control evaluation	Practical implementation challenges and optimization strategies for IT governance frameworks (COBIT 2019, RACI) within State-Owned Enterprises (SOEs) in Indonesia.
Research of Equity Pledge on the Financial Performance of Real Estate Industry Listed Companies Based on SPSS 23.0	Wumei Yi,	Yuhan Zhang	2021	Equity pledge, Financial performance	Empirical analysis using SPSS 23.0 for correlation and regression analysis	Improving the equity pledge system in China, strengthening information disclosure, diversifying financing channels to reduce risks, strengthening market supervision to regulate equity pledges and enhance corporate governance, ensuring reliable information dissemination to prevent market participants from making uninformed decisions.
Market competition and stock collapse risk	Zhiqiang, L., & Qing, H.	Liu Zhiqiang, Huang Qing	2019	Stock Market Risk	Corporate governance quality, market competition intensity, proportion of independent directors, executive compensation, large shareholder shareholding ratio	Further enhancements to governance policies to open up market access and intensify competition to mitigate stock collapse risk in China.

continued on following page

Table 1. Continued

Paper Title	Reference	Authors	Publication Year	Focus Area	Techniques/Methods Used	Proposed Future Work
A Deep Structural Model for Analyzing Correlated Multivariate Time Series	Hu, C., Hu, Y., & Seo, S. (2019). Yahoo Research.	Changwei Hu, Yifan Hu, Sungyong Seo	2019	Time Series Analysis	CNN-LSTM architecture for structural time series analysis, incorporates trend, seasonality, and event components; compares with Seasonal ARIMA, Prophet, univariate LSTM, and multivariate LSTM.	Extend the model to include additional types of events and more complex seasonality structures in future research.
A Study of the Relationship of Corporate Governance and Stock Price of the Marine Industry in Taiwan: Using the Ohlson Model	Su, Y. L., & Liu, C. T.	Yuh-Ling Su, Chien-Ting Liu	2012	Corporate Governance and Stock Price	Ohlson model, analysis of corporate book value, earnings per share (EPS), Baltic Dry Index (BDI), board size, foreign fund investor ownership percentage	Further empirical research on corporate governance's impact on stock prices and strategies to enhance governance practices.
How Do Investments in Enterprise Application Integration Drive Stock Prices?	Roztocki, N., & Weistroffer, H. R.	Narcyz Roztocki, Heinz Roland Weistroffer	2007	Impact of IT Investments on Stock Prices	Event study on EAI implementations, stock price reaction analysis, investor response based on company financial health and market conditions	Further event studies on different IT technologies, examining investor perceptions, and the effects of confounding events such as regulatory changes.
Examination of the Financial Relationship Between Overall Stock Market Value and Corporate Investments in Privacy	Squillace, J.	Joseph Squillace	2022	Privacy Investments and Stock Market Impact	Event Study Methodology (ESM), quantitative analysis of corporate investments in privacy, financial impact evaluation of privacy investments, industry-specific benefits analysis	Future research can look at different criteria for data, alternative estimation windows, alternative tests of statistics, and changes in methodology to better understand the economic effects of corporate investments in privacy.

8. CONCLUSION

Good corporate governance, employee share ownership (ESO), and corporate social responsibility (CSR) are fundamental components of sustainable business success and enhanced shareholder value. These elements foster transparency, accountability, and sound business practices, providing a solid foundation for trust and confidence among stakeholders. Governance frameworks that emphasize management integrity, high-quality audits, and balanced board structures safeguard shareholder interests, minimize risks, and bolster corporate credibility. Companies such as CG Power, Tata Group, and Yes Bank exemplify robust corporate governance practices, establishing structures resilient to malfeasance and capable of navigating market fluctuations and regulatory challenges.

Employee share ownership programs enable employees to directly share in their company's success, transforming internal culture and boosting productivity. By aligning employees' economic interests with organizational goals, ESO fosters greater engagement, reduces turnover rates, and builds a highly committed workforce that drives business success. The sense of ownership cultivated through these programs promotes long-term commitment, a critical asset for sustained growth, particularly in competitive industries. Companies like Paytm and Suzlon Energy demonstrate how ESO initiatives can simultaneously enhance performance and positively influence the organizational climate.

CSR extends these benefits by recognizing a company's broader role in addressing societal and environmental challenges. Through responsible practices and sustainable initiatives, companies can positively impact communities, enhance their brand reputation, and create value beyond profit. CSR activities strengthen relationships with stakeholders, foster customer loyalty, and position companies as socially responsible actors. As a strategic asset, CSR bolsters corporate reputation by aligning regulatory compliance with environmental sustainability.

Case studies of Indian corporations show that integrating corporate governance, ESO, and CSR fosters strong financial performance while cultivating a healthy corporate culture rooted in sustainability and ethics. In the future, organizations committed to governance excellence, employee ownership, and social responsibility will achieve superior financial resilience, stakeholder confidence, and competitive advantage. This strategic integration will drive the transformation of the Indian corporate landscape, making it more transparent, inclusive, and value-oriented.

REFERENCES

Al-Gamrh, B., Farooq, U., & Ahsan, T. (2024). Beyond the balance sheet: Assessing corporate governance through the Lens of debtholders. *International Review of Financial Analysis*, 96, 103625. Advance online publication. DOI: 10.1016/j.irfa.2024.103625

Aleissa, S., Alakkas, M., Albugeaey, Z., Alshelaly, H., Alotaibi, S., & Alzubaidi, T. (2024). Leveraging Parallel Computing for Enhanced Stock Movement Forecasting Using Machine Learning. *2024 Seventh International Women in Data Science Conference at Prince Sultan University (WiDS PSU)*, 67–72. DOI: 10.1109/WiDS-PSU61003.2024.00028

Alhydary, T., Qashqary, L., Alotaibi, S., Jaha, R., & Alansari, S. (2024a). Smart Trader: Towards an Advisory Chatbot Service for Saudi Stock Market Investment. *2024 Seventh International Women in Data Science Conference at Prince Sultan University (WiDS PSU)*, 32–35. DOI: 10.1109/WiDS-PSU61003.2024.00021

Alhydary, T., Qashqary, L., Alotaibi, S., Jaha, R., & Alansari, S. (2024b). Smart Trader: Towards an Advisory Chatbot Service for Saudi Stock Market Investment. *Proceedings - 2024 7th International Women in Data Science Conference at Prince Sultan University, WiDS-PSU 2024*, 32–35. DOI: 10.1109/WiDS-PSU61003.2024.00021

Bao, X., Sadiq, M., Tye, W., & Zhang, J. (2024). *The impact of environmental, social, and governance (ESG) rating disparities on corporate risk: The mediating role of financing constraints*. DOI: 10.1016/j.jenvman.2024.123113

Chen, Y. J., Hong, L. H., & Chen, Y. C. (2024a). Social Media Analytic-Based Corporate Credit Rating Forecasting. *6th International Conference on Artificial Intelligence in Information and Communication, ICAIIC 2024*, 1–6. DOI: 10.1109/ICAIIC60209.2024.10463454

Chen, Y. J., Hong, L. H., & Chen, Y. C. (2024b). Social Media Analytic-Based Corporate Credit Rating Forecasting. *6th International Conference on Artificial Intelligence in Information and Communication, ICAIIC 2024*, 1–6. DOI: 10.1109/ICAIIC60209.2024.10463454

Gostu, H., Parmar, M., Naik, T., & Jagtap, N. (2024). Risk Navigation in Finance: A Deep Dive into Silicon Valley Bank and Credit Suisse Strategies. *2024 3rd International Conference for Innovation in Technology, INOCON 2024*. DOI: 10.1109/INOCON60754.2024.10511378

Hu, C., Hu, Y., & Seo, S. (2019). A deep structural model for analyzing correlated multivariate time series. *Proceedings - 18th IEEE International Conference on Machine Learning and Applications, ICMLA 2019*, 69–74. DOI: 10.1109/ICMLA.2019.00020

Huang, R. (2019). Value investment in the semiconductor industry: A case study of three corporations. *Proceedings - 2019 International Conference on Economic Management and Model Engineering, ICEMME 2019*, 539–542. DOI: 10.1109/ICEMME49371.2019.00113

Kotlar, M., & Milutinovic, V. (2018). Comparing Controlflow and Dataflow for Tensor Calculus: Speed, Power, Complexity, and MTBF. *Lecture Notes in Computer Science (Including Subseries Lecture Notes in Artificial Intelligence and Lecture Notes in Bioinformatics), 11203 LNCS*, 329–346. DOI: 10.1007/978-3-030-02465-9_22

Kryzanowski, L., Li, M., Xu, S., & Zhang, J. (2024). Share pledging and corporate misconduct. *The British Accounting Review*, 101508. Advance online publication. DOI: 10.1016/j.bar.2024.101508

Liu, Y., Xu, C., Hou, M., Liu, W., Bian, J., Liu, Q., & Liu, T.-Y. (2024, December). LiuMember, Q., & LiuFellow, T. Y. (2024). Digger-Guider: High-Frequency Factor Extraction for Stock Trend Prediction. *IEEE Transactions on Knowledge and Data Engineering*, 36(12), 7973–7985. Advance online publication. DOI: 10.1109/TKDE.2024.3424475

Liu, Z., & Huang, Q. (2019). Market competition and stock collapse risk. *Proceedings - 2019 International Conference on Economic Management and Model Engineering, ICEMME 2019*, 37–41. DOI: 10.1109/ICEMME49371.2019.00016

Panda, K. (2024). Artificial Intelligence-based Analysis of Change in Public Finance between US and International Markets. *Proceedings - International Conference on Computing, Power, and Communication Technologies, IC2PCT 2024*, 1234–1238. DOI: 10.1109/IC2PCT60090.2024.10486276

Raman, R., Kumar, V., Pillai, B. G., Rabadiya, D., Divekar, R., & Vachharajani, H. (2024). Forecasting Bitcoin Value with Hybrid LSTM-GRU Neural Networks. *2024 Second International Conference on Data Science and Information System (ICDSIS)*, 1–5. DOI: 10.1109/ICDSIS61070.2024.10594710

Reddy, B. A., Kathiriya, H., Thapliyal, N., Vasuki, S., Sachdeva, M., & Shobana, A. (2024a). Predicting Financial Market Movements Through Time Series Analysis and Advanced Machine Learning Algorithms. *2024 International Conference on Advances in Modern Age Technologies for Health and Engineering Science (AMATHE)*, 1–6. DOI: 10.1109/AMATHE61652.2024.10582135

Reddy, B. A., Kathiriya, H., Thapliyal, N., Vasuki, S., Sachdeva, M., & Shobana, A. (2024b). Predicting Financial Market Movements Through Time Series Analysis and Advanced Machine Learning Algorithms. *2024 International Conference on Advances in Modern Age Technologies for Health and Engineering Science (AMATHE)*, 1–6. DOI: 10.1109/AMATHE61652.2024.10582135

Roztocki, N., & Weistroffer, H. R. (2007). *How Do Investments in Enter pr ise Application Integr ation Dr ive Stock Pr ices?* Shrieenidhi, A. M., Ruba Roshini, S., & Ranjana, P. (2024). Walmart Sales Forecasting Using Time Series Analysis. *2024 International Conference on Advances in Data Engineering and Intelligent Computing Systems, ADICS 2024*. DOI: 10.1109/ADICS58448.2024.10533547

Sinkinson, C., & Hicks, A. (2013). Unraveling the research process: social bookmarking and collaborative learning. *The Plugged-In Professor: Tips and Techniques for Teaching with Social Media*, 49–60. DOI: 10.1016/B978-1-84334-694-4.50005-3

Smits, D., & Van Hillegersberg, J. (2018). The continuing mismatch between IT governance maturity theory and practice: A new approach. *Procedia Computer Science*, 138, 549–560. DOI: 10.1016/j.procs.2018.10.075

Solaiman, S., Rahman, B. M. O., Arefin, M. F., Ahmed, C. F., Leung, C. K., & Madill, E. W. R. (2024). Unveiling Market Sentiments: A Comprehensive Analysis of Stock Market Responses to Diverse News Events Using Data Mining Techniques. *Proceedings of the 2024 18th International Conference on Ubiquitous Information Management and Communication, IMCOM 2024*. DOI: 10.1109/IMCOM60618.2024.10418389

Squillace, J. (2022). Examination of the Financial Relationship Between Overall Stock Market Value and Corporate Investments in Privacy. *Conference Proceedings - IEEE SOUTHEASTCON, 2022-March*, 339–347. DOI: 10.1109/SoutheastCon48659.2022.9764007

Su, Y. L., & Liu, C. T. (2012). A study of the relationship of corporate governance and stock price of the marine industry in Taiwan: Using the Ohlson model. *Proceedings - 3rd International Conference on Innovations in Bio-Inspired Computing and Applications, IBICA 2012*, 177–180. DOI: 10.1109/IBICA.2012.40

Subramaniam, R. K., Samuel, S. D., Seera, M., & Alam, N. (2024). Utilising machine learning for corporate social responsibility (CSR) and environmental, social, and governance (ESG) evaluation: Transitioning from committees to climate. *Sustainable Futures : An Applied Journal of Technology, Environment and Society*, 8, 100329. Advance online publication. DOI: 10.1016/j.sftr.2024.100329

Sun, Q., Xiao, Q., Jiang, J., & Huang, X. (2024). The loss of political connections and the fluctuation of corporate stock prices: Moderating effect based on media attention. *Heliyon*, 10(6), e27902. Advance online publication. DOI: 10.1016/j.heliyon.2024.e27902 PMID: 38509911

Wang, Y., & Wang, X. (2024). From ratings to action: The impact of ESG performance on corporate innovation. *Heliyon*, 10(4), e26683. Advance online publication. DOI: 10.1016/j.heliyon.2024.e26683 PMID: 38420449

Xiao, J. (2024). Risk Assessment System for Digital Inclusive Finance Based on Convolutional Neural Network. *2024 Second International Conference on Data Science and Information System (ICDSIS)*, 1–5. DOI: 10.1109/ICDSIS61070.2024.10594199

Yi, W., & Zhang, Y. (2021). Research of Equity Pledge on the Financial Performance of Real Estate Industry Listed Companies Based on SPSS 23.0. *Proceedings - 2nd International Conference on E-Commerce and Internet Technology, ECIT 2021*, 339–343. DOI: 10.1109/ECIT52743.2021.00077

Yu, X., & Fang, J. (2024). Stock transferability, the managerial learning effect and corporate innovation. *China Journal of Accounting Research*, 17(1), 100341. Advance online publication. DOI: 10.1016/j.cjar.2023.100341

Zhong, X., Zhao, Z., Yan, B., & Xu, Q. (2024). Large Language Model for Dynamic Strategy Interchange in Financial Markets. *2024 9th International Conference on Cloud Computing and Big Data Analytics, ICCCBDA 2024*, 306–312.

Chapter 3
Exploring the Benefits of Employee Share Ownership

Michael Palmieri
https://orcid.org/0000-0002-4223-2542
Kent State University, USA

ABSTRACT

This chapter asks a foundational question: How and to what extent do employee shareowners benefit from holding an equity stake in their companies? Using the U.S. General Social Survey (GSS) it examines outcomes such as income, wealth, employment stability, fringe benefits, and retirement security. Additionally, it explores how likely employee shareowners are to participate in company-sponsored training, problem-solving teams, and decision-making processes. This chapter offers an update to previous studies that used GSS data. It embeds the findings within discussions of employment precarity and economic inequality, providing a framework for understanding how workplace arrangements are connected to democratic theory. To contextualize the results, the outcomes for employee shareowners are compared to those of traditional workers and union members. The chapter finds that employee share ownership offers benefits that surpass those of traditional workers and are comparable to, or greater than, those provided by union membership.

INTRODUCTION

Economic inequality and employment precarity are key features of the United States (US) economy. Economic inequality in the US is unprecedented and continues to rise (Saez & Zucman, 2016; 2020). Similarly, the number of individuals working

DOI: 10.4018/979-8-3693-7031-5.ch003

in jobs that provide adequate wages and benefits has decreased over the last 40 years, while the number of those who find themselves working in precarious, low-quality employment arrangements has increased (Howell & Kalleberg, 2019; Oddo et al., 2021). A growing body of research has focused on how these two trends have contributed to increased political inequality, undermining a fundamental principle of democratic theory.

Labor unions are prominent in discussions at the intersection of workplace conditions and economic inequality. And for good reason. They provide their members with collective power that can be used to secure numerous benefits, including increased income in wages and retirement security (Department of Labor, 2023), better working conditions, and employment stability. Unions can act as an institution through which members can voice their concerns, learn leadership skills, and engage in democratic practice within the workplace and broader society (Ahlquist, 2017; Kochan et al., 2018). At a structural level, unions dampen economic inequality by creating company-level wage floors and lobbying for policies that benefit working people more broadly (Farber et al., 2021; Rosenfeld, 2014).

While a host of negative outcomes are associated with precarious employment (Macmillan & Shanahan, 2021) and heightened economic inequality (Wilkinson & Picket, 2009), policies designed to address either of these trends have not gained traction. In a highly polarized political climate, federal legislation designed to decrease economic inequality (e.g., progressive taxation or raising the minimum wage) or increase worker's economic security (e.g., removing barriers to union organizing or providing a more robust safety net programs) rarely garner the levels of political support needed to become law.

This chapter focuses on a lesser-known workplace-based institutional arrangement that also lies at the intersection of economic inequality and working conditions – employee ownership – where workers have a financial stake within the companies they work. The reasoning for focusing on employee ownership is three-fold. First, unlike other policy proposals that strengthen workers bargaining rights and decrease economic inequality, employee ownership receives bi-partisan support from US public officials and the broader public (Kruse & Blasi, 1999; Gowan, 2019; Rodgers, 2019). Second, the US is considered home to one of the more robust employee ownership sectors in the world. Currently, over 10 million individuals actively work at companies with employee ownership, making it more common than union membership in the private sector (National Center for Employee Ownership, 2023c). Third, despite its potential to remedy economic inequality and precarious work, employee ownership is rarely discussed in national debates regarding workplace participation and asset building, including mainstream political science literature (Mazumder & Yan, 2023).

Using the US General Social Survey, this chapter analyzes outcomes for employee-owners by comparing them to those of union members. The reason for placing employee owners alongside union members is not to establish which arrangement is "better." Instead, it is meant to demonstrate how many of the same areas in which unions are known to positively impact their members – economic security, employment stability, and workplace participation – can also be achieved through employee ownership. In doing so, this chapter moves employee ownership into discussions centered around identifying ways to ameliorate precarious employment and rising economic inequality and, by extension, bolster democracy. I find that employee-owners achieve benefits substantially higher than traditional workers across all outcomes of interest and are on par or greater than those achieved by union members.

The next section provides an overview of the impacts of rising inequality and employment precarity and how they both undermine the core assumptions of democratic theory. That section is followed by a review of previous work demonstrating how unions and employee ownership are positioned to address these issues and thus bolster democracy. The following section describes the data and research methods, and the next presents the results. The chapter concludes with a discussion of how both employee ownership and unions, while distinct workplace interventions, can be used as parallel strategies to improve workers' lives.

Economic Inequality, Precarious Work, and Democratic Theory

Over the past half-century, economic inequality in the US has risen to levels not seen in over a century (Piketty, 2014; Piketty & Saez, 2003; Saez & Zucman, 2020). While the rise of inequality within developed nations is a global phenomenon, the US is an outlier in both absolute terms and the pace of the trend (Atkinson, 2015; Hacker & Pierson, 2020). Unlike the decades following World War II through the 1970s, when incomes grew across the income ladder at similar rates, the benefits of growth over the last 50 years have accrued to a small minority. Economic inequality can be measured in various ways, but examining top-line statistics for income and wealth reveals where the US stands today. The top 1% of earners receive 24% of all income earned, a share twice as large as the bottom 50%. Wealth is even more concentrated, with the top 1% holding 40% of all wealth – twice as large as that held by the bottom 90% (Stone et al., 2020).

The economic, social, and political outcomes associated with increased economic inequality are well documented. Higher levels of economic inequality correlate with lower economic growth (Cingano, 2014; Grigoli, 2017; OECD, 2014), decreased social trust (Gallego, 2016; Bjørnskov, 2008; Kanitsar, 2022), and a wide range of health and social problems (Matthew & Brodersen, 2018; Pickett & Wilkinson, 2015; Wilkinson & Pickett, 2009). The impact of the unequal distribution of economic resources on political participation has also been investigated. Though early evidence was mixed (Brown-Iannuzzi et al., 2017), many studies find that rising economic inequality depresses various forms of political participation. Higher levels of objective income inequality, measured using the Gini coefficient, are associated with lower aggregate levels of political participation, with individuals in the poorest quintile showing larger decreases in participation. This relationship is evident in voting, political interest, and political discussion across 22 industrialized democracies (Solt, 2008), turnout in US gubernatorial elections (Solt, 2010), various forms of nonviolent protest (Solt, 2015), participation in political campaigns (Ritter & Solt, 2019). Other scholars find that higher levels of economic inequality correlate with lower membership in civic organizations (Karakoc, 2013) and lower turnout in US presidential elections (Galbraith & Hale, 2008).

In one of the most systematic studies to date, Schäfer & Schwander (2019) investigate the relationship between economic inequality and voter turnout at three different levels of analysis. First, they investigate the relationship across 21 OECD countries 1980-2014; second within a single country, Germany, across 402 administrative districts over 6 federal elections between 1998-2017; and third at the individual level, amongst voters within the same 21 OECD countries, allowing them to analyze turnout differences between income groups. Across all three levels of analysis, they find a "consistently negative effect of income inequality on turnout" and find it to be "particularly strong for low-income groups" (Schäfer & Schwander, 2019, p. 407). Others studying the relationship between economic inequality and "pro-democracy" attitudes find a negative relationship, whether they use objective measures of economic inequality (Anderson, 2012; Krieckhaus et al., 2014) or respondent's perception of the level of economic inequality (Wu & Chang, 2019).

With such wide-ranging impacts, identifying the factors contributing to the rapid increase of economic inequality in the US is crucial. Though debates around the causes of this complex, multi-decade trend still exist, a consensus has emerged that beginning in the early 1970s, changes in the labor market due to educational attainment, technology adoption, decrease in marginal tax rates, government transfers, globalization, and the steep decline in unionization rates are essential explanatory factors (Dadush et al., 2012; Putnam, 2020; Rochat, 2023; Schlozman et al., 2017). While each factor is vital to explaining increased economic inequality in the US, it is essential not to overlook changes in the workplace that took place over this same period. The workplace plays a central role in shaping individuals' day-to-day economic experiences and relationships with society, extending beyond analyses of wage income earned through work. Using the workplace as a lens to understand rising economic inequality requires and allows for an exploration of workers' changing employment conditions. More specifically, it allows for discussing the broader labor concept of precarious work and its relationship to economic inequality and political participation.

The Rise of Precarious Work

Since the 1970s, employment conditions in the US labor market have changed profoundly. Responding to economic crises, growing global competition, and technological developments, businesses and governments made drastic changes to their production and policy processes that unraveled the postwar Keynesian institutional order characterized by full-time employment with benefits and government support and protections. Guided by political and economic motivations often described as neoliberalism, businesses pursued greater employment flexibility to reduce costs while the government rolled back regulatory and social protections for workers (Hacker, 2006; Harvey, 2007; Kalleberg, 2016). As a result, the number of workers in high-quality, full-time employment receiving adequate wages and benefits has decreased, while those in temporary, low-quality positions have increased (Hewison, 2016; Katz & Krueger, 2016; Kalleberg, 2011; Oddo et al., 2021).

Precarious work, a term used to describe the growing trend of nonstandard low-quality work in the labor market, can be broadly defined as work that is "uncertain, unstable, and insecure," where "employees bear the risks of work...and receive limited social benefits and statutory protections" (Kalleberg & Vallas, 2017, p.1). As the above definition suggests, the concept of precarious work is multidimensional and can be conceptualized "as a situation of accumulated unfavorable facets of employment quality" (Julià et al., 2017, p. 391). Important dimensions include unstable non-permanent contracts, low material rewards, low job control and organizational influence, lack of access to social protections (e.g., unemployment insurance or social security), and limited opportunities for training and growth.

While early work questioned whether an objective increase in precarious work was occurring (Auer & Cazes, 2000), recent studies strongly suggest that major changes have taken place in industrialized countries. For example, a study of 26 European countries finds that half the jobs created between 1995 and 2013 and 60% of those created between 2007 and 2013 were non-standard jobs (OECD, 2015). In the US, Katz & Krueger (2016) find that 94% of net employment growth in the US economy between 2005 and 2015 occurred within non-standard work arrangements. Oddo et al. (2021), using a longitudinal dataset and multidimensional measure of precarious employment, find that between 1988 and 2016, employment precarity increased by 9% overall for respondents, with 35% of the sample in what they define as "high precarity jobs" (p. 175). While the contours of precarious employment continue to be analyzed (Benach et al., 2016), it is generally accepted that job quality is a key challenge for researchers and policymakers concerned with worker well-being and rising economic inequality (Howell & Kalleberg, 2019).

Precarious work contributes to economic inequality in various ways. From the standpoint of income, precarious work often involves low wages, irregular hours, interruptions to employment, and limited access to benefits which leads to income disparities that contribute to overall income inequality. For example, a US Government Accountability Office (GAO) study finds that those in non-standard work arrangements earn 47.9% less per year than standard workers, are two-thirds less likely to have retirement plans and health insurance and are more likely to report living in poverty (GAO, 2015). Like economic inequality, scholars have documented the impacts of employment precarity. They found it to be associated with heightened anxiety and poor mental health (Glavin & Schieman, 2021; Macmillan & Shanahan, 2021), delayed family formation and difficulty maintaining romantic relationships (Lim, 2017; Rao, 2017), increased work-life conflict (Luhr et al., 2022), challenges to forming friendships (Lewchuck, 2017), and a host of other negative health outcomes (Benach et al., 2014; Bhattacharya & Ray, 2021).

Precarious employment also contributes to wealth inequality. One way this occurs is that lower income generation results in less money that can be saved, invested in other assets, or converted into wealth (Weller & Karakilic, 2022). Additionally, those in precarious jobs are less likely to access company-sponsored retirement plans or receive benefits, including health insurance, paternity leave, or tuition assistance, which can make up a third of total compensation (Sullivan et al., 2019). Due to their lack of access to these benefits, precarious workers are likelier to take on debt to cover medical and other expenses, contributing to wealth inequality and financial insecurity (Keith et al., 2020). While the increasing precarity of work affects all workers nationally (Hacker, 2006), it is more acute for women and people of color due to persistent occupational segregation (Ross & Bateman, 2019, pp. 41-42), making it a key driver of racial disparities in income and wealth (Sullivan et al., 2019).

Though substantial research focuses on the social and economic impacts of precarious work, fewer studies directly examine its relationship with politically relevant attitudes and participation. Azzollini and Macmillan (2023) use the European Social Survey to create a multidimensional index measuring precarious work by considering the type of work contract, job control, organizational influence, employment gaps, and financial vulnerability. They analyze its relationship with individual voting in 32 countries between 2008 and 2018, finding a strong negative relationship in 29 countries, with statistical significance in 21. Using multilevel models like those for measuring economic inequality's effect on political participation, they find employment precarity is more harmful for low-income individuals. Lambert et al. (2019), using the US GSS, examine the relationship between unstable work schedules and distrust of federal institutions, including Congress, the Supreme Court, and the executive branch, finding greater distrust among those with unstable work hours. Overall, the literature underscores the workplace's critical role in social, economic, and political life. While the sub-literature on employment precarity and political participation is still in its infancy, alongside the more developed literature on economic inequality, the connection between these trends and their potential to undermine core assumptions of democratic theory becomes clearer.

Implications for Democratic Theory

The detrimental effects of rising economic inequality and employment precarity on political participation and democratic attitudes have implications for democratic theory, particularly the virtue of political equality. The more affluent are more likely to participate in politics, creating a "class bias" that permeates various forms of political participation (Leighley & Nagler, 2013; Nie et al., 1979; Schlozman et al., 2012; Verba et al., 1995; Verba et al., 1987; Wolfinger & Rosenstone, 1980). This pattern concerns scholars who view political participation, especially voting, as the means through which citizens produce a government responsive to their needs (Leighley & Nagler, 1992a).

Rising economic inequality and employment precarity negatively impact electoral participation and democratic attitudes, particularly among those with lower socioeconomic status, compounding existing participation inequalities (Azzollini & Macmillan, 2023; Schäfer & Schwander, 2019; Solt, 2008). As Schattschneider (1960) pointed out and Lijphart (1997) echoed, such dynamics create a vicious cycle where economic inequalities result in unequal political participation. This, in turn, drives unequal representation and policy responsiveness that favors the affluent, further consolidating their privileged position in society.

Inequalities in policy responsiveness benefiting the affluent are well documented (Bartels, 2016; Elkjaer & Klitgaard, 2021; Gilens & Page, 2014; Gilens, 2012) and help explain policy choices that exacerbate economic inequality and precarity for ordinary people (Bartels, 2017; Hacker & Pierson, 2010). Allowing the benefits of economic growth and innovation to accrue to a small affluent minority whilst allowing negative economic shocks to impact the less well-off disproportionately has been shown to undermine democracy by fostering authoritarian values (Ballard-Rosa et al., 2022) and increase support for right-wing populism (Autor et al., 2017). Recognizing the political ramifications of labor market changes, Rodrik and Sabel (2020) frame job quality's importance starkly: "'Where will the good jobs come from?' is perhaps the defining question of our contemporary political economy" (p. 4).

Two Workplace-based Solutions

There is no shortage of policy proposals to ease economic and political inequalities and improve workers' lives, including more progressive taxation, welfare state expansion, or raising the minimum wage. However, in a highly polarized political system, such proposals are unlikely to garner the political support required to become law (McCarty et al., 2006). While these policies undoubtedly affect income distribution, they often overlook the workplace's unique role in the economic and political inequality nexus. Workplaces generate income and, in some cases, wealth for workers, which can be used to participate in the political process. Additionally, the stability of work, the training provided, and the influence workers have within the workplace contribute to developing political identities and conceptions of self-agency, shaping interactions with the political system. This section reviews the literature on two workplace-based interventions that improve job quality and build wealth for workers. It begins with a review of unions and then discusses a lesser-known workplace arrangement – employee ownership.

The Role of Unions

One common response to Rodrik and Sabel's (2020) question is to increase the number of unionized workers in the US, and for good reason. Unions provide benefits to both members and non-members. On average, union members earn 15-20% more income (Bivens et al., 2017; Farber et al., 2021; Gittleman & Kleiner, 2016), are more likely to have pensions, employer-sponsored health insurance, and other non-wage benefits (BLS, 2019; Fieveson, 2023; Knepper, 2020), including longer tenure (Polachek & McCutcheon, 1983) and safer workplaces (Zoorob, 2018). Competing non-union firms may raise wages, benefits, and improve workplaces to attract workers, creating a "spillover effect" benefiting non-unionized workers (Banerjee et al., 2021; Fortin et al., 2021; Mahmood & Banerjee, 2023). Unions promote more equal pay schedules (Freeman & Medoff, 1984; Card, 1996), helping close racial and gender wage gaps (Rosenfeld & Kleykamp, 2012). Glass et al. (2023) find union households hold four times more median wealth than nonunion households, with nonwhite members enjoying an even larger boost, narrowing the racial wealth gap. Finally, unions flatten wage distributions (Ahlquist, 2017; Farber et al., 2021; Rosenfeld, 2014), reducing economic inequality.

The impacts of unions on economic inequality and precarity are not solely derived from economic factors alone. As Acemoglue and Robinson (2013) note, "unions do not just influence the way the labor market functions they also have important implications for the political system...which have large effects on public policy and the extent of taxation and income redistribution" (p. 174). In that vein, unions help combat economic inequality and precarious work by pushing for policies such as increases to the minimum wage, workplace safety protections, and expansion of social safety net programs, including Medicaid and unemployment insurance (Banerjee et al., 2021; Hertel-Fernandez & Gould-Werth, 2020).

Beyond wage and non-wage benefits, unions positively impact political and civic participation. Union density is associated with higher levels of aggregate turnout (Wang, 2020) and union members are more likely to vote in local elections (Moe, 2011), national elections (Freeman, 2003; Rosenfeld, 2014), and participate in civic activities such as volunteering, charitable giving, and attending community meetings (Zullo, 2011). Importantly, the observed increase in the likelihood of voting by union members is largest for those with lower SES (Kerrissey & Schofer, 2013; Leighley & Nagler, 2007; Rosenfeld, 2014), suggesting that unions have an ameliorating effect on political inequality and the class bias that exists within the electorate.

Like the non-wage benefits provided to members, the positive civic and political impacts associated with unions also extend to non-union members. Carnes and Hansen (2016) find union density is positively related to the proportion of working-class members in state legislatures. Feigenbaum et al. (2019) find the same relationship at the state and federal levels, suggesting unions help reduce inequalities in representation. Becher and Stegmueller (2020) investigate this question using data on roll call votes in the House of Representatives from the 109th to 112th Congresses and arrive at similar conclusions. The rise in union drives and strikes (Kallas et al., 2022; National Labor Relations Board, 2022), growing public support for unions (Gramlich, 2021; Van Green, 2023), and the Biden Administration's active role in boosting unions are notable developments (Kim et al., 2023). However, while the number of workers represented by unions increased by 200,000 from 2021 to 2022, the overall percentage of unionized workers fell to 11.3%. Unionization is only 6% in the private sector, far below the 1970s levels (Shierholz et al., 2023; Dinlersoz & Greenwood, 2012).

Moreover, as currently structured and implemented at the state and federal level, US labor law makes it challenging to grow union membership and density (Hertel-Fernandez, 2020; Walker, 2020). Notable are right-to-work laws, which undercut unions' financial resources and limit the amount they can invest in political activity and unionization drives (Feigenbaum et al., 2019). While there are legislative efforts at the federal level to ease these constraints, most notably the Protecting the Right to Organize Act or Pro Act, they are unlikely to gain the bipartisan support needed to become law (Fandos, 2021). This is by no means a reason to abandon such efforts. However, it underscores the need to explore other practical strategies to improve workers' lives and lessen economic inequality, work precarity, and their associated impacts.

The Role of Employee Ownership

Another way to combat employment precarity and economic inequality is to expand broad-based employee ownership. Broad-based employee ownership is a workplace arrangement that provides all or most employees with a financial stake in their company, typically through stock ownership or equity. Before elaborating on the benefits of employee ownership for workers, it should be noted that different forms confer varying levels of governance and financial rights over the firm to employees (Ben-Ner & Jones, 1995). As one scholar of employee ownership stated in testimony before the US House of Representatives, "employee ownership is not a simple, unidimensional concept that permits an easy classification of a firm as 'employee-owned' or of an employee as an 'employee-owner'" (Kruse, 2002, p. 2).

In the US, major forms of broad-based employee ownership include Employee Stock Ownership Plans (ESOPs), worker cooperatives, and employee-owned trusts (EOTs). The extent of an employee's rights and how they are exercised varies between and within models (Palmieri & Cooper, 2023). Some models provide an expansive set of governance and financial rights, as in worker cooperatives, where members share in the company's profits and vote for the board of directors. Others provide financial rights with more limited governance rights, as with ESOPs, where employees are granted stock in the company at no cost, but governance structures need not differ from typical corporations. In EOTs, a perpetual trust owns the company, and one of its purposes is the worker's well-being. Workers are the beneficiaries in this arrangement and typically receive a portion of profits each year (NCEO, 2023f). Moreover, employee-owned companies often enact various human resource policies that encourage an "ownership culture" of participation and engagement in the workplace (Weitzman & Kruse, 1990). While all forms of broad-based employee ownership seek to broaden ownership of productive assets to employees (beyond managers and the corporate suite), they do so in a multitude of ways that a single definition or prototypical example cannot capture. Instead, it is useful to highlight a characteristic they all share: providing all workers with a formal and direct way to benefit from the financial success in the companies where they work.

Key to the argument that employee ownership can serve as an alternative solution to economic inequality is the idea that employee-owned companies allow workers of all types to earn increased income and wealth. Numerous studies have found employee-owners receive between 8-20% higher wages than non-employee owners (Blasi et al., 1996; Kardas et al., 1998; Kim & Quimet, 2014; Kruse et al., 2010). Surveys of US ESOP companies find the retirement balances of employee-owners are more than twice as large as those of US residents (NCEO, 2023a; Wiefek & Nicholson, 2018), replicating earlier studies that find employee-owners have 2.2 times more in retirement wealth and 20% more in financial assets overall (Rodgers,

2010). Additionally, an analysis of the US GSS finds employee-owners have, on average, $134,000 in wealth from company stock (Rutgers School of Management and Labor Relations, 2018). Research shows pay and wealth are more equally distributed in employee-owned companies compared to conventional firms (Bernstein, 2016; Buchele et al., 2010; DAWI, 2022). Additionally, evidence suggests employee ownership can help build wealth for low- to moderate-income workers. In one of the largest qualitative studies of ESOPs, Boguslaw and Schur (2019) collected quantitative data and conducted in-depth interviews with 141 low- to moderate-income individuals from 21 companies across 16 states. Comparing their total wealth to national averages revealed significant differences. For example, Black women in the study held $55,000 in total wealth, compared to the national average of $200, with similar patterns across other racial and gender groups.

Many of the above studies are cross-sectional and do not compare differences in income and wealth over time. Two notable exceptions use longitudinal data. The first, conducted by Kim & Quimet (2014), investigates the adoption of employee ownership in 400 public companies over 30 years and finds that company-level wages increased, on average, 20% after adoption. Wiefek (2017), comparing individuals 28-34 years of age who were either employee-owners or not, finds that employee-owners have 33% higher income from wages and 92% higher household wealth. The research on income and wealth generation associated with employee ownership strongly suggests that it can improve current inequalities in income and wealth.

In addition to income and wealth, employee-owned companies provide increased employment stability. A large body of evidence shows employee-owned firms have higher survival rates than conventional counterparts and are less likely to lay off workers, particularly in crises (Brill, 2012; Blair et al., 2000; Blasi et al., 2013; Burdin, 2014; Kurtulus & Kruse, 2018; NCEO, 2023f; Park et al., 2004; Pérotin, 1987; Rosen & Rodgers, 2014). Blair et al. (2000) compared all publicly traded companies with 20% or more employee ownership to a matched sample of conventional firms from 1983 to 1991 and found that employee-owned firms have higher survival rates. Kurtulus and Kruse (2018) tracked employee-owned companies from 1991 to 2011, including two major recessions, and found that compared to conventional companies, they shed jobs at half the rate and were 25% less likely to go out of business. Wiefek (2017) found that employee-owners have 53% longer tenure than non-employee owners. The NCEO compared employee-owned companies to conventional ones in the food sector during COVID-19, finding firing and quit rates substantially lower in employee-owned firms (NCEO, 2022). Studies of worker cooperatives reach similar conclusions, finding that in response to economic shocks, these firms typically adjust hours or pay instead of laying off workers (Birchall & Ketilson, 2009; Burdin & Dean, 2009; Burdin, 2014; Craig & Pencavel, 1992, 1993, 1995; Pencavel et al., 2006), a trend that continued through the pandemic (Mankling et al., 2020).

Beyond providing wealth, income, and employment stability, employee-owned companies are more likely to offer a range of non-wage benefits than conventional firms. Wiefek (2017) finds that employee-owners are more likely to have access to flexible work schedules (52% vs. 34%), paid maternity or parental leave (65% vs. 31%), tuition reimbursement (62% vs. 24%), and childcare benefits (23% vs. 5%). Boguslaw and Schur (2019) find that basic financial education and professional development opportunities are typical at employee-owned companies. Additionally, employee-owned firms are more likely to institutionalize processes allowing worker participation in decision-making (Blasi et al., 2016; Freeman et al., 2010; Frohlich et al., 1998; Logue & Yates, 2001).

Research shows that employee-owned companies are more likely to offer an additional retirement plan beyond their employee ownership arrangement than conventional companies are to offer a single plan (Carrol, 2015; Rodgers, 2018, 2010). In a first-of-its-kind study, NCEO researchers analyzed over 300,000 tax records of retirement plan filings for employee-owned and non-employee-owned companies between 2019 and 2020 (NCEO, 2021). After matching companies with 401(k) plans of similar size, industry, and region, they found that employee-owned companies provide retirement account balances more than double those of conventional counterparts ($132,000 vs. $64,000). Together, the increased income, wealth, and employment stability that employee-owned companies provide enable employee-owners to improve their financial security and allow families to move from just making ends meet to managing life's challenges while planning for the future (Boguslaw & Schur, 2019, p. 2).

Like unions, the benefits of employee ownership extend beyond the workplace. In what is termed "workplace spillover," political scientists theorize that participatory workplaces foster democratic attitudes and skills needed for civic and political participation (Almond & Verba, 1963; Pateman, 1970; Verba et al., 1995). While early evidence faced methodological challenges (Burn & Konrad, 1987; Elden, 1981; Greenberg, 1986; Greenberg et al., 1996; Schur, 2003; Sobel, 1993), recent work has overcome many issues. It finds that participatory workplaces correlate strongly with various forms of political participation, including voting, protesting, attending community meetings, campaigning, and volunteering (Budd et al., 2018; Lopes et al., 2014), as well as pro-democratic attitudes and interest in politics (Geurkink et al., 2022; Timming & Summers, 2020). More recent studies have produced evidence suggesting that increased income, wealth, and employment stability associated with employee ownership is another factor that contributes to workplace spillover in the form of increased voting in presidential elections (Palmieri, 2024).

With roughly 6,500 companies employing 10 million employee-owners, the US has one of the most robust employee ownership sectors globally. Employee-owned companies exist across all major industries and range in size from 10 to tens of thousands of employees. Considering the private sector labor market, about 9% of workers are employee-owners, making them more common than the 6% of union members (BLS, 2024). Nevertheless, despite their long history dating to the early 19th century (Curl, 2012; Leikein, 2005; Logue & Yates, 1999) and the benefits they provide, employee ownership remains "on the fringe of both social consciousness and academic literature" (Freeman, 2007, p. 1). Political science is no exception; as Mazumder & Yan (2023) note, only eight articles in the American Political Science Review in the past decade mention corporations. They conclude that while the workplace is "a field ripe with politics," it is "bereft of political science" (Mazumder & Yan, 2023, p. 1).

Data and Measures

This chapter analyzes a pooled data set constructed from responses to the 2006, 2014, and 2018 General Social Survey (GSS). The GSS is conducted by the National Opinion Research Center at the University of Chicago in partnership with the National Science Foundation. The GSS is conducted every two years and information is obtained by face-to-face interviews of more than 1,500 randomly selected adults throughout the US. The GSS uses a split sample design where all respondents are asked a core set of identical questions, and portions of the whole sample receive different ballots that include questions associated with topical modules. In the years 2002, 2006, 2010, 2014, and 2018, a "Shared Capitalism" module was added to the GSS by scholars interested in studying employee ownership (Blasi et al., 2014). This module includes measures of employee ownership, union membership, economic resources, workplace participation in decision-making, on-the-job training, employment stability, and other measures relevant to describing workers' relationship with their workplace.

Key to this analysis is the measure of wealth and income, which serve as the two variables measuring economic resources. A measure of wealth appears only in the Shared Capitalism module in the years 2006, 2014, and 2018 GSS. After limiting the GSS data set to these three years, cases were selected based on responses to questions of interest that tap into how workers interact with their workplace via economic resource generation, employment stability, and workplace participation in training and decision-making. Selecting cases on this basis results in a sample of $n = 1959$.

Measures

Table 1 presents the dependent variables of interest used in this chapter with sample statistics. How each variable was measured in the GSS, and how it was coded for this analysis, is described in this section.

Table 1. Key variable definitions and descriptive statistics

Variable	*Scale*	*Mean*	*Std dev*
Workplace Arrangements			
Employee Share Owner	1 = yes, 0 = no	0.203	0.402
Union Member	1 = yes, 0 = no	0.102	0.302
Workplace Participation and Benefits			
Partake in decisions that affect themselves	1 = never, 4	3.044	0.950
Involved in team, committee, or task force addressing workplace issues	1 = yes, 0 = no	0.291	0.454
Received formal training sponsored by an employer	1 = yes, 0 = no	0.502	0.500
Fringe benefits are "okay"	1 = yes, 0 = no	0.729	0.445
Economic Resources			
Respondent's total wealth	1 = 0 -10th percentile, 10 = 90th -100th percentile	5.127	2.879
Respondent's income	1 = 0 -10th percentile, 10 = 90th -100th percentile	5.234	2.809
Employment Stability			
Years working with present employer	.25 = min, 67 = max	7.795	9.038
Laid off in the last 12 months	1 = yes, 0 = no	0.057	0.232

***Source*:** General Social Survey (2006, 2014, 2018).

Employee Ownership. This is the primary exogenous variable and is measured using the question "Do you own any shares of stock in the company where you now work, either directly or through some type of retirement or stock plan?". The variable is coded so that 1 = yes, and 0 = no.

Union Membership. This is a second primary exogenous variable based on the question "Do you or your spouse belong to a labor union?" This variable is coded so that union membership 1= yes and 0 = no.

Economic Resources. Three variables are used to measure this concept, wealth, income, and employment stability. Wealth is one of the primary dependent variables measuring the economic dimension of workplace participation. It is based on the question "Please estimate your total wealth". It was originally coded as an ordinal variable with values that imply the respondent's wealth within a given range with values ranging from 1 to 15 where a value of 1 implies the respondent made "Less than $5000" and a value of 15 implies the respondent made "above $10 million". The variable is recoded into deciles whose values range from 1-10, where 1 implies the respondent falls within the 0-10th percentile and 10 implies the respondent falls within the 90th-100th percentile. This helps correct changes in the relative purchasing power of a dollar that occurs from year to year. Instead of comparing ranges of dollar amounts whose relative value would change from year to year, this new measure compares the location of the respondent in the broader distribution of wealth within each sample year.

Income is the second variable measuring the economic dimension of workplace participation and is based on the question: "In which of these groups did your earnings for the last year fall? That is, before taxes or other deductions". Like wealth, respondents' income takes the form of an ordinal variable that includes income ranges. As with the variable measuring wealth, the variable measuring respondent income for each year was recoded into deciles whose values range from 1-10, where 1 implies the respondent falls within the 0-10th percentile of income and 10 implies the respondent falls within the 90-100th percentile of income in a given survey year.

Workplace Participation and Benefits. Three variables are used to measure different facets of workplace participation. Respondents were asked to evaluate 1) how often they partake in making decisions that affect themselves 2) if they were involved in a team, committee, or task force addressing workplace issues, and 3) if they received formal training sponsored by the employer. Respondents answered the first question using a 4-point scale where 1 = never and 4 = often. The second and third questions are coded so that 1 = yes and 0 = no. A fourth variable measures if workers are satisfied with their fringe benefits. This variable was recoded so that responses of "very" and "somewhat true" (values of 1 and 2) were combined to = 1 and responses of "not too true" and "not at all true" (values of 3 and 4) where combined to = 0.

Employment Stability. Employment stability is measured using two variables. The first is a measure of the respondent's tenure at their current employer. Respondents were asked the question "How long have you worked in your present job for your current employer?". The variable is continuous and measures the number of years the respondent worked at a given company. It ranges from .25 (less than six months) to 67. The second variable is based on the question, "Were you laid off in the last year?" and serves as an additional measure of employment stability. The variable is coded 1 = yes, 0 = no.

Controls. Controls for other relevant individual attributes include sex, degree, age, race, region, industry, and occupation. Table 2 below reports summary statistics for these variables.

Table 2. Control variable descriptive statistics

Variable & Scale	*Total*	*Percent*
Degree: 0-4, 0= Less than HS, 4=Graduate		
Less than high school	148	7.55
High school	1,054	53.80
Associates	193	9.85
Bachelors	410	20.93
Graduate	154	7.86
Race: 1=White, 2=Black, 3=Other		
White	1,479	75.50
Black	245	12.51
Other	235	12.00
Sex: Male=1, Female=0		
Male	1,067	54.47
Female	892	45.53
Age: Continuous, Min 19, Max 89		48.104
18-35	678	34.61
36-65	1,205	61.51
65 and over	76	3.88
Occupation: 1-6, 1=Management, 6=Military		
Management and Professional	660	33.69
Service	314	16.03
Sales and Office	476	24.30
Natural Resources, construction, and maintenance	237	12.10
Production, transportation, and material moving	271	13.83
Active Military	1	0.05
Industry: 1-16, 1=Agriculture, 16=Military		
Agriculture, Forestry, and Fishing	27	1.38
Mining, Oil, Gas Extraction	14	0.71
Utilities	25	1.28
Construction	175	8.93
Manufacturing	283	14.45
Wholesale and Retail Trade	305	15.57
Transportation	101	5.16
Information	60	3.06
Financial Activities	184	9.39

continued on following page

Table 2. Continued

Variable & Scale	*Total*	*Percent*
Professional and Technical Services	161	8.22
Management administrative and waste services	80	4.08
Education and Health Services	258	13.17
Leisure and Hospitality	182	9.29
Other Services	89	4.54
Public Administration	14	0.71
Active Military Personnel	1	0.05
Region: 1-9, 1=New England, 9=Pacific		
New England	75	3.83
Middle Atlantic	214	10.92
East North Central	354	18.07
West North Central	137	6.99
South Atlantic	400	20.42
East South Atlantic	113	5.77
West South Central	191	9.75
Mountain	186	9.49
Pacific	289	14.75

***Source*:** General Social Survey (2006, 2014, 2018).

Results

Figure 1 presents a series of bar graphs representing the mean values for key variables measuring economic resources, workplace participation, and employment stability without controls. The bar graphs separate the sample into three comparison groups: employee-owners, union members, and traditional employees (defined as those who are neither union members nor employee-owners). A clear pattern emerges across these three areas of interest – employee-owners are consistently better off than traditional employees and report outcomes that are either better or on par with those reported by union members.

Beginning first with economic resources depicted in the top two tiles, average employee-owners earn higher incomes and have more wealth than traditional employees and union members. In the case of the income variable, employee-owners have a value of 7.08 compared to traditional employees and union members, who have mean scores of 4.87 and 6.35, respectively. Recall that the wealth and income variables were recoded into deciles where 1 implies a respondent falls within the

0-10th percentile and 10 implies the respondent falls within the 90th-100th percentile. Thus, a score of 7.08 can be understood as employee owners being in the 60th percentile of overall wealth, or to place it into a dollar range, having between $100,000-$150,000, whereas traditional employees with a score of 4.65 have between $40,000-$75,000. A similar pattern emerges when looking at wealth, with the mean value for employee-owners being 6.57, larger than traditional employees and union members.

The second row of tiles reports statistics for two variables measuring workplace involvement and participation in decision-making. The left tile looks at the variable measuring workplace participation, and because it is a binary variable, it can be interpreted in percentage terms. It demonstrates it is more common for employee owners to report being part of a committee, team, or task force addressing workplace issues, with 40% of employee owners answering yes to this question, which is higher than that of union members (34%) and approaching twice that of traditional employees (24%). The next tile to the right looks at the variable measuring the respondent's ability to make decisions that affect their daily work. Though the values are relatively similar across all three groups, employee-owners have a slightly larger value (3.28).

Figure 1. Comparing employee owners with traditional employees and union members

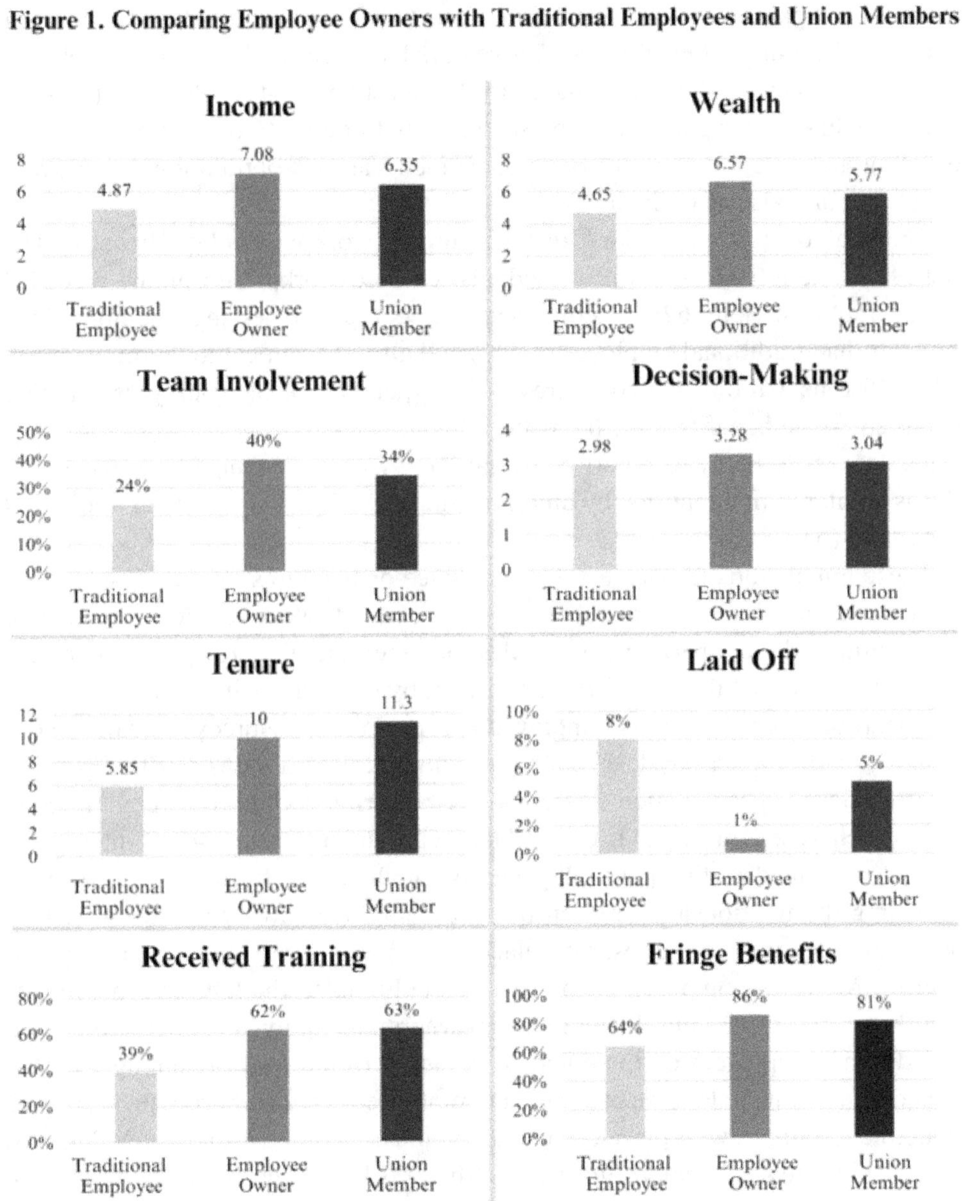

Note: Graphs report mean values of variables. Data used includes GSS (2006, 2014, 2018).

The third row of tiles looks at two measures of employment stability: tenure and layoffs. The left tile shows that the mean tenure for employee-owners (10.1 years) is lower but comparable to that of union members (11.3 years) and substantially larger than that of traditional employees (5.8 years). The second tile in this row reports whether a worker was laid off in the last year and shows that employee-owners are much less likely to report this being the case, with only 1% of employee-owners reporting such an event while 5% of union members and 8% of traditional employees reported being laid off in the last year.

The final row of tiles considers two measures of workplace-related benefits. The first tile to the left measures if individuals received workplace training provided by the employer. Here, 62% of employee owners report receiving training, which is higher than traditional employees (39%) and almost identical to union members (63%). The next tile to the right provides the percentage of employees satisfied with their fringe benefits. Like the pattern found for receiving training, employee-owners are more likely to report being satisfied with their fringe benefits (86%). This is similar to that reported by union members (81%) and larger than traditional employees (64%).

These initial statistics suggest that employee ownership serves as a workplace arrangement that, like union membership, is associated with higher levels of income and wealth, workplace participation, and employment stability. However, it can very well be the case that these statistics are driven by differences in other characteristics found between these three employee groups. Perhaps employee-owners work in regions with higher pay levels, are concentrated within industries that provide opportunities for participation or are unevenly distributed into other demographic groups such as sex, race, and age correlated with outcome variables of interest.

Table 2 considers this possibility and presents results from OLS regressions estimating the relationship between being an employee-owner and the variables measuring economic resources, workplace participation, employment stability, and controls. Model 1, composed of the first two columns to the left, presents results from bivariate regressions for employee-owners and union members compared to traditional employees on the outcome variables of interest. Beginning with the first column from the left, we can see that employee-owners report higher levels of economic resources, workplace participation, and employment stability and that all relationships are statistically significant at the .001 level. The second column from the left, which measures the same relationships for union members, tells a similar story with some caveats. Union members report higher levels of both income and wealth and are more likely to report being involved in teams and receive training. However, when looking at decision-making, the coefficient for union membership is minimal, almost zero. Likewise, while union members report longer tenure (4.10) compared to traditional employees, the estimate for being laid off, while negative (indicating a lower likelihood of being laid off), is small and insignificant.

The estimates in the first two columns suggest that while employee ownership and union membership are associated with positive outcomes for workers, the effects of employee ownership are greater than that of unions across all eight variables of interest. For example, the coefficient measuring income for employee-owners is 2.11 compared to 1.25 for union members and when looking at wealth is more than two times larger. (1.87 compared to .743). The same can be said of workplace participation, where the coefficient for the variable measuring decision-making is .315 for employee-owners and approaching zero for union members. Likewise, the coefficient for being involved in teams is nearly 3 times larger for employee-owners compared to that of union members. The same is true, though to a lesser extent, for receiving training. In the case of fringe benefits, the coefficient for employee-owners is more than two times as large as that for union members. Looking at tenure, the coefficients for employee-owners and union members are roughly similar with both types of work arrangements associated with 4 more years of tenure when compared to traditional employees. In the case of being laid off, the relationships are negative for both employee-owners and union members (suggesting both are less likely to report being laid off in the last year). However, the laid-off coefficient for employee-owners is nearly ten times larger than that of union members and statistically significant, suggesting that employee-owners experience more employment stability when compared to traditional workers than union members.

While the broader patterns laid out by the first two columns of Table 3 are compelling, these bivariate estimates can still be driven by other individual characteristics of union members and employee-owners. Model 2, which comprises the third and fourth columns, estimates the same relationships present in Model 1 but with a complete set of controls included (listed at the bottom of the table). The third column of Table 3, which reports estimates for employee-owners compared to traditional employees, shows that the coefficients for all variables are reduced when including controls, suggesting that differences in individual characteristics were indeed driving a portion of the bivariate results in Model 1. Second, though the estimates for employee-owners are reduced, their direction is unchanged and, in the case of all eight measures, remain statistically significant at the .001 level. Employee owners have higher levels of wealth and income when compared to traditional workers. For workplace participation and benefits, employee-owners are more likely to be a part of decision-making, be involved in a team, receive on-the-job training, and report being satisfied with their fringe benefits than non-employee owners. Finally, the coefficient for tenure shows that, on average, employee-owners work 1.98 years longer at the same firm and are less likely to report being laid off (-.044) when compared to traditional employees with similar characteristics.

Table 3. OLS regression: Economic benefits and job quality for employee owners

	Model 1		Model 2	
	Employee Owners	*Union Members*	*Employee Owners*	*Union Members*
Economic Resources				
Income	2.11*** (.138)	1.25*** (.131)	.907*** (.124)	.603*** (.146)
Wealth	1.87*** (.143)	.743*** (.176)	.513*** (.126)	-.109 (.147)
Workplace Participation				
Decision Making	.315*** (.047)	-.000 (.052)	.175*** (.054)	-.133** (.061)
Involved in Teams	.144*** (.021)	.052* (.026)	.081*** (.026)	.023 (.030)
Receive Training	.220*** (.023)	.151*** (.028)	.145*** (.028)	.133*** (.032)
Fringe Benefits	.193*** (.023)	.099*** (.713)	.088*** (.026)	.043*** (.023)
Employment Stability				
Tenure	4.14*** (.421)	4.10*** (.492)	1.98*** (.432)	2.67*** (.511)
Laid off	-.065*** (.0123)	-.006 (.004)	-.044*** (.014)	.005 (.015)

Source: GSS (2006, 2014, 2018).

Note: OLS coefficients estimated using STATA 17. Standard errors in parentheses. Controls in the full model include degree, race, age, sex, industry, occupational prestige, region, income, wealth, and tenure. Region and industry are operationalized using a set of dummy variables. Wealth and tenure are not included in the set of controls when they appear as dependent variables in Model 1 and Model 2.

* $p \leq .05$; ** $p \leq .01$; *** $p \leq .001$.

Another way to place these results into context is by comparing the results for employee-owners to those of union members, which are reported in the fourth column of Table 3. In all cases except that of tenure, the coefficients for employee ownership are on par or larger than those reported for union members. The coefficient for union member wealth stands out, as it is negative, though not statistically significant. This is surprising as union membership is understood to have a positive relationship with wealth, particularly retirement wealth (Glass et al., 2023). One explanation for this unanticipated result is that union member wealth may primarily take the form of a pension, which may not be as easily calculated as the value of one's stock in a company. Union members may be underreporting their overall wealth by not considering the future value of their pension payouts. Second, many employee-owned companies engage employee-owners around the company stock price and the value of individual employees' account holdings. This may make the value of their stock holdings "top of mind" and thus make them more likely to know and include the value of their stock in the overall calculation of their wealth. In other words, the coefficient for union member wealth may be an artifact of underestimation by the respondents themselves.

Nevertheless, even when comparing income, which, unlike wealth, is much easier for individuals to estimate, the coefficient for employee owners (.907) is larger than that of union members (.603). Turning to measures of workplace participation and benefits, the coefficients for employee-owners are all positive, statistically significant, and larger than those of union members across all measures. Notably, in the case of engaging in decision-making, the coefficient for union members is negative and significant (-.133). One reason this may be occurring is that job responsibilities and descriptions are much more uniform and stringent due to the collective bargaining contracts unions work under (Kirmeyer & Shirom, 1986), leaving less room for workers to decide how to complete their day-to-day work. Finally, looking at measures of employment stability, union members work 2.67 years more at the same company when compared to non-union members, which is slightly greater than the difference between employee-owners and non-employee owners (1.98). The coefficient for reporting being laid off is positive for union members, although it is small (.005) and not statistically significant. Still, this is in stark contrast to the coefficient for employee-owners which is negative and statistically significant (-.044). Recall that the measure for being laid off is binary. As such, the coefficient for employee-owners can be understood as fewer employee-owners reporting being laid off (by 4.4 percentage points).

The results from Table 3 suggest that, on average, employee-owners enjoy many of the same benefits associated with union membership when considering resource generation, workplace participation, and employment stability. In fact, in most cases, the differences between employee-owners and traditional employees are larger than those found between traditional employees and union members. This finding alone is noteworthy as employee ownership receives much less attention than unions in discussions regarding wealth building, job quality, and workplace participation. Still, the question remains as to whether this pattern holds when looking at demographic groupings, including race and sex. That is, do the differences between employee-owners and traditional workers reported in Table 2 extend to female and Black workers? Affirmative answers to this question would bolster the argument that employee ownership, like union membership, is associated with improved work quality and wealth-building opportunities for workers in both demographic groups.

Table 4 reports results from OLS regressions with the same set of controls used in Model 2 of Table 2 but using subsamples of Black and female workers. Beginning with the first column to the left, which provides estimates for Black employee owners compared to Black non-employee owners, we can see that all coefficients are moving in the expected direction. However, the coefficients for wealth, decision-making, and tenure are not statistically significant. The second column, which reports coefficients for Black union members compared to non-union members provides a more complicated story. While the estimates for economic resources are positive, and in the case of income larger than those of employee-owners, decision-making and being involved in teams are both negative, meaning that traditional workers were more likely to report they were involved in decision-making or being part of a team than union members with similar characteristics.

Moving to employment stability, the results are also mixed. On average, Black union members have a tenure of 3.5 years longer than that of traditional workers, which is nearly four times larger than the difference between employee-owners and traditional workers (.914). On the other hand, the coefficient for being laid off is positive though not statistically significant for union members (.012), meaning they were more likely than traditional workers to report being laid off in the same year. For employee owners, the opposite is the case. The coefficient is negative, statistically significant, and larger (-.082). On the whole Black employee owners are indeed better off than traditional Black employees. In many instances, the differences reported between Black employee-owners and Black non-employee owners are on par with, or greater than, those associated with union membership. The only exception to this pattern is that of tenure where the differences between union members and traditional workers are greater than that found between employee-owners and traditional workers.

Columns three and four of Table 4 report coefficients for female employee-owners and union members, respectively. The results in column three tell a similar story as those in column one – female employee owners enjoy more economic resources, higher levels of workplace participation, and increased employment stability compared to traditional workers with similar characteristics. All the coefficients move in the expected direction and are statistically significant except for decision-making and fringe benefits.

Table 4. OLS regression: Economic benefits and job quality for black and female employee owners and union members

	Black Workers		*Female Workers*	
	Employee Owners	*Union Members*	*Employee Owners*	*Union Members*
Economic Resources				
Income	.642** (.337)	.768*** (.331)	1.01*** (.189)	.672** (.146)
Wealth	.456 (.347)	.153 (.353)	.480*** (.208)	-.221 (.226)
Workplace Participation				
Decision Making	.097 (.047)	-.295 (.153)	.158 (.086)	-.163 (.091)
Involved in Teams	.211** (.071)	-.010* (.026)	.090* (.040)	-.016 (.030)
Receive Training	.158* (.080)	.101 (.081)	.182*** (.044)	.084 (.047)
Fringe Benefits	.089* (.075)	.054* (.073)	.072 (.080)	-.002 (.044)
Employment Stability				
Tenure	.914 (1.17)	3.51** (1.25)	1.44** (.643)	2.93*** (.729)
Laid off	-.082*** (.045)	.012 (.040)	-.036* (.014)	-.003 (.019)
	N=245	N=277	N=892	N=934

Source: GSS (2006,2014,2018).

Note: OLS coefficients estimated using STATA 17. Standard errors in parentheses. Controls for the first two columns from the left include degree, age, sex, industry, occupation, region, income, wealth, and tenure. Controls for the third and fourth columns include race, age, industry, occupational prestige, region, income, wealth, and tenure. Region, and industry are operationalized using a set of dummy variables. Wealth, income, and tenure are excluded from the set of controls in models where they appear as dependent variables.

* $p \leq .05$; ** $p \leq .01$; *** $p \leq .001$.

The fourth column, which provides estimates for female union members, tells a less straightforward story. Like Black union members, female union members, on average, earn more income, have longer tenure, and are more likely to receive training on the job compared to traditional workers of the same identity group. However, the coefficients are negative when it comes to wealth, decision-making, being involved in teams, or fringe benefits. Again, in the case of decision-making, this may result from the structure of collective bargaining, which limits the scope of job autonomy. The negative coefficient for being involved in teams could very well be associated with issues of gender bias within unions where women continue to be marginalized and underrepresented in leadership positions (Bryant-Anderson & Roby, 2012). For fringe benefits, this could result from union members having higher expectations for benefits, rather than an objective indicator of the benefits being worse than what traditional employees receive. With these caveats, Table 4 still demonstrates the genuine material benefits of union membership: higher wages and increased employment stability.

Based on the results presented in Table 4, the question of whether the benefits of employee ownership extend to Black and female workers can be answered in the affirmative. The employee-owners in both groups fare better than traditional workers with similar characteristics and in many instances, the differences found between female employee-owners and female traditional workers are on par, or larger than, those found between female union members and female traditional workers. The results provided in Tables 2 and 3 provide strong evidence that, like unions, employee ownership models provide higher quality jobs than those held by traditional workers. This is true if we look at the entire sample or sub-samples broken out by race and sex. Employee-owners, on average, earn more wealth and income, receive more workplace opportunities to participate in decision-making, receive more on-the-job training, are more satisfied with the fringe benefits they receive, and experience more stable employment than traditional employees, and in certain cases, union members.

DISCUSSION AND CONCLUSION

Economic inequality and employment precarity are on the rise, contributing to negative consequences for individual workers and the broader society. What is of most profound concern, from the standpoint of political science, is how both trends undermine basic assumptions of democratic theory, namely the principle of political equality. Beyond abstract principles, employment precarity and inequality are associated with various negative outcomes at the individual and societal level. These include poorer mental and physical health, financial insecurity, distrust of institutions, and lower rates of political participation. There is no shortage of policies that can remedy the current situation. However, due to the polarized nature of US politics, typical policy fixes such as expanding the social safety net or instituting progressive taxation schemes are unlikely to garner broad support from elected officials.

This chapter aims to demonstrate how economic inequality and employment precarity are connected and contribute to a widening of class biases already existing within political participation and the policy-making process. One of the contributions to the existing literature is emphasizing the important, though often overlooked, role the workplace plays in shaping the economic and political inequality nexus.

Doing so allows for a discussion of how interventions at the workplace level may serve as promising pathways by which economic inequality and precarious work can be reduced and how doing so would move us closer to achieving the principle of political equality. It introduces and examines employee ownership, a workplace arrangement rarely discussed in policy circles concerned with economic inequality and job quality into the conversation.

A sizeable literature focuses on the benefits unions provide their members and their critical role in shaping how people interact with their political system and the policy-making process. It is difficult to identify any other organized force that is as well-resourced and committed to benefiting the livelihoods of working people in the US. Still, despite the renewed interest and support that unions enjoy, they remain, if not in decline, then in a state of highly constrained growth due to features of US labor law. Moreover, changes to US labor law are, like other policies aimed at lessening economic inequality and improving the lives of working people, unlikely to be enacted by elected officials who are polarized on such topics.

On the other hand, employee ownership is one of the few policy areas that garner bi-partisan support from across the political spectrum. In the US these efforts have taken place at the municipal, state, and federal levels. In most cases the supportive policies aim to overcome the barriers common barriers. One such barrier includes a lack of awareness. This first barrier can be dealt with by funding awareness campaigns or creating employee ownership offices and centers at the state and national levels that provide reliable information regarding employee ownership models; such centers exist in over 20 states across the US, but without a reliable funding stream, they remain on shaky economic footing. Another barrier that can be overcome through policy is reducing the cost and complexity of transitions to employee ownership. A handful of US states, such as Colorado and Washington, have passed policies that aim to reduce these barriers by offering tax credits to companies that can be used to cover the costs of the transaction. Despite these recent policy wins, employee ownership remains an under-discussed and underutilized business model.

This chapter empirically demonstrates that employee ownership is another workplace-based arrangement that benefits working people in many of the same ways unions do. Employee ownership is associated with positive outcomes for workers through increased wealth and income, workplace participation, and employment stability. Considering the findings presented here and the political support that employee ownership currently receives, there is a strong case for its inclusion in policy debates centered around reducing economic inequality and improving job quality.

REFERENCES

Acemoglu, D., & Robinson, J. A. (2013). Economics versus politics: Pitfalls of policy advice. *The Journal of Economic Perspectives*, 27(2), 173–192. DOI: 10.1257/jep.27.2.173

Ahlquist, J. S. (2017). Labor unions, political representation, and economic inequality. *Annual Review of Political Science*, 20(1), 409–432. DOI: 10.1146/annurev-polisci-051215-023225

Almond, G. A., & Verba, S. (2015). *The civic culture: Political attitudes and democracy in five nations*. Princeton university press. and International Perspectives. Washington: Brookings.

Andersen, R. (2012). Support for democracy in cross-national perspective: The detrimental effect of economic inequality. *Research in Social Stratification and Mobility*, 30(4), 389–402. DOI: 10.1016/j.rssm.2012.04.002

Arrighi, B. A., & Maume, D. J. (1994). Workplace control and political participation. *Sociological Focus*, 27(2), 147–159. DOI: 10.1080/00380237.1994.10571016

Atkinson, A. (2015). *Inequality: What Can Be Done?* Harvard University Press. DOI: 10.4159/9780674287013

Auer, P., & Cazes, S. (2000). The resilience of the long-term employment relationship: Evidence from the industrialized countries. *International Labour Review*, 139(4), 379–408. DOI: 10.1111/j.1564-913X.2000.tb00525.x

Autor, D., Dorn, D., Hanson, G., & Majlesi, K. (2020). Importing political polarization? The electoral consequences of rising trade exposure. *The American Economic Review*, 110(10), 3139–3183.

Ballard-Rosa, C., Jensen, A., & Scheve, K. (2022). Economic decline, social identity, and authoritarian values in the United States. *International Studies Quarterly*, 66(1), sqab027. DOI: 10.1093/isq/sqab027

Bartels, L. M. (2008). *Unequal Democracy: The Political Economy of the New Gilded Age*. Russell Sage Foundation.

Bartels, L. M. (2017). "Political Inequality in Affluent Democracies: The Social Welfare Deficit." CSDI Working Paper 5-2017. Vanderbilt University.https://www.vanderbilt.edu/csdi/includes/Working_Paper_5_2017.pdf

Becher, M., & Stegmueller, D. (2020). Reducing unequal representation: The impact of labor unions on legislative responsiveness in the U.S. Congress. *Perspectives on Politics*, 19(1), 92–109. DOI: 10.1017/S153759272000208X

Ben-Ner, A., & Jones, D. C. (1995). Employee participation, ownership, and productivity: A theoretical framework. *Industrial Relations*, 34(4), 532–554. DOI: 10.1111/j.1468-232X.1995.tb00387.x

Benach, J., Vives, A., Tarafa, G., Delclos, C., & Muntaner, C. (2016). What should we know about precarious employment and health in 2025? Framing the agenda for the next decade of research. *International Journal of Epidemiology*, 45(1), 232–238. DOI: 10.1093/ije/dyv342 PMID: 26744486

Bernstein, J. (2016, January). *Employee Ownership, ESOPs, Wealth and Wages*. Employee-Owned S Corporations of America. http://esca.us/wp-content/uploads/2016/01/ESOP-Study-Final.pdf

Bhattacharya, A., & Ray, T. (2021). Precarious work, job stress, and health-related quality of life. *American Journal of Industrial Medicine*, 64(4), 310–319. DOI: 10.1002/ajim.23223 PMID: 33543533

Bhatti, Y., Dahlgaard, J. O., Hansen, J. H., & Hansen, K. M. (2019). Is door-to-door canvassing effective in Europe? Evidence from a meta-study across six European countries. *British Journal of Political Science*, 49(1), 279–290. DOI: 10.1017/S0007123416000521

Bivens, J., Engdahl, L., Gould, E., Kroeger, T., McNicholas, C., Mishel, L., ... & Zipperer, B. (2017). How today's unions help working people: Giving workers the power to improve their jobs and unrig the economy.

Bjørnskov, C. (2008). Social trust and fractionalization: A possible reinterpretation. *European Sociological Review*, 24(3), 271–283. DOI: 10.1093/esr/jcn004

Blasi, J. R., Freeman, R. B., & Kruse, D. (2014). *The Citizen's Share: Reducing Inequality in the 21st Century*. Yale University Press.

Blasi, J. R., Kruse, D. L., & Weltman, D. (2022). (forthcoming). Employee Share Ownership in the U.S. *Statistics, Research, and Lessons Learned.*

Brady, H. E., Verba, S., & Schlozman, K. L. (1995). Beyond SES: A resource model of political participation. *The American Political Science Review*, 89(2), 271–294. DOI: 10.2307/2082425

Budd, J., Lamare, J. R., & Timming, A. R. (2018). Learning about democracy at work: Cross-national evidence on individual employee voice influencing political participation in civil society. *Industrial & Labor Relations Review*, 71(4), 956–985. DOI: 10.1177/0019793917746619

Burn, S. M., & Konrad, A. M. (1987). Political participation: A matter of community, stress, job autonomy, and contact by political organizations. *Political Psychology*, 8(1), 125–138. DOI: 10.2307/3790989

Card, D. (1996). The effect of unions on the structure of wages: A longitudinal analysis. *Econometrica*, 64(4), 957–979. DOI: 10.2307/2171852

Carnes, N., & Hansen, E. (2016). Does paying politicians more promote economic diversity in legislatures? *The American Political Science Review*, 110(4), 699–716. DOI: 10.1017/S000305541600054X

Carter, N. (2006). Political participation and the workplace: The spillover thesis revisited. *The British Journal of Politics and International Relations, 8*(3), 410-426.

Cingano, F. (2014), "Trends in Income Inequality and Its Impact on Economic Growth", OECD SEM Working Paper No. 163, www.oecd.org/els/workingpapers

Dadush, U., Dervis, K., Milsom, S. P., & Stancil, B. 2012. Inequality in America: Facts, Trends, Democracy at Work Institute. (2022). *2021 State of the Sector: Worker Cooperatives in the U.S.*https://institute.coop/resources/2021-worker-cooperative-state-sector-report

Dow, G. K. (2003). *Governing the firm: workers' control in theory and practice.* Cambridge University Press. DOI: 10.1017/CBO9780511615849

Elden, J. M. (1981). Political efficacy at work: The connection between more autonomous forms of workplace organization and a more participatory politics. *The American Political Science Review*, 75(1), 43–58. DOI: 10.2307/1962158

Elkjær, M. A., & Klitgaard, M. B. (2021). Economic inequality and political responsiveness: A systematic review. *Perspectives on Politics*, •••, 1–20.

Fandos, N. (2021, March 10). House passes labor rights expansion, but Senate chances are slim. *The New York Times*. https://www.nytimes.com/2021/03/09/us/politics/house-labor-rights-bill.html

Farber, H. S., Herbst, D., Kuziemko, I., & Naidu, S. (2021). Unions and inequality over the twentieth century: New evidence from survey data. *The Quarterly Journal of Economics*, 136(3), 1325–1385. DOI: 10.1093/qje/qjab012

Feigenbaum, J., Hertel-Fernandez, A., & Williamson, V. (2018). *From the bargaining table to the ballot box: Political effects of right to work laws* (No. w24259). National Bureau of Economic Research.

Fieveson, L. (2023) August 28. Labor Unions and the US Economy. US Department of the Treasury. Featrued Stories. https://home.treasury.gov/news/featured-stories/labor-unions-and-the-us-economy#ftn6

Fortin, N. M., Lemieux, T., & Lloyd, N. (2021). Labor market institutions and the distribution of wages: The role of spillover effects. *Journal of Labor Economics*, 39(S2), S369–S412. DOI: 10.1086/712923

Freedman, R. B., & Medoff, J. (1984). *What do unions do?* Basic Books.

Freeman, R. B. (2003) What do unions do… to voting? National Bureau of Economic Research. Working paper no. 9992.

Gallego, A. (2016). Inequality and the erosion of trust among the Poor: Experimental evidence. *Socio-economic Review*, 14(3), 443–460. DOI: 10.1093/ser/mww010

Geurkink, B., Akkerman, A., & Sluiter, R. (2022). Political participation and workplace voice: The spillover of suppression by supervisors. *Political Studies*, 70(2), 327–347. DOI: 10.1177/0032321720960969

Gilens, M. (2005). Inequality and Democratic Responsiveness. *Public Opinion Quarterly*, 69(5), 778–796. DOI: 10.1093/poq/nfi058

Gilens, M. (2012). *Affluence and Influence: Economic Inequality and Political Power in America.* Russell Sage Foundation.

Gilens, M., & Page, B. I. (2014). Testing Theories of American Politics: Elites, Interest Groups, and Average Citizens. *Perspectives on Politics*, 12(3), 564–581. DOI: 10.1017/S1537592714001595

Gittleman, M., & Kleiner, M. M. (2016). Wage effects of unionization and occupational licensing coverage in the United States. *Industrial & Labor Relations Review*, 69(1), 142–172. DOI: 10.1177/0019793915601632

Glass, A., Weller, C. E., & Madland, D. (2023, May 3). Unions build wealth for the American working class. *Center for American Progress.* https://www.americanprogress.org/article/unions-build-wealth-for-the-american-working-class/

Glavin, P., Bierman, A., & Schieman, S. (2021). Über-Alienated: Powerless and alone in the gig economy. *Work and Occupations*, 48(4), 399–431. DOI: 10.1177/07308884211024711

Government Accountability Office. Contingent workforce: Size, characteristics, earnings, and benefits. GAO-15-168R. Retrieved from: https://www.gao.gov/products/GAO-15-168R

Gramlich, J. (2021) September 3. Majorities of Americans say unions have a positive effect on U.S. and that decline in union membership is bad. Pew Research Center. https://www.pewresearch.org/short-reads/2021/09/03/majorities-of-americans-say-unions-have-a-positive-effect-on-u-s-and-that-decline-in-union-membership-is-bad/

Greenberg, E. S. (1981). Industrial democracy and the democratic citizen. *The Journal of Politics*, 43(4), 964–981. DOI: 10.2307/2130183

Greenberg, E. S. (1986). *Workplace democracy: The political effects of participation*. Cornell University Press.

Greenberg, E. S. (2008). Spillovers from cooperative and democratic workplaces: Have the benefits been oversold. *Cooperation: The political psychology of effective human interaction*, 219-239. Edited by Snyder, M., Sullivan, B., & Sullivan, J - Mark Snyder, Brandon Sullivan, and John Sullivan

Greenberg, E. S., Grunberg, L., & Daniel, K. (1996). Industrial Work and Political Participation: Beyond "Simple Spillover". *Political Research Quarterly*, 49(2), 305–330. DOI: 10.1177/106591299604900204

Greenberg, E. S., Snyder, M., Sullivan, B., & Sullivan, J. (2008). Spillovers from cooperative and democratic workplaces: Have the benefits been oversold. *Cooperation: The political psychology of effective human interaction*, 219-239

Grigoli, F. (2017). *A New Twist in the Link Between Inequality and Economic Development. May 11th 2017*. IMF Blog.

Hacker, J. (2006). *The Great Risk Shift: The Assault on American Jobs, Families, Health Care and Retirement and How You Can Fight Back*. Oxford University Press.

Hacker, J., & Pierson, P. (2010). Winner-Take-All Politics: Public Policy, Political Organization, and the Precipitous Rise of Top Incomes in the United States. *Politics & Society*, 38(2), 152–204. DOI: 10.1177/0032329210365042

Harknett, K., Schneider, D., & Luhr, S. (2022). Who cares if parents have unpredictable work schedules?: Just-in-time work schedules and child care arrangements. *Social Problems*, 69(1), 164–183. DOI: 10.1093/socpro/spaa020 PMID: 37946720

Hertel-Fernandez, A. (2020) February 18. Aligning U.S. labor law with worker preferences for labor representation. Washington Center for Equitable Growth. https://equitablegrowth.org/aligning-u-s-labor-law-with-worker-preferences-for-labor-representation/

Hertel-Fernandez, A., & Gould-Werth, A. (2020). *Labor Organizations and Unemployment Insurance: A Virtuous Circle Supporting U.S. Workers' Voices and Reducing Disparities in Benefits*. Washington Center for Equitable Growth, October 2020.

Hirsch, B., Macpherson, D., Even, W. (2023). "Union Membership, Coverage, and Earnings from the CPS". Unionstats.com.

Howell, D. R., & Kalleberg, A. L. (2019). Declining job quality in the United States: Explanations and evidence. *The Russell Sage Foundation Journal of the Social Sciences : RSF*, 5(4), 1–53. DOI: 10.7758/rsf.2019.5.4.01

Jian, G., & Jeffres, L. (2008). Spanning the boundaries of work: Workplace participation, political efficacy, and political involvement. *Communication Studies*, 59(1), 35–50. DOI: 10.1080/10510970701849370

Julià, M., Vanroelen, C., Bosmans, K., Van Aerden, K., & Benach, J. (2017). Precarious Employment and Quality of Employment in Relation to Health and Well-being in Europe. [PubMed] [Google Scholar]. *International Journal of Health Services*, 47(3), 389–409. DOI: 10.1177/0020731417707491 PMID: 28449605

Kallas, J., Ritchie, K., & Friedman, E. (2022). Cornell-ILR Labor action tracker annual report. Accessed September 26 2023. https://www.ilr.cornell.edu/faculty-and-research/labor-action-tracker-2022?utm_source=npr_newsletter&utm_medium=email&utm_content=20230227&utm_term=8035455&utm_campaign=money&utm_id=208962&orgid=92&utm_att1=

Kalleberg, A. (2016). *December 21*. Institutions, Precarious Work, and Inequality. Russel Sage Foundation.

Kalleberg, A. L. (2011). *Good jobs, bad jobs: The rise of polarized and precarious employment systems in the United States*. Russell Sage Foundation.

Kalleberg, A. L., & Vallas, S. P. (2018). Probing precarious work: Theory, research, and politics. *Research in the Sociology of Work*, 31, 1–30. DOI: 10.1108/S0277-283320170000031017

Kanitsar, G. (2022). The inequality-trust nexus revisited: At what level of aggregation does income inequality matter for social trust? *Social Indicators Research*, 163(1), 171–195. DOI: 10.1007/s11205-022-02894-w

Karasek, R. A.Jr. (1976). *The Impact of the Work Environment on Life Outside the Job. Ph.D. Disseration.* Massachusetts Institute of Technology.

Kardas, P., Scharf, A. L., & Keogh, J. (1998). Wealth and income consequences of ESOPs and employee ownership: a comparative study from Washington State. *Journal of Employee Ownership Law and Finance*,10(4), Keith, M. G., Harms, P. D., & Long, A. C. (2020). Worker health and well-being in the gig economy: A proposed framework and research agenda. In Perrewé, P. L., Harms, P. D., & Chang, C.-H. (Eds.), *Entrepreneurial and small business stressors, experienced stress, and well being* (pp. 1–33). Emerald Publishing., DOI: 10.1108/S1479-355520200000018002

Kerrissey, J., & Schofer, E. (2013). Union membership and political participation in the United States. *Social Forces*, 91(3), 895–928. DOI: 10.1093/sf/sos187

Kim, E. H., & Ouimet, P. (2014). Broad-based employee stock ownership: Motives and outcomes. *The Journal of Finance*, 69(3), 1273–1319. DOI: 10.1111/jofi.12150

Kim, S. M., Krisher, T., & Megerian, C. (2023) September 26th Biden to show solidarity with striking UAW workers in historic move. Associated Press. https://www.pbs.org/newshour/politics/biden-to-show-solidarity-with-striking-uaw-workers-in-historic-move

Knepper, M. (2020). From the fringe to the fore: Labor unions and employee compensation. *The Review of Economics and Statistics*, 102(1), 98–112. DOI: 10.1162/rest_a_00803

Kochan, T. A., Yang, D., Kimball, W., & Kelly, E. (2018). Worker Voice in America: Is There a Gap between What Workers Expect and What They Experience? *Industrial & Labor Relations Review*, 72(1), 3–38. DOI: 10.1177/0019793918806250

Krieckhaus, J., Son, B., Bellinger, N. M., & Wells, J. M. (2014). Economic inequality and democratic support. *The Journal of Politics*, 76(1), 139–151. DOI: 10.1017/S0022381613001229

Lafferty, W. (1985). Decision making involvement and socioeconomic resources in Norway: A normative–empirical analysis. *Scandinavian Political Studies*, 8(4), 1–32. DOI: 10.1111/j.1467-9477.1985.tb00325.x

Lafferty, W. M. (1989). Work as a source of political learning among wage-laborers and lower-level employees. *Political learning in adulthood*, 89-101. In Sigel, R. S. (Ed.), *Political Learning in Adulthood.* University of Chicago Press.

Leighley, J. E., & Nagler, J. (1992). Individual and systemic influences on turnout: Who votes? 1984. *The Journal of Politics*, 54(3), 718–740. DOI: 10.2307/2132308

Leighley, J. E., & Nagler, J. (2007). Unions, voter turnout, and class bias in the US electorate, 1964–2004. *The Journal of Politics*, 69(2), 430–441. DOI: 10.1111/j.1468-2508.2007.00541.x

Leighley, J. E., & Nagler, J. (2013). *Who votes now?: Demographics, issues, inequality, and turnout in the United States*. Princeton University Press. DOI: 10.23943/princeton/9780691159348.001.0001

Lewchuk, W., Clarke, M., & De Wolff, A. (2008). Working without commitments: Precarious employment and health. *Work, Employment and Society*, 22(3), 387–406. DOI: 10.1177/0950017008093477

Lim, S. (2017). "Bad jobs" for marriage: Precarious work and the transition to first marriage. *Research in the Sociology of Work*, 31, 399–427. DOI: 10.1108/S0277-283320170000031015

Lopes, H., Lagoa, S., & Calapez, T. (2014). Declining autonomy at work in the EU and its effect on civic behavior. *Economic and Industrial Democracy*, 35(2), 341–366. DOI: 10.1177/0143831X13484606

Macmillan, R., & Shanahan, M. J. (2021). Why precarious work is bad for health: Social marginality as key mechanisms in a multi-national context. *Social Forces*, 100(2), 821–851. DOI: 10.1093/sf/soab006

Mason, R. M. (1982). *Participatory and workplace democracy: A theoretical development in critique of liberalism*. Southern Illinois University Press.

Mazumder, S., & Yan, A. (2023). What Do Americans Want from (Private) Government? Experimental Evidence Demonstrates that Americans Want Workplace Democracy. *The American Political Science Review*, •••, 1–17. DOI: 10.1017/S0003055423000667

McCarty, N., Poole, K. T., & Rosenthal, H. (2006). *Polarized America: the dance of ideology and unequal riches*. MIT Press.

Moe, T. M. (2011). *Special interest: Teachers unions and America's public schools*. Brookings Institution Press.

National Center for Employee Ownership. (n.d.). *ESOP (Employee Stock Ownership Plan) Facts*. https://www.esop.org/#:%7E:text=As%20of%202020%2C%20we%20at,in%20the%20number%20of%20participants

National Labor Relations Board (NLRB). (2022). "Election Petitions Up 53%, Board Continues to Reduce Case Processing Time in FY22" (news release). October 6, 2022 https://www.nlrb.gov/news-outreach/news-story/election-petitions-up-53-board-continues-to-reduce-case-processing-time-in

OECD. (2014), "Focus on Inequality and Growth - December 2014" https://www.oecd.org/social/Focus-Inequality-and-Growth-2014.pdf

Palmieri, M., & Cooper, C. (2023). Employee Ownership: What it is and what it can achieve. In Hernandez Gutierrez, G., & Zuloaga Fernandez Del Valle, R. (Eds.), *Employee ownership in the Americas: A path to shared prosperity* (pp. 1–23). ITESO, Universidad Jesuita de Guadalajara. DOI: 10.31391/JDTD1733.6

Palmieri, M. L. (2024). Retheorizing workplace spillover theory: Does an economic-based pathway exist? *International Review of Applied Economics*, •••, 1–23. DOI: 10.1080/02692171.2024.2406354

Pateman, C. (1970). *Participation and democratic theory*. Cambridge University Press. DOI: 10.1017/CBO9780511720444

Peterson, S. A. (1992). Workplace politicization and its political spillovers: A research note. *Economic and Industrial Democracy*, 13(4), 511–524. DOI: 10.1177/0143831X92134004

Polachek, S. W., & McCutcheon, E. P. (1983). Union effects on employment stability: A comparison of panel versus cross-sectional data. *Journal of Labor Research*, 4(3), 273–287. DOI: 10.1007/BF02685213

Putnam, R. D. (2020). *The upswing: How America came together a century ago and how we can do it again*. Simon and Schuster.

Rao, A. H. (2017). "You Don't Dare Plan Much": Contract work and personal life for international early-career professionals. *Research in the Sociology of Work*, 31, 429–453. DOI: 10.1108/S0277-283320170000031016

Rochat, M. (2023). The determinants of growing economic inequality within advanced democracies. *International Review of Economics*, 70(4), 1–19. DOI: 10.1007/s12232-023-00427-6

Rodgers, L. (2019) "New Data on Employee Ownership from the General Social Survey". https://www.nceo.org/employee-ownership-blog/article/new-data-employee-ownership-general-social-survey

Rosalsky, G. (2023) February 28 2023. You may have heard of the 'union boom'. The numbers tell a different story. NPR. https://www.npr.org/sections/money/2023/02/28/1159663461/you-may-have-heard-of-the-union-boom-the-numbers-tell-a-different-story

Rosenfeld, J. (2014). *What unions no longer do*. Harvard University Press. DOI: 10.4159/harvard.9780674726215

Rosenfeld, J., & Kleykamp, M. (2012). Organized labor and racial wage inequality in the United States. *American Journal of Sociology*, 117(5), 1460–1502. DOI: 10.1086/663673 PMID: 25620802

Ross, M., & Bateman, N. (2019, November). Meet the Low-Wage Workforce. Metropolitan Policy Program at Brookings. https://www.brookings.edu/wp-content/uploads/2019/11/201911_Brookings-Metro_low-wage-workforce_Ross-Bateman.pdf

Ross, M., & Bateman, N. (2019, November). Meet the Low-Wage Workforce. Metropolitan Policy Program at Brookings. https://www.brookings.edu/wp-content/uploads/2019/11/201911_Brookings-Metro_low-wage-workforce_Ross-Bateman.pdf

Saez, E., & Zucman, G. (2020). The rise of income and wealth inequality in America: Evidence from distributional macroeconomic accounts. *The Journal of Economic Perspectives*, 34(4), 3–26. DOI: 10.1257/jep.34.4.3

Schlozman, K. L., Brady, H. E., & Verba, S. (2018). Unequal and Unrepresented. In *Unequal and Unrepresented*. Princeton University Press.

Shierholz, H., Poydock, M., & McNicholas, C. (2023). January 19th. Unionization increased by 200,000 in 2022. Economic Policy Institute. https://www.epi.org/publication/unionization-2022/#:~:text=During%20fiscal%20year%202022%2C%20the,year%202016%20(NLRB%202022)

Sobel, R. (1993). From occupational involvement to political participation: An exploratory analysis. *Political Behavior*, 15(4), 339–353. DOI: 10.1007/BF00992102

Standing, G. (2011). *The precariat: The new dangerous class* (p. 208). Bloomsbury academic.

Stone, C., Trisi, D., Sherman, A., & Beltran, J. (2020, January). A Guide to Statistics on Historical Trends in Income Inequality. Center on Budget Policy Priorities. https://www.cbpp.org/research/poverty-and-inequality/a-guide-to-statistics-on-historical-trends-in-income-inequality

Sullivan, L., Meschede, T., Shapiro, T., Kroeger, T., & Escobar, F. (2019, April). Occupational Segregation, Benefits, and the Racial Wealth Gap. Institute on Assets and Social Policy. http://www.appam.org/assets/1/7/occupational_segregation_report_40219.pdf

The Hewison. K. (2016). Precarious work. *The SAGE handbook of the sociology of work and employment*, 428-443.

Timming, A., & Summers, J. (2020). Is workplace democracy associated with wider pro-democracy affect? A structural equation model. *Economic and Industrial Democracy*, 41(3), 709–726. DOI: 10.1177/0143831X17744028

Van Green, T. (2023) April 19th. Majorities of adults see decline of union membership as bad for the U.S. and working people. Pew Research Center. https://www.pewresearch.org/short-reads/2023/04/19/majorities-of-adults-see-decline-of-union-membership-as-bad-for-the-u-s-and-working-people/

Verba, S., & Almond, G. (1963). *The civic culture: Political attitudes and democracy in five nations*. Princeton University Press.

Verba, S., Schlozman, K. L., & Brady, H. E. (1995). *Voice and equality: Civic voluntarism in American politics*. Harvard University Press. DOI: 10.2307/j.ctv1pnc1k7

Walker, A. N. (2020). *Divided unions: The Wagner Act, federalism, and organized labor*. University of Pennsylvania Press. DOI: 10.9783/9780812296662

Wang, T. (2020). *Union Impact on Voter Participation–And How to Expand It*. Harvard Kennedy School Ash Center for Democratic Governance and Innovation.

Weitzman, M., & Kruse, D. (1990). Profit sharing and productivity. In Blinder, A. (Ed.), *Paying for productivity: A look at the evidence* (pp. 95–140). Brookings Institution.

Weller, C. E., & Karakilic, E. (2022). Wealth Inequality, Precariousness, Household Debt, and Macroeconomic Stability. *Journal of Economic Issues*, LVI(2), 599–606. DOI: 10.1080/00213624.2022.2065864

Wilkinson, R. G., & Pickett, K. E. (2009). Income inequality and social dysfunction. *Annual Review of Sociology*, 35(1), 493–511. DOI: 10.1146/annurev-soc-070308-115926

Wilson, J., & Musick, M. A. (1997). Work and volunteering: The long arm of the job. *Social Forces*, 76(1), 251–272. DOI: 10.2307/2580325

Wolfinger, R. E., & Rosenstone, S. J. (1980). *Who votes?* Yale University Press.

Zoorob, M. (2018). Does 'right to work'imperil the right to health? The effect of labour unions on workplace fatalities. *Occupational and Environmental Medicine*, 75(10), 736–738. DOI: 10.1136/oemed-2017-104747 PMID: 29898957

Zullo, R. (2011). Labor unions and charity. *Industrial & Labor Relations Review*, 64(4), 699–711. DOI: 10.1177/001979391106400404

ADDITIONAL READINGS

Blasi, J. R., Freeman, R. B., & Kruse, D. L. (2013). *The citizen's share: Reducing inequality in the 21st century*. Yale University Press.

Freeman, R. B., & Medoff, J. L. (1984). *What Do Unions Do?* Basic Books.

Kruse, D. L., Freeman, R. B., & Blasi, J. R. (Eds.). (2010). *Shared capitalism at work: Employee ownership, profit and gain sharing, and broad-based stock options*. University of Chicago Press. DOI: 10.7208/chicago/9780226056968.001.0001

Rosen, C., & Case, J. (2022). *Ownership: Reinventing companies, capitalism, and who owns what*. Berrett-Koehler Publishers.

Rosenfeld, J. (2014). *What Unions No Longer Do*. Harvard University Press. DOI: 10.4159/harvard.9780674726215

Schlozman, K. L., Verba, S., & Brady, H. E. (2012). *The unheavenly chorus: Unequal political voice and the broken promise of American democracy*. Princeton University Press. Kalleberg, A. L. (2011). *Good Jobs, Bad Jobs: The Rise of Polarized and Precarious Employment Systems in the United States, 1970s–2000s*. Russell Sage Foundation. Bhimji, F., & Baird, I. (Eds.). (2019). *Precarious Work: Understanding the New Normal*. Palgrave Macmillan.

KEY TERMS AND DEFINITIONS

Broad-based employee ownership: Broad-based employee ownership is a form of corporate structure where a significant portion of employees own stock or hold an equity stake in the company. This ownership can take various forms, such as Employee Stock Ownership Plans (ESOPs), worker cooperatives, or Employee Ownership Trusts (EOTs), and is designed to spread wealth creation and decision-making power among a broad range of employees rather than being concentrated at the top.

Economic Inequality: Economic inequality refers to the unequal distribution of resources, wealth, and income within a society. It manifests in disparities in access to economic opportunities, employment, education, and wealth accumulation and is often measured through metrics such as the Gini coefficient, wealth distribution percentiles, and income gaps.

Gini coefficient: The Gini coefficient is a statistical measure used to represent the level of income or wealth inequality within a population. It ranges from 0 to 1, where 0 signifies perfect equality (everyone has the same income or wealth), and 1 signifies perfect inequality (one person has all the income or wealth, while everyone else has none). The Gini coefficient is widely used in economics and social sciences to quantify inequality across different societies or groups.

Income Inequality: Income inequality refers to the uneven distribution of income earned through wages, salaries, and other financial returns across a population. It is often measured using ratios of income between different percentiles of earners (e.g., top 1% vs. bottom 50%) or using statistical tools like the Gini coefficient.

Political Inequality: Political inequality refers to unequal access to political resources and influence, resulting in the unequal ability to affect political decision-making processes. It is measured by disparities in political participation, representation, and the extent to which individuals or groups can shape public policies.

Precarious Employment: Precarious employment refers to work arrangements characterized by instability, insecurity, low wages, and limited access to benefits such as health care, paid leave, and retirement plans. Precarious jobs often include part-time, temporary, freelance, or gig work and contribute to income volatility and limited job security, exacerbating economic inequality and worker vulnerability.

Wealth Inequality: Wealth inequality refers to the unequal distribution of assets and property among individuals and groups within a society. It includes disparities in the ownership of financial assets (e.g., stocks, bonds) and tangible assets (e.g., real estate), which accumulate over time and often surpass income inequalities in their impact on long-term economic stability and opportunity.

Workplace Spillover: Workplace spillover refers to the idea that workplace structures and practices can influence behaviors, attitudes, and participation outside the workplace, particularly in civic and political life. Research suggests that workplaces with participatory structures, like employee-owned firms or cooperative enterprises, can foster democratic attitudes, social trust, and skills that spill over into increased civic engagement and political participation.

Chapter 4
Synergizing Employee Share Ownership With Corporate Governance and CSR:
Pathways to Enhanced Organizational Performance and Sustainable Value Creation

Ramya H. P.
https://orcid.org/0000-0002-2048-807X
Dayananda Sagar College of Engineering, India

Hemalatha K. G.
https://orcid.org/0000-0003-0092-0715
Dayananda Sagar College of Engineering, India

R. Deepak
https://orcid.org/0000-0003-2344-6550
Ramaiah Institute of Technology, India

ABSTRACT

Over the past three decades, employee share ownership has gained traction in both industrialized and emerging economies, drawing interest from academics, policy-makers, and practitioners (Dondi, 1992). This phenomenon has sparked significant interest across academic circles and among policymakers and business practitioners (Kuvaas, 2003; Pendleton et al., 1998).This chapter explores the synergies between Employee Share Ownership (ESO), corporate governance, and Corporate Social

DOI: 10.4018/979-8-3693-7031-5.ch004

Responsibility (CSR), demonstrating how ESO can drive organizational performance and long-term value creation. By integrating agency theory and evidence-based research, it presents best practices for implementing ESO, analyzing its effects on employee engagement, financial performance, and sustainability while addressing potential challenges in stakeholder alignment.

INTRODUCTION

In recent years the intersection of Employee Share Ownership (ESO), Corporate Governance and Corporate Social Responsibility has gathered increasing attention from scholars and practitioners alike. The evolving landscape of corporate governance emphasizes the need for inclusive practices that not only align the interests of shareholders and management but also empower employees as key stakeholders. This shift is particularly relevant in the context of sustainable value creation, where organizations are called to balance economic performance with social and environmental responsibilities. In an increasingly interconnected global economy businesses are being pushed beyond traditional financial objectives to adopt strategies that encompass a broader array of stakeholder interests. As companies strive to balance profitability with social responsibility the concepts of Employee Share Ownership (ESO), Corporate Governance (CG), and Corporate Social Responsibility (CSR) have emerged as key drivers of long-term sustainability and enhanced organizational performance. The convergence of these three elements creates a powerful framework through which organizations not only have financial growth but also social and ethical leadership.

An Employee Stock Ownership Plan (ESOP) is a type of employee benefit plan that provides employees with an ownership stake in the company. Under this plan, qualified employees receive a predetermined percentage of the company's equity shares from their employer at no upfront cost. The distribution of shares may be based on factors such as length of service, employee salary, or other allocation methods. The shares allocated to employees are held in a trust for security and growth until the employee leaves the company or retires. If an employee resigns, the company repurchases their shares, which can then be redistributed to other departing employees. Employee Stock Ownership Plans (ESOPs) were introduced by corporate lawyer Louis Kelso in 1956 as a means to transfer ownership of Peninsula Newspapers Incorporation from its founders to their successors, specifically the managers and employees. Kelso firmly believed that the employees were integral to the company's success, making it logical and justifiable for them to ultimately hold the shares of the enterprise.

Under an ESOP, employees are allocated shares that are held for them based on the plan's specific terms. The financing for these shares can come from employee contributions, employer funding, or external loans. ESOPs offer several advantages for employees, including fostering a deeper involvement in company operations and providing direct financial incentives tied to their productivity and innovation. For companies, ESOPs enhance employee recruitment and retention, while also contributing to improved economic performance. From a policy perspective, ESOPs serve as a valuable tool for promoting stakeholder capitalism, boosting corporate performance, and delivering broader societal benefits, such as better Environmental, Social, and Governance (ESG) outcomes. ESOP schemes align well with global goals, particularly the UN's Sustainable Development Goals (SDGs), including SDG 10, which focuses on reducing inequalities. (Kong et al., 2024) found that offering Employee Stock Ownership Plans (ESOPs) to non-executive staff promotes greater corporate environmental engagement, particularly when considering expenditures on environmental protection, the quality of disclosed environmental information, and environmental, social, and governance (ESG) ratings. ESOPs foster a sense of unity among members, empowering them to advocate for management to reduce carbon emissions, which enhances their well-being and sustains their interest in long-term corporate value. Moreover, companies that prioritize environmental preservation can increase their long-term value, even if they forgo short-term profits due to substantial initial investments. The positive outcomes are attributed to ESOP plans that maintain ownership over longer periods, have higher employee participation rates, and provide more non-executive employees with shares. These plans also create strong incentives that effectively address the free-rider problem. Although ESO is not a comprehensive solution, it can contribute to incremental improvements across various SDGs, particularly in fostering sustainable and resilient communities. Public policy can support the establishment and success of ESOPs through four key areas: education, legislation, taxation, and research.

Literature Reviews

The literature on employee share ownership, corporate governance, and corporate social responsibility has evolved significantly over the past few decades, reflecting changing attitudes toward stakeholder engagement and organizational accountability. This review synthesizes key findings from the existing body of research, highlighting the interconnections between these domains.

Employee Share Ownership (ESO) refers to the practice of granting employees ownership stakes in the company, typically through stock options or employee stock ownership plans (ESOPs). (Wen et al., 2021) describe Employee Stock Ownership Plans (ESOPs) as a strategic employee welfare policy that enables employees to share in the profits and benefits derived from the growth of the enterprise by acquiring company shares. By aligning personal interests with organizational goals, ESOPs contribute to the sustainable growth of a company. Additionally, ESOPs play a crucial role in overseeing operational activities and reducing agency costs within the enterprise.

Research has shown that ESO can lead to increased employee motivation, commitment, and productivity, as employees feel a greater sense of ownership and responsibility towards the organization (Pierce et al., 1991; Blasi et al., 2016). ESOPs provide employers with the opportunity to reward high performers for their contributions to business growth by offering equity or a cash payout based on that equity. Employee stock options are commonly included in total compensation packages as an effective way to encourage long-term commitment from recipients. Consequently, they play a vital role in the success of any expanding company.

1. Motivational Theories: Theories such as agency theory and social cognitive theory provide a foundation for understanding how ESO aligns employee interests with those of the organization. By sharing financial risks and rewards, ESO can mitigate agency problems and enhance collaboration (Akerlof, 1982; Rousseau & Shperling, 2003).
2. Impact on Performance: Empirical studies have demonstrated a positive correlation between ESO and organizational performance metrics, including profitability, employee retention, and innovation (Richter & Schrader, 2017). However, the mechanisms through which these outcomes are achieved remain underexplored.

Corporate Governance encompasses the systems and processes that direct and control organizations, ensuring accountability and transparency to stakeholders. Traditional governance models have focused primarily on shareholder interests, often at the expense of other stakeholders, including employees and the community.

1. Evolving Governance Models: Recent literature has advocated for more inclusive governance models that consider the interests of a broader range of stakeholders, including employees (Aguilera et al., 2008). This shift aligns with the principles of CSR, which emphasize ethical practices and social responsibility.
2. Role of Employee Participation: Studies have highlighted the importance of employee participation in governance processes, suggesting that involving employees in decision-making can lead to better outcomes and increased organizational commitment (Pugliese et al., 2009). However, the integration of ESO into governance structures remains under-researched.

One significant area of research is the role of board diversity in corporate governance. (Amin et al., 2022) found that the presence of females in corporate governance positively influences organizational performance, particularly when moderated by family ownership. This suggests that diverse boards may bring different perspectives that enhance decision-making and performance outcomes. Similarly, (Arora & Sharma, 2016) highlighted the importance of board structure in developing countries, indicating that effective governance structures can lead to improved financial performance. The size and effectiveness of audit committees have also been extensively studied. (Detthamrong et al., 2017) argued that larger audit committees tend to have broader knowledge and authority, which can enhance their monitoring capabilities. However, some researchers, such as (Al-Ahdal & Hashim, 2022), noted that excessively large audit committees might lead to inefficiencies and increased costs, thereby negatively impacting firm performance. This contradiction underscores the need for a balanced approach to audit committee composition.

Moreover, the frequency of audit meetings has been linked to organizational performance. (Darko et al., 2016) and (Shrivastav, 2022) found that higher audit meeting frequency correlates positively with firm performance, as it allows for more effective oversight of management activities. Ownership structure is another critical factor influencing corporate governance and firm performance. (Anderson & Reeb, 2003) demonstrated that founding-family ownership can have a positive impact on organizational performance, as these owners often have a vested interest in the long-term success of the company. Conversely, the concentration of ownership can lead to agency problems, where the interests of majority shareholders may not align with those of minority shareholders (Agrawal & Knoeber, 1996).

Corporate Social Responsibility (CSR) refers to the ethical obligation of organizations to consider the social and environmental impacts of their operations. The literature on CSR has expanded to include discussions on stakeholder theory, which posits that organizations should create value for all stakeholders, not just shareholders. (Achour, 2024) identified a positive correlation between employee stock ownership (ESO) and firm financial performance (FFP), indicating that ESO contributes to improved FFP. Additionally, Corporate Social Responsibility (CSR) plays a mediating role in the relationship between ESO and FFP.

1. CSR and Employee Engagement: Research indicates that CSR initiatives can enhance employee engagement and satisfaction, as employees are more likely to feel proud of their organization when it is perceived as socially responsible (Quarrey et al., 1986). However, the interplay between CSR and ESO in fostering employee engagement is not well understood.

2. Sustainable Value Creation: The integration of CSR into corporate governance frameworks has been shown to contribute to sustainable value creation, as organizations that prioritize social responsibility often experience long-term benefits, including enhanced reputation and customer loyalty (Simsek et al., 2022). Yet, the role of ESO in this process remains largely unexplored.

Research Gap

While significant research has been conducted on Employee Share Ownership (ESO), Corporate Governance, and Corporate Social Responsibility (CSR) as individual concepts, there is a notable gap in understanding the synergistic integration of these elements and their collective impact on organizational performance and sustainable value creation. Most existing studies examine these topics in isolation, often focusing on their individual effects on financial metrics or stakeholder engagement. However, empirical evidence on the interaction between ESO, governance frameworks, and CSR initiatives remains limited. Specifically, there is a lack of comprehensive analysis on how ESO, when embedded within corporate governance and aligned with CSR, can drive both economic performance and social responsibility. This research aims to bridge this gap by exploring the interconnectedness of these three elements and providing a roadmap for leveraging their synergy for long-term value creation.

Objectives

1. To Explore the Synergies Between Employee Share Ownership and Corporate Governance.
2. To Analyze the Role of Corporate Social Responsibility in Enhancing Employee Engagement.
3. To Identify Pathways for Sustainable Value Creation.
4. To Assess the Impact of Integrated Approaches on Organizational Performance.

Research Methodology

A comprehensive review of existing literature on ESO, corporate governance, and CSR will be conducted to understand their individual and collective roles in organizational success. Key theories, models, and frameworks (e.g., agency theory, and stakeholder theory) will be analyzed to provide a theoretical basis for understanding the potential synergies among these elements.

Overview of Employee Share Ownership (ESO)

ESO are formal mechanisms that allow employees to acquire ownership of their company through various methods. These programs offer different ways for employees to gain shares, including:

- **Direct Purchase Plans**: These plans encourage employees to buy shares using their funds. Many countries have tax-qualified schemes to support this by offering shares at a discount or providing matching shares. For example, in the U.S., employee stock purchase plans (ESPPs) allow employees to save money over a set period (usually 6 to 12 months) and then purchase shares at a discount of up to 15%. In the UK, share incentive plans allow companies to match the shares purchased by employees.
- **Stock Options**: Stock options grant employees the ability to purchase shares at a fixed price for a set number of years in the future. If the share price rises, employees can benefit by purchasing shares below the current market value. In most countries, companies have the flexibility to establish stock option rules, making them a popular employee incentive.
- **Restricted Stock**: This category includes shares or stock units that employees can acquire once certain conditions are met, such as achieving performance goals or working for a specific number of years.
- **Share Gifting Schemes**: In these programs, companies give shares to employees at no cost. Typically, these shares must be held in a trust for a designated period.

Stock options have also faced criticism for being inconsistent with the true spirit of employee ownership. While their appeal has waned due to changes in accounting rules requiring companies to report option expenses, stock options may not always align with shareholder interests. Because stock option value increases with volatility, they can reward managers for creating volatility in the company's share price, even though shareholders typically prefer stability. Empirical research shows that shareholders value firms with lower volatility, meaning stock options can misalign the interests of managers and shareholders. Therefore, restricted stock and long-term performance incentives tied to competitive benchmarks are considered more beneficial for fostering genuine employee ownership. Despite these concerns, stock options remain in use, particularly where they offer tax advantages, though they may not be the optimal approach for aligning employee and shareholder interests. Listed companies must comply with the Securities and Exchange Board of India (SEBI) Guidelines for Employee Stock Option Schemes and Employee Stock Purchase Schemes, which were established in 1999 and updated as of September 3, 2009.

Private and unlisted companies are required to follow Rule 12 of the Companies (Share Capital and Debenture) Rules 2014 and Section 62(1)(b) of the Companies Act 2013. Additionally, compliance with the Companies Act of 2013, along with the SEBI (Share Based Employee Benefit & Sweat Equity) Regulations, 2021, and the SEBI (Listing Obligations and Disclosure Requirements) Regulations, 2015, is mandatory for listed companies. These regulations are designed to ensure that ESOPs are implemented fairly for the benefit of employees, enabling them to qualify for tax advantages.

Employee-Owned Companies: Employee ownership refers to a business structure where all employees hold a significant stake in the company. However, merely having an employee share ownership scheme does not automatically qualify a company as employee-owned. The classification depends on various factors, including the company's capital structure, control mechanisms, listing rules, and share options, among other triggers. When employees do own shares, this ownership can take two forms: direct or indirect.

- **Direct employee ownership** occurs when employees individually hold shares that grant them the same rights as other shareholders, allowing them to influence company management. Example - Publix Super Markets, Penmac Staffing, Brookshire Brothers, WinCo Foods, Robert W. Baird & Co. etc. These rights may include:
  - Attending general meetings or appointing proxies to attend, speak, and vote on their behalf.
  - Voting on company matters, and if employees own more than 50% of the shares, they can pass ordinary resolutions.
  - Inspecting directors' service contracts.
- **Indirect employee ownership** involves the company being partially or fully owned by a trust, which holds shares on behalf of the employees. This trust acts in the employees' interests in overseeing company management. Example - Amul, Banas Dairy, Co-optex, Dabbawala etc.

In both models, employee interests are often safeguarded through representation, such as employee councils or consultation groups. The company's relationship with its employees may be formalized in a constitution, which outlines the company's values and governance structure. In some cases, this leads to the appointment of employee representatives as directors on the company's board, with the same responsibilities as other board members.

Reasons for a Company to Choose Employee Share Ownership

Companies typically adopt ESOP schemes for two main reasons:

1. **Enhancing Employee Recruitment and Retention:** This is crucial for both large organizations and start-ups with limited cash flow. In today's competitive business environment, talent retention is increasingly important. Companies with ESOPs excel in recruitment and retention by upholding high employment standards, investing in their workforce, and fostering employee engagement, making them attractive to skilled, dedicated staff.
2. **Succession Planning and Ownership Transition**: ESOPs are commonly used for succession planning in smaller, privately-owned businesses when the owner is preparing to retire. Instead of shutting down or selling to a competitor, owners may choose to sell the company to their employees through an Employee Ownership Trust (EOT), facilitating a smooth transfer of ownership to contributing staff members.

Corporate Governance: Strengthening Accountability

Corporate governance encompasses the policies, rules, and processes that control and direct a corporation. It defines the relationships among the company's stakeholders—shareholders, management, employees, and the board of directors—and ensures that decisions are made transparently and ethically. Corporate governance (CG) and ethics are interconnected concepts that play a crucial role in managing a company's operations. Together, they establish a foundation for accountability, transparency, full disclosure, and sustainable practices. Key aspects of governance include the accountability and transparency of financial information provided by company administrators to stakeholders. An ethical organization ensures the accuracy of financial information and promotes transparency in both financial and non-financial disclosures, enhancing the company's reputation and societal value. As a corporate citizen, a company has a responsibility to uphold ethical standards and maintain respectable governance within society. This commitment to ethics and accountability safeguards against misconduct. Financial disclosures should comply with global standards such as International Financial Reporting Standards (IFRS) and Indian Accounting Standards (IND AS), while non-financial disclosures should address Environmental, Social, and Governance (ESG) practices. ESG goals focus on environmentally friendly practices and social responsibility to achieve ethical and improved governance.

Corporate governance encompasses the guidelines and processes that boards of directors must follow to manage a company's affairs effectively. Directors are responsible for safeguarding the interests of both internal stakeholders—such as owners, employees, and managers—and external stakeholders, including customers, society, government, creditors, suppliers, and investors. Good governance is reflected in accountability, integrity, and values, and increasingly incorporates sustainability and ethical practices. Strong corporate governance fosters resilience, enhances the company's reputation, and facilitates capital raising while reducing potential financial losses. The board's role is vital in ensuring shareholder value and implementing governance practices effectively, especially in closely held companies where ownership and control often reside with the same individuals. In companies owned by Employee Stock Ownership Plans (ESOPs), governance is still managed by a board of directors, which may include independent trustees acting on behalf of ESOP participants. An independent board is crucial for preventing conflicts of interest and ensuring fair executive compensation practices. While management oversees daily operations, incorporating employee feedback fosters a culture of ownership that benefits the organization. Companies can implement ESOPs via a Direct Route or Trust Route, following a structured approval process and ensuring compliance with the Companies Act of 2013. In either approach, transparency or adherence to governance standards are essential for unlocking employee potential and sustaining business growth in India.

Corporate Social Responsibility (CSR): Beyond Profit

CSR reflects a company's commitment to operating in a socially responsible manner, taking into account the environmental, social, and ethical impacts of its actions. CSR initiatives typically focus on reducing environmental harm, improving social welfare, and ensuring fair business practices.

- **Ethical Corporate Behavior**: CSR is becoming an essential part of corporate strategies, as businesses face pressure from consumers, investors, and regulators to adopt practices that go beyond profit maximization.
- **Value Creation for Society**: Integrating CSR into corporate strategies allows companies to contribute positively to societal issues, such as climate change, inequality, and community development, thus enhancing their reputation and fostering goodwill among stakeholders.

The following key theories provide a robust theoretical foundation for analyzing the synergy between ESO, Corporate governance, and CSR:

1. Employee Share Ownership (ESO)

The recognition of the critical role played by various stakeholders, especially employees, has naturally prompted a reevaluation of the sole focus on maximizing shareholder value. This shift advocates for a partnership approach that seeks to balance the interests of all stakeholders. However, the responsibility for making these trade-offs ultimately rests with the manager. With that in mind (Hill and Jones, 1992) advance a broad or generalized agency theory where all partners are explicitly taken into account.

I. Agency theory: The concept of agency theory deals with the potential conflicts of interest between owners or shareholders (principals) and employees or managers (agents). Economists like Michael Jensen and William Meckling introduced the theory in their influential 1976 paper. The theory aims to align the often goals of these two groups to minimize in efficiency and costs resulting from separation of ownership and control. It suggests that conflicts of interest arise between shareholders and employees. Employee Stock Ownership is a mechanism to align the interests of employees with those of shareholders reducing agency costs by motivating employees in the best interests of the organization (Jensen and Meckling, 1976). Granting ownership rights to employees encourages behaviours that enhance organizational performance as they directly benefit from the company's success.

Key Concepts of Agency Theory:

Principal-agent relationship: shareholders delegate decision-making authority to managers or employees as they do not run the day-to-day operations of the organization.

Agency Problem: In Agency Theory, the agency problem arises from a misalignment of incentives between the principal and the agent. Agents may prioritize their interests over those of the principals, especially if their goals differ from those of shareholders.

Information Asymmetry: Information asymmetry exacerbates agency problems by giving agents more information about the organization's operations than principals, making it difficult for shareholders to monitor agents' actions in their best interests.

Agency Costs: These are the costs incurred due to agency problems. They include:

- Monitoring Costs: Expenses incurred by principals to monitor agents' behavior, such as implementing corporate governance mechanisms or performance reviews.
- Bonding Costs: Costs associated with incentivizing agents to align their interests with those of principals, often through contracts or incentive-based compensation like stock options.
- Residual Loss: The remaining losses to shareholder value due to agents not acting fully in the principal's interest, even after monitoring and bonding efforts.

Employee Share Ownership (ESO) as a Solution to the Agency Problem:

ESO aligns employee and shareholder interests by giving employees ownership in the company, incentivizing them to act in ways that benefit the organization and its shareholders. This shared interest improves performance and value. Here's how ESO helps address key aspects of Agency Theory:

1. Alignment of Interests: ESO aligns employees' goals with shareholders by making employees partial owners of the company. This creates a shared objective of increasing the company's value and reduces agency problems by ensuring that the incentives of both employees and shareholders converge.
2. Increased Motivation and Commitment: ESO can increase employee motivation and commitment, leading to greater effort, higher productivity, and increased innovation, benefiting shareholders directly. Employees with a stake in the company are more likely to take initiatives that improve operational efficiency and innovation, crucial for long-term shareholder value.
3. Reduction of monetary cost ESOP monitoring cost as employees' financial incentives become aligned with shareholder objectives in the need for the extensive external monitoring system.
4. Mitigating information Asymmetry ESO health mitigates this by transforming employees into stakeholders who are more likely to share relevant information openly. When employees own shares they are encouraged to think and act like shareholders leading to Greater transparency and collaboration between management and employees. this reduces the risk of employees acting opportunistically or withholding important information that could affect company performance.
5. Long-Term Focus: ESO fosters a long-term focus in employee decision-making. Unlike traditional compensation structures which may incentivize short-term gains (for example performance bonuses tied to quarterly targets), ESO Encourages employees to focus on long term value creation. since employees

have a financial stake in the future value of the company there more likely to support strategies that enhance sustainable growth and profitability benefiting both themselves and shareholders.

6. Bonding costs: agency theory suggest that principles can inker bonding cost to encourage agents to act in their interest. ESO effectively serves as a bonding mechanism by offering employees ownership in the company. This form of incentive-based compensation reduces the need for complex performance contracts and other mechanisms that principals might otherwise use to ensure alignment. Employees are naturally bonded to the organization's goals as their financial rewards are tied to the company's success.

ESO's Impact on Organizational Performance:

Numerous studies have shown that organizations with employee share ownership programs tend to experience better performance, lower turnover, and higher employee satisfaction. This is partly because ESO directly addresses the root of agency problems by turning employees into partners in the company's success. Some of the key outcomes include:

- **Reduced Turnover and Retention of Talent:** Employees with equity in the company are more likely to remain committed to the organization for the long term, reducing turnover rates and the associated costs of recruiting and training new employees.
- **Improved Corporate Governance:** By involving employees in ownership, ESO can lead to better corporate governance. Employees have a vested interest in ensuring that management makes sound decisions that align with shareholder goals. This collective oversight contributes to better decision-making processes and limits the risks of managerial opportunism.
- **Enhanced Organizational Culture:** ESO can foster a sense of unity and collaboration within the organization. Employees who feel they are co-owners of the business are more likely to participate in decision-making, contribute ideas, and take responsibility for outcomes, leading to a more engaged and high-performing workforce.

Potential Challenges and Limitations of ESO in Agency Theory:

While ESO is a powerful tool for aligning interests between principals and agents, it is not without challenges:

- **Dilution of Ownership:** As employees receive ownership stakes, existing shareholders may face dilution of their equity. This could potentially lead to concerns among shareholders, especially if the distribution of shares is not well managed.
- **Short-Term Pressure:** While ESO generally encourages long-term thinking, it can sometimes create short-term pressures if employees become overly focused on share price fluctuations. This can lead to undesirable behavior, such as a focus on short-term gains at the expense of long-term strategy.
- **Complexity in Implementation:** Designing and managing employee share ownership plans can be complex and costly, especially for smaller organizations. There is also the risk of creating unrealistic expectations among employees regarding the financial value of their shares, especially if the company faces market challenges.
- **Risk of Decoupling:** In some cases, the psychological ownership and alignment that ESO aims to create may not materialize if employees do not perceive their ownership stake as significant or meaningful. This can lead to a situation where ESO is in place but fails to deliver the desired reduction in agency costs.

II. Social Cognitive Theory: developed by Albert Bandura in the 1980s, is a psychological model that emphasizes the interaction between individual cognitive processes and social environments in shaping behavior. The theory asserts that behavior is not just a product of internal psychological factors (like motivation and knowledge) or external environmental factors (like rewards and punishments), but rather a dynamic interaction between these influences. This concept is often referred to as reciprocal determinism, where cognitive processes, social environment, and behavior mutually influence one another.

The key elements of Social Cognitive Theory include:

- Observational Learning: People learn behaviors by observing others in their environment.
- Cognitive Processes: Individuals actively interpret and assess their environment, adjusting their behavior based on perceived outcomes and expectations.
- Self-Efficacy: Belief in one's ability to perform tasks and achieve goals boosts motivation and resilience.
- Reciprocal Determinism: Behavior, personal factors, and environmental factors are intertwined and mutually influential.

Application to Employee Behavior and Ownership:

When employees feel a sense of ownership—either psychological ownership (mental or emotional ownership) or actual financial ownership through mechanisms like employee share ownership (ESO)—their attitudes and behaviors can be positively transformed. According to (Pierce et al., 2001), this sense of ownership triggers deeper psychological processes that lead to psychological ownership, which can significantly enhance employee commitment and motivation.

III. Stakeholder Theory: This theory expands the focus behind shareholders to include all stakeholders including employees. ESO can be viewed as a stakeholder engagement strategy that recognizes employees as critical stakeholders. Whose interests must be considered in governance and decision-making processes (Freeman, 1984). By involving employees in ownership, organizations can foster a sense of belonging and commitment, which can enhance performance.

- ESO Expands the concept of Stakeholder Inclusion: By making employees shareholders, ESO transforms them into key stakeholders whose interests align with those of traditional shareholders. This creates a deeper connection between employees and the company's mission, fostering a culture of shared responsibility.
- Synergy with CSR: ESO fits seamlessly with CSR, as both focus on value creation for broader stakeholder groups. When employees are shareholders, they are more likely to support CSR initiatives that benefit the community, the environment, and society at large, knowing that these actions contribute to long-term sustainable value creation.
- Employee Ownership and Corporate Decision-Making: Stakeholder theory suggests that firms should consider the interests of employees in corporate decisions. ESO provides employees with a direct mechanism to influence governance and CSR initiatives, ensuring that their voices are heard and incorporated into strategic decision-making.

2. Corporate Governance (CG)

Corporate Governance encompasses the systems and processes that direct and control organizations, ensuring accountability and transparency to stakeholders. The theoretical frameworks relevant to CG include:

I. Stewardship Theory: This theory posits that managers (or stewards) are motivated to act in the best interests of the organization and its stakeholders, rather than solely pursuing personal gains. ESO can enhance stewardship by aligning the interests of employees with those of the organization, fostering a culture of collaboration and shared goals (Davis et al., 1997).

ESO and Stewardship Behavior: ESO can foster a culture of stewardship, where employees view themselves as caretakers of the organization. As shareholders, they are more likely to prioritize long-term growth and sustainability, adopting a stewardship mentality rather than acting as mere agents seeking short-term rewards.

Enhanced Governance through Stewardship: Stewardship theory implies that when employees have a direct stake in the company, they are more likely to engage in governance processes that promote transparency, accountability, and ethical decision-making. This strengthens corporate governance structures, as employees play a proactive role in safeguarding the company's future.

CSR as Part of Stewardship: CSR aligns with stewardship theory by emphasizing the responsibility of the company to act as a steward of social and environmental resources. When employees are part-owners, they are more likely to support CSR initiatives that reflect their shared values and contribute to the company's long-term sustainability.

II. Contingency Theory: Contingency Theory is a management theory that suggests there is no one-size-fits-all approach to organizational structures and leadership. Instead, the effectiveness of a particular governance or management structure is contingent upon specific contextual factors such as organizational size, industry dynamics, external environment, technology, and organizational culture. This means that organizational success depends on finding the right "fit" between these contextual factors and the governance or management practices in place.

Core Principles of Contingency Theory:

- No Universal Solution: Contingency Theory rejects the idea of a one-size-fits-all approach to organizing or managing.
- Fit between context and structure: Success is determined by how well organizational characteristics align with the organizational structures or strategies employed.
- Adaptability and Flexibility: The theory stresses the importance of adaptability. Organizations need to continuously adjust their governance structures and processes in response to changes.

Contingency Factors Influencing ESO's Effectiveness:

- Organizational Size: In small and medium-sized enterprises (SMEs), ESO schemes might foster a stronger sense of ownership and accountability because employees have a more direct influence on the organization's success.

In larger organizations, ESO may be less personal but still contribute to alignment between employees and the company's goals.

- Industry: In industries that rely on innovation (e.g., tech companies), ESO can encourage employees to think like owners and take calculated risks, which may lead to greater innovation. Conversely, in more stable, mature industries (e.g., utilities), ESO might focus on maintaining employee loyalty and commitment to the organization's long-term goals.
- Corporate Culture: If an organization has a participative, collaborative culture, integrating ESO into its governance framework might reinforce shared decision-making and collective responsibility for performance. In more hierarchical organizations, ESO may require adjustments to governance structures to ensure that employees' interests are adequately represented at higher levels.

In corporate governance, effectiveness depends on factors such as organizational size, complexity, industry characteristics, competitive landscape, and corporate culture. Larger organizations require more formalized governance structures, while industry and culture influence governance designs. The integration of Employee Share Ownership (ESO) into corporate governance frameworks can be viewed as a contingent strategy. ESO involves providing employees with shares of the company, giving them a financial stake in the organization's success. The benefits of ESO depend on how well this strategy aligns with the organization's unique characteristics and contextual factors.

III. Resource Dependency Theory: RDT introduced by Jeffrey Pfeffer and Gerald Salancik in 1970 posits that organizations are not self-sufficient entities. Instead, there embedded in a broader external environment in which they depend on crucial resources to survive and thrive. These resources might include capital information human talent Technology and even legitimacy. According to RDT the success and stability of an organization are largely determined by its ability to manage relationships with external stakeholders and secure essential resources.

The key Idea behind the resource dependency theory is that organizations must strategically manage their dependency on external entities by forming collaborations and other types of relationships. These external stakeholders' example suppliers, regulators, and partners. Employees hold significant power because they control the resources that the organization needs to function. In response, organizations seek to reduce the dependence and uncertainty by developing strategies that either ensure access to these resources or reduce the vulnerability to external influences.

ESO (Employee Stock Ownership) enhances organizational resources by creating a stronger sense of ownership and commitment among employees leading to increased knowledge sharing improved processes and innovative ideas. it also improves employee retention aligns the interest of employees with shareholders and reduces dependence on external resources by enhancing the internal resource base.

Strategic Benefits of ESO through the Lens of Resource Dependence Theory:

- Reducing External Dependence: Organizations often rely on external stakeholders, such as investors, lenders, or regulators, to provide critical resources like funding, legitimacy, and market access. However, by strengthening internal resources through ESO, organizations can become more self-reliant. For example, higher employee productivity and innovation can reduce the need for external financing by improving profitability. This diminishes the power that external financial stakeholders hold over the organization, giving it greater flexibility and control over its strategic direction.
- Improving Organizational Resilience: Organizations with strong internal resources are better able to withstand external shocks, such as economic downturns or shifts in market demand. ESO fosters a stronger commitment from employees, leading to higher levels of productivity, adaptability, and problem-solving capabilities during times of crisis. This resilience reduces the organization's vulnerability to external threats and helps it maintain access to essential resources, even in challenging environments.
- Strategic Alliances and Stakeholder Engagement: Resource Dependence Theory highlights the importance of strategic alliances and stakeholder relationships in securing resources. ESO can enhance an organization's ability to form partnerships with other key stakeholders by demonstrating a commitment to shared governance and inclusive decision-making. For instance, companies with employee ownership are often seen as more ethical and socially responsible, which can improve their relationships with external stakeholders such as customers, regulators, and the broader community. These enhanced relationships can, in turn, improve access to external resources such as market share, regulatory support, and community goodwill.
- Mitigating Power Imbalances: One of the key challenges that organizations face, according to RDT, is the imbalance of power between them and the external entities on which they depend. By fostering employee ownership, organizations can distribute power more equitably within their internal governance structures, reducing the potential for conflicts between employees and management. This internal balance of power can also reduce the organization's susceptibility to external pressures, as it can demonstrate greater cohesion and stability in its internal governance and decision-making processes.

3. Corporate Social Responsibility (CSR)

CSR refers to the ethical obligation of organizations to consider the social and environmental impacts of their operations. Theoretical frameworks relevant to CSR include:

I. **Triple Bottom Line Theory (TBL):** This theory was introduced by John Elkington in 1994, and broadens the concept of business performance beyond the traditional financial bottom line to include two additional dimensions: social and environmental performance. This framework encourages organizations to balance profitability (economic dimension) with social responsibility and environmental stewardship. By adopting the TBL approach, companies can pursue sustainable business strategies that generate long-term value across multiple dimensions, rather than focusing solely on short-term financial gains.

Core Dimensions of the Triple Bottom Line Theory:

- **Economic Dimension:** This refers to the financial performance of an organization, measured in terms of profitability, return on investment (ROI), and shareholder value. While economic performance is still critical under the TBL framework, it is integrated with broader goals, ensuring that financial success is not achieved at the expense of societal or environmental well-being.
- **Social Dimension:** The social aspect focuses on the organization's impact on people, both internally (e.g., employees, stakeholders) and externally (e.g., communities, society at large). Key elements include employee welfare, fair labor practices, community engagement, and contributions to societal well-being. Organizations are encouraged to consider how their operations affect various stakeholders and take proactive steps to enhance positive social outcomes.
- **Environmental Dimension:** This dimension emphasizes environmental sustainability, including the responsible use of natural resources, pollution prevention, and minimizing the organization's ecological footprint. Companies are expected to mitigate negative environmental impacts through sustainable practices, energy efficiency, waste reduction, and the adoption of clean technologies.

Together, these three dimensions create a more holistic view of performance and success, where an organization's long-term viability is judged not only by its financial returns but also by its contributions to social equity and environmental sustainability.

Synergizing Employee Share Ownership (ESO) with Corporate Social Responsibility (CSR) Initiatives:

By synergizing Employee Share Ownership (ESO) with Corporate Social Responsibility (CSR) initiatives, organizations can enhance their ability to create value across all three dimensions of the Triple Bottom Line—economic, social, and environmental. This integration can lead to more sustainable outcomes that benefit not only the company but also its employees, society, and the planet.

1. Economic Dimension - Enhancing Financial Performance and Stakeholder Alignment: ESO provides employees with a financial stake in the organization's success, which can improve both individual and organizational performance. When employees are also shareholders, they have a vested interest in the economic well-being of the company, which often results in increased productivity, innovation, and cost efficiency. This alignment of interests between employees and shareholders creates a sense of shared responsibility and enhances financial outcomes.

- **Increased Productivity and Profitability:** Employees who own shares in the company are likely to be more motivated and engaged, as their financial success is tied directly to the organization's performance. This can lead to higher levels of productivity and profitability. Employees are more inclined to adopt entrepreneurial behaviors, seek efficiencies, and work collaboratively to achieve financial goals.
- **Long-Term Financial Stability:** ESO schemes can foster long-term commitment to the company, reducing employee turnover and strengthening organizational stability. This ensures that human capital, a critical resource for the company's economic success, is preserved and nurtured.
- **Enhanced stakeholder relationships:** ESO and CSR together can enhance relationships with key external stakeholders including investor's customers and suppliers. Companies that demonstrate a commitment to social responsibility, employee welfare, and sustainable practices are more attractive to investors and customers whose priority is ethical and sustainable business practices.

2. Social Dimension - Empowering Employees and Strengthening Social Impact

CSR initiatives that focus on social outcomes aim to create positive impacts for employees, communities and Society at large by integrating ESO into these initiatives companies can amplify those social contributions.

- **Employee Empowerment and Welfare:** ESO provides Employees with direct financial stake in the organisation increasing their sense of belonging and empowerment. this can improve employee moral job satisfaction and overall being. When employees feel valued as both contributors and owners, they are more likely to be engaged and committed to the company's social mission.
- **Social Equity and Inclusion:** ESO, especially when extended to all employees regardless of their rank or role, promotes social equity within the organization by distributing ownership and wealth more broadly. This helps to reduce income inequality within the company, contributing to broader social goals of fairness and inclusivity. The democratization of ownership can lead to more inclusive decision-making processes, giving employees a stronger voice in how the organization is governed.
- **Community Engagement:** A socially responsible company that integrates ESO can better engage with its surrounding community. Employees with a stake in the company's success are more likely to support CSR activities such as volunteerism, charity initiatives, and local development projects. By giving employees ownership, organizations can foster a culture of social responsibility that extends beyond the company to the broader community.

3. Environmental Dimension - Fostering Environmental Stewardship

The environmental component of CSR focuses on sustainability and the responsible use of natural resources. By integrating ESO into environmental initiatives, companies can mobilize their workforce to actively participate in sustainability efforts, contributing to the long-term protection of the environment.

- **Employee-Driven Sustainability Initiatives:** Employees who have an ownership stake in the company are more likely to take initiative in identifying and implementing sustainable practices. Whether it's energy-saving measures, waste reduction, or process innovations, employees can become powerful advocates for sustainability within the organization. The shared sense of responsibility, fostered through ESO, can motivate employees to act as stewards of the company's environmental performance.
- **Corporate Commitment to Sustainability:** Companies that integrate ESO with a strong environmental CSR agenda demonstrate a commitment to both their workforce and the planet. This dual focus can strengthen the organization's reputation as an environmentally conscious business. For example, organizations can align employee incentives with sustainability goals, encour-

aging employees to participate in reducing the company's carbon footprint, supporting renewable energy projects, or minimizing resource consumption.

- **Long-Term Environmental Strategy:** As employee-owners, individuals are more likely to prioritize the company's long-term environmental strategy over short-term financial gains. This can lead to more sustainable decision-making, with a focus on long-term environmental impacts rather than immediate profits. Employee owners are more likely to advocate for responsible environmental practices, recognizing that the future health of the company is tied to the health of the planet.

Synergy of ESO and CSR Leading to Sustainable Outcomes:

The integration of ESO with CSR initiatives can generate value across all three dimensions of the Triple Bottom Line, leading to sustainable outcomes that benefit the company, employees, society, and the environment. By aligning economic, social, and environmental goals, organizations can achieve sustainable value creation. This framework posits that organizations should focus on three dimensions of performance: economic, social, and environmental. By synergizing ESO with CSR initiatives, organizations can create value across all three dimensions, leading to sustainable outcomes (Elkington, 1997). Employees who are engaged in ownership are more likely to support CSR initiatives, as they feel a personal stake in the organization's reputation and success.

II. Social Exchange Theory (SET): initially developed by George Homans in the 1950s and further refined by scholars like Peter Blau and Richard Emerson, provides a framework for understanding human behavior and relationships in terms of reciprocal exchanges. According to this theory, social relationships are formed through interactions that involve a series of exchanges where individuals give and receive benefits. These exchanges can be tangible, like financial rewards, or intangible, such as emotional support, trust, and recognition. The key principle is reciprocity, which posits that individuals engage in exchanges with the expectation that their contributions will be rewarded by others, creating mutually beneficial relationships.

Key Concepts of Social Exchange Theory:

- Reciprocity: Central to SET is the idea of reciprocity, meaning that when one party provides a benefit to another, the recipient feels an obligation to return the favor. In organizations, this can be seen in the relationship between employers and employees, where employers provide resources, support, or rewards, and employees reciprocate with loyalty, effort, and commitment.

- Mutual Dependence: Relationships in SET are built on mutual dependence. Both parties need something from each other and are willing to engage in exchanges to fulfill those needs. In the workplace, employees depend on the organization for compensation, development opportunities, and a sense of belonging, while the organization depends on employees for their skills, labor, and creativity.
- Trust and Commitment: Successful exchanges rely on trust and the belief that the other party will reciprocate fairly. Over time, these positive exchanges build commitment and foster long-term relationships. In organizations, trust and commitment can lead to increased employee engagement, reduced turnover, and higher performance levels.
- Cost-Benefit Analysis: Individuals in exchange relationships constantly evaluate the costs and benefits of their interactions. If the perceived benefits outweigh the costs, they are more likely to maintain and strengthen the relationship. In contrast, if the costs (e.g., effort, time) consistently exceed the benefits (e.g., rewards, recognition), the relationship may deteriorate.

Applying Social Exchange Theory to Employee Ownership and Corporate Social Responsibility (CSR): In the context of organizations, Employee Share Ownership (ESO) and Corporate Social Responsibility (CSR) initiatives represent two significant investments that companies can make in their employees. By offering ESO, companies give employees a direct financial stake in the organization's success, while CSR initiatives reflect the company's commitment to ethical practices and social impact. When organizations invest in both ESO and CSR, they create a foundation for positive exchange relationships with their employees, fostering loyalty, engagement, and enhanced performance.

Key Benefits of Using Social Exchange Theory in ESO and CSR:

- Increased Employee Engagement: SET suggests that when employees receive benefits from the organization, they are more likely to reciprocate with engagement and commitment. By offering ESO and engaging in CSR, companies create reciprocal relationships where employees feel invested and motivated to contribute more to the company's success.
- Enhanced Organizational Performance: The positive reciprocal relationships fostered by ESO and CSR can lead to enhanced performance. Employees who feel a sense of ownership and ethical alignment with the organization are more likely to go above and beyond in their roles, contributing to innovation, productivity, and overall organizational performance.

- Higher Levels of Employee Retention and Loyalty: SET indicates that when employees receive valuable benefits, they develop a sense of obligation to stay with the organization. ESO and CSR create a powerful combination of financial and social rewards that can significantly reduce turnover and increase loyalty.
- Improved Organizational Reputation: A company that integrates ESO and CSR is likely to build a strong reputation as an ethical, responsible employer. This positive external image can enhance the organization's ability to attract talent, investors, and customers who prioritize ethical and sustainable practices.

Challenges of Applying Social Exchange Theory:

- Ensuring Perceived Fairness: For social exchanges to work effectively, employees must perceive the benefits they receive as fair and meaningful. If employees feel that ESO is not fairly distributed or that CSR initiatives are tokenistic, the reciprocal relationship may break down, leading to disengagement.
- Balancing Financial and Social Investments: Organizations need to carefully balance financial rewards with social and ethical investments. Overemphasis on one dimension may reduce the perceived value of the other, weakening the overall exchange relationship.
- Long-Term Commitment: SET relies on the development of long-term relationships. Organizations must be consistent in their commitment to both ESO and CSR to maintain trust and reciprocity with employees over time.

This theory posits that relationships are built on reciprocal exchanges. When organizations invest in employee ownership and CSR, they foster a positive exchange relationship with employees, leading to increased loyalty, engagement, and performance (Blau, 1964). Employees are more likely to reciprocate these investments with higher levels of commitment and productivity.

III. Institutional Theory: This perspective emphasizes the role of social norms and values in shaping organizational behavior. As societal expectations regarding corporate responsibility evolve, organizations that integrate ESO with CSR are better positioned to meet these expectations, enhancing their legitimacy and reputation (DiMaggio & Powell, 1983). Institutional Theory is a framework for understanding how organizational behavior is shaped by broader social norms, values, and rules that exist within society. Rooted in sociology, this theory explores how organizations respond to external pressures, such as cultural expectations, regulations, and standards, to gain legitimacy and ensure their survival. Organizations are seen not merely as economic actors but as entities embedded in social and cultural environments that influence their behavior, practices, and structures.

According to Institutional Theory, organizations are influenced by the need to conform to societal norms and expectations to gain legitimacy, which is crucial for their continued existence and success. Legitimacy is the perceived appropriateness or desirability of an organization's actions, as judged by external stakeholders such as customers, investors, regulators, and society at large. Organizations that fail to align with social expectations risk losing support, facing regulatory challenges, and damaging their reputation, which can jeopardize their performance and survival.

Key Concepts of Institutional Theory:

- Legitimacy: This is the central concept of Institutional Theory. Organizations seek to be seen as legitimate actors in their environment by conforming to societal norms, values, and expectations. Legitimacy provides organizations with social approval, which is necessary for attracting resources, customers, and investment, as well as maintaining stakeholder trust.
- Isomorphism: Institutional Theory highlights a process called isomorphism, where organizations become more similar to each other over time as they adopt similar structures, practices, and behaviors to meet external pressures. There are three types of isomorphism:

    1. Coercive Isomorphism: Driven by legal and regulatory pressures.
    2. Normative Isomorphism: Driven by professional standards and social expectations.
    3. Mimetic Isomorphism: Driven by uncertainty, leading organizations to imitate successful peers or competitors.

- Institutional Pressures: These are external forces that compel organizations to adopt certain practices or behaviors. Pressures can come from various sources, including government regulations, industry standards, public opinion, and the expectations of key stakeholders such as employees, customers, and investors.
- Decoupling: Sometimes organizations may adopt practices or policies superficially to appear legitimate without genuinely integrating them into their core operations. This is known as decoupling, where there is a gap between formal practices and actual behavior. For example, an organization may claim to follow sustainability practices for reputational purposes without fully committing to them in practice.

Applying Institutional Theory to Employee Share Ownership (ESO) and Corporate Social Responsibility (CSR): In the context of Employee Share Ownership (ESO) and Corporate Social Responsibility (CSR), Institutional Theory provides insights into how organizations can adapt to changing societal expectations regarding corporate responsibility. As social norms evolve, particularly around issues of employee empowerment, social equity, and environmental sustainability, organizations that integrate ESO with CSR initiatives are better positioned to align with these expectations, thereby enhancing their legitimacy and reputation.

Challenges of Applying Institutional Theory:

- **Decoupling Risk:** One challenge of Institutional Theory is the risk of decoupling, where organizations may adopt ESO and CSR initiatives superficially to gain legitimacy without genuinely committing to these practices. This can lead to a gap between formal policies and actual behavior, undermining the organization's credibility.
- **Balancing Competing Institutional Pressures:** Organizations may face competing institutional pressures, such as the need to balance profitability with social responsibility. Navigating these pressures effectively is crucial for maintaining legitimacy without sacrificing financial performance.
- **Adapting to Changing Norms:** Societal norms and values are constantly evolving. Organizations need to be agile and responsive to these changes to maintain legitimacy. What is considered socially responsible today may change in the future, requiring organizations to continuously adapt their CSR and ESO strategies.

Importance of Integrating ESO, Corporate Governance, and CSR

The intersection of ESO, governance, and CSR is more than a strategic alignment—it is a synergistic relationship that can transform organizations into responsible, accountable, and high-performing entities. Each of these elements, when integrated effectively, strengthens the others:

- **ESO as a Catalyst for Better Governance and CSR:** Employee ownership fosters a more democratic and inclusive approach to corporate governance, as employees become active participants in decision-making. Additionally, employees who own shares are more likely to support CSR initiatives that benefit both the company and society, knowing that long-term sustainability enhances their financial wellbeing.

- **Corporate Governance as a Framework for Sustainable ESO:** Good governance ensures that ESO programs are designed and managed effectively, promoting fair distribution of shares and avoiding potential pitfalls such as stock price volatility or employee disenchantment.
- **CSR as a Platform for Inclusive Growth:** CSR initiatives aligned with ESO contribute to creating shared value, where employees, shareholders, and the community benefit from the company's success.

The Path to Enhanced Organizational Performance and Sustainable Value Creation

When ESO is synergized with robust governance frameworks and CSR initiatives, the potential for enhanced organizational performance is substantial. Several pathways illustrate this potential:

- **Increased Employee Engagement:** ESO deepens employees' emotional and financial investment in the company, which in turn drives higher engagement, lower turnover rates, and greater innovation.
- **Improved Corporate Reputation:** Firms that integrate ESO with CSR not only promote social responsibility but also build a stronger, more resilient corporate reputation. This can attract socially conscious investors and customers, further enhancing the company's market position.
- **Sustainable Value Creation:** The alignment of ESO, governance, and CSR creates a virtuous cycle of value creation—where employee ownership fosters higher productivity, better governance promotes responsible business practices, and CSR ensures that the company's impact extends beyond the financial bottom line to create long-lasting social and environmental benefits.

CONCLUSION

The theoretical framework for integrating Employee Share Ownership with Corporate Governance and Corporate Social Responsibility emphasizes the interconnectedness of these concepts in driving improved organizational performance and sustainable value creation. Drawing from agency theory, stewardship theory, stakeholder theory, and CSR frameworks, organizations can develop comprehensive strategies that align employee interests with broader governance and social responsibility objectives. This approach not only fosters a culture of ownership and accountability but also positions organizations to excel in a complex and socially conscious business environment. Future research should continue to explore these connections, providing empirical evidence and practical frameworks for organizations looking to implement these strategies effectively.

In summary, while there is a growing body of literature on employee share ownership, corporate governance, and corporate social responsibility, there are still significant research gaps in understanding how these elements can be combined to enhance organizational performance and create sustainable value. Future research should concentrate on developing comprehensive frameworks that integrate these concepts, explore the mechanisms of interaction, and provide empirical evidence of their combined impact across various contexts. By addressing these gaps, scholars and practitioners can gain a better understanding of the potential of ESO as a catalyst for improved governance and CSR practices, ultimately leading to more sustainable organizational outcomes.

REFERENCES

Achour, Z. (2024). Impact of employee stock ownership on firm financial performance: Does corporate social responsibility matter? *International Journal of Management and Enterprise Development*, 23(2), 155–170. DOI: 10.1504/IJMED.2024.139275

Agrawal, A., & Knoeber, C. R. (1996). Firm performance and mechanisms to control agency problems between managers and shareholders. *Journal of Financial and Quantitative Analysis*, 31(3), 377–397. DOI: 10.2307/2331397

Al-Ahdal, A. A., & Hashim, H. A. (2022). The impact of audit reputation on firm performance: Evidence from Indian non-financial firms. *Journal of Financial Reporting and Accounting*, 20(5), 866–896. DOI: 10.1108/JFRA-12-2020-0361

Amin, A., Ali, R., Rehman, R., Naseem, M. A., & Ahmad, M. I. (2022). Female presence in corporate governance, firm performance, and the moderating role of family ownership. *Ekonomska Istrazivanja*, 35(1), 929–948. DOI: 10.1080/1331677X.2021.1952086

Anderson, R. C., & Reeb, D. M. (2003). Founding-family ownership and firm performance: Evidence from the S&P 500. *The Journal of Finance*, 58(3), 1301–1328. DOI: 10.1111/1540-6261.00567

Arora, A., & Sharma, C. (2016). Corporate governance and firm performance in developing countries: Evidence from India. *Corporate Governance (Bradford)*, 16(2), 420–436. DOI: 10.1108/CG-01-2016-0018

Blau, P. M. (1964). *Exchange and power in social life*. Wiley.

Darko, A.. (2016). The impact of audit committee characteristics on firm performance: Evidence from Ghana. *International Journal of Accounting and Financial Reporting*, 6(1), 1–20.

Davis, J. H., Schoorman, F. D., & Donaldson, L. (1997). Toward a stewardship theory of management. *Academy of Management Review*, 22(1), 20–47. DOI: 10.2307/259223

Detthamrong, A.. (2017). The impact of audit committee characteristics on financial performance: Evidence from Thailand. *International Journal of Business and Management*, 12(3), 1–12.

DiMaggio, P. J., & Powell, W. W. (1983). The iron cage revisited: Institutional isomorphism and collective rationality in organizational fields. *American Sociological Review*, 48(2), 147–160. DOI: 10.2307/2095101

Donaldson, L., & Davis, J. H. (1991). Stewardship theory or agency theory: CEO governance and shareholder returns. *Australian Journal of Management*, 16(1), 49–64. DOI: 10.1177/031289629101600103

Dondi, J. (1992), Contribution to the knowledge of employee ownership: theoretical and empirical approach, PhD Thesis, University of Bordeaux IV.

Elkington, J. (1997). *Cannibals with forks: The triple bottom line of 21st century business.* Capstone.

Freeman, R. E. (1984). *Strategic management: A stakeholder approach.* Pitman.

Hill, C. W. L., & Jones, T. M. (1992). STAKEHOLDER-AGENCY THEORY. *Journal of Management Studies*, 29(2), 131–154. Advance online publication. DOI: 10.1111/j.1467-6486.1992.tb00657.x

Jensen, M., & Meckling, W. (1976). The Theory of Firm: Managerial Behavior, Agency Costs and Ownership Structure. *Journal of Financial Economics*, 3(4), 305–360. DOI: 10.1016/0304-405X(76)90026-X

Jensen, M. C., & Meckling, W. H. (1976). Theory of the firm: Managerial behavior, agency costs, and ownership structure. *Journal of Financial Economics*, 3(4), 305–360. DOI: 10.1016/0304-405X(76)90026-X

Kong, D., Liu, J., Wang, Y., & Zhu, L. (2024). Employee stock ownership plans and corporate environmental engagement. *Journal of Business Ethics*, 189(1), 177–199. DOI: 10.1007/s10551-023-05334-y

Kuvaas, B. (2003). Employee ownership and affective organizational commitment: Employees' perceptions of fairness and their preference for company shares over cash. *Scandinavian Journal of Management*, 19(2), 193–212. Advance online publication. DOI: 10.1016/S0956-5221(01)00044-6

Pendleton, A., Wilson, N., & Wright, M. (1998). The perception and effects of share ownership: Empirical evidence from employee buy-outs. *British Journal of Industrial Relations*, 36(1), 99–123. Advance online publication. DOI: 10.1111/1467-8543.00082

Pfeffer, J., & Salancik, G. R. (1978). *The external control of organizations: A resource dependence perspective*. Harper & Row.

Pierce, J. L., Kostova, T., & Dirks, K. T. (2001). Toward a theory of psychological ownership in organizations. *Academy of Management Review*, 26(2), 298–310. DOI: 10.2307/259124

Saylor, T. (2017) *Esops Help Some CPA Firms With Retention, Succession,* Journal Of Accountancy. https://tinyurl.com/pkv6e54t

Shrivastav, A. (2022). Audit meeting frequency and firm performance: Evidence from Indian firms. *Journal of Business Research*, 112, 65–80. DOI: 10.1016/j.jbusres.2020.02.041

Smith, A. (1776). *The wealth of nations*. Methuen & Co., Ltd.

Wen, X., Li, Z., Zhang, Y., & Shen, S. (2021). ESOP and corporate sustainable growth. In *E3S Web of Conferences* (Vol. 253, p. 03039). EDP Sciences.

Chapter 5

Influence of Employee Ownership on Environmental and Social Sustainability

P. Selvakumar
https://orcid.org/0000-0002-3650-4548
Department of Science and Humanities, Nehru Institute of Technology, Coimbatore, India

Sudhanshu Chandra
Maulana Azad National Urdu University, India

Saumyaa Pandey
Maulana Azad National Urdu University, India

Krishna Charan J.
Vel Tech Rangarajan Dr. Sagunthala R&D Institute of Science and Technology University, India

Nitika Malik
Maharshi Dayanand University, India

Rishi Chaudhry
Maharshi Dayanand University, India

ABSTRACT

Employee ownership represents a strategic approach that aligns the interests of employees with those of the organization through direct or indirect ownership stakes. This ownership can manifest in various forms, including employee stock ownership plans (ESOPs), stock options, and worker cooperatives, each offering unique benefits and implications for both employees and the organization. The fundamental idea behind employee ownership is to foster a deeper sense of commitment and responsibility among employees, leveraging their stake in the company's success to drive higher productivity, innovation, and job satisfaction. An ESOP is a prevalent model where employees are granted shares of the company, typically through a trust

DOI: 10.4018/979-8-3693-7031-5.ch005

fund, which holds the shares on behalf of employees until they retire or leave the company. ESOPs can serve as both an employee benefit and a financial strategy for companies, providing a mechanism for business owners to sell their stake while retaining employee engagement and continuity.

10. INTRODUCTION TO EMPLOYEE OWNERSHIP: CONCEPTS AND MODELS

Worker cooperatives represent a more extensive form of employee ownership where the workers not only hold shares but also have a significant say in the company's governance. In a cooperative, employees typically elect a board of directors and participate in key decisions, reflecting a democratic approach to business management. This model promotes equity and can enhance collective decision-making, potentially leading to greater innovation and alignment with employee interests. Cooperatives can be particularly effective in creating sustainable and resilient organizations, as they align the goals of the business with the well-being of its workers. Each of these models comes with its own set of advantages and challenges. For example, while ESOPs can be beneficial for both employees and employers, they may also lead to a lack of liquidity for the company if not managed properly. Stock options can motivate employees but might create challenges in terms of dilution of ownership and can sometimes lead to short-term thinking if employees are focused solely on share price fluctuations. Worker cooperatives, while fostering a high level of engagement and satisfaction, may face difficulties in achieving the same level of efficiency and scalability as traditional hierarchical companies (Henseler, J., et al., 2015). Understanding the various concepts and models of employee ownership is crucial for organizations considering this strategy. It involves assessing the company's goals, financial structure, and the desired level of employee involvement and empowerment. By carefully selecting and implementing the appropriate model, organizations can create a more motivated and aligned workforce, potentially leading to improved performance, retention, and long-term success. Employee ownership, when implemented effectively, can transform the dynamics within a company, contributing to a more collaborative and committed organizational culture.

10.1. Environmental Sustainability: The Role of Employee Ownership

Environmental sustainability is increasingly recognized as a crucial element for modern businesses, and employee ownership can play a significant role in advancing this agenda. When employees hold a stake in their company, they are more likely to be invested in its long-term success, which often includes a commitment to sustainable practices. This heightened sense of ownership can lead to innovative approaches to environmental stewardship, as employees are motivated to ensure that their company thrives not only economically but also environmentally. Employee ownership can foster a culture of accountability and responsibility, driving organizations to adopt greener practices (Ketelaar, E., et al., 2013). When employees are shareholders or co-owners, they have a vested interest in the company's performance, including its environmental impact. This ownership can lead to a greater emphasis on sustainability initiatives, as employees may push for practices that reduce waste, conserve resources, and minimize the company's carbon footprint. For example, in a worker cooperative or an ESOP structure, employees might advocate for investments in energy-efficient technologies or support initiatives aimed at reducing the company's environmental impact, knowing that these efforts can lead to long-term benefits for the organization and its stakeholders. Moreover, employee-owned companies often exhibit a higher level of engagement in corporate social responsibility (CSR) efforts. These organizations may be more inclined to integrate environmental sustainability into their core business strategies, recognizing that their commitment to sustainability can enhance the company's reputation and, consequently, its success (Islam, G., et al., 2021).

The alignment of employees' interests with the company's success can also lead to more effective implementation of sustainable practices. When employees feel a sense of ownership, they are more likely to contribute innovative ideas and solutions to environmental challenges. They might engage in continuous improvement practices, seek out efficiencies, and drive initiatives that reduce the company's environmental impact. Additionally, employee-owned companies may experience higher levels of employee retention, which can result in a more consistent and dedicated workforce focused on achieving long-term sustainability goals. However, integrating environmental sustainability into employee-owned businesses does present challenges. It requires a cultural shift towards viewing sustainability as integral to the company's success rather than as an additional or secondary consideration. There must be a clear alignment between the company's sustainability goals and the values of its employees. Employee owners need to be provided with the necessary resources, training, and support to actively participate in and drive sustainability initiatives. Furthermore, companies must develop clear metrics and reporting mechanisms to track progress and demonstrate the impact of their sustainability efforts. The potential for employee ownership to contribute to environmental sustainability is significant, but it depends on the commitment and involvement of the employees (Lu, C. S., et al., 2014). When employees have a stake in the company's success, they are more likely to advocate for and implement sustainable practices that benefit both the environment and the organization. By fostering a culture of shared responsibility and long-term thinking, employee ownership can drive substantial advancements in environmental sustainability, creating a positive impact on the planet while also enhancing the company's resilience and success.

10.1.1. Social Sustainability: Employee Ownership and Community Impact

Social sustainability, which emphasizes the well-being and stability of communities, is increasingly recognized as a critical component of a company's overall sustainability strategy. Employee ownership can significantly enhance social sustainability by fostering a more inclusive and equitable workplace, strengthening community ties, and contributing to broader social impact goals (Gartenberg, C., et al., 2019). This approach aligns the interests of employees with the long-term success of the company, often leading to a more engaged, motivated, and socially responsible workforce. One of the primary ways employee ownership promotes social sustainability is by creating a more equitable distribution of wealth. In employee-owned companies, workers share in the company's financial success, which can help reduce income inequality and provide employees with greater economic security. This financial stake encourages a sense of fairness and inclusion, as employees see a direct correlation between their efforts and the company's success. By enhancing economic stability among employees, these organizations contribute to the broader goal of reducing social inequality and fostering community resilience. Employee ownership also strengthens community impact through the development of a more invested workforce (Edinger, J., et al., 2019). When employees own a stake in the company, they are more likely to engage in activities that benefit their local communities.

These activities not only enhance the company's reputation but also create tangible benefits for the community, fostering a positive relationship between the organization and its surrounding area. In addition to financial and community engagement benefits, employee ownership can promote a more inclusive workplace culture. Employee-owned companies often emphasize democratic decision-making and participatory management, which can lead to more diverse and equitable work environments. By involving employees in governance and strategic decisions, these organizations can create a workplace that values different perspectives and experiences, contributing to a more inclusive and supportive work culture (Dutton, J. E., et al., 1994). However, achieving these social sustainability benefits requires intentional effort and commitment from employee-owned companies. It involves creating structures that ensure meaningful employee participation and fostering a culture that supports social responsibility. Companies must also develop strategies to engage with and invest in their communities actively. This includes setting clear goals for social impact, measuring progress, and adapting practices to address emerging community needs. Employee ownership has the potential to make significant contributions to social sustainability by aligning employee interests with broader social goals. By promoting economic equity, enhancing community engagement, and fostering inclusive workplace cultures, employee-owned companies can drive positive social change (Chan, K. W., et al., 2011). The benefits of employee ownership extend beyond the company itself, creating ripple effects that enhance the well-being and resilience of communities. Through a commitment to shared values and mutual benefit, employee ownership can play a pivotal role in advancing social sustainability and building stronger, more equitable societies.

10.2.Employee Engagement and Motivation: Driving Sustainability Efforts

The synergy between employee engagement and sustainability not only enhances the organization's environmental performance but also fosters a culture of shared responsibility and commitment to long-term goals. Engagement and motivation stem from a variety of factors, including meaningful work, alignment with personal values, and recognition of contributions. When employees perceive their roles as integral to achieving the company's sustainability goals, they are more likely to be invested in these efforts. For instance, employees who understand how their daily tasks contribute to larger environmental objectives are more motivated to adopt sustainable practices, such as reducing waste, conserving energy, and supporting sustainable sourcing. This sense of purpose and connection to broader sustainability goals can transform routine tasks into meaningful contributions, fostering a proactive approach to environmental stewardship. Moreover, organizations that actively involve employees in sustainability initiatives often experience higher levels of engagement (Bartlett, C. A., et al., 1994). Providing opportunities for employees to participate in sustainability programs, such as green teams, eco-challenges, and volunteer projects, can enhance their commitment to these efforts. When employees are given a voice in shaping sustainability strategies and implementing solutions, they are more likely to feel valued and empowered. This participatory approach not only boosts morale but also leverages the diverse perspectives and ideas of employees, leading to more innovative and effective sustainability practices.

Recognition and reward systems also play a crucial role in sustaining employee motivation for environmental and social initiatives. Recognizing and celebrating achievements related to sustainability—whether through formal awards, public acknowledgment, or performance-based incentives—can reinforce the importance of these efforts and encourage ongoing participation. By aligning reward systems with sustainability goals, organizations can motivate employees to pursue and excel in initiatives that contribute to environmental and social impact. The integration of sustainability into the core values and mission of the organization further enhances employee engagement. When sustainability is embedded in the company's culture and strategic objectives, it becomes a shared goal that all employees can rally around (Kaptein, M.,2008). This alignment creates a sense of collective purpose, where employees are driven by a commitment to making a positive difference. A clear and compelling sustainability vision, communicated effectively throughout the organization, can inspire employees to contribute their best efforts towards achieving these goals. However, fostering employee engagement in sustainability requires more than just motivation—it also demands a supportive organizational environment.

10.2.1. Ownership Culture and Sustainability Values: Aligning Goals

Ownership culture and sustainability values are increasingly recognized as synergistic components in achieving organizational excellence and long-term success. Cultivating an ownership culture within a company entails fostering a sense of personal investment and accountability among employees, which aligns their individual goals with the organization's strategic objectives. This culture is characterized by employees treating the company's resources and success as if they were their own, leading to enhanced performance and a stronger commitment to the company's values. When integrated with sustainability values, an ownership culture can significantly amplify the impact of environmental and social initiatives, creating a powerful framework for achieving comprehensive and lasting sustainability goals. At the heart of an ownership culture is the principle of shared responsibility (Pierce, J. L., et al., 2001). Employees who feel a sense of ownership are more likely to take initiative and be proactive in their roles. This heightened engagement can translate into a stronger commitment to sustainability, as employees recognize that their actions directly affect the company's environmental and social performance. When employees see their contributions as integral to achieving sustainability targets, they are more motivated to adopt and advocate for eco-friendly practices, such as reducing energy consumption, minimizing waste, and supporting sustainable sourcing.

Moreover, integrating sustainability into performance metrics and reward systems reinforces the alignment of ownership culture with sustainability values. By incorporating sustainability criteria into performance evaluations and recognition programs, organizations can incentivize employees to prioritize and excel in sustainability efforts. Rewards and recognition for contributions to sustainability goals not only motivate employees but also highlight the company's commitment to these values, further embedding sustainability into the organizational culture. Challenges may arise in aligning ownership culture with sustainability values, particularly in balancing short-term objectives with long-term sustainability goals (Pellegrini,

C., et al., 2018). Companies must navigate potential conflicts between immediate business needs and the pursuit of comprehensive sustainability targets. Effective communication and strategic planning are essential to ensure that sustainability efforts are integrated into the company's overall strategy and that employees understand the importance of balancing both short-term and long-term considerations. In conclusion, aligning ownership culture with sustainability values creates a robust foundation for achieving organizational success and advancing environmental and social objectives (Ramakrishnan T.,et al., 2022). By fostering a culture of shared responsibility, embedding sustainability into core values, empowering employee involvement, and integrating sustainability into performance metrics, organizations can harness the full potential of an ownership culture to drive meaningful and lasting sustainability outcomes.

10.2.2. Decision-Making and Governance: Employee Ownership and Sustainability

Decision-making and governance are pivotal elements in the intersection of employee ownership and sustainability, shaping how organizations implement and prioritize environmental and social initiatives. Employee ownership fundamentally transforms traditional decision-making processes by introducing a shared responsibility model, where employees are not only stakeholders but also active participants in governance. This participatory approach can enhance sustainability efforts by aligning organizational strategies with both employee values and broader environmental and social goals. In employee-owned companies, decision-making often becomes more democratic, with employees having a significant role in shaping policies and strategies. This inclusive approach to governance ensures that sustainability considerations are integrated into key decisions at various levels of the organization. Employees, who are directly impacted by and invested in the company's outcomes, bring valuable insights and diverse perspectives to sustainability discussions. Their involvement can lead to more comprehensive and effective sustainability strategies, as they are likely to advocate for practices that align with their values and the long-term health of the organization. The governance structures in employee-owned companies, such as worker cooperatives or ESOPs (Employee Stock Ownership Plans), often feature mechanisms that facilitate employee participation. For instance, in worker cooperatives, employees typically elect a board of directors and have a say in major business decisions, including those related to sustainability. This participatory governance model ensures that sustainability is not merely a top-down directive but a shared objective that reflects the collective commitment of the workforce. Similarly, in ESOPs, while employees may not be involved in day-to-day decisions, they often influence broader strategic decisions through their representation on boards or committees, ensuring that sustainability goals are considered in corporate strategies.

The alignment of employee ownership with sustainability values requires effective decision-making processes that balance short-term business needs with long-term environmental and social goals. Employee-owned companies are often better positioned to adopt and sustain long-term sustainability initiatives because the ownership structure encourages a focus on enduring success rather than immediate financial gains. Employees who have a stake in the company's future are more likely to support investments in sustainable technologies, practices, and initiatives that may not yield immediate returns but are crucial for long-term viability and corporate responsibility (Schaufeli, W. B., et al., 2002). Furthermore, transparency and accountability in governance are enhanced in employee-owned companies, which supports more robust sustainability efforts. When employees are involved in decision-making, there is a greater emphasis on transparent communication and accountability for sustainability outcomes. This transparency helps build trust among employees and stakeholders, as they can see the direct impact of their contributions and the company's commitment to sustainability. Additionally, clear reporting and feedback mechanisms allow employees to monitor progress and hold the organization accountable for meeting its sustainability targets. Challenges in integrating employee ownership with sustainability governance may arise, particularly in balancing diverse perspectives and interests. Effective governance structures must manage potential conflicts between competing priorities, such as short-term profitability versus long-term sustainability.

10.3. Innovation and Risk-Taking: Employee Ownership and Sustainable Practices

Innovation and risk-taking are critical drivers of progress in sustainable practices, and employee ownership can significantly influence how these factors are approached within organizations. When employees have a stake in the company, their motivation and engagement often lead to a more proactive approach to innovation and a greater willingness to embrace and manage risks associated with sustainable practices (Paille, P., et al., 2019). This ownership perspective not only fosters a culture of continuous improvement but also enables organizations to explore and implement novel solutions to environmental and social challenges. In employee-owned companies, the alignment of personal and organizational interests creates an environment conducive to innovation. Employees who feel a sense of ownership are more likely to invest their time and energy in developing creative solutions that advance sustainability. This is because they directly benefit from the company's success and are motivated to contribute to its long-term viability. This increased engagement can lead to a more dynamic and forward-thinking approach, where employees actively seek out and experiment with new technologies, processes, and practices that support sustainable development. The inherent risk-taking culture in employee-owned companies is another key factor that supports sustainable innovation. Traditional corporate structures often prioritize minimizing risk to protect short-term profits, which can stifle innovation. In contrast, employee-owned organizations tend to focus on long-term success, encouraging a more calculated approach to risk-taking. Employees, knowing that they will share in the rewards and consequences of their decisions, are more willing to engage in experimental and potentially disruptive initiatives. This willingness to take risks can lead to significant breakthroughs in sustainability, such as the development of new eco-friendly products, processes, or business models that might not have been pursued in a more risk-averse environment.

Moreover, the collaborative nature of employee-owned organizations enhances their capacity for innovation. In these companies, employees often work together more closely and share knowledge and expertise across departments. This collaborative environment facilitates the exchange of ideas and fosters a culture where innovative solutions can emerge from diverse perspectives. When employees are encouraged to contribute ideas and collaborate on sustainability projects, it leads to more holistic and effective solutions that address a range of environmental and social issues (Moore, C., et al., 2012). Employee ownership also affects the approach to managing and mitigating risks associated with sustainable practices. Since employees have a direct stake in the company's success, they are more likely to adopt a strategic approach to risk management, balancing potential rewards with associated risks. This can lead to more thoughtful and deliberate decision-making processes when it comes to investing in new sustainable technologies or practices. Employees are often more inclined to engage in scenario planning, risk assessment, and iterative testing to ensure that sustainable innovations are implemented effectively and responsibly (Mahadev Madgule, et al., 2023). However, integrating innovation and risk-taking with employee ownership requires careful management. The organization must foster an environment where employees feel empowered to experiment and propose new ideas without fear of negative repercussions if those ideas do not succeed. This involves creating a culture that views failure as a learning opportunity rather than a setback, thereby encouraging continuous experimentation and improvement. Providing the necessary resources, support, and recognition for innovative efforts is also crucial in sustaining a culture of innovation.

Furthermore, organizations must balance the immediate challenges and constraints of implementing new sustainable practices with their long-term goals. While employee ownership can drive innovation, it is essential to align new initiatives with the company's strategic objectives and ensure that they are financially viable and operationally feasible. Effective communication and alignment between leadership and employees are necessary to navigate these complexities and ensure that innovation efforts contribute to the company's overall sustainability goals. In conclusion, employee ownership plays a significant role in enhancing innovation and risk-taking related to sustainable practices . By aligning employees' interests with the company's long-term success, fostering a collaborative and supportive environment, and encouraging a strategic approach to risk management, employee-owned organizations can drive meaningful advancements in sustainability. This alignment not only benefits the organization through improved environmental and social outcomes but also contributes to a culture of continuous improvement and innovation. As employee-owned companies leverage these dynamics, they can achieve substantial progress in their sustainability efforts and build a more resilient and forward-thinking business model.

10.3.1.Supply Chain Management: Employee Ownership and Sustainable Sourcing

Supply chain management is a critical area where employee ownership can significantly influence sustainable sourcing practices, driving both environmental and social responsibility throughout the supply chain. Employee ownership transforms traditional supply chain dynamics by fostering a deep sense of accountability and shared commitment to sustainability among employees. This shift in perspective can lead to more rigorous efforts in sourcing practices, ensuring that sustainability considerations are embedded throughout the supply chain from procurement to delivery (Sugumaran K. M, D., et al., 2019). In employee-owned organizations, the alignment between employees' personal interests and the company's long-term goals often translates into a stronger focus on sustainable sourcing. Employees who have a stake in the company's success are more likely to advocate for and participate in sustainable procurement practices. This involves selecting suppliers who adhere to environmental and social standards, minimizing the carbon footprint of the supply chain, and supporting ethical labor practices. The sense of ownership encourages employees to consider the broader implications of their sourcing decisions, promoting transparency and accountability. Such measures help to ensure that sourcing practices remain aligned with the company's sustainability goals and provide opportunities for continuous improvement. However, integrating employee ownership with sustainable sourcing practices can present challenges. Balancing short-term cost considerations with long-term sustainability goals requires careful management (Spreitzer, G. M., 1995). Sustainable sourcing often involves higher costs or more complex logistics, which can be challenging for employee-owned companies that must also consider financial performance and profitability.

Moreover, successful implementation of sustainable sourcing practices requires a comprehensive approach that includes training and development. Employees need to be equipped with the knowledge and skills to evaluate suppliers, understand sustainability standards, and apply best practices in procurement. Training programs and resources can help employees make informed decisions and contribute effectively to sustainability initiatives, ensuring that the company's sourcing practices reflect its commitment to environmental and social responsibility. In conclusion, employee ownership can significantly impact supply chain management by enhancing sustainable sourcing practices. The alignment of employee interests with the company's long-term success fosters a deeper commitment to sustainability, leading to more rigorous and effective procurement processes. By leveraging the collaborative nature of employee-owned organizations, implementing robust monitoring systems, and addressing the challenges associated with sustainable sourcing, companies can build supply chains that are not only efficient but also environmentally and socially responsible. This alignment between employee ownership and sustainable sourcing not only benefits the company but also contributes to a more ethical and sustainable global supply chain.

10.4. Stakeholder Engagement: Employee Ownership and Community Involvement

Stakeholder engagement is a crucial aspect of fostering strong relationships between organizations and their broader communities, and employee ownership can significantly enhance community involvement efforts. Employee-owned companies, by nature of their structure, often exhibit a heightened sense of responsibility and investment in their local environments. This commitment manifests in more proactive and meaningful engagement with community stakeholders, driving positive social impact and strengthening the bonds between the organization and its surrounding community. In employee-owned companies, the alignment of employee interests with organizational goals leads to a natural inclination towards active community involvement. Employees who have a stake in the company's success are more likely to engage in activities that benefit the community, as they understand that these efforts contribute to the company's long-term health and stability. This can include supporting local charities, participating in community service projects, and collaborating with local organizations to address pressing social issues. The sense of ownership and responsibility drives employees to contribute their time, skills, and resources to initiatives that enhance the well-being of their communities.

The collaborative nature of employee-owned companies also enhances their ability to build strong relationships with community stakeholders. When employees are actively involved in community engagement efforts, they bring their unique insights and connections to the table, fostering deeper and more authentic relationships with local organizations and residents. This collaborative approach can lead to more successful partnerships and initiatives that address specific community needs and contribute to local development. For example, employee-owned companies might collaborate with local schools to provide educational programs, partner with community groups to address environmental challenges, or support local businesses through joint ventures and sponsorships (Van Tuin, L., et al., 2020). Furthermore, employee-owned companies often exhibit a long-term commitment to community involvement, driven by their focus on sustainable success. Unlike traditional businesses that may prioritize short-term gains, employee-owned organizations are more likely to invest in long-term community relationships and initiatives. This long-term perspective allows companies to build deeper connections with stakeholders and contribute to sustainable community development. Employees, as co-owners, are invested in the company's future and are motivated to support initiatives that create lasting positive impacts in their communities. Despite these advantages, integrating employee ownership with effective stakeholder engagement requires careful planning and management. Companies must develop clear strategies and frameworks for community involvement that align with their values and objectives (Vijayakumar G, et al., 2024). This involves setting specific goals for community engagement, establishing metrics to measure the impact of initiatives, and ensuring that resources are allocated effectively. Additionally, organizations must navigate potential challenges such as balancing community involvement with business priorities and addressing diverse stakeholder expectations.

Training and development also play a crucial role in enhancing stakeholder engagement. Employees need to be equipped with the skills and knowledge to effectively participate in community initiatives and represent the company in interactions with stakeholders. Providing training on community engagement best practices, communication skills, and stakeholder management can help employees contribute more effectively to community efforts and build stronger relationships with local organizations and residents. In conclusion, employee ownership significantly enhances stakeholder engagement and community involvement by fostering a culture of responsibility, transparency, and long-term commitment. The alignment of employee interests with organizational goals leads to more proactive and meaningful engagement with community stakeholders, driving positive social impact and strengthening community relationships (Zoghbi-Manrique-de-Lara, P., 2010).

By leveraging the collaborative nature of employee-owned companies, developing clear strategies for community involvement, and providing training and support, organizations can effectively integrate employee ownership with community engagement efforts, contributing to both organizational success and sustainable community development.

10.4.1. Case Studies: Successful Employee-Owned Companies and Sustainability

Examining successful employee-owned companies provides valuable insights into how such organizations effectively integrate sustainability into their business models, demonstrating the powerful synergy between employee ownership and environmental responsibility. These case studies highlight how employee ownership can drive meaningful advancements in sustainable practices while enhancing organizational performance and community impact. The experiences of these companies offer practical examples of how ownership structures can align with and reinforce sustainability goals. One prominent example is Ben & Jerry's, the well-known ice cream company that has long been recognized for its commitment to social and environmental issues (Wilden, R., et al., 2015). While Ben & Jerry's is not fully employee-owned, its partial employee ownership structure has contributed to its robust sustainability initiatives. The company's employees are actively involved in decision-making processes related to sustainability, resulting in the development of innovative practices such as using Fairtrade-certified ingredients and implementing extensive waste reduction programs. The company's commitment to environmental stewardship is reflected in its efforts to reduce greenhouse gas emissions, support climate justice initiatives, and advocate for policy changes that address environmental challenges. The alignment between employee interests and sustainability goals has enabled Ben & Jerry's to effectively integrate social responsibility into its core business strategy.

The John Lewis Partnership, which includes John Lewis & Partners and Waitrose & Partners, is known for its extensive employee ownership structure and strong commitment to sustainability. The company has implemented numerous initiatives to reduce its environmental impact, such as reducing carbon emissions, minimizing waste, and promoting ethical sourcing. Employee engagement in these initiatives is high, with employees actively participating in sustainability programs and contributing to decision-making processes (Avey, J. B., et al., 2012). The partnership model encourages a shared vision of sustainability, leading to significant progress in environmental stewardship and corporate responsibility.New Belgium Brewing Company exemplifies how employee ownership can drive sustainability in the beverage industry. As a 100% employee-owned craft brewery, New Belgium Brewing has integrated sustainability into every aspect of its operations, from sourcing ingredients to managing waste. The company's employees are actively involved in sustainability efforts, including initiatives to reduce energy consumption, support renewable energy projects, and engage in community-based environmental programs. New Belgium Brewing's commitment to sustainability is further reflected in its certification as a B Corporation and its recognition as one of the most sustainable companies in the brewing industry. The employee ownership structure has fostered a culture of innovation and accountability, enabling the company to achieve significant environmental and social impact.

10.4.2.Challenges and Limitations: Implementing Sustainability in Employee-Owned Companies

Implementing sustainability in employee-owned companies presents a unique set of challenges and limitations that organizations must navigate to achieve their environmental and social goals. While the employee ownership model offers several advantages, such as heightened engagement and a long-term focus, it also introduces complexities that can impact the effectiveness of sustainability initiatives (Abhilasha A., et al., 2022). Understanding and addressing these challenges is crucial for leveraging the full potential of employee ownership in driving sustainable practices. One significant challenge is balancing short-term financial pressures with long-term sustainability goals. Employee-owned companies often face the same economic pressures as traditional businesses, including the need to maintain profitability and manage operational costs. Sustainable practices, such as investing in renewable energy or adopting eco-friendly materials, may require substantial upfront costs and may not yield immediate financial returns. Employee-owned companies must carefully navigate these financial considerations, ensuring that their sustainability initiatives are strategically aligned with both their long-term vision and their immediate financial realities. This balancing act requires effective communication and planning to ensure that sustainability investments are viewed as integral to the company's long-term success rather than as burdensome expenses. Another challenge is the potential for conflicting priorities among employees.

In addition, integrating sustainability into existing processes and systems can be complex and time-consuming. Employee-owned companies may need to overhaul their operations, supply chains, and management practices to align with sustainability goals. This can involve significant changes in how resources are allocated, how suppliers are selected, and how products are designed and manufactured. Such transitions require careful planning, extensive training, and potentially substantial investments in new technologies or processes. Ensuring that employees are adequately prepared and supported during these transitions is crucial for successful implementation.

Comprehensive training programs and change management strategies can help employees adapt to new practices and ensure that sustainability initiatives are effectively integrated into daily operations. Resistance to change is another potential barrier to implementing sustainability in employee-owned companies. Even with strong employee engagement, some individuals may resist new sustainability initiatives due to uncertainty or a perceived threat to their current roles and responsibilities. Overcoming this resistance requires a transparent approach to communication and a focus on demonstrating the long-term benefits of sustainability initiatives. Engaging employees early in the process, addressing their concerns, and highlighting the positive impacts of sustainability on both the company and the community can help build support and reduce resistance.

10.5. Policy and Regulatory Frameworks: Supporting Employee Ownership and Sustainability

Policy and regulatory frameworks play a pivotal role in supporting employee ownership and sustainability, providing the necessary structure and incentives for organizations to integrate these principles effectively. By shaping the legal and financial environment in which employee-owned companies operate, these frameworks can facilitate the adoption of sustainable practices and ensure that employee ownership contributes to both economic resilience and environmental responsibility. A well-designed policy landscape not only encourages the growth of employee ownership but also aligns these ownership structures with broader sustainability goals. First and foremost, supportive policy frameworks can promote the establishment and expansion of employee ownership models, such as Employee Stock Ownership Plans (ESOPs) and worker cooperatives. Tax incentives, grants, and subsidies can provide financial benefits to companies that adopt employee ownership structures, making it more feasible for businesses to transition to or establish these models. For example, favorable tax treatment for ESOP contributions and capital gains can reduce the financial burden associated with setting up and maintaining employee ownership programs. Such policies not only make employee ownership more attractive but also help ensure that companies have the resources necessary to invest in sustainability initiatives.

Supportive policies can also include incentives for companies that demonstrate leadership in sustainability. For instance, public recognition programs, sustainability certifications, and awards can highlight the achievements of employee-owned companies that excel in environmental and social performance. These recognitions not only serve as a benchmark for best practices but also encourage other organizations to follow suit. By creating a positive feedback loop where sustainability is celebrated and rewarded, regulatory frameworks can motivate employee-owned companies to continually improve their practices and contribute to broader sustainability goals. Furthermore, policies that facilitate access to funding and resources for sustainability projects are essential. Employee-owned companies, particularly smaller or newly established ones, may face challenges in securing the capital needed to invest in green technologies or sustainable practices. Government-backed loans, grants, and investment programs can help mitigate these barriers, enabling companies to pursue innovative solutions and enhance their sustainability performance. Such financial support can be crucial for implementing energy-efficient technologies, developing sustainable products, and achieving other key sustainability objectives. On the other hand, regulatory frameworks must be carefully designed to avoid unintended consequences that could hinder the effectiveness of employee ownership and sustainability efforts. Overly complex or restrictive regulations can impose significant compliance costs and administrative burdens on employee-owned companies, potentially detracting from their ability to focus on sustainability initiatives. Simplified regulatory processes, streamlined reporting requirements, and clear guidelines can help ensure that companies can meet their obligations without being overwhelmed by bureaucratic challenges.

Additionally, policies that promote collaboration between employee-owned companies and external stakeholders, such as industry associations, non-governmental organizations, and academic institutions, can enhance the effectiveness of sustainability efforts. Support for partnerships and collaborative initiatives can facilitate knowledge sharing, best practice development, and joint projects that advance sustainability goals. By fostering an ecosystem of support and collaboration, policy frameworks can amplify the impact of employee ownership in driving sustainability. Finally, ongoing evaluation and adaptation of policies and regulations are crucial to ensuring their continued relevance and effectiveness. As sustainability challenges evolve and new best practices emerge, policy frameworks must be flexible and responsive to changing circumstances. Engaging with stakeholders, including employee-owned companies, in the policy development process can ensure that regulations address current needs and support ongoing improvements in sustainability practices. In conclusion, well-crafted policy and regulatory frameworks are fundamental to supporting employee ownership and sustainability. By providing financial incentives, establishing clear standards, facilitating access to resources, and promoting collaboration, these frameworks can enable employee-owned companies to integrate sustainability into their core operations effectively. Ensuring that policies are balanced, adaptable, and supportive of both employee ownership and sustainability goals will help create a conducive environment for organizations to thrive while making meaningful contributions to environmental and social well-being.

10.5.1 . International Perspectives: Employee Ownership and Sustainability Globally

Employee ownership and sustainability are increasingly recognized as interconnected concepts with global relevance, influencing how companies operate and contribute to sustainable development across diverse regions. Different countries have developed unique approaches to integrating employee ownership with sustainability, reflecting varying cultural, economic, and regulatory contexts. By examining international perspectives, we can gain insights into how employee-owned companies worldwide address sustainability challenges and opportunities and identify best practices that could be adapted across borders. In the United States, employee ownership is primarily facilitated through mechanisms like Employee Stock Ownership Plans (ESOPs) and worker cooperatives. Many ESOPs have adopted strong sustainability practices, driven by both the financial benefits of long-term planning and the employees' vested interest in the company's success. Companies like New Belgium Brewing and Clif Bar have leveraged their employee ownership structures to support comprehensive sustainability initiatives, from reducing carbon footprints to sourcing organic ingredients. U.S. policies, such as tax incentives for ESOPs, have supported these efforts, though challenges remain in balancing sustainability investments with short-term financial pressures. In Europe, employee ownership often intersects with robust social and environmental regulations, leading to diverse models of sustainable business practices. For example, The John Lewis Partnership in the UK, a major employee-owned retailer, integrates sustainability deeply into its operations, driven by its cooperative ownership model and stringent sustainability reporting requirements. Similarly, Ecovia Intelligence in France highlights how worker cooperatives are leveraging employee ownership to drive innovations in green technologies and sustainable practices. European countries generally have supportive frameworks for employee ownership, with regulations encouraging transparency and sustainability, although the effectiveness of these measures can vary between nations.

10.5.2. Measuring Sustainability Performance: Metrics and Evaluation Methods

Measuring sustainability performance is critical for organizations seeking to assess and enhance their environmental and social impacts. Effective metrics and evaluation methods enable companies to track progress, identify areas for improvement, and demonstrate their commitment to sustainability. To achieve comprehensive measurement, organizations must develop a robust framework that incorporates quantitative and qualitative indicators, integrates various aspects of sustainability, and aligns with both internal goals and external standards. A fundamental aspect of measuring sustainability performance is selecting relevant metrics that reflect the organization's sustainability goals. Environmental metrics typically include measures such as carbon footprint, energy consumption, water usage, waste generation, and resource efficiency. These metrics provide insights into the organization's environmental impact and help identify opportunities for reducing resource use and emissions. To evaluate these metrics effectively, organizations must implement robust data collection and reporting systems. Consistent and accurate data collection is crucial for reliable measurement and analysis. Companies often use software tools and sustainability management systems to automate data collection, track performance, and generate reports. These systems help ensure that data is collected systematically and can be analyzed in a meaningful way. Regular monitoring and periodic reviews of sustainability performance are essential to maintain accuracy and relevance. Benchmarking is another important method for evaluating sustainability performance. By comparing their metrics to industry standards, best practices, or peer organizations, companies can assess their performance relative to others and identify areas for improvement. Benchmarking can provide valuable context for understanding performance and setting realistic targets. Organizations may use external databases, industry reports, and sustainability indexes to gather benchmarking data and make informed comparisons. In addition to quantitative metrics, qualitative assessments provide valuable insights into sustainability performance. Qualitative evaluation methods can include stakeholder interviews, case studies, and narrative reporting. These approaches offer a deeper understanding of the context and impact of sustainability initiatives, capturing nuances that quantitative metrics might overlook.

Moreover, third-party verification and certification can enhance the credibility of sustainability performance claims. External audits and certifications, such as ISO 14001 for environmental management or B Corporation certification, provide independent validation of sustainability practices and performance. These certifications not only validate the organization's efforts but also improve stakeholder trust and confidence in the reported data. Finally, integrating sustainability performance into strategic decision-making is essential for driving continuous improvement. Organizations should use performance data to set ambitious yet achievable sustainability goals, develop action plans, and monitor progress. Regular reviews of sustainability performance help organizations adjust their strategies, address challenges, and capitalize on opportunities for improvement. In conclusion, measuring sustainability performance requires a comprehensive approach that incorporates both quantitative and qualitative metrics, integrates various aspects of sustainability, and aligns with established standards and frameworks. By implementing robust data collection systems, benchmarking against industry standards, and leveraging qualitative assessments, organizations can effectively evaluate their sustainability efforts and drive meaningful progress. Transparency through reporting and external verification further enhances credibility, while integrating performance data into strategic decision-making ensures continuous improvement and alignment with sustainability goals.

10.6. Future Directions: Emerging Trends and Research in Employee Ownership and Sustainability

As the global focus on sustainability intensifies, the intersection of employee ownership and sustainability is emerging as a critical area of research and development. This evolving field reflects the growing recognition of how employee ownership models can significantly contribute to sustainable business practices while addressing pressing environmental and social challenges. Future directions in this area are shaped by several key trends and research avenues that promise to advance our understanding and implementation of sustainable practices within employee-owned companies. One prominent trend is the increasing integration of Environmental, Social, and Governance (ESG) criteria into employee ownership models. ESG frameworks provide comprehensive guidelines for measuring and managing sustainability performance across various dimensions. Research is increasingly exploring how employee-owned companies can align with ESG principles to enhance their environmental stewardship, social responsibility, and governance practices. This integration is expected to lead to more robust sustainability strategies, with employee ownership structures facilitating deeper engagement with ESG goals and practices.

Collaboration and partnerships are emerging as key strategies for advancing sustainability in employee-owned companies. Future trends are likely to include increased collaboration with external stakeholders, such as non-governmental organizations, academic institutions, and industry associations, to drive sustainability initiatives. These partnerships can provide valuable resources, expertise, and networks that enhance the effectiveness of sustainability efforts. Research is focusing on how employee-owned companies can leverage these collaborations to access new technologies, share best practices, and amplify their impact on sustainability. Additionally, the concept of "sustainable finance" is gaining traction within the realm of employee ownership. Sustainable finance refers to investments that consider environmental, social, and governance factors alongside financial returns. Employee-owned companies are exploring how to access sustainable finance opportunities, such as green bonds or impact investments, to fund their sustainability initiatives. Research is examining how these financial instruments can support the growth of employee-owned businesses while advancing their sustainability objectives.

10.7. CONCLUSION

The influence of employee ownership on environmental and social sustainability is profound and multifaceted, reflecting the unique synergies between ownership structures and sustainable practices. Employee ownership, characterized by employees having a stake in the company's equity, inherently aligns personal and organizational goals, fostering a strong commitment to long-term sustainability. This alignment creates a framework where sustainability is not only a strategic priority but also a shared value among employees, influencing organizational culture, decision-making, and operational practices. In terms of environmental sustainability, employee ownership often leads to enhanced efforts in reducing ecological footprints and improving resource efficiency. Employee-owned companies tend to adopt more ambitious environmental goals, driven by the vested interest of employees in the company's long-term viability and reputation. The participatory nature of employee ownership models facilitates a collaborative approach to environmental initiatives, with employees actively contributing to and supporting sustainability programs. This can result in innovative solutions, such as the implementation of energy-efficient technologies, waste reduction practices, and sustainable product designs, that might be more challenging to achieve in traditional ownership structures.

Social sustainability benefits similarly from the employee ownership model. Employee-owned companies are often better positioned to promote fair labor practices, equitable treatment, and community engagement. The direct stake that employees have in the company translates into a stronger commitment to fostering inclusive and supportive work environments. Additionally, the focus on long-term success inherent in employee ownership structures can lead to more stable employment practices, improved job security, and enhanced worker well-being. This focus on social sustainability extends beyond the workplace, as employee-owned companies frequently engage in community development initiatives, supporting local causes and contributing to societal well-being. Furthermore, employee ownership encourages transparency and accountability, which are crucial for both environmental and social sustainability. Employees, as stakeholders in the company's success, are more likely to advocate for and support transparent reporting practices, ethical business conduct, and responsible resource management. This transparency helps build trust with external stakeholders, including customers, investors, and regulatory bodies, reinforcing the company's commitment to sustainability.

However, the relationship between employee ownership and sustainability is not without its challenges. Balancing immediate financial pressures with long-term sustainability goals can be difficult, particularly in industries with tight margins or high operational costs. Employee-owned companies must navigate these challenges by integrating sustainability into their core business strategies and leveraging the collective insights and commitment of their employee-owners to drive progress. Additionally, the effectiveness of employee ownership in promoting sustainability can vary based on factors such as the company's size, industry, and geographic location. While larger employee-owned firms may have the resources and influence to implement comprehensive sustainability initiatives, smaller firms might face constraints related to funding and expertise. Similarly, regulatory environments and cultural attitudes toward sustainability can impact how employee ownership models align with environmental and social goals. In conclusion, the influence of employee ownership on environmental and social sustainability is significant, providing a framework that aligns employee interests with long-term sustainability objectives. Employee ownership fosters a culture of collaboration, accountability, and innovation, which can lead to meaningful advancements in both environmental stewardship and social responsibility.

REFERENCES

Abhilasha, A., Sreenivasulu, A., & Manimozhi, T. Satheesh kumar P., Selvakumar P. and Singh P.,(2022). "The Model of Smart Sensing Device For Sensitive Nano-clusters Modification in Sensing Properties," 2022 2nd International Conference on Advance Computing and Innovative Technologies in Engineering (ICACITE), Greater Noida, India, 2022, pp. 1043-1047, DOI: 10.1109/ICACITE53722.2022.9823846

Avey, J. B., Wernsing, T. S., & Palanski, M. E. (2012). Exploring the process of ethical leadership: The mediating role of employee voice and psychological ownership. *Journal of Business Ethics*, 107(1), 21–34. DOI: 10.1007/s10551-012-1298-2

Bartlett, C. A., & Ghoshal, S. (1994). Changing the role of top management: Beyond strategy to purpose. *Harvard Business Review*, 72(6), 79–88.

Chan, K. W., & Lam, W. (2011). The trade-off of servicing empowerment on employees' service performance: Examining the underlying motivation and workload mechanisms. *Journal of the Academy of Marketing Science*, 39(4), 609–628. DOI: 10.1007/s11747-011-0250-9

Dutton, J. E., Dukerich, J. M., & Harquail, C. V. (1994). Organizational images and member identification. *Administrative Science Quarterly*, 39(2), 239–263. DOI: 10.2307/2393235

Edinger, J., Edinger-Schons, L. M., Schäfer, D., Stelmaszczyk, A., & Becker, C. (2019). Of money and morals—The contingent effect of monetary incentives in peer-to-peer volunteer computing. *Proceedings of the 52nd Hawaii International Conference on System Sciences*. DOI: 10.24251/HICSS.2019.115

Gartenberg, C., Prat, A., & Serafeim, G. (2019). Corporate purpose and financial performance. *Organization Science*, 30(1), 1–18. DOI: 10.1287/orsc.2018.1230

Henseler, J., Ringle, C. M., & Sarstedt, M. (2015). A new criterion for assessing discriminant validity in variance-based structural equation modeling. *Journal of the Academy of Marketing Science*, 43(1), 115–135. DOI: 10.1007/s11747-014-0403-8

Islam, G., & Greenwood, M. (2021). Reconnecting to the social in business ethics. *Journal of Business Ethics*, 170(1), 1–4. DOI: 10.1007/s10551-021-04775-7

Kaptein, M. (2008). Developing a measure of unethical behavior in the workplace: A stakeholder perspective. *Journal of Management*, 34(5), 978–1008. DOI: 10.1177/0149206308318614

Ketelaar, E., Beijaard, D., den Brok, P. J., & Boshuizen, H. P. A. (2013). Teachers' implementation of the coaching role: Do teachers' ownership, sensemaking, and agency make a difference? *European Journal of Psychology of Education*, 28(3), 991–1006. DOI: 10.1007/s10212-012-0150-5

Lu, C. S., & Lin, C. C. (2014). The effects of ethical leadership and ethical climate on ethical behavior in the international port context. *Journal of Business Ethics*, 124(2), 209–223. DOI: 10.1007/s10551-013-1868-y

Mahadev Madgule, N. (2023). Vinayaka, Yeshwant M. Sonkhaskar, Dhiren Ramanbhai Patel, R. Karthikeyan, P. Selvakumar,(2023). Mechanical properties and microstructure of activated TIG welded similar joints of Inconel alloys by desirability approaches. *Materials Today: Proceedings*, 77, 528–533. DOI: 10.1016/j.matpr.2022.12.250

Moore, C., Mayer, D. M., Chiang, F. F. T., Crossley, C., Karlesky, M. J., & Birtch, T. A. (2019). Leaders matter morally: The role of ethical leadership in shaping employee moral cognition and misconduct. *The Journal of Applied Psychology*, 104(1), 123–145. DOI: 10.1037/apl0000341 PMID: 30221953

Ones, D. S., & Dilchert, S. (2012). Employee green behaviors. In Jackson, S. E., Ones, D. S., & Dilchert, S. (Eds.), *Managing human resources for environmental sustainability* (pp. 85–116). Jossey-Bass.

Paille, P., Morelos, J. H. M., Raineri, N., & Stinglhamber, F. (2019). The influence of the immediate manager on the avoidance of non-green behaviors in the workplace: A three-wave moderated-mediation model. *Journal of Business Ethics*, 155(3), 723–740. DOI: 10.1007/s10551-017-3519-1

Pellegrini, C., Rizzi, F., & Frey, M. (2018). The role of sustainable human resource practices in influencing employee behavior for corporate sustainability. *Business Strategy and the Environment*, 27(8), 1221–1232. DOI: 10.1002/bse.2064

Pierce, J. L., Kostava, T., & Dirks, K. T. (2001). Toward a theory of psychological ownership in organizations. *Academy of Management Review*, 26(2), 298–310. DOI: 10.2307/259124

Ramakrishnan, T., Mohan Gift, M. D., Chitradevi, S., Jegan, R., & Subha Hency Jose, P. Nagaraja, Rajneesh Sharma H.N., Selvakumar P., Sintayehu Mekuria Hailegiorgis, (2022). "Study of Numerous Resins Used in Polymer Matrix Composite Materials", Advances in Materials Science and Engineering, vol. 2022, Article ID 1088926, 8 pages, 2022. DOI: 10.1155/2022/1088926

Schaufeli, W. B., Salanova, M., Gonzalez-Roma, V., & Bakker, A. B. (2002). The measurement of engagement and burnout: A two sample confirmatory factor analytic approach. *Journal of Happiness Studies*, 3(1), 71–92. DOI: 10.1023/A:1015630930326

Spreitzer, G. M. (1995). Psychological empowerment in the workplace: Dimensions, measurement, and validation. *Academy of Management Journal*, 38(5), 1442–1465. DOI: 10.2307/256865

Sugumaran, K. M. D., Pandiyarajan V., Y. B S, Selvakumar P. and M. S, (2024). "Analysis of Electromyography Signals for Control of Mechanical Prosthesis using Machine Learning Techniques," 2024 2nd International Conference on Intelligent Data Communication Technologies and Internet of Things (IDCIoT), Bengaluru, India, 2024, pp. 1059-1067, DOI: 10.1109/IDCIoT59759.2024.10467707

Tollin, K., & Christensen, L. B. (2019). Sustainability marketing commitment: Empirical insights about its drivers at the corporate and functional level of marketing. *Journal of Business Ethics*, 156(4), 1165–1185. DOI: 10.1007/s10551-017-3591-6

Van Tuin, L., Schaufeli, W. B., Van den Broeck, A., & van Rhenen, W. (2020). A corporate purpose as an antecedent to employee motivation and work engagement. *Frontiers in Psychology*, 11, 572343. DOI: 10.3389/fpsyg.2020.572343 PMID: 33071907

Vijayakumar, G., Rajkumar, M., Rajiv Chandar, N., Selvakumar, P., & Duraisamy, R. (2024). Muniyandi Rajkumar, Rajiv Chandar N, Selvakumar P and Ramesh Duraisamy, (2024). Environmentally friendly TDS removal from waste water by electrochemical ion exchange batch-type recirculation (EIR) technique. *Environmental Science. Water Research & Technology*, 10(4), 826–835. DOI: 10.1039/D3EW00793F

Wilden, R., & Gudergan, S. P. (2015). The impact of dynamic capabilities on operational marketing and technological capabilities: Investigating the role of environmental turbulence. *Journal of the Academy of Marketing Science*, 43(2), 181–199. DOI: 10.1007/s11747-014-0380-y

Zoghbi-Manrique-de-Lara, P. (2010). Do unfair procedures predict employees' ethical behavior by deactivating formal regulations? *Journal of Business Ethics*, 94(3), 411–425. DOI: 10.1007/s10551-009-0273-z

Chapter 6
A Framework for Assessing the Environmental and Social Benefits of Employee Ownership

Siriyama Kanthi Herath
https://orcid.org/0000-0002-6443-9739
Clark Atlanta University, USA

Hewa Gamage Eranga Ravihara Kulathunga
https://orcid.org/0009-0003-5577-5823
DeVry University, USA

ABSTRACT

This research develops a framework to assess the environmental and social benefits of employee ownership models. By reviewing literature, we identify factors that contribute to positive sustainability outcomes and examine supporting evidence. Our goal is to inform policymakers, business managers, and scholars seeking to advance sustainable and equitable business practices. Additionally, we will explore the potential challenges and limitations associated with employee ownership models, such as financial risks and governance issues. Our findings will provide practical recommendations for businesses and policymakers interested in implementing or enhancing employee ownership programs.

DOI: 10.4018/979-8-3693-7031-5.ch006

1. INTRODUCTION

Employee ownership involves employees participating in the company's operations while holding a financial stake in its success. This ownership can assume many forms, for instance, Employee Stock Ownership Plans (ESOPs); 'co-ops'; or profit-sharing (Mackin, 2024). One key advantage of employee equity ownership is that it fosters responsibility and self-motivation among employees to enhance the company's performance. This business model, whereby employees have a large share of stocks in the organization, has been on the rise in recent years.

Evaluating the effects of employee ownership on the external environment and for the individuals involved has several reasons. First, it can be beneficial to know how employee ownership can be positive for those goals of sustainability. Secondly, it might be of great use to policymakers, businesses, and investors who are interested in supporting securitization that is sustainable. Lastly, a comparative analysis can be made concerning the overall effects of employee ownership on the environment and social setting in which the company operates to determine how such an aspect can further be developed to foster beneficial impacts. A business model for sustainability builds on positive financial, social, and environmental return for stakeholders (Bocken et al., 2013), thus including employees as value beneficiaries where they improve the value offering through sustainable efforts.

Although the use of gamification is known to improve employee engagement and motivation, its effects on environmental and social sustainability are still largely under-researched (Yetim & Gur, 2023; Martell & Gielen, 2000). Since the issues described above are becoming increasingly urgent, there is a need to explore how adopting the principles of employee ownership can help to achieve a better future for businesses and employees.

1.2 Objectives and Target Audience

The primary objective of this chapter is to establish a robust framework for evaluating the environmental and social benefits of employee ownership. By conducting a comprehensive literature review, we aim to:

Identify specific factors within employee ownership models that contribute to positive sustainability outcomes.

Examine the existing evidence supporting these relationships.

Highlight areas where further research is needed to strengthen our understanding.

Through this analysis, we will provide practical recommendations for policymakers, business managers, and scholars interested in advancing sustainable and equitable business practices. This literature review aims to contribute to the field of sustainability and business studies in several ways.

Synthesizing Existing Knowledge: This chapter conducts a systematic literature review to analyze existing studies on employee ownership and its impact on sustainability. These syntheses will assist us in finding out such common features as trends, patterns, and emerging themes in the given research area. For example, O'Boyle et al., (2016) indicated that employee-owned organizations have a better environmental performance.

Identifying Research Gaps: This chapter will present some inconsistencies, shortcomings, and gaps in literature by conducting a critical appraisal of current literature. The following areas of overlap have in this analysis been emphasized to demonstrate directions for future research on the link between employee ownership and sustainability. For example, although prior studies have shown that employee ownership enhances the organization's environmental responsibilities, the subject of social sustainability remains underexplored.

Informing Policy and Practice: By understanding the benefits and challenges of adopting the mentioned approach, policymakers, practitioners, and researchers involved in the development of the sustainable business model can use the finding of this review to enrich the knowledge acquired. In addition, using this information, policymakers can design adequate measures that will encourage employee ownership as well as environmentally sustainable economies. It is thus plausible that practitioners could learn from this review and apply employee ownership models that improve their organizations' sustainability performance. It is vital for the researchers to establish the research gaps identified above that can enable him/her to generate new knowledge in this area.

Mainly, the target audience for research on the environmental and social benefits of employee ownership would consist of scholars, policymakers, and businessmen. Business scholars, economists and sociologists would be a few of the scholars attracted to theoretical and empirical results in such research work. These insights can be used by policymakers to create new policies and or revise the existing ones to encourage employees' ownership as well as its benefits. The research might be useful for business leaders, first, for those who are planning to introduce the models of employee ownership or improve their CSR strategies, as the results of the research shed light on the environmental and social effects of employee ownership schemes. Finally, investors, and other stakeholders interested in sustainable business and ethics could also consider this study useful. Having outlined the objectives and intended audience, the discussion now shifts to the theoretical underpinnings that shape our understanding of the relationship between employee ownership and sustainability.

2. THEORETICAL FOUNDATION

2.1 Employee Ownership Theories

Employee Ownership theories focus on the construct and instruments of employee ownership, such as cooperatives, profit-sharing plans, or stock ownership plans. Researchers from areas of business, economics and sociology will find the theoretical and empirical aspects of such findings useful. It is in this area that the policymakers could direct their efforts in either coming up with policies and or regulations that support employee ownership of organizations or fine-tune existing ones accordingly. The research will benefit business leaders, especially those contemplating the adoption of employee ownership scheme or those who would wish to improve on their corporate social responsibility profiles to appreciate the possible environmental and social effects of the schemes. Also, investors and other interested parties who are interested in sustainability and ethical corporations could make use of this study.

The basic forms of employee ownership schemes which exist are the most popular one is the 'Employee Stock Ownership Plan' or 'ESOP', whereby the employee is given an opportunity to own shares in the company through contributions made by the employer. Cooperatives, on the other hand, are organizations that are owned and run by members, basically the employees or the buyers of products. Others involve allowing employees to own a portion of company stock, cash-bonus plans and others that grant employees a portion of the firm's profits. Contemporary discourse on employee ownership in the workplace employs four interrelated yet distinct concepts: ownership as compensation, ownership as investment, ownership as retirement benefit, and ownership as membership (Mackin, 2024).

Each model has unique features and sustainability implications Martell and Gielen (2000) argue that ESOPs promote employee autonomy and long-term organizational perspectives. Bonal and Cooper (2008) have pointed out that through the Co-operatives, democratic principles of governance can be applied to ensure a balance of majority, minority, and the public as well as the environment. It also helps to increase the performance of employees, as well as minimize costs since employees can gain from the profits (Jensen & Meckling, 1976).

Stakeholder Theory: Originated by Freeman (1984) the concept of stakeholder theory focuses on the idea that the company success is measured with reference to the stakeholders, which may comprise of employees, the communities, the customers, the shareholders, as well as the environment. As applied to the EWPs, this theory assumes that employees have direct stock purchase rights, giving them more reason to care about the organization's performance. The key benefits of employee ownership are the sense of responsibility and control, motivation of the business goals congruence and commitment to organizational objectives (Jensen & Meckling, 1976). As with stakeholder theory, the concept of sustainability is tightly linked, mainly because SST supports business models that imply an equal maximization of both financial and non-financial value (Hörisch et al., 2014; Freudenreich et al., 2020; Herath & Herath, 2024). Through the involvement of the employees in the decision-making processes, giving them ownership hence stake in the organization fosters stakeholder engagements hence Sustainability since the organization will always have in mind how its operations will impact the rest of the society and the environment.

Agency Theory: First proposed by Jensen and Meckling in 1976, this theory exists in response to the principal-agent conflict typical of conventional organizations where managers may not always hold the owner's best interest at heart. Thus, retaining a closer link of agency between owners and employees decreases the agency gap and fosters sustainable decision-making due to concerned and more directly involved interest. As outlined by Jensen and Meckling (1976), agency theory posits that there is a principal-agent problem between owners (principals) and managers (agents) in traditional corporate structures. This can cause potential problems in organizational relationships and corrupt decision-making processes with the goal of maximizing short-term profits with little regard to long-term consequences. This issue can be dealt with through employee ownership because this only helps bring the employees' and owners' self-interests in the company to parity. This may result in increases in such values as sustainability since people are receptive to the end results of their choices.

Social Identity Theory: Tajfel and Turner (1979) presented the social identity theory under which people gain a sense of the self from associations with the groups. This theory looks at how people get their identification by belonging to a specific group. When employees own the company, they identify with it hence working cohesively, being happier and committed especially where organizational goals include sustainability. When people are shareholders in the organization, they develop an organizational commitment toward it. This may cause a higher level of employee satisfaction and motivation and better attitudes towards sustainable policies at a company.

Institutional Theory: DiMaggio and Powell (1983) carried out work on institutional theory which states that organizations are embedded in the social and institutional environment and hence are affected by the norms, values, and expectations of such an environment. DiMaggio and Powell (1983) maintained that institutions exert pressure on organizations. Employee ownership might be considered as an institutional solution that influences conventional corporate culture and inspires saving the environment and having regard to social needs. Thus, employee ownership can be regarded as institutional innovation that goes against the existing tendencies in the sphere of corporate management and emphasizes eco-friendlier forms of business activity. In using the concept of employee ownership, organizations can then display their corporate social responsibility and get other organizations to follow as well.

2. 2 Sustainability Theories

Triple Bottom Line (TBL): John Elkington developed the TBL in 1994, as a new way of looking at organizational performance indicators. Unlike a narrow concentration on economic performance, Elkington insisted that firms should monitor how they are faring in social and environmental capitals. The TBL model recognizes measures as Profit, People and Planet, which implies that firms should evaluate their effects on economic justice, social accountability, and ecological efficiency (Friant et al., 2024). Employee ownership models are in tune with TBL since employee ownership practices increase economic justice for employees, enhance socially sensitive practice and ensure proper usage of resources for success while maintaining the natural environment.

Sustainability Theory: From the general context of the Brundtland report (1987) this theory identifies sustainability as the capability of fulfilling the needs of the existing generations without draining the resources for those of the other generations. SEEBs are inclined more toward the long-period view, and this makes them have a view different from that of stock markets where profits are valued more than the continuance of the business. Sustainability theory states that business organizations should aim to achieve economic, environmental, and social performance objectives (Elkington, 1997). So, we can define that results of employee ownership can include such factors as employment, length of tenures of the managers, customers, shareholders, community involvement and sustainable thinking. This is particularly the case when the employees have an equity interest in the firm and are therefore more likely to consider both the organization's long-term implications of their decisions as well as the impact they would have on the environment of the business (Martell & Gielen, 2000).

Circular Economy Theory: The Circular Economy (CE) theory has been brought from ecological economics and industrial economics and a systemic way has been proposed to eliminate clumsy circulation. It opposes the established ''take-make-dispose'' approach in which products and resources are consumed, disassembled, and discarded, by focusing on products and materials that are recovered, recycled, refurbished, remanufactured, and repurposed to have longer life cycles (Friant et al., 2024). Companies owned by persons who work for them may exhibit a higher level of circular economy because it is in the best interests of the employee's owners who work in those companies to ensure that they work for companies that do not have to incur expenses on things that they do not need to use though the methods of circular economy are correct (Friant at al., 2020). This management system encourages organizational members to adopt behaviors aligned with the company's sustainable practices. For instance, Qalati et al., (2023) revealed that firms that had participative decision-making system like the employee-owned structures had improved eco-innovation capabilities.

Behavioral Theories of Sustainability: One branch of sustainability theory analyzes abilities and actions people take to affect the environment. These theories focus on the motivational, social cognitive and cultural factors involved in sustainable behavior change such as motivations, perceptions and recognition of standard behavioral patterns (Mastria et al., 2023). Relevance to Employee Ownership: Since everyone in an employee-owned organization has a strong claim on that organization's success, everyone shall be eager to ensure sustainable practices. They found that this attributed sense of ownership and responsibility leads to many environmentally friendly behaviors like recycling, energy saving, and supporting green technology. Furthermore, the highly participative organizational culture of the firms fully engages all stakeholders in the sustainable initiatives made in the companies, thus ensuring that individual and organizational values are congruent. Research shows that specifically the arising of employees' organizational identification realized through the perception of purpose and ethical values increases the likelihood of sustainable behaviors of their organizations (Bhattacharya et al., 2023).

Employee ownership and sustainability models explore the connections between employee ownership and practices such as environmental performance, social responsibility, and economic resilience. The next section explores the critical environmental, social, and economic indicators that reflect the sustainability performance of employee-owned businesses.

3. KEY SUSTAINABILITY INDICATORS FOR EMPLOYEE-OWNED BUSINESSES

Employee-owned businesses are also excellent for increasing sustainability as they are based on the principles of inclusiveness, and stakeholders' initiatives and actions. The following heads show how these businesses can check their social, environmental, and economic impression, according to the GRI and SASB standards.

3.1 Environmental Indicators

Several employee-owned companies adopt a proactive measure to environmental conservation since employee-owners are aware of the firm's commitment. Key environmental indicators include:

Energy Use: Reducing energy consumption is essential for sustainability and can be measured in kWh per production unit. Employee ownership encourages innovation in energy conservation technologies well as the generation of renewable energy sources (Friant et al., 2024).

Emissions: Monitoring of GHG is essential in the effort to minimize carbon intensity of organizations. As a result, the extent of emissions shrinks in employee-owned firms, which act sustainably in the long run (Bhattacharya et al., 2023).

Waste Management: Quantifying the volume and sorts of waste generated, as well as the quantity of recycling and composting, shows that a company is eager to decrease landfill additions. Integrated responsibility entails that employees have ownership of waste minimization activities, and thus would be motivated to engage themselves in these activities (Qalati et al., 2023).

Water Usage: The water assessment by withdrawal and discharge levels, as well as reusing levels, can help identify areas that can be conserved. Top-down codes of conduct in resource-intensive industries are programs that can be driven by the employees, and enhance water management (Friant et al., 2024).

3.2 Social Indicators

This has made social sustainability the natural next step after the models of employee ownership since they foster the inclusiveness of communities. Key social indicators include:

Employee Satisfaction: Self-report measures collected through bi-annual organizational climate surveys of job satisfaction, work-life, and employee engagement demonstrate the positive aspects of the shared governance structures. Bhattacharya et al., (2023) has found out that studies reveal that often, in employee-owned firms, satisfaction with their jobs and organizational commitment are higher.

Community Engagement: The volume of volunteers, number of contributions provided, and cooperation with local non-profit organizations illustrate the commitment of a firm to improve the community's welfare. The empirical research shows that the sampled EoBs have better community relations as compared to conventionally owned firms because of the localized employee decision making (Friant et al., 2024).

Social Equity: Indicators related to diversity, equity, and inclusion (DEI) are used to refer to how a business responds to social inequality; DEI indicators are used to measure response to social inequality. Firms possessed by employees are normally pioneers of fair distribution of wealth and proper polices in the workplace (Qalati et al., 2023).

3.3 Economic Indicators

In this chapter, economic sustainability is identified as the key to the survival of companies under the employee ownership system. Key economic indicators include:

Return on Investment (ROI): Checking the financial returns against the investment guarantees economic returns while working within the parameters of the employee ownership model (Bhattacharya et al., 2023).

Profitability: The return accounting metrics are the measures of a company's financial performance, including net profit margin and earnings growth. Long term profitability may be achieved through the concept of employee ownership as it directs organizational goals towards the attainment of laser focus (Vermeulen and Salomone, 2023).

Financial Stability: Measures such as debt/equity ratio and liquidity ratios expose an organization's' resilience to the adverse effect of the difficult economic conditions. The stability of OES arises from theoretical economic concepts, such as business ownership occurring through the orders, self-organized value preservation, and rational economic behavior (Qalati et al., 2023).

3.4 Linking Indicators to Global Frameworks

To enhance transparency and accountability, employee-owned businesses can align their sustainability reporting with recognized global frameworks:

Global Reporting Initiative (GRI): The GRI standards offer guidelines for measuring and comparing economic, environmental, and social performance.

Sustainability Accounting Standards Board (SASB): SASB's industry standards guide companies and organizations in assessing and reporting on issues that are most significant to their industries.

Task Force on Climate-Related Financial Disclosures (TCFD): Embracing TCFD recommendations helps businesses and other organizations face climate risks and related opportunities systematically and thus improve their robustness and management. The following section outlines the research design, data collection, and analytical methods employed to examine the sustainability impacts of employee ownership.

4. METHODOLOGY

This chapter employs a systematic literature review to examine the external and internal benefits of employee share ownership (EO). Literature reviews are particularly effective for conceptual integration and the evaluation of existing research to identify trends, changes, and gaps. This transformative methodological approach constructs a conceptual foundation for establishing sustainability performance metrics for EO. The methodology is structured into five key components: research design, literature review approach, data collection and extraction, analytical framework and study limitations.

4.1 Research Design

The evidence in this research is compiled and accredited from academic and industrial standpoints using a systematic literature review methodology. This way, the review is more transparent, which helps to replicate it within the launch of other projects in response to specific research agendas. Key elements of the research design include:

Determining the impact of EOP for environmental, social, and economic sustainable development.

Only studies exploring models like ESOPs, cooperatives and profit sharing were considered samples for this review.

The results are useful for the creation of assessment criteria in sustainability in employee-owned firms. Consequently, this design offers a clear guide of how knowledge is categorized, how existing knowledge is examined, and where future research should be focused.

4.2 Literature Search Strategy

The literature search was conducted using a structured and systematic approach to ensure the inclusion of high-quality and relevant studies. Scholarly databases such as JSTOR, Emerald Insight, Scopus, and Web of Science were used to locate peer-reviewed articles and industry reports. Keywords included "employee ownership," "sustainability," "environmental performance," "social performance," "stakeholder engagement," and "sustainable business practices." The search used articles published between 2010 and 2024 to consider its recent data.

4.3 Data Collection and Extraction

The elements of sustainability were derived from each research work depending on sustainability measures related to employees 'shares. Key areas of focus included:

Environmental Indicators: Measures involve consumption of energy, emissions to atmosphere, disposal of wastes, conversation of water, and meeting environmental standards.

Social Indicators: KPI of quality of life, satisfaction, equity, and diversity of the employees, and community benefits related to ESOP.

Economic Indicators: Predictive financial effects associated with sustainable performance, economic measures of overall performance, and the viability of the ESOP model.

For every source, the information on whether the aspects under each indicator evidence a positive or negative influence from employee ownership on sustainability was obtained. Consequently, methodology, analysis, and conclusion of each research were outlined, which facilitated comparison and synthesis.

4.4 Analytical Framework

The systematic review of the literature involved Analysis of themes therefore the results that follow are deduced from the thematic synthesis of the literature to elicit the frequent outcomes of sustainability in employee-owned firms. Studies were categorized by sustainability dimension (environmental, social, economic), with the following analytical steps:

Some of the commonalities, regularities, and outcomes connected with each sustainability dimension were summarized and served as a foundation for the framework.

Data reported from EO firms were contrasted with results from other qualitative research conducted on non-EO structured firms, with the latter used to give focus on the distinctive outcomes of employee ownership

Using the synthesized findings, the set of guidelines, options and recommended indicators were identified that will form the basis for creating a conceptual framework for evaluation of models of employee ownership about sustainability.

4.5 Limitations of the Review

A possibility of bias in the papers sampled may be derived from the fact that only published articles were included and where necessary only the English language papers were considered which may have led to increased; Some of the findings made in this chapter were based on secondary data hence some empirical tests may not have been effectively carried. Thirdly, only recent papers were selected, which might reduce the coverage of the role and effects of employee ownership in the context of sustainability over the long history. The next section presents the key findings of the study and discusses their implications for advancing sustainability through employee ownership models.

5. CASE STUDIES IN EMPLOYEE OWNERSHIP AND SUSTAINABILITY

Employee ownership models provide a unique foundation for integrating sustainability into business practices. This section presents two prominent case studies—Mondragon Corporation and John Lewis Partnership—that exemplify how employee ownership can drive environmental, social, and economic sustainability. The analysis concludes with comparative insights and broader implications.

5.1 Mondragon Corporation (Spain)

The best and well-known example of a worker owned organization is the Mondragon Cooperative from Spain which is currently a federation of companies. Its organizational structure is based on decentralization of power, participation, and a focus on the environment.

Environmental Initiatives: Waste reduction, recycling, and resource efficiency are noticeable and distinctive in Mondragon as a firm embraces circular economy principles. In investments in renewable energy and energy-efficient technologies are visible evidence that its seeks to achieve minimum negative effects on the natural environment (Friant et al., 2024). It also has sustainability objectives within its production systems as a way of making the cooperative to align its operations to sustainable practices all over the world.

Social Responsibility: Being a cooperative with a mission of worker ownership, Mondragon has restricted wealth creation to fair distribution for reinvestment back into the organization and the members. The cooperative developed an organizational culture that is welcoming and offers support to local communities through education, housing, and social services (Heras-Saizarbitoria, 2014). This further underlines the fact that through the activities of the cooperative, social equity and resilience will always be promoted.

Economic Stability: Having business in almost all sectors of the economy; industrial; retail; and service makes Mondragon more resistant to economic shocks. Democracy guarantees that any decisions made involving money are sustainable in the long haul, which is especially useful in a depression.

5.2 John Lewis Partnership (United Kingdom)

John Lewis Partnership provides a good example to help understand how employee ownership can contribute to increasing sustainability while relying on a more participatory business organization model.

Environmental Practices: John Lewis is committed to achieving net-zero carbon emissions by 2035, implementing energy-efficient operations and renewable energy sourcing. Waste is another crucial area, and the company has a clear policy toward sustainable procurement and circular fixing, including but not limited to repair of products, recycling services (John Lewis Partnership Sustainability Report, 2023).

Social Contributions: In a way, employee ownership gives purpose to all employees of John Lewis, which are known as "partners". Job satisfaction and job involvement are highly correlated to the participative governance structure (Bhattacharya et al., 2023). Bridging with the community; the company has observed to shows its communal relations as its status in philanthropic services like volunteering and finance given to the charitable organizations.

Economic Outcomes: John Lewis invests the profits in its staff in the form of improved remuneration, training and the opportunity to advance in their career. This strategy is sustainable to financial management and improves the company's image in the labor market.

5.3 Comparative Insights

The comparison of Mondragon Corporation and John Lewis Partnership reveals key insights into how employee ownership supports sustainability:

Environmental Commitment: Both organizations provide explicit examples on environmental performance by controlling energy use and waste production. Job satisfaction and engagement are attributed to the participatory governance structure (Bhattacharya et al., 2023). The company's strong community ties are evident in its philanthropic initiatives, such as volunteering programs and financial support for local charities.

Social Equity: Ethical responsibilities are part of the platform for both organizations. The Mondragon cooperative model concentrates on the distribution of the profits generated to the employees and the overall community while for John Lewis the main concern is to improve of the employees' satisfaction and the social contributing.

Economic Resilience: Widespread employment share ownership plan is good for economic stability in both examples. Mondragon has many operating fields, which are effective in sustaining its profits; John Lewis relies on brand identity and good employee relations as leading factors to financial security.

Employee Engagement: Employee involvement in decision-making in both organizations leads to increased morale, creativity and resp

5.4 Lessons and Broader Implications

These case studies point to the change that is possible when more employees become owners of the businesses they work for. The central focus of participatory governance arrangement is integrating sustainability strategy into business activities. The characteristics of the models of employee-ownership contain a provision of TBL principles to address environmental, social and economic challenges. Key takeaways include:

The critical role of participatory governance in aligning business practices with sustainability objectives.

The ability of employee-owned models to balance environmental, social, and economic goals, as reflected in the Triple Bottom Line (TBL) framework.

The importance of fostering employee engagement to drive innovation and sustainability at all levels of the organization.

From the Mondragon and John Lewis example other organizations can follow their example on how sustainability can be obtained by suppressing employee ownership. These examples demonstrate that collective responsibility, and shared ownership can buck the trend and build robust, fair, and sustainable organizations.

Employee Ownership Plans (ESOPs): An ESOP is a plan in which a company forms a trust and uses it to buy shares for its employees in the company's stock. Through its operation, the employees are allowed to buy stakes in the company through the ESOP. These types of programs can be used not only as a reward management employee engagement but also as an entrenchment mechanism (Aubert et al., 2014).

Cooperatives: Cooperatives are organizations that operate as business entities and are formed by members with buying or using alike status, usually employees or consumers. It includes the sharing of profits and our management of the enterprise.

Profit-Sharing: The idea of a profit-sharing plan involves declaring a portion of the company profits for the purpose of distribution to workers based on their productivity or the company profitability. Nevertheless, profit sharing does include ownership of a business, but it is also an incentive by way of cash, which is related to performance.

5.5 Potential Impact on Environmental and Social Performance

Employee ownership models can positively influence environmental and social performance in several ways:

Increased Employee Engagement: When the employees of the company have bought into the company, they are likely to be motivated more to increase their commitment towards environmentalism and social responsibility.

Long-Term Perspective: An example of an authorization that can evoke a lengthy outlook, thereby promoting durability and social and competitive justice, is the ownership of corporations by the employees.

Community Involvement: Research further shows that companies with employee ownership have a close link with communities, hence, leading to participation in most of the issues affecting societies and involvement in most of the societal outcomes.

Shared Decision-Making: Common features of cooperatives and ESOPs are that they empower employees in decision-making, which in its turn, contributes to increased sustainability and non-anti-social performance.

Financial Stability: Another advantage is that ownership can mitigate the/herd-mentality problem since a company's employees are not as likely to take dangerous short-term risk for the sake of getting a large amount of money that they do not own or control.

Although these are the advantages that could be expected from using the models, employee ownership concepts depend on certain factors in relation to the effectiveness in enhancing the company's environmental and social performances such as culture and intensions, industry type and implementation practices. The next section explores how employee ownership can contribute to sustainability, encompassing environmental and social benefits that align with long-term societal and ecological goals.

6. SUSTAINABILITY BENEFITS OF EMPLOYEE OWNERSHIP

6.1 Environmental Benefits

To understand the environmental benefits of employee ownership, it's essential to first define environmental sustainability. Environmental sustainability is the responsible use and management of natural resources to meet the needs of the present without compromising the ability of future generations to meet their own needs (Prasad & Gupta, 2024). It involves balancing economic, social, and ecological goals, such as reducing carbon emissions, promoting renewable energy, and ensuring equitable access to resources. To accurately measure the environmental benefits of employee ownership, we must identify key performance indicators (KPIs) that reflect the company's impact on the natural environment.

Resource Efficiency: Thus, the concept of employee ownership can influence resource efficiency since it makes the employees better understand their duties and be more accountable for them (Martell & Gielen, 2000). This kind of stake means that the employees understand the implications of resource utilization and proper utilization of the available resources will be observed to the later effect of reducing wastage. For instance, Cooper and Bonal (2008) found that there are new indications minimizing energy use and emissions by companies that are owned by the employees as compared to conventional owned companies. Reduced waste generation and renewable energy adoption are prime examples of efficient use of resources.

Green Innovation: There is also another way how employee ownership can support green innovation that refers to the incentive of the employees to pam design and create new products and, in many cases, new processes that would ultimately be more environmentally friendly. Anytime the employees of the firm are allowed to participate in organizational decisions regarding the firm's direction, then the employees can proffer as well as endorse radical solutions to environmental issues.

6.2 Corporate Social Responsibility (CSR)

Work-Family culture can be essential in enhancing CSR programs, especially those to do with environmental preservation. By involving those employees in decisions for the organization, then they will back plans that will be a benefit to society. Work-Family culture can be essential in enhancing CSR programs, especially those to do with environmental preservation. By involving those employees in decisions for the organization, then they will back plans that will be a benefit to society. For instance, case studies involving the subject of Performance Evaluation Systems demonstrate that employee-owned businesses are more likely to engage in the usage of renewable energy, greenhouse reduction, or participation in environmental conservation projects as highlighted by Aubert et al., (2014).

Social Benefits: Social sustainability involves a society's capacity for addressing the needs of the current population and at the same time do not hindering the capabilities of other generations in the future. It involves numerous aspects that are associated with equality, fairness and individual or group rights.

However, to ascertain the extent of the impact of employee ownership, there is the need to develop suitable KPIs that will assist in the evaluation of the impact to the employees, and the wider society. KPIs for social sustainability include:

Equity: It all boils down, however, to the principle of distributive justice meaning equal access to resources and opportunities for every member of society.

Justice: Promoting the culture of abiding to fair and equal treatment of people, and human rights.

Well-being: The health of people and Communities with especial focus on their physical, Mental, and social wellbeing.

Community development: Assisting in building the capacity of vibrant and sustainable communities.

Social inclusion: Ensuring that all individuals, regardless of their background, can participate fully in society.

In essence, social sustainability is about creating a just, equitable, and inclusive society that can thrive over the long term. To evaluate the social impact of employee ownership, it is essential to identify key performance indicators (KPIs) that measure the positive outcomes for employees, communities, and society.

Community Involvement

For instance, Bonal & Cooper (2008) noted that employee-owned businesses are especially socially responsible for their regional communities. It can be explained with the idea that a person becomes more responsible for the fate of a company if he or she is a shareholder in this company, therefore, such employees will also be concerned about their community. That could result in a higher level of participation in local endeavors, donation and support for social causes and other community enhancement programs.

Social Equity

Employee ownership helps enhance social equity because the employees will have more profits and other benefits in the company. Thereby aiding in the prevention of income disparity so that the distribution of wealth subject to its originators befit the employees. Furthermore, employee ownership brings democratic basis in decision making that allows employees to take a stand in the company's affairs, which in turn may lead to formation of equity and democratic work environment (Bonal & Cooper, 2008).

6.3 Key Indicators and Measurement Examples

1. Environmental Performance Indicators

Energy Use: Expressed in the number of kilowatt-hours (kWhs) or another measurement unit of energy used throughout a company or its divisions or departments. This could assist the identification of sectors that may be targeted and improved on, to reduce energy wastage. o Greenhouse Gas Emissions: Hazardous by nature and obtained from emissions data of CO_2, methane, etc., direct and indirect sources may also be difficult to standardize across facilities due to measurement differences. o Waste Management: Defined in terms of tonnage and kind of waste produced, collected or treated through recycling or composting. Some of the data issues include sorting waste stream correctly and final disposal or recovery status confirmation.

Water Usage: Evaluated through tracking the total volume of water that has been withdrawn, reused and discharged over time. It may take time to solicit reliable data especially if several sites employ divergent reporting format or if indirect sources of water use are applied.

2. Social Performance Indicators

Employee Retention and Turnover: Assessed by measuring the attrition rates and turnover Coefficients and may be broken down based on rankings of service periods, divisions or other characteristics. This data can work to signal organizational health but relies on agreed upon definitions of ‘retention’ and ‘turnover.’

Employee Well-being and Satisfaction: Based on self-completion questionnaires can be administered at appropriate intervals to determine satisfaction with the job, mental and physical health and quality of the work-life balance. However, it is possible to obtain biased information if employees feel uncomfortable providing feedback, especially if they fear repercussions or their identities are known to the employer. Christian et al (1976) found out that employee ownership can have strong positive correlation with job satisfaction, morale, motivation, individual and organizational performance. When employees are employed in the organization, there will be better performance, provided they understand the risks they are incurring. Also, giving the employees ownership of the company will mean that they have control and freedom over what they do, which can lead to an increase in job satisfaction, hence the reduction in turnover (Jensen & Meckling, 1976).

Community Engagement: Measured in terms of the number and kinds of community involvement sponsored, hours donated, or funds contributed. Some of the issues arising from the measurement of social impacts include the level of reported engagement and its impact on society needs to be measured fully.

3. Economic Performance Indicators

Return on Investment (ROI): Calculated using profit data relative to capital invested, which can help measure the financial success of employee ownership models. However, gathering consistent ROI data can be challenging due to the variability in financial reporting standards.

Employee Share Value: Evaluates the monetary value of employee-held stock or profit-sharing plans, providing insight into financial stability. Data challenges include fluctuating market values and discrepancies in how share ownership is managed across companies.

6.4 Challenges Associated with Data Collection and Analysis

Data Inconsistency: Employee-owned companies may vary significantly in how they collect, categorize, and report on these metrics, making cross-company or longitudinal comparisons complex.

Access to Data: Some performance indicators require sensitive financial or operational data that may not be easily accessible due to confidentiality agreements or privacy regulations.

Resource Constraints: Smaller employee-owned organizations may lack the necessary resources or expertise to collect and analyze data comprehensively, potentially leading to gaps or inaccuracies.

By expanding on these indicators with concrete examples and acknowledging challenges, the framework offers a practical, nuanced approach to assessing the environmental and social benefits of employee ownership. This will aid in making informed, data-driven recommendations for stakeholders. The next section introduces a structured framework for evaluating the environmental and social impacts of employee ownership, integrating theoretical foundations, performance indicators, and data collection methods.

7. FRAMEWORK FOR ASSESSING SUSTAINABILITY IN EMPLOYEE-OWNED BUSINESSES

To support a comprehensive analysis of the environmental and social gains of employee ownership model, we put forward the following framework based on the company's practices, social impacts, and sustainable development goals. Drawing from the theoretical framework developed in section 2, our framework adopts a multi- dimensional perspective to measure environmental and social impacts. While supporting the proposed framework of evaluating the environmental and social effects of employee ownership, case studies and empirical studies are used throughout the chapter.

Key Indicators

Accordingly, to evaluate the environmental and social effectiveness of EO, one must also define variables of sustainability performance, which would allow measuring effects among employees. Some potential indicators include:

Environmental performance: The sectors under environmental concern include Energy; Greenhouse emissions; Wastes; Water; and Environmental compliance (WBCSD, 2019).

Social performance: Employment, turnover, social, and demographic, and adherence with ethical standards (Global Reporting Initiative, 2021).

Economic performance: Owners' profits, return on investment and selling activity (Jensen & Meckling, 1976).

Data Collection Methods

To collect data on these indicators, a variety of methods can be employed, including:

Surveys: The surveys can be used to get the perception of the various stakeholders including the employees, customers and the public on the company's performance in terms of the environment and social impact.

Case studies: Examples can also be given which may involve an illustration of how some specific employee-owned business operates and what sort of sustainability initiatives it follows.

Financial data: Data relative to the employee's financial profitability, including incomes statements and balance sheets, can be used to establish the economic performance of employee-owned businesses.

Environmental and social reporting: Almost every business, including the employee-ownership ones, release sustainability reports that contain information on their environmental and social impact.

Framework Structure

The proposed framework for assessing the environmental and social benefits of employee ownership consists of the following components:

Theoretical foundation: This component presents the literature review, how the concept of employee ownership works and the benefits it may bring to sustainability.

Key indicators: In this component, an indication of the measurement environmental and social performance is made.

Data collection methods: This component examines the possible means to gather data for the evaluation of these indicators.

Analysis and evaluation: This component involves assessment of data collected for the purpose of evaluating the environmental and social impact of employee ownership and this is done by comparing it with ordinary businesses.

Recommendations: The implication of this component is to highlight recommendations based on the conclusion of the analysis to; policy makers, businesses as well as researchers.

In adhering to this framework (**Table 1**), researchers shall be better placed to analyze the social benefits of employee ownership to the environment and society at large, which would help provide a comprehensive view of the role of the concept in rehabilitating business systems for sustainable and equitable processes.

Table 1. Framework for assessing environmental and social benefits of employee ownership

Component	Description
Theoretical Foundation	Literature review, employee ownership concept, potential sustainability benefits.
Key Indicators	Environmental performance, social performance, economic performance.
Data Collection	Surveys, case studies, financial data, environmental & social reports.
Analysis & Evaluation	Data assessment, comparison with ordinary businesses, evaluation of environmental and social impact.
Recommendations	Policy implications, business practices, future research directions.

The next section outlines diverse data collection approaches, including case studies, surveys, and financial and social reporting.

8. DATA COLLECTION METHODS

To measure the environmental and social benefits of employee ownership effectively, we need to implement a variety of data collection methods that provide accurate and reliable data.

Case Studies

There are quite a few cases which illustrate that employee ownership means sustainability in terms of environment and social relationships. For instance, the Mondragon Corporation, a large-scale cooperative organization in operation in Spain, adopts a relatively sound environmental performance, such as investment on renewable energy, and other environmental measures. Mondragon has also been recognized for its efforts towards social responsibility and any issues regarding its employees (Cooper & Bidelman, 2014; Qalati et a., 2024).

One more example can be mentioned – the John Lewis Partnership, which is an employee-owned retail company based in the United Kingdom. As for sustainability strategies that John Lewis has pursued, it is possible to list the following: a reduction of the company's carbon footprint and fighting for ethical sourcing. The company has also been applauded for its concern on the welfare of employees and the society in large (Lewis, 2019).

Empirical Research

The literature on the impact of EOs on organizations' performance has continued to be supported by empirical studies, and especially on sustainability performance. For instance, Martell & Gielen (2000) identified that general studies meta-analysis of shares had shown that performance in employee and conventionally owned business was substantially higher in firms or employee-owned business in both financial and social performances.

Some studies that were conducted in the recent past have also looked at the relationship between employee ownership and environmental aspects. For instance, Bonal and Cooper (2008) employed research which compared the environmental performance of the worker cooperatives to the conventional firms. The authors discovered that through their analysis that the worker cooperatives agreed to conserve the environment and reduce their effect on the environment than other organizational structures.

Financial Data Analysis

This chapter demonstrates that traditional quantitative financial analysis, as well as qualitative analysis, can be used to measure the employment-based stock ownership and environmental and social effects of the companies. By analyzing the financial data, it is possible to look for some patterns, correlations and, in some cases, link between EE and corporate sustainability performance. Some key financial metrics that can be used to assess environmental and social benefits include:

Return on investment (ROI): Cross-sectional comparisons of employee-owned businesses with those of conventional firms can be made to determine if there is a correlation between financial performance and financial returns.

Cost-benefit analysis: Because employee ownership is a form of investment, there may be certain costs to sustainability initiatives that can be quantified, revealing their overall cash costs.

Financial ratios: Data about some key financial variables, including debt to equity and current ratios, may be useful for determining the stability of employee-owned companies.

Social accounting Most of the effects of employee ownership are hard to quantify; therefore, an evaluation of social and environmental costs, as well as benefits of business activities can contribute to determining the impact of the subject.

By analyzing the financial data, the researchers can state possible connections between the EOP implementation and such indicators as resource utilization, employees' satisfaction level, and community engagement. These financial issues can even further be an issue for small business as they tend to suffer from downside of the problem as they can ill-afford anticipate the impact of the problem.

Environmental and Social Reporting

The assessment of the impact of managing employees on the environment and society is impossible without environmental and social reporting. Therefore, the information discussed in this chapter about sustainability practices of the company shows its social corporate responsibility and provides relevant information about its performance to the stakeholders. Key aspects of environmental and social reporting include:

Sustainability reporting: Presenting complete analysis reports which show the environmental, social, governance performance of a firm.

Materiality assessment: The enhancement of the awareness of the environmental and social MIS that may be important to the company and every actor vested in the undertaking.

Data collection and verification: Acquiring data of the firm's environmental and social performance, as well as ensuring the correctness of the acquired data through verification.

Stakeholder engagement: To ensure that the sustainability information to be delivered and timely is relevant and accountable the suggested approach is to involve the stakeholders in the process of designing and presenting the sustainability information.

In this regard employee-owned organizations are advantageously placed because robust environmental and social reporting practices enhance the following.

Enhance transparency: Give stakeholders a timely and accurate report on the performance of the organization in terms of sustainability.

Improve reputation: Establish credibility with stakeholders in the organization (Syamlal, 2023).

Improve reputation: Build trust and credibility with customers, investors, and other stakeholders.

Identify risks and opportunities: Identify potential risks and opportunities related to environmental and social factors.

Drive sustainability performance: Set goals, track progress, and make informed decisions to improve sustainability performance.

Sustainability reporting frameworks and standards

To ensure transparency and accountability when evaluating and reporting environmental and social performance sustainable reporting frameworks standards have been established.

Global Reporting Initiative (GRI): An important framework of sustainability reporting that offers practices to companies looked for on reporting information on economic, environmental and social impacts.

Sustainability Accounting Standards Board (SASB): A standards top-down setting organization that generates industry special sustainability standards.

Task Force on Climate-Related Financial Disclosures (TCFD): Proposed rules on the reporting of information related to the climate.

Through compliance with these frameworks and standards, the sustainability report produced by employee-owned businesses can be made to be consistent, compatible as well as more credible. Despite its numerous benefits, the implementation of employee ownership models is not without challenges, as organizations often face significant financial, regulatory, and cultural barriers that require thoughtful solutions to overcome as discussed in the following section.

9. CHALLENGES AND BARRIERS TO EMPLOYEE OWNERSHIP AND SOLUTIONS

9.1 Challenges and Barriers to Employee Ownership

Like any other strategic approach, employee ownership has several problems and issues attached to it even as firms stand to gain in a big way. These obstacles can also be analyzed in terms of financial, regulatory and culture constrains.

Financial Hurdles

Employee ownership models can include financial risks in organizations, particularly where it is used to practice the concept. Among the challenges, one can indicate the possibility to acquire shares or establish Employee Stock Ownership Plan (ESOPs). Some of the costs associated with implementing the new structures of employee motivational tools such as the Employee Stock Ownership Plans are shown below. This can be a challenge that is most especially demanding of small entities that may have small capital to fund their needs. In the third party, should the management intend to undertake the implementation of the employee ownership program may be forced to incur expensive costs in other professionals such as lawyers and accountants. These costs can include:

Acquiring shares: Purchasing shares for employees can be a considerable expense, especially in larger companies.

Setting up ESOPs: Establishing and administering an ESOP involves legal fees, accounting costs, and ongoing administrative expenses.

Financing the transition: Going for an EOP means a huge amount of capital may be needed to purchase out the current shareholders or to acquire the shares for the employees.

These financial issues can be even more so as an issue for small business as they are less likely to be able to absorb the effects of the problem.

Regulatory Barriers

One of the possible causes of administrative and legal problems can be employee ownership which can depend on the location. These barriers may include:

Tax implications: Employee ownership further brings in taxation issues which may present a great challenge for organizations that intend to adopt such models.

Labor laws: Existing legal provisions relating to employees restrict the level of participation in share ownership or decision-making.

Corporate governance regulations: The corporate governance regulations can simply limit employee management or even demand certain procedures for implementing such patterns.

Complex regulations: Complicated regulations surrounding ESOPs or other employee ownership models can increase the administrative burden and costs.

Legal requirements: Adhering to legal requirements, such as disclosure obligations and fiduciary duties, can be challenging.

Employee ownership can be a reason for administrative and legal challenges which may be location dependent. These barriers may include:

Cultural Barriers

Eradicating stereotypes and prejudice mean crossing barriers of communication, raising consciousness and enthusiasm to embrace diversity in the workplace. There are however other cultural and societal factors that can influence the level of adoption of employee ownership. At some phase organizational culture and society can also limit the acceptance of employee ownership in some regions or industries. These barriers may include:

Resistance to change: Employees may be resistant to the idea of owning a stake in the company, particularly if they are accustomed to a traditional employer-employee relationship.

Lack of understanding: Employers may decide not to agree with the concept of employee ownership, feeling that the benefits are small, or it is the other way round, the employees may lack belief in the necessity of the program.

Cultural norms: In some cultures, the concept of employee ownership does not conform with acceptable standard practice of work and ownership.

Traditional management styles: Organizations with well-entrenched bureaucratic-authoritarian organizational culture may have problems implementing bottom-up or decentralization based on EMP employee ownership.

Risk aversion: An employee or an investor might be hesitant to participate in employee ownership because of perceived risks as for instance loss making.

Lack of trust: This means that often there can be a level of mistrust between the workforce and the management teams wherein employee ownership models cannot be implemented.

These are some of the important financial, regulatory, and cultural challenges that need to be met by organizations that are interested in using employee share-ownership to deepen organizational sustainability and engagement.

9.2 Challenges and Solutions for Implementing Employee Ownership

Although more and more companies embrace the strength of employee ownership as a tool towards sustainability, its use in an organization is not without some challenges. The advantages of such programs can still be optimized for sustainability issues if the above-listed obstacles are addressed following certain strategies. Mehak & Batcha (2024) analyze how various management practices, such as employee ownership or engagement strategies, can contribute to sustainable development.

Key challenges and proposed solutions are as follows:

Financial Hurdles

***Challenge*:** While the models of EE schemes generally do not necessarily entail high initial outlay, the development of ESOPs and similar forms could wear a high price tag. These costs are purchasing of shares, putting in place activation of ESOPs and other operating costs which may be economically suicidal for most SMEs.

Solutions:

Policy Incentives: It is possible for governments to give a tax exemption or grant subsidies to all companies that decide to incorporate the models of employee ownership. For instance, the tax credit on contributions to the ESOP or credit for the administration costs reduces the financial constraints.

Access to Low-Interest Loans: For purposes of establishing the initial costs, there should be provision of loan facilities that are targeted at the employee-owned businesses whether offered by the government or other financial institutions. Lower-interest loans decrease the related costs for conversion to an employee ownership scheme. There are also advantages that come with taking a gradual approach to putting in place structures of employee ownership: management style may find it difficult to transition to a more participatory model of employee ownership.

Phased Ownership Implementation: Employee ownership can be gradually put into practice, thus eliminating the financial load in one year, as well as gradually creating the necessary organizational infrastructure.

Regulatory Barriers

Challenge: Regulatory systems are multidimensional, and there can be laws that could slow down or even obstruct the shifts to employee ownership models. For example, taxes, legal systems and institutions regarding employment, and corporate governance policies may differ across jurisdictions and thus act as barriers to ownership transfers.

Solutions:

Regulatory Reforms and Simplification: It could be that governments pass employee ownership friendly legislation that either provides a clearer rule on tax treatment, employee rights, or corporate responsibility on firms that are employee owned.

Standardized Guidelines: To promote strategies of employee stock ownership, it might be reasonable to create simplified legal frameworks that would allow the transition to adoption, regarding the national and international aims for sustainability. It would also establish a best practice framework for how more selective models of employee ownership are implemented and managed.

Advisory Services and Legal Support: Advisory services or affiliations with legal and fiscal professionals, backed by government, may help corporate entities in dealing with ordinances, primarily if the problems are experienced by small businesses that probably do not have adequate internal knowledge.

Cultural Barriers

***Challenge*:** Moving to the EOM can be a major culture transformation which can be quite a challenge especially if the company has a conventional top-down organizational culture. There may be culture of noncompliance with changes, or lack of appreciation of Ownership, or disbelief on shared decision making, among others.

Solutions:

Education and Training Programs: Additional capability involves providing awareness sessions such as workshops or training sessions that seek to elaborate on the reasons why the goals of employee ownership are noble and lead to sustainability. These programs could include issues such as decision making, ownership responsibilities, and ownership and sustainable business.

Leadership Development and Succession Planning: Leaders should also be trained in how to lead a less centralized work culture and engage them in the process of adopting employee ownership can assist in filling those gaps. It is possible to have succession planning that guarantees the successful implementation of employee ownership concepts and practices for perpetuity, and not for the benefit of the present generation only.

Incentives for Cultural Change: Creating financial/non-financial incentives stating them for strong employee ownership feelings will help to introduce more responsiveness. This may range from incentives based on the achievement of sustainability goals, to rewards for organizational cross-functional decisions.

Data and Performance Measurement Challenges

***Challenge*:** Assessing and marking environmental and social effects of employee ownership can be challenging, including a mere comparison of changed outcomes with the regular financial rates.

Solutions:

Development of Customized KPIs: These aspects can be discussed and defined with the help of experts, and then organizations can use special key performance indicators (KPI) that would cover the environmental and social effect of employee ownership. Such KPIs may include retention rates of employees, number of interactions with people with local communities, and levels of CO2 emissions.

Integrated Reporting Standards: One way of making it easier is by implementing or supporting the implementation of IFRs for integrated reporting which encompass both Financial, Social and Environmental data. This chapter also helps to render sourcing of financial reports more transparent and comparable in terms of the sustainability effect of employee-owned firms.

Use of Digital Tools for Data Collection: This section offers an overview of how the empirical evidence supports the theoretical arguments regarding the link between employee-ownership and sustainability, with particular focus to use of available research and best practice cases to demonstrate positive environmental impact of employee-ownership.

The next section highlights how insights from the study can guide policymakers, practitioners, and researchers in leveraging employee ownership as a sustainable business strategy.

10. POLICY AND PRACTICAL IMPLICATIONS

Therefore, the information derived from this review could be useful to policymakers, practitioners, and researchers to understand the opportunities and risks of adopting employee ownership as a long-term business strategy. For instance, Wang and Liu (2021) demonstrated that employees' ownership can improve the CSR. This information can be utilized by policymakers to come up with policies that will encourage participation in employee ownership and sustainable management practices. This chapter on employee ownership models can help the practitioners to introduce these models into organizations to improve organizational sustainability performance. The above-mentioned gaps can be helpful for further research to provide contributions to the creation of new knowledge in this field. These research studies are important to alert readers to the significance of the research and what the results may mean to policy, practice and other future research.

Employee Ownership and Climate Change Mitigation

It is the prerogative of all employees and shareholders to address this global social issue as an imperative that companies should take the lead by preventing climate change.

Therefore, there is an important role of employee ownership in climate change mitigation. Which is why if the employees have a substantive interest in the long-term viability of their company and therefore the long-run, their decision making is likely to be longer-run oriented and therefore consider the environmental impacts of their decisions. It can also result in increased responsibility and a positive attitude towards environmental conservation and management and people's ability to support programs that might be financially costly, but healthier for the natural environment in the longer run.

Overall research has indicated that employee-owned companies are typically environmentally superior to traditionally owned firms. For instance, O'Boyle et al., (2016) discovered that firms where employees are shareholders emit less greenhouse gas, as well as generate less waste. This may be because employees of the said companies will feel compelled to garner higher responsibility and assume the responsibility of the company's environmental accountability.

Also, on the aspect of organization environment, climate change mitigation measures could further be improved in the employee-owned business enterprises since it presents several chances of which innovative measures could be applied. Employees are more encouraged to assume responsibility when used in decision-making, more so if they are allowed to propose or implement change within an organization. This may lead to the development of specific approaches to addressing the problems affecting the environment such as support for green energy sources, reduction in the usage and purchasing of energy, and acquisition of environmentally friendly supply chain.

Employee Ownership and Resource Efficiency

Another comparatively less explored area but potentially useful source of information is that employee ownership can also help in resource efficiency, which is crucial for controlling climate change and achieving sustainable development. This is because when people are given an incentive to or are motivated to care about an organization's performance, they are naturally concerned about costs or expenses incurred in the organization including wastage. This can lead to increased attention being paid to energy conservation, water and material conservation.

Research work reveals that the resourced efficiency performance of establishments is usually better in the employee-owned firms than the conventionally owned ones. For instance, Buhl, C; Geeliminar; F; & K; (2016) made a discovery that showed that firms that are owned by the employees are associated with lesser energy utilization and production of wastes. This may be so because the employees in those companies feel directly responsible for the environmental impact of the company and hence show appreciation of policies and measures aimed at achieving better environmental performance.

Also, -subjective factors regarding employee-owned business may pursue more innovative resource efficiency. Self-managed work teams introduce the policy that empowers the employees to offer and authorize the implementation of change. At the same time, it can generate novel approaches to solution of the problems connected with usage of resources, for example, energy-saving technologies use, replenishment of water resources, and circular economy.

The Role of Employee Ownership in Driving Sustainable Innovation

Worker participation has also been found to increase resource efficiency which is a fundamental area that must be addressed to de carbonize the economy and support sustainable development. If employees have stock in the company, they will easily ensure that they do not consume a lot of resources and do not dispose of waste material. This can lead to a paradigm shift in energy efficiency, water consumption and efficient utilization of materials.

Research has revealed that firms with employee ownership mechanisms possess superior stock of resource efficiency performance than firms with conventional modes of ownership. For instance, Buhl et al., (2016) emphasize the alignment of employees' values with organizational goals, leading to resource-efficient practices and reduced environmental impact. Furthermore, employee-owned organizations could be more likely to have long-term outlook when it comes to issues of innovation. Since the employees have something to gain in the future of the company, they do not have to engage in the generation of immediate profits, and this would probably lead to more spendings on research and development that could benefit the environment in the future than could be sponsored by a greedy profit-motivated company.

Cross-Country Comparisons of Employee Ownership and Environmental Performance

Comparative studies between different countries will thus help in understanding the effect of employee ownership on environmental performance. For example, while conducting comparative cross cultural, cross economic and cross regulatory analysis, researchers can map out the factors that impact on the effectiveness of implementing employee ownership in enhancing the results on the environment.

It has been found that the link between employee ownership and environmental performance depends on the country. Environmental performance of employee-owned firms is relatively higher in some countries as compared to others. This may be due to differences in cultures, laws or economic systems respectively.

Thus, when comparing countries one can identify what has the highest efficiency among the strategies used to respect the environmentally friendly employee ownership models. Thus, when analyzing the different cases of best of practice or examples of firms that are employee-owned, in different countries, it is possible for scholars to identify the factors that may help the enhancement of the positive environmental performance of these firms. The section to follow presents global empirical evidence and best practices linking employee ownership with environmental and social sustainability outcomes.

11. EMPIRICAL EVIDENCE FOR EMPLOYEE OWNERSHIP AND SUSTAINABILITY: GLOBAL TRENDS AND BEST PRACTICES

This section presents concrete examples of empirical evidence that highlight the impact of employee ownership on sustainability, drawing on studies and real-world cases to support the theoretical link between employee ownership and positive environmental and social outcomes.

11.1 Global Trends in Employee Ownership and Sustainability

Numerous empirical studies and case evidence have suggested that the environment and social performance of the firms owned by employees are better than that of the traditional business organizations. This trend is evident across nations, sectors, and regions, with some variations influenced by local contexts. Key examples include:

Mondragon Corporation (Spain)

The Mondragon Corporation is a large federation of worker co-operatives in Spain and remains one of the best studied models of how EO has affected sustainability. Currently, Mondragon has taken it upon itself to support sustainability in terms of energy, gas emissions, and wastes. In a study done by Kasmir (2016), Mondragon reportedly practiced much more effective measures of environmental sustainability than traditional corporations because of Mondragon's sustainable organizational cooperative long-term stakeholder values goals.

John Lewis Partnership (United Kingdom)

The A case in point of the social sustainability that can be realized by the John Lewis Partnership is through employee ownership. This company has been considered as one of the UK's longest standing employee-owned companies owing to its continued practice of employee ownership, and has attracted attention from academic, professional, and policy circles (for example, EOA, 2022; Flanders et al, 1968; Basterretxea and Storey, 2018). Research reveals that John Lewis is significantly higher in terms of its employees' satisfaction, health, and social involvement compared to its more traditional competitors. Information and communication technologies are utilized by the company's employee-owners who are involved in sustainability activities all the way from resource efficiency to sourcing sustainably. Employees making the social connection in 2019: Carbon emissions were down by 12%; waste recycling up by 20% to employee-led initiatives (John Lewis Sustainability Report, 2019). Pendleton et al., (2023) reveal that there has been a sharp rise in the number of UK employee-owned firms since 2014 and the authors concluded that, increasing employee ownership beyond the current level might produce considerable economic and social dividends in the British private and public sectors.

11.2 Empirical Studies Supporting the Impact on Environmental Sustainability

A theoretical and empirical literature linkage suggests that there is a positive correlation between the degree of employee ownership and environmental sustainability. In a meta-analysis of research articles, Tingle & Wharton (2023) study focuses on whether employee-owned businesses are best suited in attaining Environmental, Social, and Governance (ESG) objectives. Findings include a strong positive correlation between Employee Stock Ownership Plans (ESOPs). and increased effectiveness of environmental management, disclosure and decision-making accountability. These firms studied tend to exhibit better ESG performance because of a good relationship between the employee and firms' management, which ensures sustainable environmental performance. Meaningful stakeholder engagement, historical environmental performance, social initiatives, sustainability, and, most importantly, improved commitment and motivation can all be attributed to employee ownership. Promoting employee ownership will help in ensuring that the management and workforce work towards realizing long-term sustainable goals of a business and thereby avoid pollution.

11.3 Social Sustainability and Employee Well-being

Research shows that employee ownership positively impacts social sustainability through improved employee well-being and community engagement. A study by O'Boyle et al. (2016) compared the employee satisfaction levels in employee-owned companies with those in traditional firms. They found that employee-owned firms scored higher in employee engagement and well-being metrics, largely due to the participatory work culture fostered by ownership. They further revealed that the effect of employee ownership on performance has strengthened over time and the effect of employee ownership was consistent across different firm sizes. Employees in these firms reported a stronger sense of purpose and commitment to social initiatives, as evidenced by:

Community Involvement: Employee-owned companies, such as Namaste Solar in the United States, often demonstrate a strong commitment to community involvement. For instance, Namaste Solar's 2021 ES report highlights employee-led initiatives aimed at providing renewable energy access to disadvantaged communities. These efforts demonstrate the positive impact that employee ownership can have on corporate social responsibility and community development (Namaste Solar, 2021).

Workplace Inclusivity and Equity: Studies According to the findings made by Rosen et al. (2020), it was revealed that the organizations, which are owned by employees, have a greater tendency of implementing fair workplace policies including equal opportunity for employment, sharing of profits. Similarly, Rosen et al., (2020) argue that employee ownership fosters a sense of ownership and responsibility among workers, which can lead to increased focus on long-term sustainability goals. This commitment to equity is aligned with social sustainable development targets and overall provides subject employees' quality work experience and satisfaction.

11.4 Comparative Analysis of Employee-Owned and Traditional Firms

According to Buhl et al (2016) survey of manufacturing firms, it was revealed that firms operated under employee-ownership model had a higher likelihood of implementing sustainable production methodologies. For the former, specific measurable values were decreased usage of water, increased recycling of materials and high possibility of adopting green innovation. Specific metrics included reduced water usage, higher recycling rates, and a greater likelihood of implementing green innovation. This study underscores the tendency of employee-owned businesses to prioritize long-term environmental and social gains over short-term profits. Key findings include:

Employee involvement fosters innovative solutions for sustainability challenges.

Eco-innovation driven by employees enhances resource efficiency and environmental performance.

Such initiatives improve organizational competitiveness by reducing costs and increasing market differentiation.

Success depends on supportive leadership and a culture encouraging employee participation.

11.5 Cross-Cultural Evidence

Cross-cultural research also gives a sample of the relation between employee ownership and sustainability. A cross-sectional study by undertook a description of the analysis six employee-owned firms from Germany, Japan and America. Findings showed that employee-owned firms in each country exhibited enhanced social responsibility, albeit in culturally specific ways:

Germany: German employee-owned firms tend to emphasize eco-friendly supply chains and sustainable product design, influenced by strong national sustainability policies.

Japan: Japanese employee-owned businesses showed a higher commitment to community welfare and employee well-being, consistent with cultural values of collectivism.

United States: U.S. employee-owned companies focused more on innovation in renewable energy and waste reduction, reflecting the country's emphasis on technological advancements in sustainability.

11.6 Lessons from International Case Studies

There are numerous forms in which employee ownership exists, and these forms differ across countries or regions due to cultural, economic, or legal factors. A comparative study may prove helpful in identifying examples as well as risks and vulnerabilities.

Mondragon Corporation (Spain)

A prime example is the Mondragon Corporation Cooperativa in Spain, which is an umbrella organization that has been operating across various sectors and countries promoting the causes of employee ownership for several decades now. The key factors that have contributed to Mondragon's success include democracy within its administration, the value of education and training for its employees and its policy on social and environmental responsibility towards society.

Germany: Germany has a long-standing tradition of employee ownership, primarily through codetermination statutes that grant employees representation in managerial decision-making (OECD, 2021).

Canada: Canada has witnessed a significant surge in employee ownership, particularly through Employee Stock Ownership Plans (ESOPs) (National Center for Employee Ownership, 2023).

United States: While the United States has a robust ESOP market, challenges such as legal and regulatory complexities can hinder the widespread adoption of employee ownership (Rosen et al., 2020). Research from the Rutgers School of Management and Labor Relations and the Employee Ownership Foundation in 2020 revealed that employee-owned businesses had better performance in terms of job preservation, pay, and workplace health safety during the Covid-19 period. The survey revealed that ESOP companies were more likely to retain employees, less likely to implement pay cut measures (26.9percent as compared to 57.3%), and more likely to introduce protective measures against COVID-19 (98.3% in contrast to 88.9%).

There is literature and empirical evidence to suggest that the environmental and social performances of firms that are owned by the employees are higher than that of firms that are owned conventionally. Multiple studies have established that companies that are operated with employees' equity have more favorable environmental performances such as emission of greenhouse gases and wastes besides consuming less energy. A qualitative synthesis of the effect of employee ownership on environmental performance and established that employee-owned business outperforms conventionally owned business if the intent of the latter is environmental performance.

Besides, it has also been found that firms where employees have stock ownership have better social performance. Research done shows that such firms tend to be socially responsible, for instance in labor policies, community issues, and employee welfare. Firms with majority shares owned by employees have a tendency of providing their employees furbearer benefits such as medical care and insurance policies, pension plans, and paid vacations.

One essential factor to appreciate about this study is that the connection between employee ownership and sustainability is multifaceted and not universal, and it may, therefore, depend on several factors such as industrial classification, firm size, and even culture. Still, the plethora of empirical findings enforces the idea that employee-ownership can be a valuable mechanism for enhancing environmental as well as social responsibility.

11.7 Key Factors Influencing EO and Sustainability

Several factors mediate the relationship between EO and sustainability outcomes:

Organizational Culture: Organizational culture has considerable influence on the extent to which the employee ownership models are successful and can be defined by a very strong culture in favor of sustainability. Decision-making is one of the forms of employee involvement that helps managers engage employees in work and focus on improving the company's sustainability performance. For instance, O'Boyle et al., (2016) note that companies that have a good sustainability culture equally exhibit better performance in the implementation of the employee-owned programs.

Employee Engagement: It was also acknowledged that employee engagement is critical for the success of the employee ownership programs. When employees have vested interest in the company then understanding the company' sustainability goals they are motivated to work in achieving the set goals. It has been found that firms having employees as shareholders possess higher engaged employees, which directly improve environmental as well as social responsibilities. Authors such as Appelbaum and Berg (2001) state that through understanding sustainability, employee ownership is one critical area that must be examined with regards to the role that HPWS can have in promoting sustainable business practices. The human resource management practices that include the practices of High-Performance Work System (HPWS) which involves the management practices based on people strategies such as employee involvement, skill development, and incentives can create workforce for sustainability. Through implementation of these systems, organizations can foster a unique culture and approach where employee ownership no longer must be created but is rather amplified and in turn increases sustainability. Thus, the approach enhances the overall motivation of employees and the general interest in successful solutions that will guarantee sustainability.

Governance Structures: The internal structures of the firms being governed by their employees can also impact on their sustainability performance. Proper management systems facilitate achievement of sustainability objectives by having organizational structures that correspond to that of the company's strategic plans as well as employees' participation. For instance, Lee, J. & Park, J. (2022). determined that when the governance structures of the companies with employees' stakes were sound the firms' environmental and social performance impressed.

Evidence from diverse global contexts affirms the potential of EO as a mechanism for advancing environmental and social sustainability. While results vary across industries and cultures, EO consistently fosters long-term, responsible practices that benefit employees, communities, and the planet.

12. CONCLUSION LIMITATIONS AND FUTURE RESEARCH

The following conclusions can therefore be made regarding the relationship between sustainable employment and employee ownership according to the findings of this study. However, it is worth mentioning the limitations of this work and discussing possible areas for further research.

12.1 Limitations

It is also pertinent to identify the following limitations pertaining to this research study and its conclusions about the link between employee ownership and sustainability. There is limitation of data to work on and this was seen in this study. Research on the direct impact of employee ownership and sustainability has not fully evolved and is well documented therefore there might be little statistics collected in some areas of study or industries.

The other weakness is that it is not immune to some methods of methodological difficulties. Therefore, it can be challenging to compare the performance of an employee-owned business against a conventional business since there might be other variables which could have contributed to the results like the sector, size or business practices. The above factors should be kept constant during empirical research thus requiring efforts to control them.

Finally, they found generalizability of the findings could be a concern. The studies and findings included in this review suggest that the results may not be generalizable across all employee-owned businesses (EOBs) or settings. The next section summarizes findings, acknowledges limitations, and outlines future research directions to advance understanding of employee ownership's role in sustainability.

12.2 Future Research Directions

There are several ways in which new avenues for research can assist to increment the research about the idea of employee ownership and sustainability. These include:

Longitudinal studies: Field surveys can make use of cross-sectional and longitudinal methods to analyze the results of employee-owned businesses in due time to determine the effects of employee ownership on their sustainability.

Expanding the sample size: Conducting larger-scale studies involving a diverse range of employee-owned businesses to improve the generalizability of findings.

Cross-cultural comparisons: Cross-cultural research between different nations can assist in defining the similarities and trends in the connection between employee ownership and sustainability.

Utilizing mixed methods: Combining case studies with quantitative research to leverage the strengths of both approaches and address potential biases.

Developing standardized metrics: Creating standardized metrics for measuring environmental and social performance to facilitate comparisons across different studies.

Industry-specific analysis: Industry level studies may help to identify advantages and disadvantages of employee ownership in distinct fields of industry.

Quantitative analysis: More convoluted studies such as meta-analyses and regression analyses should be employed to come up with more concrete evidence as to the correlation between employee ownership and sustainability.

In this regard, to eliminate such shortcomings and outline the directions of further research, it will be possible to enhance the knowledge of the further positive impact of employee ownership to a more sustainable and fair business environment.

Employee ownership to some extent has been in existence for the last few centuries but it has just been in the last few decades that the role it can play in sustainability has been well recognized. Research also finds out that there is a propensity for high environmental and social performance in companies owned by the employees as compared to other conventional business ownership structures. For instance, O'Boyle et al., (2016) confirmed that there is a positive correlation between employee-owned firms and better environmental performance as indicated by low emission and wastes outputs. In the same way, Buhl et al., 2016 stated that number of research showed that employee-owned companies are more concerned on social responsibilities including labor standards and the community.

Regarding the hypothesis that it may be the case that employee ownership is positive related to sustainability several factors may be accounted for. One of these is the self-interest of the employees with respect to the long term of the health of the business. Research has also indicated that when employees have an interest in the business, they are more likely to have a longer perspective of the firm, meaning that they are able to estimate the impacts of their decisions that they impose on the environment and the societies. Baum et al (1997) clarify that collaborative relationship can result a higher level of organizational commitment to sustainable environmental practices and the propensity to fund sustainable activities that entail up-front costs while yielding higher returns in the future.

Another possible channel could be the enhanced autonomy and participation of employees that are typical for employee-ownership organizations. Self-organized governance empowers employees to participate actively in the functioning of the company, hence they are motivated to work. It can culminate in improved workers' output, less untoward from work, and responsibility to uphold firms environmental and social responsibility.

REFERENCES

Acquah, I. S. K., Issau, K., Dei Mensah, R., & Vanderpuye, F. (2023, September 21). When stakeholder orientations matter: Modelling employee orientation, shareholder orientation and supply chain orientation as necessary and sufficient conditions for firm performance. *Heliyon*, 9(10), e20359. DOI: 10.1016/j.heliyon.2023.e20359 PMID: 37771530

Appelbaum, E., & Berg, P. (2001). High-Performance Work Systems and Labor Market Structures. In Berg, I., & Kalleberg, A. L. (Eds.), *Sourcebook of Labor Markets. Plenum Studies in Work and Industry*. Springer., DOI: 10.1007/978-1-4615-1225-7_11

Attanasio, G., Preghenella, N., De Toni, A. F., & Battistella, C. (2022). Stakeholder engagement in business models for sustainability: The stakeholder value flow model for sustainable development. *Business Strategy and the Environment*, 31(3), 860–874. DOI: 10.1002/bse.2922

Aubert, N., Garnotel, G., Lapied, A., & Rousseau, P. (2014). Employee ownership: A theoretical and empirical investigation of management entrenchment vs. reward management. *Economic Modelling*, 40, 423–434. DOI: 10.1016/j.econmod.2013.12.011

Basterretxea, I., & Storey, J. (2018). Do employee-owned firms produce more positive employee behavioural outcomes? If not, why not? A British-Spanish comparative analysis. *British Journal of Industrial Relations*, 56(2), 292–319. DOI: 10.1111/bjir.12247

Becker, C. (2021). Environmental performance boosts market value, but a firm's collective reputation may sink it. Wisconsin School of Business. https://business.wisc.edu/news/environmental-performance-boosts-market-value-but-a-firms-collective-reputation-may-sink-it/

Bhattacharya, C. B., Sen, S., Edinger-Schons, L. M., & Neureiter, M. (2023). Corporate purpose and employee sustainability behaviors. *Journal of Business Ethics*, 183(3), 963–981. DOI: 10.1007/s10551-022-05090-5

Blasi, J., Kruse, D., & Freeman, R. B. (2017). *The Citizen's Share: Reducing Inequality in the 21st Century*. Yale University Press. DOI: 10.12987/9780300195064

Blasi, J. R., Kruse, D. L., & Weltmann, D. (2013). "Firm Survival and Performance in Privately Held ESOP Companies." In Sharing Ownership, Profits, and Decision-Making in the 21st Century, Douglas L. Kruse, ed. Vol. 14 in the series Advances in the Economic Analysis of Participatory and Labor-Managed Firms, Takao Kato, ed. Bingley, UK: Emerald Group Publishing, pp. 109-124. DOI: 10.1108/S0885-3339(2013)0000014006

Bocken, N. M. P., Short, S., Rana, P., & Evans, S. (2013). A value mapping tool for sustainable business modelling. *Corporate Governance (Bradford)*, 13(5), 482–497. DOI: 10.1108/CG-06-2013-0078

Bonal, X., & Cooper, D. (2008). The cooperative advantage: A comparative study of the performance of worker cooperatives and conventional firms. *International Journal of Cooperative Studies*, 22, 1–26.

Buhl, A., Blazejewski, S., & Dittmer, F. (2016). The More, the Merrier: Why and How Employee-Driven Eco-Innovation Enhances Environmental and Competitive Advantage. *Sustainability (Basel)*, 8(9), 946. DOI: 10.3390/su8090946

Chartered Management Institute. The MoralDNA of Employee-Owned Companies. (2019). https://moraldna.org/wp-content/uploads/2019/06/CMI-Managers-and-Their-MoralDNA.pdf

Christian, J., Meckling, W. H., & Jensen, M. C. (1976). Theory of the firm: Managerial behavior, agency costs, and ownership structure. *Journal of Financial Economics*, 3(4), 305–360. DOI: 10.1016/0304-405X(76)90026-X

Cooper, D., & Bidelman, P. (2014). *The Mondragon experience: Lessons from a cooperative enterprise*. Routledge.

Cooperative Development Foundation. (2020). The Power of Employee Ownership: A Guide to Cooperative Business Models. Cooperative Development Foundation. Retrieved from https://www.cdf.coop/3. Comparative Analysis of Different Employee Ownership Models

DiMaggio, P. J., & Powell, W. W. (1983). The Iron Cage Revisited: Institutional Isomorphism and Collective Rationality in Organizational Fields. *American Sociological Review*, 48(2), 147–160. DOI: 10.2307/2095101

Dudley, T., & Rouen, E. (2021, July 12). The big benefits of employee ownership. *Harvard Business Review*.

Elkington, J. (1997). *Cannibals with forks: The triple bottom line of 21st century business*. Capstone.

Employee Ownership Foundation. (2020). COVID-19 and employee-owned companies: Research findings. Employee Ownership Foundation, https://assets-eof.s3.us-east-2.amazonaws.com/assets/public/2020-10/EOF_CovidResearch_Oct23b.pdf

EOA. (2022). John Lewis partnership. https://employeeownership.co.uk/case-studies/john-lewis-partnership

FasterCapital (N.D). Choosing the Right ESOP Structure for Your Business. https://fastercapital.com/keyword/esop-structure.html

FCLTGlobal. (2023). The Long-term Payoff of Employee Ownership. FCLTGlobal. Retrieved from https://hbr.org/2021/05/the-big-benefits-of-employee-ownership

Fieldfisher: Ethics matters more to managers in employee-owned companies, new research reveals. (n.d.). https://www.fieldfisher.com/en/services/employee-ownership-solutions

Flanders, A., Pomeranz, R., & Woodward, J. (1968). *Experiment in Industrial Democracy: A Study of the John Lewis Partnership*. Faber and Faber.

Freeman, R. E. (1984). *Strategic management: A stakeholder approach*. Pitman Publishing.

Freudenreich, B., Lüdeke-Freund, F., & Schaltegger, S. (2020). A stakeholder theory perspective on business models: Value creation for sustainability. *Journal of Business Ethics*, 166(1), 3–18. DOI: 10.1007/s10551-019-04112-z

Friant, M. C., Vermeulen, W. J. V., & Salomone, R. (2020). A typology of circular economy discourses: Navigating the diverse visions of a contested paradigm. *Resources, Conservation and Recycling*, 161, 104917. DOI: 10.1016/j.resconrec.2020.104917

Friant, M. C., Vermeulen, W. J. V., & Salomone, R. (2024). Transition to a sustainable circular society: More than just resource efficiency. *Circular Economy and Sustainability*, 4(1), 23–42. DOI: 10.1007/s43615-023-00272-3

Global Reporting Initiative. (2021). GRI Standards. https://www.globalreporting.org/standards/

Herath, S. K., & Herath, L. M. (2024). Accounting for Sustainability: The Measurements and Financial Reporting Disclosure. In Sun, L. (Ed.), *Contemporary Research and Practices for Promoting Financial Literacy and Sustainability* (pp. 50–91). IGI Global., DOI: 10.4018/979-8-3693-0863-9.ch003

Herath, S. K., & Kulathunga, H. G. E. R. (2024). Integrating ESG Metrics With Ecosystem Services Valuation: A Pathway to Sustainable Development. In Castanho, R. (Ed.), *ESG and Ecosystem Services for Sustainability* (pp. 143–170). IGI Global., DOI: 10.4018/979-8-3693-3771-4.ch006

Hörisch, J., Freeman, E., & Schaltegger, S. (2014). Applying stakeholder theory in sustainability management: Links, similarities, and a conceptual framework. *Organization & Environment*, 27(4), 1–19. DOI: 10.1177/1086026614535786

Jensen, M. C., & Meckling, W. H. (1976). Theory of the firm: Managerial behavior, agency costs and ownership structure. *Journal of Financial Economics*, 3(4), 305–360. DOI: 10.1016/0304-405X(76)90026-X

John Lewis Partnership. (2019). John Lewis Partnership Ethics & Sustainability Report 2019. John Lewis Partnership. Retrieved from https://www.johnlewispartnership.co.uk/content/dam/cws/pdfs/Juniper/ethics-and-sustainability/progress-report-2019-20.pdf

John Lewis Partnership. (2023).. . *Sustainability Report*, 2023, •••. https://www.johnlewispartnership.co.uk

Kasmir, S. (2016). The Mondragon cooperatives and global capitalism: A critical analysis. *New Labor Forum*, 25(1), 52–59. DOI: 10.1177/1095796015620424

Kolkowska, N. (2023, January 25). Employee engagement in sustainable business. Sustainable Review. https://sustainablereview.com/employee-engagement-in-sustainable-business/

Lee, J., & Park, J. (2022). Employee ownership and corporate social responsibility: A meta-analysis. *Journal of Business Ethics*, 110(3), 599–614.

. Lewis, J. (2019). John Lewis Partnership Annual Report.

Lozano, R. (2018). Sustainable business models: Providing a more holistic perspective. *Business Strategy and the Environment*, 27(8), 1159–1166. DOI: 10.1002/bse.2059

Mackin, C. (2024). Defining employee ownership: Four meanings and two models. *Journal of Participation and Employee Ownership*, 7(1), 1–25. DOI: 10.1108/JPEO-10-2022-0019

Martell, K., & Gielen, N. (2000). Employee ownership and firm performance: A meta-analysis. *International Journal of Management Reviews*, 2, 117–139.

Mehak, S. S., & Batcha, H. M. (2024). Analyzing the influence of green human resource practices on organizational sustainability: The role of green attitudes and performance of employees. *Environment, Development and Sustainability*. Advance online publication. DOI: 10.1007/s10668-024-05157-5

Mondragon Corporation. (2024). Mondragon today annual report 2024. https://www.mondragon-corporation.com/en/

. National Center for Employee Ownership. (2023). Employee Ownership in Canada.

NCEO. (2017). Research on Employee Ownership. National Center for Employee Ownership. Retrieved from https://www.nceo.org/employee-ownership-data/academic-research

O'Boyle, E. H., Patel, P. C., & Gonzalez-Mulé, E. (2016). Employee ownership and firm performance: A meta-analysis. *Human Resource Management Journal*, 26(4), 425–448. DOI: 10.1111/1748-8583.12115

O'Boyle, E. H., Patel, P. C., & Gonzalez-Mulé, E. (2016). Employee ownership and firm performance: A meta-analysis. *Human Resource Management Journal*, 26(4), 425–448. DOI: 10.1111/1748-8583.12115

OECD. (2021). OECD Reviews of Labour Market and Social Policies: Germany 2021. OECD Publishing.

Olson, D. G. (n.d.). Sustainable businesses, employee ownership & cooperatives. ESOP Law. https://www.esoplaw.com/sustainable-businesses-employee-ownership-cooperatives

Pendleton, A., Robinson, A., & Nuttall, G. (2023). Employee ownership in the UK. *Journal of Participation and Employee Ownership*, 6(3), 194–214. DOI: 10.1108/JPEO-11-2022-0030

Prasad, R. T., & Gupta, J. (2024). Recent Advances in the Application of Nanomaterials for Environmental Sustainability. In Verma, A., Gupta, H. S., & Sethi, S. K. (Eds.), *Hybrid Composite Materials*. Springer., DOI: 10.1007/978-981-97-2104-7_14

Qalati, S. A., Barbosa, B., & Iqbal, S. (2023). The effect of firms' environmentally sustainable practices on economic performance. *Ekonomska Istrazivanja*, 36(3), 2199822. Advance online publication. DOI: 10.1080/1331677X.2023.2199822

Rosen, C., Case, J., & Staubus, M. (2020). *Ownership culture: How employee ownership can drive inclusive growth and social responsibility*. Beyster Institute Press.

Solar, N. (2021). 2021 Public Benefit Report. Retrieved from https://info.namastesolar.com/hubfs/2021_Namaste_Solar_Public_Benefit_Report_Final.pdf

Stranahan, S., & Kelly, M. (n.d.). Ownership design for a sustainable economy. Fifty by Fifty. https://www.fiftybyfifty.org/2018/05/employee-ownership-and-ecological-sustainability/

Syamlal, V. S. V. (2023). The impact of sustainable branding using big data and business analytics in the market research industry (Publication No. 31134975) [Doctoral dissertation, University of Wales Trinity Saint David]. ProQuest Dissertations & Theses.

Tajfel, H., & Turner, J. C. (1979). An integrative theory of intergroup conflict. In Austin, W. G., & Worchel, S. (Eds.), *The social psychology of intergroup relations* (pp. 33–75). Brooks/Cole.

Tingle, K., & Wharton, E. S. G. Initiative. (2023). The power of shared ownership: How employee-owned businesses achieve sustainability goals. Retrieved from https://esg.wharton.upenn.edu/news/the-power-of-shared-ownership-how-employee-owned-businesses-achieve-esg-goals/

Wang, Y., & Liu, Y. (2021). Does employee ownership enhance corporate social responsibility? Evidence from China. *Journal of Business Ethics*, 103(4), 753–776.

World Business Council for Sustainable Development. (2019). WBCSD's 2019 Sustainability Leadership Report. https://www.wbcsd.org/

Yetim, M. A., & Gur, F. A. (2024). When they are more than just employees: Environmentally conscious decision-making in employee-owned organizations. *Business Strategy and the Environment*, 33(4), 2694–2711. Advance online publication. DOI: 10.1002/bse.3626

Zhang, R., Aljumah, A. I., Ghardallou, W., Li, Z., Li, J., & Cifuentes-Faura, J. (2023). How does economic development promote the sustainability targets? Role of natural resources utilization. *Resources Policy*, 156, 102856.

Chapter 7
Employee Stock Ownership:
Demystifying Corporate Social Responsibility and Taxation in India

R. Amudha
SASTRA University, India

S. Dinesh
https://orcid.org/0000-0003-1751-7973
Sri Ramachandra Institute of Higher Education and Research, India

N. Shobhana
School of Management, SASTRA University (Deemed), Thanjavur, India

ABSTRACT

An Employee Stock Ownership Plan (ESOP) is a strategic welfare extended to the employees in a company in the form of sharing the profits and progress of a company. The managerial personnel who have decided to go for ESOP strategy have to decide about the centre for power of control in day-to-day business operations. Thus, corporate decision making is made crucial when ESOP is decided to be followed to strengthen the ownership of an enterprise. The main challenge in issuing ESOP is the dilution in the management. This chapter deals with the corporate social responsibility, corporate governance and tax implications associated with ESOP.

DOI: 10.4018/979-8-3693-7031-5.ch007

INTRODUCTION

Any form of business organisation is incorporated by the motivated entrepreneurs and led by competent leadership. The success of the organisation also depends upon the dedicated employees who carries out the mission and propel the growth of the organisation. Employees are considered as internal customers and only satisfied employees will render the better productivity and profitability. These contented employees will make the organisation to have a sustainable competitive advantage in the market and lead to a constant elevation towards the mission. As parents nurture their children, the employees nurture their organisation with their values and heartfelt efforts. The contented employees will have a feeling of oneness with the organisation and they celebrate the success of the organisation as their own. The emotional bonding, dedication and commitment of the employees could not be measured in monetary terms. The employees may reach the targets, meet the expectations of the consumers and at times they also innovate new techniques in production and marketing. Thus, the skills, knowledge and experience of the employees should be recognised by the top management as the employees are considered to be the valuable asset of the organisation.

A company which appreciates its own employees will be reciprocally appreciated by them. This will lead to enhanced productivity and loyalty of the employees. The retention of the employees will also be high as they are satisfied with the positive work environment and the attitude of the top management. The consistent performance evaluation of the employees will make to understand about their progress over a period of time. The employees will always expect recognitions and rewards for their high performance. These rewards will also motivate them to exceed their own targets of the previous period.

An Employee Stock Ownership Plan (ESOP) is a strategic welfare extended to the employees in a company in the form of sharing the profits and progress of a company. ESOP is one of the rewards extended to the employees as a strategic benefit plan. It implies that the interest in the ownership of the company is given to the employees aligning them with the interest of the shareholders. It is a profit-sharing plan designed by the management recognising the efforts of the employees. ESOP will attract, motivate, and retain the employees and this is an option given to them but not an obligation. It is an option given to the permanent employees and whole-time directors the right to buy the stock at a predetermined rate over a particular period. The ESOPs were found by a corporate lawyer Louis Kelso in the year 1956 as a shift of ownership of Peninsula Newspapers Incorporation from their founders to the successors, namely, the managers and employees. He strongly believed that the employees of the company are the ones who had made the company to be successful. So, it is logical and reasonable that they should be the ultimate holders of the shares in the enterprise.

Infosys, Tata Consultancy Services, Reliance Industries Limited, HDFC Bank, Wipro, Mahindra & Mahindra, Axis Bank, Larsen and Toubro, Amul, Aavin and Bajaj Auto are the Indian companies offering ESOP to its employees. Rica Bhattacharyya, ET Bureau (September 2024) has said that the successful ESOPs increased the wealth of top executives at large Indian corporations by more than INR 10,300 crore. Companies such as L&T, Infosys, and ICICI Bank adopted ESOPs to reward and retain talent reflecting the increasing significance of stock-linked incentives in compensation packages.[1] Sixteen Indian new-age tech companies have announced ESOP buybacks till October 2024, giving their employees more than 148 million dollars in wealth.[2]

Employee Stock Ownership Plan

According to Rule 12(1) of the Companies (Share Capital and Debentures) Rules, 2014, ESOP can be issued to employees, directors (apart from independent directors), and employees of holding or subsidiary companies. The directors and promoters who own more than 10% of the company's shares are not eligible. However, a notified start-up company is exempt from this requirement. A firm may offer additional capital to its employees through an employees' stock option plan under Section 62(1)(b) of the Companies Act, 2013 as long as a special resolution is enacted, and the requirements are met. Foreign Exchange Management Act (FEMA)1999 and Foreign Exchange Management (Overseas Investment) Regulations (FEMA OI)2022 governs the purchase of equity by residents in India. Overseas investment rules permit foreign entities to grant ESOPs to resident Indian employees and the individuals must be directors or employees of the foreign entity's Indian office, branch, or subsidiary, or of an Indian entity in which the foreign entity has direct or indirect equity interests.

An employee benefit plan which grants employees' a share of the company's equity is known as an ESOP (Employee stock option plans). Each qualified employee receives from the employer a specified percentage of the company's equity shares at no initial cost. The conditions of service, the employee's pay scale, or some other allocation method may be used to determine how the shares are distributed. Until the employee leaves the company or retires, the shares for an employee stock ownership plan are kept in a trust unit for safety and growth. In the event of their resignation, the firm buys back their shares, which are then given to other departing employees.

Workers' share in the business allows them to go from being mere employees to owners of the business. Employee-owned corporations, which resemble worker cooperatives, are businesses in which most of the stock is held by the employees themselves. Newly hired people have less voting power at shareholder meetings since senior employees are allotted more shares than the newly hired employees.

ESOP give employers the chance to reward top performers for contributing to the expansion of their businesses by offering them equity or a cash pay-out based on that equity. As part of the total compensation package, employee stock options are frequently used as an effective means of encouraging long-term commitments from the individuals to whom they are granted. This forms a crucial component of the success story of any growing company.

In India, ESOP Trusts have become a powerful tool for empowering employees and companies alike through the promotion of a long-term commitment and shared ownership culture. To establish an ESOP, a company must first establish a trust to which it can contribute cash or additional company stock in exchange for present shares. Up to a certain amount, these trust donations are tax deductible. After then, the shares are sent to each employee's personal account. The most popular allocation formulae are based on years of service, remuneration, or both. Newly hired people typically become members of the plan and begin to receive allocations following the completion of at least a full year of employment.

Before employees are eligible to obtain the shares in an ESOP, the shares must be vested. Vesting refers to the growing rights that employees receive on their shares as their seniority inside the company increases. Members of the ESOP should get their equity back when they leave the company. Within 60 days following the employee's leave, private enterprises are required to repurchase the leaving employee's shares at fair market value. Each year, the corporations are required to conduct a stock valuation to establish the share price. In situations where the company is losing some of its long-term employees and the share price has increased significantly, the corporation must ensure that it has the funds to cover all the repurchasing shares.

If a company intends to issue shares under the ESOP scheme, it must make sure that the Articles of Association permit the issuing of shares through ESOP. If the company's articles do not permit, it should call an extraordinary general meeting to amend them to include the clause allowing for the issuance of shares through ESOP. Later, the board meeting should be held to pass a resolution and obtain shareholder approval for the ESOP scheme.

The employees in an organisation have two options at the time of obtaining shares under ESOP. They can sell the shares immediately or hold them to get appreciation in the future. When the employee opts for selling immediately, the sales proceeds less the tax on the gain will be given to them. If they wish to retain the shares, they will receive dividends on their holdings or capital gains if there is increase in prices.

The morale of the employees will be enhanced and results in increased productivity in the workplace. The employees will always have an intention of retaining in the company as the ESOP, a stock-based option is an investment in a long-term.

This will also enable the companies to achieve their long-term goals with sufficient financial background.

The ESOP can be extended by way of issuing equity shares to the employees directly as and when they exercise this option. The company can also issue shares to Employee Welfare Trust which administers ESOP and the trust in turn transfers the shares to employees who exercises the option to buy the shares. The company must enter into an ESOP agreement which comprises of all provisions regarding the issue of shares namely, grant date, vesting date, number of shares to be granted, vesting period, exercise date, exercise period and exercise price.

The grant date is the agreement date giving the option to employees to own the shares at a future date. The vesting date is the date on which employees are entitled to buy the shares after fulfilling all the conditions. This date can also be called as agreed-on grant date. The vesting period is a definite period during which ESOP will remain in the trust fund. The employees should remain in the organisation during the vesting period to gain the ownership of the stock under ESOP. The exercise date is the date when the employees exercise their option. The Exercise period starts from the completion of the vesting period and the employees can use their right to apply for the shares under ESOP which are approved by the shareholders in the annual general meeting by passing a special resolution. The exercise price is the price payable by the employees to exercise this option. The employees can purchase the shares at an exercise rate which can be lesser than fair market value. The employees can also compute their potential profit if they wish to sell in the stock market. Thus, ESOP is always considered to be a best retention strategy of the company through proper recognition of the employee.

The listed companies should adhere Securities Exchange Board of India (Employee Stock Option Scheme and Employee Stock Purchase Scheme) Guidelines 1999 which is updated up to 3rd September 2009 and the private and unlisted companies should adhere Rule 12 of Companies (Share Capital and Debenture) Rules 2014 and Section 62(1)(b) of the Companies Act 2013. The Companies Act of 2013 and Part G of Schedule 1 of SEBI (Share Based Employee Benefit & Sweat Equity) Regulations, 2021, SEBI (Listing Obligations and Disclosure Requirements) Regulations, 2015, and any rules imposed thereunder, pertaining to Listed Companies, must be complied with. These legal regulations are framed to ensure that ESOPs are implemented for the benefit of the employees in a fair manner to qualify themselves for the tax advantages.

The Securities Exchange Board of India (SEBI) also ensures that transparency of financial information is to be maintained at the time of issue of the stock options in the interest of the shareholders. The employees should be provided with financial information necessary to understand about the value of shares held by them. They could understand the profitability and performance of the company by knowing the value of shares from the financial statements. Providing the relevant financial information to the employees may make them to feel oneness towards the organisation and understand that their efforts will augment the value of the shares. The growth of the company depends upon employee ownership and participative management.

The ESOP Trust functions is a process for issuing shares in accordance with the ESOP program's implementation. To carry out the ESOP Plan, an ESOP Trust is created and registered especially for that reason. A plan is developed by the company and approved by its members. Simultaneously, an ESOP Trust is established in accordance with the Trusts Act of India, 1882, and registered to function as a middleman between the organization and its workers. Employee shares are issued by the ESOP trust when option holders execute their options.

Determining the eligibility to serve as an ESOP trust trustee is crucial. Acting as trustees is prohibited for directors, senior executives and their families, and anyone economically possessing 10% or more of the paid-up share capital. Additional requirements and conformity are imposed on listed companies in accordance with SEBI laws about voting rights, secondary acquisitions, the value of acquired shares, and the purpose of calling general meetings. The regulatory requirements for ESOP trust paths are more complicated and include things like ESOP Trust and PAN Registration, preparation of ESOP Trust Deed, and the like.

For the ESOP Trust, it is imperative to set up a strong governance framework, which includes appointing trustees who have fiduciary duties. To ensure compliance, there should be regular audits and transparent reporting procedures in place. For the purpose of purchasing shares or fulfilling other ESOP scheme requirements, the company must provide the ESOP Trust with sufficient funding. To prevent any financial hardship on the business, a thorough financial planning is required. Finding the fair value of the shares that the ESOP Trust owns is crucial to maintaining equity and following legal requirements. For this reason, businesses may use independent valuers. Employers should properly explain to staff members the specifics of the ESOP plan, highlighting both its advantages and disadvantages. Maximizing employee participation and fostering trust will require a clear knowledge of the plan.

When adopting employee stock ownership plans, both listed and unlisted companies can benefit greatly from using ESOP trusts. Although the process is frequently used by publicly traded companies to purchase shares on the secondary market without reducing their current capital base, it also offers unlisted businesses great chances to reward and retain talent.

Listed firms can reward their employees in a flexible and effective way by acquiring shares without altering their capital structure through the ESOP Trust mechanism. Listed companies can give their staff members a chance to contribute to the expansion and success of the company while keeping control over their current shareholding using the secondary market.

Still, unlisted companies can benefit greatly from ESOP Trusts. These privately held businesses can set up an Employee Stock Ownership Plan (ESOP) Trust to facilitate employee ownership and match workers' interests with the organization's long-term growth goals.

For both listed and unlisted businesses, the ESOP Trust structure streamlines employee exit procedures. Employees can easily access the value of their shares when they exercise their stock options since the trust provides an effective and transparent procedure for liquidity. Regardless of the company's listing status, this liquidity factor is constant, allowing employees to quickly reap the rewards of their ownership. The ESOP Trust mechanism provides an adaptable solution that meets the unique needs of listed and unlisted Indian companies, enabling the creation of employee stock ownership plans that promote employee engagement, retention, and alignment of employee interests with the company's long-term growth goals.

Corporate Governance and ESOP

Corporate governance (CG) and ethics are closely related phenomenon and play a significant role in managing the affairs of the company. The governance and ethics form a fundamental base in maintain accountability, transparency, full disclosure and sustainable practices in a company. The main aspects of the governance are the accountability and transparency of financial information by the administrators of the company to their stakeholders. An ethical organisation can ensure the accuracy of the financial information with utmost responsibility. This transparency and complete disclosure of the financial and non-financial information will build a good image on the company and increases the value of the company in the society.

As a corporate citizen, it is the responsibility of the company to be more ethical and maintain a respectable governance in the society. These ethical standards and accountability together with responsibility will protect against any misconduct in the affairs of the company. The financial disclosure should be as per global accounting standards namely, International Financial Reporting Standards (IFRS) and Indian Accounting standards (IND AS). The non-financial disclosure includes the information relating to Environmental, Social and Governance (ESG) practices. The ESG goals relate to environment amicable practices with social responsibility to attain ethical and improved governance.

Corporate governance is the total system of guidelines and processes to be followed by board of directors in directing and controlling the affairs of a company. During the implementation of corporate governance practices, the directors should ensure the protection of internal and external stakeholders. The internal stakeholders include the owners, employees and managers. The external stakeholders include customers, society, government, creditors, suppliers and investors. The stakeholders generally view governance practices as a replication of the accountability, integrity and values of a company. Of late, the sustainability and ethical practices in relation to environment are also considered to a establish a good governance. A best corporate governance will always lead to resilience with enduring success. It will form a base of integrity of the company and build a trust among the stakeholders. The ease of raising capital in the market and possibility of increasing prices of the shares are to be also feasible with good governance. Thus, long-term financial feasibility is assured, and the potential financial loss can be reduced.

In terms of pure governance, the role of the directors in any corporation is essential to the expansion and improvement of the company. The board is responsible for making every effort to guarantee that the corporation's stockholders will continue to gain value. Many boards of closely held companies simply convene virtually using the template minutes provided by corporate counsel, carrying out their crucial duties with little more consideration than what is necessary to sign off.

The shareholders, the real owners of the enterprise are the prime responsible persons to elect the board of directors. The directors are responsible for the accountable persons for governance practices, and they delegate powers to officers for implementation. The fiduciary affiliation of directors towards shareholders leads to a principal agency relationship among them. As agents, the directors are morally responsible to the shareholders and their responsibility in the implementation of governance practices in the corporates is emphasised.

Corporate governance differs based on the ownership of the company whether the company is privately or publicly held. Employees at a public company are permitted to own stock, but they are not permitted to advise the company board on the operations of the company. The executives of the company are directly accountable to the board of directors who take governance decisions.

The interests of ownership and the positions in top management were in the hands of same group of personnel in case of closely held companies. Therefore, the ownership and control will be twinned, and decision-making power goes with the same hands. At times, the personnel concerned may wish to come out of ownership before forgoing the managerial power. The role of corporate governance is felt while ESOP is decided to follow for the succession in ownership in an organisation. The managerial personnel who have decided to go for ESOP strategy have to decide about the centre for power of control in day-to-day business operations. Thus, corporate decision making is made crucial when ESOP is decided to be followed to strengthen the ownership of an enterprise.

As public and private enterprises are governed by a board of directors, ESOP-owned businesses are also governed by directors. An independent trustee is designated as the authorized shareholder and acts in a fiduciary role on behalf of the ESOP participants as part of the governance of an ESOP. In this capacity, the trustee selects and nominates internal and external directors to the business's board of directors, the majority of whom are chosen for their operational and/or industry experience by the management team and the firm itself.

In a 100% owned by the ESOP, the duties performed by the board of directors includes the protection of interest of the shareholders, ensuring the identification and implementation of the business's strategic plans, executive hiring, supervision, and evaluation, examining and pursuing specific business decisions and monitoring the operations of ESOP trustee.

The establishment of an independent board is especially vital to the better operation of corporate governance. If the board were exclusively made up of corporate insiders, conflicts of interest may naturally arise. For instance, the executive compensation committee should be made up of independent directors.

The most flourishing ESOPs see the requirement for independent directors as a chance to appoint highly skilled directors with pertinent business and industry experience. Independent directors who meet the requirements can be a great source of contacts, ideas, and establish for appropriate practices which contribute to the development of value.

The Chief Executive Officers may feel that some employees may make irrational demands of the company due to their increased rights as ESOP recipients while an ESOP is issued. In fact, after the sale to an ESOP, daily operations will not be altered, and the company's management team will be supervising the day-to-day operations. They continue to discuss with the board to determine the strategic guidance of the company. However, the most thriving ESOP-owned businesses incorporate employee input and involvement into their procedures and culture, recognizing that creating an atmosphere of employee ownership is a crucial approach.

A corporation may provide ESOP to its employees via the Direct Route or the Trust Route in accordance with the Companies Act of 2013. In case of direct route, the employees receive their options straight from the corporation. The qualifying employees receive new equity shares at the time of exercise. As a result, the direct approach involves direct communication between the employer and employees.

The company's board of directors drafts the ESOP plan and approves it with a resolution. After that, the plan is presented to the Remuneration Committee for approval. Following receipt of the permission, the board will convene a shareholder meeting. The plan will be presented to all shareholders at the meeting, and a separate resolution will be voted to establish the trust. The notification that is given must include information about the employees who are eligible for the ESOP and its cost. The plan must be approved by the shareholders through a special resolution. The board sends a letter of offer to the appropriate staff following approvals. Next, draft the proposed trust's Trust Deed in accordance with the Indian Trusts Act and file it with the relevant Sub-Registrar. PAN is to be applied for the trust and a bank account to be opened with the received PAN. The quantity and value of shares must be ascertained and assigned to the Trust as the employees have to receive them later. The trust can only purchase a share of a firm that is listed on the Indian Stock Exchange through the secondary market. If the company is not publicly traded, the trust may be able to buy the shares by using an independent registered valuer's assessment. At no point in time may the total number of shares held by the trust exceed 5% of the paid-in capital and free reserves of the business. Then, the process of lending money to the Trust will start and it can buy the necessary number and type of shares at the agreed upon price. After that, the trust will sell or transfer the shares to the qualified workers at the exercise price that is decided in line with the ESOP Scheme. The trust will reimburse the company for the loan upon receipt of the exercise price. The trust established can purchase shares from an employee who wants to sell them, preventing the corporation from transferring them to an unidentified third party.

In India, ESOP Trusts are essential to the implementation of effective employee stock ownership schemes. ESOP Trusts establish a win-win scenario for businesses and employees by managing the capital structure, offering ownership, offering incentives to employees, and offering tax benefits. It is imperative that businesses create and manage the trust in compliance with the law while maintaining openness and efficient governance. ESOP Trusts have the potential to unleash employee wealth and support the sustained expansion and prosperity of Indian businesses via meticulous design and implementation.

Review of Literature: ESOP and CG

Kurland, N. (2018) has opined that the laissez-faire system for the stakeholders can be of ESOP and a benefit corporation. A B.Corp is a profit oriented corporation which aims to build a positive social impact based on the operational activities of the enterprise. The benefit corporation is also be considered as a traditional one with obligations transformed to meet advanced standards of its purpose, transparency, and accountability. The objective of B.corp is to have extended stakeholders' interest and it can be achieved only at the cost of wealth of employee owners. The B.Corp can also fortify the culture of the company by way of engaging the employees in a profound work environment. The company which combines ESOP and B.Corp can create a layer of responsibility for the employee owners to achieve the objective of extended stakeholders' interest. [3]

Wen et.al (2021) have said that ESOP is a strategic employee welfare policy which allows the sharing of profits and benefits of growth of an enterprise by employees by acquiring shares in the enterprise. The sustainable growth of a company is enhanced by ESOP as it links the personal interests with organisational interests.

ESOP also plays a significant role in the supervising the operational activities and decrease the agency costs in an enterprise. [4]

Kaswan (2022) has said that the two forms of ownership can be considered in legal and psychological arena. Though the legal ownership gives an innate participation right, the shareholder can only have the rights over the property. The psychological ownership gives an accountability together with the right to control. The findings of his study revealed that the ESOP is more of property oriented and he has suggested that decision making along with governance should be highlighted in ESOP.[5]

Wu et.al (2023) discovered that ESOPs greatly lower corporate financial malfeasance. The reason for this is that non-executives possess more shares than executives do. The underlying methods by which ESOPs restrain executives' opportunistic behaviour include increased internal and external supervision.[6]

Employee ownership of stock has a substantial anti-corporate fraud effect, but other internal and external governance systems also play a role in this regard. Consequently, employee stock ownership should be implemented as a key corporate governance mechanism in companies with inadequate governance systems, such as those without institutional investors, in order to enhance governance and foster long-term business development.

Organizations that intend to implement ESOPs should make sure that they are carefully drafted, with careful thought about the arrangement of shareholding structure. A company's propensity to break the law is correlated with both a larger percentage of common employee stock ownership and a higher proportion of ESOPs in total shares (as opposed to a smaller percentage of common employee stock ownership and a lower proportion of ESOPs). Therefore, businesses should suitably raise the number of shares held in ESOPs as well as the shareholding ratio of regular employees to maximize the governance function of employee stock ownership.

ESOP and Corporate Social Responsibility

Relationship issues between management and business owners are in-built in firm management, and this is mirrored in the conflicting interests of the management and owners' groups. This association is explained by the agency theory, which highlights the conflict of interest in these two groups. Employees become owners of the company under ESOP and they have the right to take part in decision-making processes at different corporate levels and net profit distribution. This results in a change in the conventional dynamic relation between employees, management, and owners, raising employee motivation and helping them to identify with the owners' objectives. The performance of the business, employee engagement and the societal impact are influenced by the ESOP blended with corporate social responsibility (CSR). ESOP, as referred to the practice of providing employees the degree of stake in the business will align a sense of ownership, responsibility, and motivation among the employees. Instead of extending incentives for their efficient performance, the employees are given the stock options and allow them to have a stake in the business. The CSR integrates the social and environmental concerns into their operations which ultimately is influenced by the interactions of the stakeholders. An efficient CSR program should always cover environmental sustainability, labour engagement and other ethical practices towards the society. It will also enhance the reputation of the company, customer attraction and improved relationships with the stakeholders.

The integration of CSR and ESOP motivates the companies to operate the business with a high degree of responsibility towards the society and the environment. The combination of responsibility and accountability will become the culture of any organisation which enhance the engagement of the employees in the financial stake in the business and improves the morale of the employees. The employees will always feel oneness in the company and operate in line with the mission of the company. This will also result in the high degree of job satisfaction, motivation, and retention of the employees. This positive contribution of the employees towards the mission of the company will be the outcome of sharing values between the company and employees. When CSR emphasises sustainable practices which are beneficial to the society and the environment, ESOP promotes employees' loyalty and their interest in the sustained success of the company. This mutual endurance among ESOP and CSR will enhance the stability, reputation, and competitive edge of the organisation.

ESOP and CSR integration is essential to protect the interests of the employee-owners and align their interests with the long-term success of the company. The properly structured policy of corporate governance is very much critical for the maintenance of transparency, accountability and fairness within an ESOP. The ESOP committee is having a fiduciary responsibility of managing ESOP assets in pursuit of safeguarding the financial stake and it must ensure that the company stock is managed in the interest of the employee-owners.

The ESOP trustees may be constituted internally or externally. The internal trustee may be headed by executives and the managing executives must be careful in avoiding the conflicts of interest. The external trustee is an independent third party with the expertise and operate in an unbiased manner. They should ensure that they will deduce the conflicts of interests and impartiality. The ESOP trust must act with prudence, diligence, and loyalty. They are responsible with fiduciary capacity to the employee-owners for the financial stake they possess in the company. The board of directors continue to be the govern the company and they should keep in mind that they have a dual responsibility to both the company and the employee-owners. The board of directors appoints the ESOP trustee, and this trustee manages the assets of ESOP. The board of directors will be continuously responsible for all strategic decisions of the company. The company will also establish a EOP committee to manage the day-to-day affairs of the ESOP and it will maintain the rapport with ESOP trustee. The ESOP committee consists of the executives of the company and the representatives of the employees. This composition is mainly formed to protect the interests of both the parties. The mechanism of ESOP should be communicated to the employees to increase their literacy level about this employee-owner relationship.

Review of Literature: ESOP and CSR

Achour (2024) has found that there exists a positive relationship between employee stock ownership (ESO) and firm financial performance (FFP) and ESO increases the FFP. CSR has a mediating role in the relationship between ESO and FFP.[7]

Corporate financialization is impacted by the macroeconomic environment, regulatory uncertainty, and the greater return gap among financial assets and tangible investments. Feng et.al (2022) discovered that ESOP implementation significantly reduces company financialization, and ESOPs improve internal control and lower management agency expenses to reduce business financialization. According to heterogeneity analyses, ESOPs have a significantly stronger negative impact on corporate financialization in companies with greater funding restrictions, a lower quality external audit, and higher percentages of shareholdings by CEO and self-funded worker ownership.[8]

The founders of the company are, of course, the ones who decide on its legal structure. They can choose to utilize a structure that makes all subsequent employees as co-owners or just employees. Naturally, the founders will choose to hire the remaining workers because they lack a strong moral compass. This is the primary cause of the dearth of employee-owned businesses. Employee-owned businesses typically offer better working conditions, are more competitive, and have greater environmental, employee, and community responsibility.

Kong et.al (2024) have revealed that when considering environmental protection expenditures, the quality of environmental information disclosed, and environmental, social, and governance (ESG) ratings, giving ESOPs to non-executive staff encourages increased corporate ecological engagement. ESOPs give members a sense of unity around a shared goal, enabling them to exert pressure on management to lower carbon emissions, improving their health and attracting their remaining interest in enduring corporate value. Furthermore, businesses who invest in environmental preservation increase their long-term firm worth despite forgoing short-term profit due to high initial expenditures. The ESOP plans that have sustained validity times of ownership, greater employee subscription rates, and more non-executive employees awarded to them are responsible for these good benefits. These schemes also have an incentive effect that is strong enough to counteract the free-rider issue.[9]

Zhou et al (2022) have found that public companies in China extend ESOPs which give their employees both internal psychological and external financial incentives and boosts their desire to participate in CSR activities and eventually contributes to CSR.[10]

Pan (2020) has said that when ESOPs are put into place, workers become owners of the company and have the similar privileges as the investors who provide the money. As a result, the ESOP itself is one way for businesses to uphold their social responsibility while also empowering workers' human rights and promoting their social mobility. However, when there is a transition from employees to owners, their interests will be more tightly constrained by the expansion of the company. As a result, the deployment of ESOPs will align the conflicts of interest resulting from agency problems, allowing enterprises to improve financial performance, reduce working staff turnover, and increase management efficiency. Ultimately, as financial results show an increase, people and businesses can afford to engage in social and environmental activities. As people and businesses pay more taxes, the government can improve services for the public, the environment, and technological development.[11]

Syariati et.al (2017) discovered that the ESOP program's ability to increase compensation was positively impacted by earnings management. Enhanced earnings management occurs when management aims to increase profits at year-end so that it can generate substantial profits by raising the share price and implementing the ESOP program. The management ownership and board of directors' authority can offset the ESOP program's increased earnings management. Institutional ownership and the audit committee have no influence in the way in which earnings are managed.[12]

Benefits of an ESOP

The tax benefit that employees receive is one of the advantages of employee stock ownership plans. Taxes are not withheld from employee contributions made to an ESOP. Workers are only subject to taxes when they leave the company in another way or get a dividend from their ESOP upon retirement. Capital gains are subject to taxation over time. A 10% penalty will be applied to any cash distributions they choose to take before reaching the standard retirement age.

Employee involvement and engagement are typically higher in companies that have an ESOP in its place. Employee awareness is increased because they have the chance to weigh in on choices about goods and services. Workers can offer suggestions on the direction the company should go in and view the organization's future ambitions in a broad sense. Additionally, an ESOP boosts staff confidence in the business.

Plans for employee stock ownership benefit the organization as a whole in addition to the employees. The adoption of ESOPs led to a 2.4% rise in annual revenue growth, a 2.3% increase in job growth, and an improved chance of company survival, per the Rutgers University National ESOP Comparison Study. Better organizational performance raises the company's share price and, eventually, the amount in each employee's ESOP account.[13]

Through ESOPs, an employee can purchase firm shares at face value and then sell them for a profit (after a predetermined amount of time determined by his employer). There are numerous examples of employees becoming extremely wealthy alongside the company founders. A prime example is Google's initial public offering. Even the employees who held shares in the company, Sergey Brin and Larry Page, became the richest people in the globe.

An organization will provide its staff stock options as a means of encouraging them. Employees would have a motivation to give it their all since they would stand to gain financially from the company's rapid share price growth. While the main advantages an ESOP offers firms are incentive, employee retention, and recognizing hard work, there are a number of other significant benefits as well. Organizations might avoid paying out cash as a reward by using ESOP options, which would reduce their immediate cash outlay. Offering ESOPs instead of cash rewards would be the most practical choice for companies that are growing or initiating larger-scale operations.

Employee stock ownership programs are a common strategy used by organizations to draw in and keep top talent. Typically, organizations distribute the stocks gradually. As an example, a business might give its workers stock at the end of the fiscal year as a perk for sticking with the company and earning that award. Businesses that provide ESOPs have long-term goals. Employers want to keep their staff members around for the long run, but they also want to turn them into stakeholders. The worrying attrition rates of the majority of information technology organizations could be reduced with the use of ESOPs. Startups use stocks as a tool to draw in talent. These companies frequently lack funding and are not able to provide competitive compensation. However, they differentiate their remuneration package by providing a share in their company.

Drawbacks of an ESOP

If employees depend on their ESOP for retirement, a drop in the company's stock value could cause an imbalance in their investment portfolio. The employee runs the danger of losing their savings as well as their income in the event that the company fails. Examples are the corporate failures of Enron and WorldCom, where workers lost the majority of their retirement funds.

In an Employee Stock Ownership Plan, each share's percentage of ownership decreases due to dilutive share ownership. Employees face financial risk as the value of ESOPs can change depending on the performance of the company. Any profits from ESOPs are subject to capital gains tax payable by the employees resulting in tax burden and this may lower the overall benefit if the price of the share doesn't rise significantly. The employees also have limited liquidity as they cannot trade their shares if the company is not publicly traded. Companies might have less flexibility to lower its cash demand and be required to make larger contributions to an ESOP than to retirement plans.

Conflicts of interest may arise because employees may anticipate a voice in the company's decision-making process after becoming shareholders resulting in governance problems in companies. An ESOP's trustees could also be exposed to fiduciary risk. The company also face administrative burden in setting and managing an ESOP as it is subject to statutory regulations.

Taxation of ESOP in India

For seven decades, the ESOP has existed. Louis O. Kelso, a political economist and corporate lawyer best known as the Father of the Employee Stock Ownership Concept, created an unorthodox type of ownership in the 1950s. The general word ESOP refers to a bundle of investments or incentives intended for a company's workers. According to Company Law, it is a right to subscribe for its securities at a future date, though at a fixed rate, is offered to full-time directors, officers, or workers. It is a creative approach to staff retention, compensation, incentive, and motivation.

A group of workers will be given ownership of the company in this manner. One of the most focal resources for managing any business is human capital. Companies have been paying their employees in unusual ways for the past few decades, such as through Sweat Equity, Employee Stock Purchase Scheme (ESPS), and Employee Stock Option Scheme (ESOS). A number of statutes, including the Company Law, the Income-tax Law, Securities Laws, Foreign Exchange Regulations, and, International Financial Reporting Standards (IFRS) and Statement of Financial Accounting Standards (SFAS), must be considered when it comes to the regulatory aspects of ESOP in India. Only ESPS and ESOS were previously under the purview of SEBI, the stock market regulator.

The Employee Stock Option Plan (ESOP), Employee Share Purchase Plan (ESPP), Sweat Equity, Stock Appreciation Rights Plan (SAR), Phantom ESOPs, Compensation Plans, Incentive Plans are examples of ESOP. However, because of regulatory limitations, the ESOP plan is widely used in India. While in ESPP, a listed entity offers the right to purchase its shares immediately, in contrast to ESOP, later for a lower price than current market prices with a lock-in period, in ESPP an entity gives its eligible employees the option to purchase its shares at a forthcoming date but at a different price. The shares will not be provided to its employees under SAR; but, as an incentive, they will get the appreciation in share value between two designated dates. The SAR option is closely related to the overall performance of the company. An offer of restricted stock is subject to specific requirements, such as the employer's authority to revoke the entitlement if the requirements are not fulfilled. Shares granted to its employees and/or directors at a discount or in exchange for something other than cash in exchange for their expertise or rights related to intellectual property, etc., are known as sweat equity shares.

Accepting or using the offered choice is not required. If the current share price is less than the exercise price, the employee is free to decide whether to exercise the option or let it expire. In either event, the worker will have a set amount of time to choose to exercise or forfeit his rights. The term exercise date refers to the day an employee opts to purchase them. An employee's offer of securities under an Employee Stock Option Plan (ESOP) scheme, whether at no cost or at a discounted rate, is taxable as a benefit in the year in which the employee receives the securities. However, if an employee of a qualified start-up is involved, the obligation to pay or deduct taxes on such a perquisite may be postponed. The market worth of the perk on the date the ESOP was exercised, less the sum that was recovered from the employee, is the perquisite's value. Gains from securities granted under ESOPs that are later transferred by the employee are subject to taxation under the "Capital Gains" heading. [Section 17(2)(vi)]

Tax Implications When Allotment of Shares Was Made

Any business that pays employee salaries must deduct taxes at the average tax rate at the moment of payment. Benefits that employee receive from their employers are also included in the definition of salary. ESOPs are taxed at two different points of time in the hands of employees. The first is when the employee receives their securities, and the second is when they are sold.

ESOPs were subject to Fringe Benefit Tax (FBT) prior to changes made by the Finance Act of 2009. Since then, under specific circumstances, it has become taxable for employees as perquisites. Any stocks (ESOP) that are given to employees for free or at a discounted rate would be considered perquisite. When determining perquisite value, the FMV of the securities on the date of allocation is irrelevant. Rather, the FMV of the securities at the time of option exercise is taken into account. When securities are allocated, the initial tax instance will occur. When an employee exercises their option, the difference between the stocks' Fair Market Value (FMV) on the exercise date and the amount they paid for them is taxable as perquisite and subject to taxation under the head salary at the time of securities allocation. As a result, in the year that securities are distributed, the employer must deduct the tax (TDS) on the perquisite amount from the employee's wage under section 192 of Income Tax Act. The quoted and unquoted shares allocated under the ESOP plan will have their fair market value determined in accordance with Rule 3 of Income Tax Act.

The cost of acquiring such shares shall be the Fair Market Value (FMV) on the day on which the employee exercises the option, unless the capital gain results from the transfer of specified security or sweat equity shares as mentioned in clause (vi) of subsection (2) of section 17 of the Income Tax Act. If foreign firms issue an Indian resident an ESOP (Cross border ESOP), the ESOP is taxable in India and is subject to any applicable double taxation avoidance agreements. These Cross-border ESOPs are governed by FEMA 1999 and FEMA OI Regulations 2022.

Tax Implications When Transfer of Shares by The Employees

Gains from securities granted under ESOPs that are later transferred by the employee are subject to taxation under the "Capital Gains" heading. The security type and the length of time it is held will determine whether capital gains are taxable. The time frame for holding stocks will start on the day the securities are allocated, not the day the option is exercised, and terminate on the day the employees transfer the shares. In order to calculate the capital gain, the cost of acquiring the securities will be determined by their fair market value on the day the option is exercised.

Tax Treatment of ESOPS For a Start-Up

Since employees do not immediately benefit from securities granted under ESOPs, the tax deduction on those securities in the year of allocation itself was quite onerous for them because it decreased their cash flow. Tax Deduction at Source (TDS) on salary (Section 192), self-assessment tax (Section 140A), direct payment of tax by the employee (Section 191), and Section 156 (notice of demand) are among the provisions of the Income-tax Act that have been amended to postpone the deduction and payment of tax on income in the form of perquisites arising from ESOPs in order to lessen the tax burden.

The delay of TDS and tax payment on perquisite arising from ESOPs will only be available to qualifying start-ups as defined under Section 80-IAC and their employees. Eligible start-ups must deduct taxes from income arising from ESOP perquisites within 14 days of the occurrence of any of the following events, whichever occurs first, according to Section 192, which allows employers to deduct taxes from employee salaries: a) after 48 months have passed from the conclusion of the assessment year in which securities are distributed under ESOPs; b) after the assessee's employment with the company ends; or c) following the sale of securities distributed under ESOP.

The tax will be subtracted for this purpose using the rates that apply to the fiscal year in which securities are distributed or transferred under ESOPs. Therefore, in his income return for the year in which securities are distributed, an employee must declare the value of the perquisite from ESOPs. However, the employee will not be obliged to pay tax on benefits resulting from ESOPs in that year due to the tax payment postponement.

In case of employers, tax deduction is available for the cost of the shares issued under ESOP and is available in the year in which the option is exercised by the employees. The company can avail up to 25% of an employee's compensation as a deduction for taxation purpose and can reducing the liability of tax. The company can invest in new ventures or pay off the debts by having the advantage of tax reduction and augmenting the amount from ESOP. The company can also defer the payment of taxes on capital gains through ESOP.

When the securities are extended to the employees by the employer as per ESOP scheme at cost free or at concessional rates, the value of securities is taxable as a perquisite in the financial year in which such shares are issued to them.

For the employees, ESOPs are taxed at the time of exercising the option. The difference between the fair market value and the exercise price is considered as income from salary for taxation purpose. This tax amount is deducted at source from the income of the employees. ESOPs are also taxed as a capital gain at the time of sale by the employees. The difference between sale price and fair market value on the date of exercise is calculated as capital gains.

The gain from the selling of shares that have been held for less than or equal to a year is known as a short-term capital gain. Consequently, they will be subject to a 15% tax rate, which is a concession under Section 111A of the Income Tax Act of 1961.

The gain from the selling of shares that have been held for more than a year is known as a long-term capital gain. The IT Act added Section 112A, which became operative on April 1, 2018. When gains exceed Rs. 1 lakh, this clause levies an LTCG tax at a rate of 10% without indexation. According to Section 10(38), LTCGs originating from listed shares were exempt prior to the Finance Act of 2018 as long as the selling transaction was subject to Securities Transaction Tax (STT). Later, when Section 112A was introduced, the exemption was removed.[14]

From the fiscal year 2024-25, there will only be two holding periods: 12 months and 24 months. The holding term for all listed securities is 12 months, while all other assets are 24 months. Hence, listed shares held for more than 12 months are considered long-term. From fiscal year 2024-25, the limit on the exemption of Long-Term Capital Gains on the equity shares transfer, equity-oriented units, or Business Trust units is proposed to be enhanced from Rs.1 lakh to Rs.1.25 lakh each year. The tax rate has also been hiked from 10% to 12.5%. While the tax rate changed on July 23, 2024, the exemption amount was raised to Rs. 1.25 lakhs for the entire year.[15]

For unlisted enterprises, selling shares acquired through ESOPs can be challenging because there might be few buyers and merchant bankers determine the FMV. Moreover, capital gains are subject to taxation based on borrowed money. This means that short-term capital gains, which are subject to taxation at a marginal tax rate, are generated when shares are sold within 36 months of their exercise. Capital gains that are generated after a period of 36 months are subject to a 20% indexation tax. Nonetheless, staff members will have more options to pay out their shares once the company is listed. Moreover, FMV is impacted by changes in the market.[16]

A buyback of ESOP occurs when a business chooses to repurchase the option prior to it being exercised into equity shares. This is rather typical among Indian startups and unlisted businesses. An Indian company offers its employees an ESOP as an incentive, but only in the case of a liquidation event (such as an IPO or additional financing rounds) does it permit conversion into stock. Employers may choose to buy back options before they are exercised in order to give their employees liquidity because the shares are not available owing to an inactive market.

Employers deduct tax at source (TDS) under Section 192 and classify such buy-back income under the Salary heading. As a result, it will appear on your Form 16 and does not require separate disclosure in employee's Income Tax Return (ITR).[17]

Challenges in Issuing ESOP

The main challenge in issuing ESOP is the dilution in the management. In July 2023, Sonal Bhutra in CNBCTV 18, has told that the India faces a shareholder activism, and the institutional shareholders has raised their dissents to 44%, the major reason being the ESOP.[18] The management perceives ESOP issued at discount as a compensation to be deferred. While the investors perceive a risk element in salary payments and wish to issue ESOP at a price nearer to market price. ESOP will be successful only if the prices of the shares increase in future. Simultaneously, the burden of tax also increases resulting in insignificant net gain. Moreover, the companies offer ESOP instead of paying competitive salary package to its employees. Unless the employees get an exit option, selling of shares acquired under ESOP is difficult. At times of resignations or terminations within the vesting period, a large portion of ESOP could not be received by the employees.

An employee may have to sell the granted ESOP shares to pay taxes if they quit the company. If an employee's employment is terminated because of a disability or death, it will have a huge impact on them. The employee may be taxed on a higher value upon exercise if the share price was higher at the time of allocation but decreased at the time of tax withholding. In this case, the employee must pay perquisite tax even though they are receiving a notional benefit rather than an actual benefit.[19]

Huili Zhang et.al (2023) have stated that an ESOP is more likely to be adopted by a company with significant agency issues or a high margin of call risk. This results in abusing ESOPs by the shareholders having control to pursue personal gain at the expense of other shareholders.[20]

CONCLUSION

Employers typically give ESOPs to staff members as a reward to help them retain outstanding talent. After having a stake in the business, it serves as a motivating tool for staff members, making them feel accountable for its success. Start-ups that are unable to pay significant salaries to staff during the initial phase are especially prefer ESOPs. ESOPs enable start-ups to hire highly skilled workers for comparatively cheap salaries, with ESOPs covering the remaining balance.

The participation of the employees in ESOP is mainly triggered by the cashless transactions as a token of their performance incentives. This may foster a degree of commitment and ownership among the employees. The incorporation of worker engagement in the ownership will definitely result in the long-term success of the organisation. This in turn helps the company to expand its capital base and lever its capital structure facilitating the expansion and diversification of the projects. The taxation nuances should be clearly understood by the employers while opting for ESOP, thereby maintaining the responsibility towards the society as a corporate citizen.

The organization that chooses ESOP funding offers enticing financial advantages. Firstly, its contributions are tax deductible. Second, dividends made on ESOP stock that are distributed to staff members or utilized to pay back the ESOP loan are deductible as well. Employers and employees can benefit from ESOPs in a variety of ways. The main benefits of ESOPs for an organization include tax advantages, employee retention, and employee motivation. When a skilled workforce is retained, the business will thrive and the underlying shares will generate a healthy return, which encourages employees to stay with the company. It will result in increased productivity, efficiency, and profits, and it will undoubtedly benefit all parties involved. It is a helpful tool for attracting skilled human resources for new businesses or those in the expansion stage. It can be applied to expansion, acquisitions, the establishment of new divisions, and the like. ESOPs have been one of the empowerment schemes and widely accepted as a component of both public and private businesses worldwide. While there are other types of employee ownership programs available, ESOPs are successful in this regard. ESOPs have been effectively implemented by numerous multinational corporations across various industries.

REFERENCES

https://economictimes.indiatimes.com/news/company/corporate-trends/esop-culture-making-india-inc-top-execs-richer/articleshow/113104554.cms?from=mdr (Accessed in October 2024)

https://inc42.com/features/indian-startup-employees-made-at-least-inr-1250-cr-via-esop-buybacks-in-2024/# (Accessed in October 2024)

https://cleartax.in/s/tax-deductibility-esop-expenses (Accessed in October 2024)

https://cleartax.in/s/long-term-capital-gains-on-shares (Accessed in October 2024)

https://cleartax.in/s/esop (Accessed in October 2024)

https://cleartax.in/s/taxation-on-esop-rsu-stock-options (Accessed in October 2024)

https://www.cnbctv18.com/business/esop-full-form-employee-stock-option-big-shareholders-dissent-17115661.htm (Accessed in October 2024)

https://eqvista.com/esop/employee-stock-ownership-plan-india/ (Accessed in October 2024)

Achour, Z. (2024). Impact of employee stock ownership on firm financial performance: Does corporate social responsibility matter? *International Journal of Management and Enterprise Development*, 23(2), 155–170. DOI: 10.1504/IJMED.2024.139275

Feng, Y., Yu, Q., Nan, X., & Cai, Y. (2022). Can employee stock ownership plans reduce corporate financialization? Evidence from China. *Economic Analysis and Policy*, 73, 140–151. DOI: 10.1016/j.eap.2021.11.002

Kaswan, M. J. (2022). Property, ownership, and employee ownership: Employee control in ESOPs. *Journal of Participation and Employee Ownership*, 5(1), 14–31. DOI: 10.1108/JPEO-11-2020-0028

Kong, D., Liu, J., Wang, Y., & Zhu, L. (2024). Employee stock ownership plans and corporate environmental engagement. *Journal of Business Ethics*, 189(1), 177–199. DOI: 10.1007/s10551-023-05334-y

Kurland, N. (2018). ESOP plus benefit corporation: Ownership culture with benefit accountability. *California Management Review*, 60(4), 51–73. DOI: 10.1177/0008125618778853

Pan, H. ESOPs in the cycle of sustainability: Evidence of Chinese firms. *Book of Abstracts ARTEM OCC 2020 Edition*, 338.

Syariati, N. E., Subroto, B., & Andayani, W. (2017). The Role of Employee Stock Option Plan to Reduce Earnings Management Actions. Jurnal Keuangan dan Perbankan, 21(3), 425-435

https://cleo.rutgers.edu/articles/largest-study-yet-shows-esops-improve-performance-and-employee-benefits/

Wen, X., Li, Z., Zhang, Y., & Shen, S. (2021). ESOP and corporate sustainable growth. In *E3S Web of Conferences* (Vol. 253, p. 03039). EDP Sciences.

Wu, F., Cao, J., & Zhang, X. (2023). Do non-executive employees matter in curbing corporate financial fraud? *Journal of Business Research*, 163, 113922. DOI: 10.1016/j.jbusres.2023.113922

Zhang, H., He, J., Zhu, J., & Chan, K. C. Used as a Tool: When Esops Meet Controlling Shareholders' Share Pledging in an Emerging Market. Available at *SSRN* 4583067. DOI: 10.2139/ssrn.4583067

Zhou, L., Wei, F., & Kong, Y. (2022). Do employee stock ownership plans affect corporate social responsibility? Evidence from China. *International Journal of Environmental Research and Public Health*, 19(3), 1055. DOI: 10.3390/ijerph19031055 PMID: 35162079

Chapter 8
Significant Employee Share Ownership and Corporate Governance:
Evidence From French Firms

Oussama Moustabchir
https://orcid.org/0009-0007-9259-2814
University of Grenoble Alpes, France

ABSTRACT

In France, over the years, employees have acquired an increasingly significant stake in the capital of their companies, often to the point of becoming a key shareholder group. French legislation has made it compulsory for employee shareholders to be represented on the board of directors once they collectively hold more than 3% of the capital. This chapter examines the effects of significant employee share ownership and the resulting board representation on the overall performance of the corporate governance system. The empirical results show that significant employee share ownership has positive effects on corporate governance. The results also show that employee shareholding representation on the board of directors has negative effects in terms of governance. These results suggest a number of recommendations that could help companies in their choice of ownership structure, and that could enlighten regulators about good governance practices.

DOI: 10.4018/979-8-3693-7031-5.ch008

INTRODUCTION

In France, more and more employees are holding a financial stake in their companies. The 2023 census by the European Federation of Employee Share Ownership (EFES) shows that there are around 3 million employee shareholders in France, owning around €110 billion[1], placing France at the top of European countries in terms of both the total value of capital held by employees and the total number of employee shareholders. According to EFES, the proportion of employee shareholders in relation to the total number of employees is 34% in France, compared with a European average of around 19.6% (Figure 1). These figures clearly show that employee share ownership tends to make employees a key shareholder group in France.

Figure 1. Democratization rate of employee share ownership in Europe (Annual economic survey EFES, 2023, p.70, graph 29)

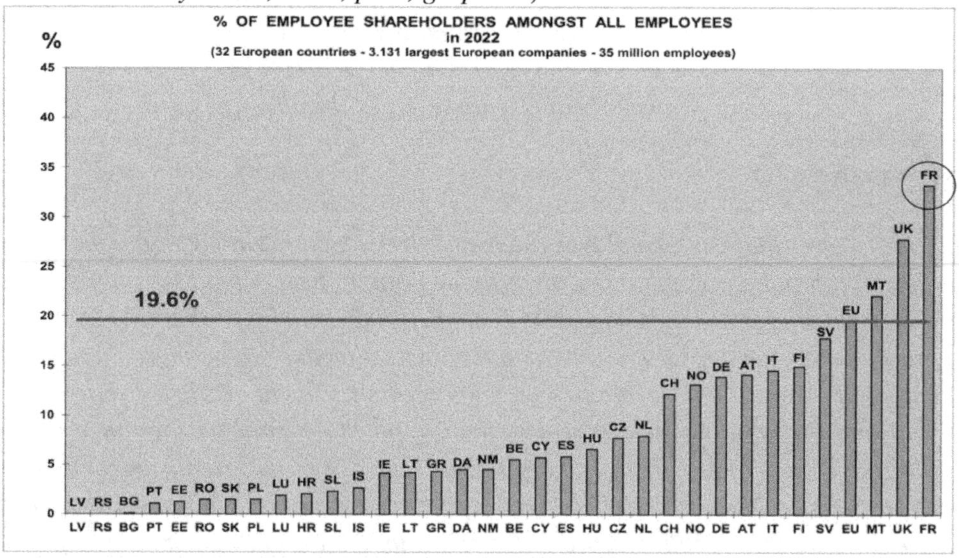

This rise in employee share ownership in France is the result of a threefold determination: That of the company, which adopts it to stimulate the efforts of its employees and align their interests with those of the company and its shareholders; that of the employee, who becomes a shareholder to ensure a more profitable and equitable sharing of the value created through his or her work; and that of the State, which encourages and facilitates its development for its positive long-term effects on job stability, the reduction of social inequalities, the easing of pension systems and, more generally, on the sharing of the value created by companies (Hollandts and Guedri, 2008). The 2019 PACTE Act encourages the further development of the number of employee shareholders and the strengthening of their role in corporate governance and reflects the French legislator's ambition to achieve a 10% employee shareholding in the capital of major companies by 2030. As a result, employee share ownership occupies a special place in current debates on corporate governance in France (Cardoni, 2021).

The relationship between employee ownership and corporate governance is neither recent nor devoid of ambiguity. Since corporate governance became a subject of academic study, a great deal of thought has been given to the consequences of separating the ownership of capital from the management of the company (Berle and Means, 1932; Jensen and Meckling, 1976). Basically, it is accepted that most corporate governance problems stem from this dismemberment, which gives rise to divergent interests that limit the potential for creating and sharing value on a sustainable basis. Employee share ownership can be seen as one of the best mechanisms for aligning interests, helping to bring capital and labour closer together in companies and limiting the sources of conflict (Desbrières, 2002). In the current context marked by a general craze for employee share ownership, some recent works on the subject openly question the impact of a high or even majority employee shareholding in their company (Toe et *al.*, 2017; Garfatta and Zorgati, 2021; Abdelnour et *al.*, 2022; Kaswan, 2022). Although there is an abundant literature on employee ownership, very few studies analyse changes in corporate governance in the context of significant employee ownership (Toe et *al.*, 2017; Guery and Stevenot, 2017). Yet the issue is fundamental because, in principle, significant shareholding gives employees more control and ownership rights and may lead them to participate in corporate governance bodies (Desbrières, 2002; Cardoni, 2021). As a result, it can affect the structure and overall operation of the company's governance system.

French legislation introduced employee ownership of at least 3% of the capital as the threshold above which employee shareholder representation on the board of directors becomes mandatory for large, listed companies. Recently, the 2019 PACTE law reaffirmed this legal threshold of 3% employee share ownership and extended the scope of this obligation to large French non-listed companies. This obligation on large French companies to include employee shareholder representatives on their boards is based on the increasingly significant weight of employees in the capital of French companies (Hollandts et *al.*, 2011; Ginglinger et *al.*, 2011). This legislative specificity bears witness to a French originality in the sense that employee shareholding representation on the board of directors is virtually absent in the European and international landscape (Crifo and Rebérioux, 2019). This gives our research an international perspective and justifies the interest of studying the French context. All the more so since, in terms of significant employee share ownership, France is a typical case in this respect (Figure 2).

Figure 2. Employee share ownership levels in Europe (Annual economic survey EFES, 2023, p.61, graph 20)

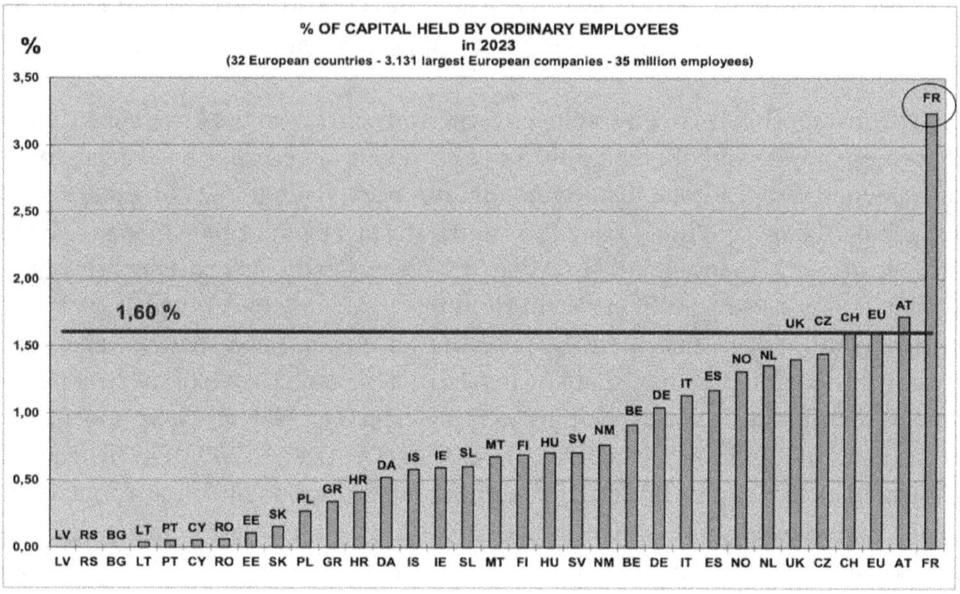

The contribution of this chapter is to focus on the phenomenon of significant employee ownership, i.e. the case where employees hold a high or even majority fraction of their company's capital (Toe, et *al.*, 2017). We study the effect of significant employee ownership on the overall performance of the governance system of French companies. We also examine the effect of mandatory employee shareholding representation on the board of directors in terms of governance. To do this, we refer to the field of corporate governance theories, in particular agency theory. Empirically, we use regression analyses on panel data from a sample of French companies belonging to the SBF 120 stock market index, over the period from 2012 to 2021. The data on governance come from the Refinitiv database (formerly Thomson-Eikon). Data on significant employee share ownership are collected from companies' universal registration documents. To take into account the endogeneity biases that most empirical studies on employee ownership suffer from (Toe et *al.*, 2017), the Generalized Method of Moments (GMM) system estimator was employed in our regression analyses (Blundell and Bond, 1998). To further investigate and better understand the relationship significant employee ownership and the overall performance of the governance system, we analyzed the potential threshold effect related to employee ownership.

The remainder of this chapter is organized as follows. In the first section, we present the analytical framework, the literature review and set out the research hypotheses. The second section presents the empirical approach adopted and describes the sample and data sources. The results are presented and discussed in the third section.

1. LITERATURE REVIEW, THEORETICAL FRAMEWORK AND HYPOTHESES

Before analyzing the impact of significant employee share ownership on corporate governance, it seems necessary first of all to return to the theoretical foundations of corporate governance and to look at what employee share ownership covers as a mechanism for creating and sharing value.

1.1. Employee share ownership in the light of corporate governance theories

In the academic literature on management science, it is customary to attribute the emergence of corporate governance and, more broadly, the governance of organizations to the debate opened by Berle and Means (1932) on what they called "*passive ownership*". In their seminal work "*The modern corporation and private property*", the authors noted that the managerial company[2] was becoming the dominant organizational form. They observe that 65% of companies in the United States are managerial and point out that one of the major specificities of this organizational form lies in the separation of the ownership of capital and the management of the company. For these authors, this dismemberment was at the root of a divergence - partial or total - of interests between shareholders and managers. Their analyses raise two important questions, which remain unanswered: who really bears the residual risk? and who should appropriate the residual gains? With these two questions, Berle and Means (1932) launched the debate on corporate governance and, since then, various conceptualizations and theoretical perspectives have been put forward.

Building on the insights of Berle and Means, Jensen and Meckling (1976), in their seminal work on agency theory, propose a framework for analyzing the realistic effects of this disaggregation of the functions of ownership of capital and management of the firm. The idea underlying their analytical framework is that this dismemberment gives rise to a divergence of interests between shareholders and managers, which necessarily leads to conflicts that generate agency costs that limit the potential for improving the company's performance. Drawing heavily on the analyses of Alchian and Demsetz (1972), the authors explain that this dismemberment makes it necessary for shareholders to put in place governance mechanisms

- of control and incentives - to counter the opportunistic behaviour of managers and limit their attempts to expropriate the value generated. On this basis, the theoretical field of corporate governance has focused on mechanisms relating to the way in which value is created and shared, the distribution and exercise of power and responsibilities, the regulation of conflicts of interest, the prevention of biases affecting decision-making, the reliability of information disclosed, the fight against fraud and corruption, the conditions for the sustainability of the company's activity, etc. (Charreaux, 1997, 2011).

A detailed analysis of the field of corporate governance theories reveals the existence of four theoretical approaches (Charreaux, 2011). Firstly, the shareholder approach to governance, which suggests that governance mechanisms aim only to defend the interests of shareholders through the discipline - control and incentive - of managers (Jensen and Meckling, 1976; Fama, 1980; Charreaux, 1997). Secondly, the partnership approach to governance, which broadens the scope of interests to be defended to include different stakeholders (employees, shareholders, managers, etc.) with a view to ensuring a fair distribution of value. This is an analytical framework which argues that the sustainability of the company's activity cannot be ensured without obtaining the support and taking into account the legitimate interests of the various stakeholders (Freeman, 1984). Thirdly, the cognitive approach to governance, which focuses on cognitive arguments - knowledge and skills - to explain the origin of the value to be distributed (Charreaux, 2002; Wirtz, 2011). Finally, the behavioral approach to governance, which focuses on the cognitive/behavioral and emotional biases affecting the decisions of the company and its managers (Charreaux, 2005).

In the academic literature on employee share ownership, the most widely used frame of reference is agency theory (Jensen and Meckling, 1976). Underpinning the shareholder approach to governance, this theory considers that employee share ownership is a mechanism which can lead employees to act in the interests of shareholders and can limit the sources of conflict (Cardoni, 2021). Given the alignment of interests that it can foster within the company, employee share ownership can also be a channel for exchanging information that can improve the decisions taken within the company (Guery and Stevenot, 2017). Taking advantage of their dual status and therefore of the confrontation of several sources of information, employee shareholders can help to reduce information asymmetry and increase transparency within the company, particularly at general meetings. In addition, as Desbrières (2002) points out, employee share ownership can foster collective control and mutual monitoring among employees, which is likely to encourage other employees (non-shareholders) to make the necessary efforts and execute the company's strategies effectively. From the point of view of this theory, if employee ownership aligns the interests of employees with those of shareholders and ensures a better flow of information within the company, it should help to minimize sources of conflict and improve corporate governance and performance (Cardoni, 2020; Abdelnour et *al.*, 2022).

1.2. Employee share ownership as a mechanism for creating and sharing value

Employee share ownership has long been recognized as a mechanism for involving employees financially and on a long-term basis in the destiny and performance of their company (Guedri and Hollandts, 2008). By associating employees with the capital, employee share ownership offers several advantages, both for employees and for the companies which use it (Mygind and Poulsen, 2021). For companies, employee share ownership serves as an incentive mechanism that stimulates employees' efforts and helps align their interests with those of the company and its shareholders (Aubert et *al.*, 2016). It can also be an alternative form of financing which contributes to the stability of the shareholder structure, particularly in the event of financial difficulties or the risk of a takeover (Pugh et *al.*, 1999). For employees, share ownership offers an additional financial reward likely to lead to a more profitable sharing of the value created (Hollandts and Guedri, 2008). It sometimes even serves as a defensive mechanism which can help employees to protect their employment relationship (Kruse, 2022). Employee share ownership also gives employees certain rights of control and ownership which can help to rebalance power within the company (Desbrières, 1997a).

Offering employees the opportunity to become shareholders reflects the desire to create a "community of interest" within the company (Poulain-Rehm and Lepers, 2013). In this way, employee share ownership can be a meeting point for initially divergent interests, helping the company to move its internal stakeholders from a state of conflict to a climate of trust and cooperation (Desbrières, 2002). Given the capital-labour convergence it fosters in companies, employee share ownership can be a channel for exchanging valuable, less costly to transfer, and credible information between shareholders and employees (Guery and Stevenot, 2017). Compared with other shareholders, who may have only limited knowledge of the implementation of their company's strategies, employee shareholders have an informational advantage by being both employees and shareholders. Seen from this angle, the presence of employees at shareholder meetings may prevent managers from taking advantage of their informational advantage over other shareholders, by encouraging them to maximize the company's performance rather than their personal remuneration (Hollandts, 2018). According to Desbrières (2002), employee shareholders have a dual incentive to improve the effectiveness of their company's governance. To protect their dual investment, they can contribute to the alignment of interests between shareholders and managers, help to reduce information asymmetries and, above all, make the governance system preventive of potential conflicts and behavioral biases affecting decisions (Cardoni, 2020).

While employee ownership can be beneficial in a number of ways, it is not exempt from certain deviant behaviors, or even risks, for the companies that practice it. Employee share ownership can encourage the development of free rider behavior and make it easier for employees and managers to become entrenched (Desbrières, 2002; Aubert et *al.*, 2014). It can even sometimes discourage unionization and, at the same time, create conflicts between different groups of employees (Mygind and Poulsen, 2021). Employee ownership can also represent ownership without control on the part of employees, and thus constitute a transfer of financial risk onto them (Kaswan, 2022; Kruse, 2022). Added to this is the fact that it confers on employees an increased risk since they invest both human and financial capital in the same company (Blair, 1999; Blair et *al.*, 2000). These negative aspects of employee ownership have given rise to much debate, and their consideration generally conditions the nature of the relationship between employee ownership and corporate governance (Desbrières, 2002; Aubert et *al.*, 2014).

Furthermore, the literature indicates that employee shareholders generally have a low capacity for influence compared to other shareholders (Trébucq, 2002). The influence and role that employees can play in terms of governance may be insignificant when they only hold a small fraction of the capital (Faleye et *al.*, 2006). In this context, the literature indicates that the effects of employee share ownership vary according to the fraction of capital held by employees, the proportion of voting rights emanating from them and their potential representation on governance bodies (Toe et *al.*, 2017). Several researchers have shown that the capacity of employee shareholding to influence corporate governance is strictly linked to the levels it represents in the company's capital (Hollandts and Guedri, 2008; Kim and Ouimet, 2014; Garfatta and Zorgati, 2021).

1.3. The case of significant employee share ownership

While the question of the influence of employee shareholding on corporate governance has been widely studied in the literature (Desbrières, 2002; Guery and Stevenot, 2017; Cardoni, 2020; Abdelnoor et *al.*, 2022), the case of significant employee shareholding has so far rarely been addressed (Toe et *al.*, 2017). Significant employee ownership, as defined by Toe et *al.* (2017, p. 1), is: "*the impact of a major or even majority presence of employees in the capital and in the governance bodies*". It can strengthen employees' willingness and ability to exert pressure on their company from a governance point of view. Linking significant employee shareholding to corporate governance is tantamount to including the reflection on employee shareholding in its contribution to the overall performance of the corporate governance system. A review of the literature reveals that the case of significant employee share ownership can be analyzed from two perspectives. According to the first, employee-controlled companies are inefficient for various reasons and their rarity demonstrates that they are not a viable organizational form. Firstly, Jensen and Meckling (1979) argue that when employees become a major or even controlling shareholder group, this encourages entrenchment behavior and makes it difficult and less effective to exercise control within the company. In this vein, Hansmann (2000) has put forward the idea that decision-making becomes difficult and ineffective in employee-controlled companies because of the heterogeneity of their interests. Other studies warn of the presence of overall negative effects when employee ownership reaches a certain level and highlight a dark side of employee ownership (Guedri and Hollandts, 2008). In the United States, Faleye et *al* (2006) find that companies with a high fraction of capital (below 5%) held by employees invest less, take fewer risks, grow more slowly, create fewer new jobs, deviate more from the objective of maximizing shareholder value and are less productive. Indeed, when employees hold a high fraction of the capital, they can push managers to favor employees' interests, which can lead to a risk of loss of competitiveness for the company (Jensen and Meckling, 1979; Toe et *al.*, 2017). Furthermore, employee shareholders are generally reluctant to take risks because of their dual investment in the company (Bova et *al.*, 2015), and this risk aversion can lead to poor decision-making, particularly with regard to investment (Faleye et *al.*, 2006). On the other hand, Winkler et *al* (2019) point out that above a certain level, the benefits of employee share ownership can outweigh its drawbacks and create a climate of cooperation within the company. More recently, Wu et *al.* (2023) find that the probability of corporate financial fraud decreases significantly after adoption of ESO plans.

According to the second perspective, holding a significant or even majority shareholding gives employees significant bargaining power and a more profitable distribution of value (Rajan and Zingales, 1998; Blair et *al.*, 2000). In the case of France, Abdelnour et *al.* (2022) found that high levels of employee share ownership reduce agency costs. In this sense, Guery and Stevenot (2017) point out that employee share ownership, when it involves a significant share of the capital, is generally associated with a better circulation of information in the company. For these authors, employee share ownership can improve corporate governance by reducing information asymmetry within the company. Similarly, Cardoni (2020) shows that employee ownership contributes to strengthening the disciplinary and cognitive roles of the corporate governance system and leads to the prospect of more balanced and less conflictual governance. As pointed out by Blair et al (2000, p. 251) "*employee ownership, if widespread, is likely to encourage employees to monitor their colleagues and to use social pressure on them to encourage them to make efforts*". In this vein, Pugh et al (1999) note that employee shareholders can play an important role in minimizing "short-termist" management and excessive risk-taking. By becoming a major shareholder group, employees can help to improve corporate governance, by helping to mitigate conflicts of interest and reduce the information asymmetry experienced by other shareholders (Aubert et *al.*, 2016; Cardoni, 2020). This is likely to increase their power to act and may strengthen their willingness and ability to put pressure on their company and its management to comply with good governance practices (Ginglinger et *al.*, 2011). Some studies indicate that employee share ownership only has positive effects when employees hold a high fraction or even a majority of their company's capital (Aubert et *al.*, 2017; Abdenour et *al.*, 2022). For example, the work of Aubert et *al.* (2017), as well as that of Abdenour et *al.* (2022), shows that employee share ownership only reduces the company's agency costs when it is at a high level. For these authors, employee share ownership only becomes a real mechanism for aligning interests between shareholders and employees when the latter hold a high fraction, or even a majority, of the capital.

So, depending on whether we take the first or the second view, significant employee share ownership can be seen either as a source of inefficiency or as a factor for improving corporate governance. It is therefore possible to pose the following hypothesis:

Hypothesis 1: Significant employee share ownership influences the overall performance of the company's governance system.

1.4. The effect of employee shareholder representation on governance bodies

A notable feature of significant employee ownership is that it allows employees to sit on their company's board of directors (Toe et *al.*, 2017). In France, the Breton Act (2006) introduced employee ownership of at least 3% of the capital as the threshold above which the appointment of an employee shareholder representative to the board of directors becomes mandatory for listed companies. More recently, the PACTE Act (2019) reaffirmed this legal threshold of 3% employee share ownership and extended the scope of this obligation to large French non-listed companies. This obligation on large French companies to have employee shareholder representatives on the board of directors is based on the increasingly significant weight of employees in the capital of French companies (Hollandts et *al.*, 2011; Ginglinger et *al.*, 2011). This compulsory representation of employee share ownership on the boards of directors of large companies is today a "French originality", in the sense that it is virtually absent from the European and international landscape (EFES, 2021).

The Notat Sénard Report (2018, p.57, note 157) states that directors representing employee shareholders "*do not represent labor but a particular form of shareholding*". The participation of employees in governance bodies due to their significant weight in the capital of their company is of particular interest in the sense that it must take into account not only the interests of employees but also those of the company's shareholders (Cardoni, 2021). Directors representing employee shareholders have an interest in making the governance of their company more accountable, since this accountability depends not only on the value of their human capital but also on the value of their financial investment (Desbrières, 2002). However, the fact that this practice is virtually absent in the other European countries, and that it is imposed by law and not implemented voluntarily by companies, suggests that such representation does not only have advantages. The literature highlights the risk of possible attempts at collusion between directors representing employee shareholders and managers, which could make the exercise of control within the board of directors less effective (Desbrières, 1997; Toe et *al.*, 2017).

From the point of view of agency theory, the hierarchical dependency link between employee-shareholders and managers is likely to impair independence, create a climate of slackness, weaken the board's disciplinary function, and facilitate managerial entrenchment (Aubert et *al.*, 2014; Hollandts et *al.*, 2018). Indeed, directors representing employee shareholders are not sufficiently independent of their managers to exercise their governance role effectively and objectively (Hollandts et *al.*, 2011). In this context, Hollandts and Guedri (2008) show that the presence of directors representing employee shareholders weakens the positive effects of employee ownership on company performance. Gharbi and Lepers (2008) show that managers rely on employee ownership to become entrenched. Hollandts et *al.* (2018) show that employee shareholding representation on the board of directors weakens control mechanisms and encourages entrenchment behavior. Cardoni (2021) shows that employee shareholder representation on the board of directors also offers an opportunity for managerial entrenchment. On the other hand, the heterogeneity of employee shareholders' preferences due to their dual status, and the resulting ambiguity, overload, and role conflicts, may prevent directors representing employee ownership from effectively exercising their mandate (Desbrières, 2002; Toe et *al.*, 2017). Based on these arguments, we can pose the following hypothesis:

Hypothesis 2: Employee shareholder representation on the Board of Directors influences the overall performance of the company's governance system.

2. EMPIRICAL APPROACH

In this section, we present the sample, the variables and data sources, and the econometric approach adopted.

2.1. Sample

The research sample is made up of a panel of 102 listed French companies whose governance scores were surveyed over the period 2012-2021. The phenomenon of significant employee share ownership is particularly developed in large companies in France, which justifies restricting the sample mainly to listed companies. Moreover, collecting data on the performance of corporate governance systems becomes particularly difficult beyond companies belonging to the French SBF 120 stock market index. The initial sample for this study was subject to certain restrictions. We had to remove a number of companies whose data were missing. As a result, after adjustments, the sample is made up of 739 "company-year" observations, representing 102 SBF 120 companies, 33 of which belong to the CAC 40, over the 10 years studied. The sectoral breakdown of the sample is shown in table 1.

Table 1. Sectoral breakdown of the sample according to the GICS classification

GICS sectors	Companies		Observations	
	N	%	N	%
1-Energy	8	7.8	61	7.3
2-Consumer goods	12	11.8	106	12.4
3-Basic materials	6	5.9	57	6.6
4-Industry	21	20.6	182	21.2
5-Consumer services	13	12.7	108	12.6
6-Telecommunications	6	5.9	57	6.6
7-Health	7	6.9	42	4.9
8-Technology	16	15.6	136	15.8
9-Community services	13	12.7	108	12.6
Total	**102**	**100**	**739**	**100**

2.2. Variables and data sources

2.2.1. Dependent variable

The overall performance of the corporate governance system "GOV_Perf" is the dependent variable of the research. Given its multi-dimensional nature, we propose to assess it through the governance scores attributed by Refinitiv (formerly Thomson-Eikon). Refinitiv gathers information from various sources, such as registration reports, NGOs, the media, disclosures, company websites, etc., and covers more than 85% of the world's listed companies. With regard to governance data, Refinitiv provides each company, for each year, with a governance score ranging from 0 to 100 measured by 138 criteria, with a specific weighting for each criterion. More specifically, this score assesses the relevance of the commitments made in terms of governance by examining the practices adopted and questioning their scope within the company. Refinitiv's governance scores have recently been used by several researchers (Tangjitprom, 2013; Jahmane et *al.*, 2021; Guney et *al.*, 2020). Refinitiv evaluates companies in relation to their peers in the sector and in relation to context (national and international). This ensures that the data is not biased by institutional factors - particularly regulatory factors - specific to the countries and sectors in which the companies operate. This specificity of Refinitiv makes it possible to see how the company performs in relation to its peers in the sector, and to compare the performance of its governance system with that of other companies in the country and sector of activity. Refinitiv data is therefore used to establish the link between significant employee shareholding and corporate governance.

2.2.2. Independent variable

Significant employee share ownership is the independent variable of the research. Two approaches are considered to operationalize it. A first approach consists of relating the fraction of capital held by employees to the fraction of capital held by the majority shareholder (Toe et *al.*, 2017). This approach makes it possible to capture the significant weight of employee shareholding in relation to the controlling shareholder. Following the example of Toe et *al.* (2017) and Trébucq (2002), the percentage of capital held by employees is related to the percentage held by the majority shareholder "SIGN_ESO". A second approach consists of using a dummy variable which takes the value 1 if the employees hold a significant fraction of their company's capital. Researchers have highlighted the need to adopt the fraction of voting rights granted to employees as a measure of employee ownership (Faleye et *al.*, 2006; Guedri and Hollandts, 2008). Voting rights reflect the direct involvement of employees in company decision-making (Klein, 1987). Thus, levels of employee shareholding exceeding 3% of the capital in voting rights are used as significant employee shareholding thresholds "ESO $\geq$ 3" (Kim and Ouimet, 2014; Garfatta and Zorgati, 2021). The choice of the 3% threshold is justified by the fact that in France the legislator has introduced employee ownership of at least 3% of the capital as the threshold above which employee shareholding representation on the board of directors becomes mandatory for large companies (Loi PACTE, 2019). In addition, employee shareholding representation "ESO_Board" is measured by a binary variable which takes the value 1 if the company has at least one employee shareholding representative on the board of directors and 0 if it does not (Hollandts and Guedri, 2008; Hollandts et *al.*, 2011).

2.2.3. Control variables

Several corporate characteristics are associated with corporate governance and should therefore be included as control variables. Thus, we include several control variables likely to influence the relationship between significant employee ownership and corporate governance. These are, on the one hand, variables linked to the characteristics of the company, and, on the other hand, those linked to the ownership structure. Regarding firm characteristics, previous literature shows that firm size, debt, industry, and financial performance are important control variables in corporate governance (Guery and Stévenot, 2017; Abdelnoor et *al.*, 2022). Following Gillet-Monjarret and Martinez (2012), firm size "SIZE" is measured by the logarithm of sales. Financial performance "ROE" is measured by return on equity. Debt" is measured by the ratio of total debt to total assets. In addition, the existence of a CSR committee among the governance bodies reflects the quality of the company's governance (Gillet-Monjarret and Martinez, 2012). The "CSR_COMIT" variable is measured by a dichotomous variable that takes the value 1 if the company has a CSR committee, and 0 otherwise. Finally, the duality of the leader "DUAL" is also likely to influence the operation of the company's governance bodies (Abdelnoor et *al.*, 2022). This is operationalized by a binary variable that takes the value 1 if the executive is also chairman of the board of directors and 0 otherwise. With regard to ownership structure, the literature shows that the nature of the controlling shareholders is likely to influence the effectiveness and functioning of the corporate governance system (Gillet-Monjarret and Martinez, 2012). In the French context, most companies are controlled by managers and their families, and by institutional investors (Mard et *al.*, 2014). Following Elage and Dardour (2021), we used three binary variables to identify the nature of controlling ownership: "FAM" for controlling family ownership, "STATE" for controlling state ownership and "INST" for controlling institutional ownership. In this study, 10% of voting rights is used as the minimum threshold of control to distinguish the main shareholder (Boubaker and Sami, 2011).

2.3. Models and econometric approach

To analyse the influence of significant employee share ownership on the performance of the corporate governance system, the following econometric model is tested:

$$GOV\_Perf_{i,t} = \beta_0 + \beta_1\, SIGN\_ESO_{i,t} + \beta_2\, CONTROLS_{i,t} + \varepsilon_{i,t}$$

With: GOV_Perf = Overall performance of the governance system (Refinitiv scores); SIGN_ESO = Significant employee ownership; CONTROLS = Control variables; i = Index ranging from 1 to 102 companies; t = Annual changes 2012-2021; ε = Standard residual term.

In order to test hypothesis 2, a second econometric model incorporating the representation of employee share ownership on the Board of Directors "ESO_Board" and the same control variables is estimated. The model is as follows:

$$GOV\_Perf_{i,t} = \beta_0 + \beta_1\, ESO\_Board_{i,t} + \beta_2\, CONTROLS_{i,t} + \varepsilon_{i,t}$$

The econometric approach consists of conducting regression analyses on panel data for French companies in the SBF 120 stock market index over the period 2012-2021.

3. Results and discussion

In this section, we present the descriptive statistics, the regression results, and the robustness tests.

3.1. Descriptive Statistics

Table 2 presents the descriptive statistics for the sample. On average, the overall governance performance is 53. We can therefore deduce that the companies in the sample are characterized by an intermediate level of governance (according to the Refinitiv evaluation grid). This suggests that there is still room for improvement and that the companies in the sample need to continue their efforts in the area of corporate governance. We can see that this performance increases between 2013 and 2021 (Figure 2): the average was 48.48 in 2013, rising to 68.18 in 2021.

Table 2. Descriptive statistics

Variable	Mean	Standard deviation	Median	Minimum	Maximum
GOV_Perf	53.32	22.37	58.76	4.5	94.63
SIGN_ESO	0.096	0.17	0.035	0	1
SIZE	8.905	1.36	8.888	5.232	12.138
DEBT	0.476	0.56	0.317	0	5.351
ROE	0.084	0.28	0.091	-3.88	1.641
CSR_COMIT (binaire)	0.93				
INST (binaire)	0.242				
FAM (binaire)	0.330				
STATE (binaire)	0.118				
DUAL (binaire)	0.621				
ESO ≥ 3 (binaire)	0.332				
ESO_Board (binaire)	0.258				

The descriptive analysis of significant employee ownership indicates that, compared to controlling shareholders, employees hold an average percentage of voting rights of 9.6%, with a disparity of 1.7%. Figure 3 shows the evolution of the overall performance of the governance system and the average level of employee share ownership for the companies in the sample over the study period.

Figure 3. Evolution of employee share ownership and governance performance (Refinitiv score) between 2012 and 2021

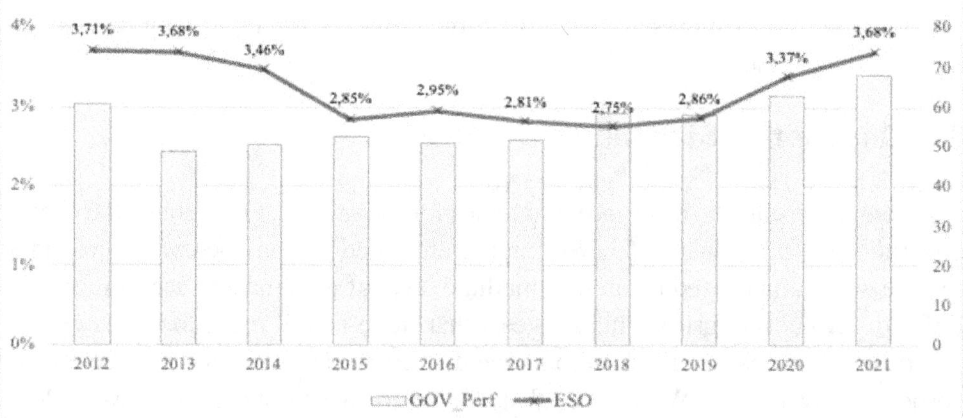

It should also be noted that a third of the companies in the sample have employee share ownership exceeding 3% of the capital. It then appears that 25.8% of the companies in the sample have at least one director representing employee shareholders on the board of directors. This means that there are still companies that do not have any employee shareholder directors, even though they have an employee share ownership exceeding the legal threshold of 3% of the capital. Figure 4 shows the evolution of the average level of employee shareholding representation on the board of the companies in the sample over the study period. The representation of employee share ownership on boards of directors has been increasing in recent years. A significant increase in the number of companies with directors representing employee shareholders has been noted since 2020. This can be attributed to the entry into force of the PACTE Act in 2019. It should be noted that directors representing employee shareholders now sit in 37 SBF 120 companies, compared with 21 in 2012.

Figure 4. Change in employee shareholder representation on the board of directors and governance performance (Refinitiv score) between 2012 and 2021

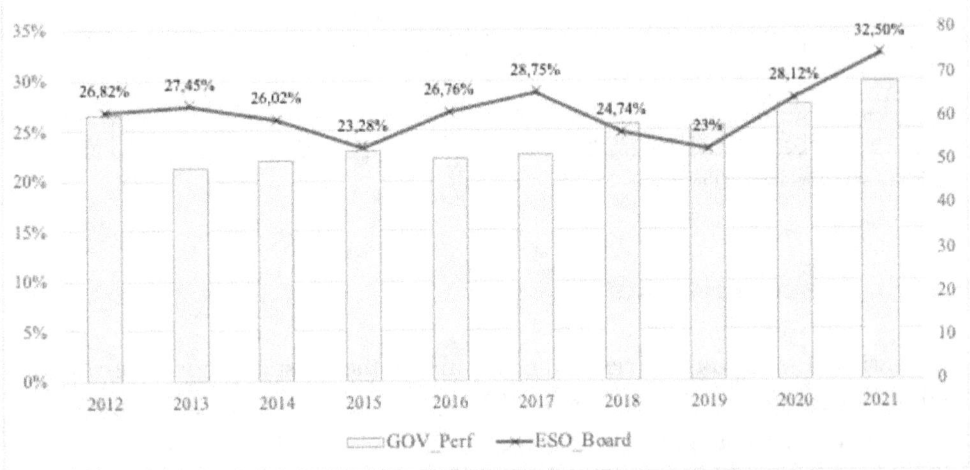

In terms of company characteristics, the statistical results (table 3) show an average financial performance of 8.40%. In addition, the companies in the sample vary widely in size, with a high degree of dispersion, since the standard deviation is 1.36. It should also be noted that 93% of the companies in the sample have a CSR committee. Lastly, table 3 shows that the majority of companies are controlled by families and institutional investors, which reflects the specificity of the French context in terms of ownership structure (Mard et *al.*, 2014). In fact, 33.2% of the companies in the sample have a controlling family shareholding, and 24.2% are controlled by institutional investors.

The Pearson correlation coefficients are presented in Table 3. The results show that the various correlation coefficients are below 0.8, the limit set by Kennedy (1992), indicating the absence of bi-variate multi-colinearity between the various independent variables.

Table 3. Variable correlation matrix

	1	2	3	4	5	6	7	8	9	10	11
1.GOV_Perf	1										
2. SIGN_ESO	0.06	1									
3.ESO_Board	-0.07*	0.49*	1								
4.SIZE	0.11	0.22*	0.40	1							
5.DEBT	0.05	-0.04	0.01	-0.05	1						
6.ROE	-0.02	-0.02	-0.06	-0.01*	-0.16*	1					
7.CSR_COMIT	0.19*	0.08	0.12	0.19	-0.01	0.04*	1				
8.INST	0.06*	-0.09	-0.15	-0.03	0.00*	0.01	0.00*	1			
9.FAM	-0.30	-0.13*	-0.22	-0.08*	-0.02*	0.03	-0.01	-0.04	1		
10.STATE	-0.18	0.14*	0.11	0.12*	0.03	0.02*	0.04	0.07	0.05	1	
11.DUAL	-0.22*	0.01	0.00	0.08	-0.01	0.05	-0.19	-0.20	0.22*	0.11	1

*Significant correlation at threshold ≤10%.

3.2. Regression Results

A series of tests were carried out to determine the most appropriate estimation method. According to Wooldridge (2010), it is appropriate to use the method of quasi-generalized least squares (Feasible GLS) to solve the heteroscedasticity problem. Table 4 presents the results of the FGLS regression analyses. It can be seen from this table that the effect of significant employee ownership on the performance of the governance system is positive and significant (model 1: $\beta = 3.94$; $p < 5\%$), which validates hypothesis 1. This result is consistent with those of Aubert et *al.* (2017), as well as those of Abdenour et *al.* (2022), showing that employee share ownership reduces agency costs in the company only when it is at a high level. This implies that employee share ownership becomes a real mechanism for aligning interests between shareholders and employees when the latter hold a significant or even majority fraction of the capital. In fact, holding a significant or even major fraction of the capital seems to offer employees significant bargaining power, which may lead them to improve corporate governance by helping to mitigate conflicts of interest and reduce information asymmetry within the company (Blair et *al.*, 2000). Contrary to the work of Faleye et *al.* (2006) and Toe et *al.* (2017), it seems that high employee share ownership improves corporate governance in French companies.

The results also show that companies with employees holding at least 3% of the capital in exercisable voting rights perform well in terms of governance (model 2: $\beta = 3.74$; $p < 1\%$), which corroborates hypothesis 1. This result is in line with the analyses of Abdelnour et *al.* (2022) and Winkler et *al.* (2019), who emphasize that above a certain level, the benefits of employee share ownership can offset its drawbacks and create a climate of cooperation within the company. Ownership of a significant proportion of the capital is accompanied by an increase in voting rights and guarantees them representation on the board of directors, which makes it possible to exercise closer control over management (Desbrières, 2002). It should be remembered that in France, the Breton Act (2006) only requires employee shareholding to be represented on the Board of Directors when employees hold at least 3% of the capital. On this point, Nekhili et *al* (2021) show that the presence of employee shareholders on the board has a positive impact on governance performance. When they hold a high proportion of the capital and therefore of the voting rights on decisions, employees can exert considerable influence on the direction and choices of the company (Kaswan, 2022).

Furthermore, model 3 shows a negative and significant effect of employee shareholding representation on the board of directors on the overall performance of the company's governance system (β= -49.4; $p < 1\%$). This result can be attributed to the entrenchment of managers. Indeed, directors representing employee shareholders are not sufficiently independent from their managers to properly and objectively exercise their governance role (Aubert et *al.*, 2014). According to Desbrières (1997a), collusion may exist between managers and employee shareholder representatives on the board of directors with the aim of making the exercise of control within the board of directors less effective. According to Gharbi and Lepers (2008), the hierarchical dependency link between employee shareholders and managers may encourage the latter to rally the directors representing employee shareholders to their own causes. In this sense, the presence of implicit contracts (promises of promotion, extra pay or job retention, for example) can reinforce the dependence of employees on their managers (Cardoni, 2020). This is consistent with the perspective of agency theory, which considers that this lack of independence is likely to weaken the disciplinary function of the Board, create a climate of relaxation and facilitate managerial entrenchment (Hollandts et *al.*, 2011). This result is in line with that of Hollandts et *al.* (2018), who argue that directors representing employee shareholders strengthen managerial entrenchment and that their presence weakens control mechanisms.

These different aspects can to a large extent explain the negative effect of directors representing employee ownership (Hollandts et *al.*, 2018).

Table 4. FGLS regression results

Variables	(1) GOV_Perf	(2) GOV_Perf	(3) GOV_Perf
SIGN_ESO	**3.94**** (2.33)**	–	44.88** (5.61)
ESO ≥ 3	–	**3.47*** (2.73)**	–
ESO_Board	–	–	**-49.4*** (-5.63)**
SIZE	1.51*** (4.64)	1.61*** (4.04)	1.818*** (4.10)
INST	38.6*** (20.37)	4.35*** (3.17)	3.197** (2.41)
FAM	-6.99*** (-7.50)	-11.2*** (-9.12)	-11.11*** (-9.40)
STATE	-4.12** (2.42)	-11.02* (1.98)	-5.66** (2,22)
CSR_COMIT	14.2*** (-5.46)	15.21*** (7.69)	-19.2** (-5.46)
DEBT	-0.880 (-1.30)	-0.378 (-0.47)	2.653 (1.07)
ROE	-0.020 (-0.01)	-0.103 (-0.05)	-1.776 (-0.30)
DUAL	-6.77*** (-7.00)	-7.95*** (-6.76)	-7.255** (-2.23)
Intercept	41.10*** (4.23)	43.95*** (8.65)	-42.87*** (-8.57)
Year	Yes	Yes	Yes
Sector	Yes	Yes	Yes
N observations	739	739	739
N companies	102	102	102
Hausman test (p-value)	0.000	0.012	0.001
Breusch–Pagan test (p-value)	0.018	0.036	0.022
Wooldridge test (p-value)	0.612	0.877	0.824
Wald $\chi 2$	1157.09***	515.49***	561.44***

***, **, * represent significance at 1%, 5% and 10% thresholds respectively.

With regard to the control variables, Table 4 shows that company size has a positive and significant influence on corporate governance. According to Elage and Dardour (2021), large companies are often subject to external pressure to comply with "good" governance practices. In addition, companies with a CSR committee have better governance performance. It can also be seen that dual leadership has a negative effect on corporate governance. When the executive is also chairman of the board, this can weaken control mechanisms and restrict the ability of directors to exercise their roles effectively and objectively (Krause et *al.*, 2014). With regard to ownership structure variables, the presence of controlling institutional shareholding has a positive influence on governance. The results also indicate that controlling state ownership has a negative effect on the quality of corporate governance. In line with Barnea and Rubin (2010), the state generally pursues divergent objectives (notably political) that may be in conflict with good corporate governance. Finally, the results show that family-controlled firms are characterized by poor corporate governance performance. In fact, governance problems are often present in family businesses because of the transmission issues (Abdelnour et *al.*, 2022).

3.3. Robustness analysis: checking endogeneity

In this research, it is possible that other unobservable factors affect the study variables. There is therefore the possibility of a problem of unobserved heterogeneity. In addition, the risk of delayed causality between variables cannot be ruled out (Semadeni et *al.,* 2014). Faced with these endogeneity problems from which most econometric studies on corporate governance suffer (Guery and Stevenot, 2017) and which are likely to arise in this research, the Generalized Method of Moments (GMM) estimator is employed in regression analyses (Blundell and Bond, 1998). The use of the GMM estimator is appropriate given the structure of the data.

Model 1 (Table 5) shows that significant employee ownership has a positive effect on the performance of the governance system ($\beta = 21.36$; $p < 5\%$), which confirms hypothesis 1. It also emerges that employee share ownership exceeding 3% in voting rights has a positive effect on corporate governance (model 2: $\beta = 4.98$; $p < 5\%$). It can also be noted that the presence of directors representing employee shareholders negatively affects the overall performance of the company's governance system (model 4: $\beta = -78.58$; $p < 5\%$). In sum, it can be seen that the main results of the GMM estimates presented in Table 5 are similar to those of the FGLS regressions (Table 4), which confirms the results by controlling for the endogeneity of the models tested.

Table 5. GMM regression results

Variables	**(4) GOV_Perf**	**(5) GOV_Perf**	**(6) GOV_Perf**
GOV_Perf t-1	0.037*** (5.84)	0.04*** (5.83)	0.062*** (5.46)
SIGN_ESO	**21.3603**** **(2.02)**	–	–
ESO ≥ 3	–	**4.986**** **(2.70)**	–
ESO_ Board	–	–	**-78.58**** **(-2.90)**
SIZE	-0.8745 (-0.76)	-0.8872 (-0.75)	3.842*** (3.09)
FAM	1.6671 (0.33)	2.719 (0.55)	-9.566** (-2.75)
INST	72.855*** (9.45)	74.17*** (9.42)	4.284 (1.53)
STATE	-9.91* (-1.98)	-11.47** (-2.02)	-4.35** (-2.32)
DUAL	-11.07*** (-3.21)	-12.83*** (-3.80)	-14.0*** (-4.14)
DEBT	0.84* (1.97)	0.824 (0.39)	-0.1688 (-0.08)
CSR_COMIT	24.54*** (3.50)	24.94*** (3.48)	25.53*** (3.71)
ROE	6.159* (1.78)	7.69** (2.23)	2.041 (0.60)
Intercept	37.92*** (6.59)	38.09*** (6.47)	-40.42*** (-7.32)
Year	Yes	Yes	Yes
Sector	Yes	Yes	Yes
N observations	606	606	606
N companies	102	102	102
AR 1 test (p-value)	0.000	0.000	0.000
AR 2 test (p-value)	0.861	0.612	0.511
Sargan test (p-value)	0.791	0.601	0.998

***, **, * represent significance at 1%, 5% and 10% thresholds respectively.

3.4. Additional analysis: the threshold effect of employee share ownership

To further investigate and better understand the relationship between significant employee ownership and the overall performance of the governance system, the potential threshold effect related to employee ownership was analyzed. In line with previous work (Faleye et *al.,* 2006; Kim and Ouimet, 2014; Garfatta and Zorgati, 2021), we used binary variables that take the value 1 if the employee shareholding belongs, alternatively, to the level: [0% - 3%]; [3% - 10%]; [10% - 15%]; [15% and more] of the capital in voting rights, and 0 in the opposite case.

Table 6 presents the results of GMM regressions testing the threshold effect between employee ownership and the overall performance of the corporate governance system. The results show that employee ownership levels below 3% have no significant effect on the overall performance of the corporate governance system (model 7). This can be explained by the low levels of employee shareholding compared to the shareholding structure of large companies. Indeed, if they only have a limited fraction of the capital and therefore of the voting rights in decisions, employee shareholders find themselves in a situation of powerlessness in the face of the controlling shareholders who exert a decisive influence on the company's orientations and choices (Kaswan, 2022). The results also show that employee shareholding levels of between 3% and 10% of voting rights have a positive and significant effect on the overall performance of the company's governance system (model 8: β= 5.0003; $p < 5\%$). This result is consistent with that of Aubert et *al.* (2017) and Abdenour et *al.* (2022), who show that employee share ownership only reduces agency costs in the company when it is at a high level. Secondly, we find that levels of employee shareholding of between 10% and 15% of voting rights have no significant effect on the overall performance of the corporate governance system. This result is in line with that of Dondi (1992), who observes that employee share ownership has beneficial effects as the proportion of capital held by employees increases, until it reaches 10%. Beyond this threshold, the beneficial effects of employee share ownership tend to decrease. Nonetheless, model 10 shows that companies with employee share ownership levels exceeding 15% of capital by voting rights are characterized by good governance performance (β= 19.569; $p < 1\%$). In this respect, Winkler et *al.* (2019) point out that above a certain level, the benefits of employee ownership can outweigh its drawbacks and create a climate of cooperation within the company.

In summary, the results clearly illustrate the existence of a threshold effect in the relationship between employee ownership and the overall performance of the corporate governance system. Taken together, the results show that employee ownership of less than 3% of the capital has no effect on corporate governance. On the other hand, levels of employee share ownership between 3% and 10% and exceeding

15% of the capital in terms of voting rights have positive and significant effects on the overall performance of the company's governance system.

Table 6. GMM regressions testing the threshold effect of employee share ownership

Variables	**(7)**	**(8)**	**(9)**	**(10)**
	GOV_Perf	**GOV_Perf**	**GOV_Perf**	**GOV_Perf**
GOV_Perf t-1	-0.1237***	-0.0793**	-0.1468***	-0.156***
	(-3.24)	(-2.12)	(-3.91)	(-3.97)
ESO [0 – 3%]	**-1.7320**	–	–	–
	(-0.90)			
ESO [3% - 10%]	–	**5.0003****	–	–
		(2.51)		
ESO [10% – 15%]	–	–	**4.3371**	–
			(1.53)	
ESO [15% et +]	–	–	–	**19.569*****
				(3.23)
DUAL	-7.330***	-5.6015**	-14.773***	-14.688***
	(-2.65)	(-2.09)	(-5.78)	(-4.21)
FAM	-11.066***	-10.109***	-14.532***	-18.602***
	(-3.90)	(-3.05)	(-5.24)	(-5.14)
INST	43.223***	52.973***	35.149***	61.976***
	(5.31)	(6.17)	(3.70)	(5.54)
STATE	-11.44* (-1.98)	-10.02 (-1.40)	12.05** (-2.32)	-11.12* (-1.97)
CSR_COMIT	-10.628	-22.652**	-12.602	-8.1488
	(-1.35)	(-2.59)	(-1.39)	(-0.86)
DEBT	-3.1346**	-4.0337**	-3.697**	-5.2138**
	(-1.84)	(-2.28)	(-2.25)	(-2.80)
SIZE	-2.7382**	-4.0955***	-0.2512	-0.6457
	(-2.59)	(-3.59)	(-0.28)	(0.48)
ROE	-10.68***	-7.680**	-5.6119	-6.4679
	(-2.73)	(-1.99)	(-1.38)	(-1.50)
Intercept	-59,37***	-65.79***	-57.12***	-61.41***
	(-10.51)	(-11.30)	(-10.67)	(-10.72)
Year	Yes	Yes	Yes	Yes
Sector	Yes	Yes	Yes	Yes

continued on following page

Table 6. Continued

Variables	(7)	(8)	(9)	(10)
N observations	627	627	627	627
N companies	102	102	102	102
AR (1) test (p-value)	0.000	0.000	0.001	0.002
AR (2) test (p-value)	0.056	0.138	0.155	0.082
Sargan test (p-value)	0.442	0.118	0.284	0.415

***, **, * represent significance at 1%, 5% and 10% thresholds respectively.

CONCLUSION

The aim of this research was to examine the impact of high or even majority employee share ownership on the overall performance of the company's governance system. Although there is an abundant literature linking employee ownership to corporate governance, very few studies have focused on analyzing changes in corporate governance in the context of significant employee ownership (Toe et *al.*, 2017; Guery and Stevenot, 2017). This research is based on arguments suggesting that employee shareholders have a twofold incentive to improve the effectiveness of their company's governance, since this improvement depends not only on their investment in financial capital, but also in human capital (Desbrières, 2002). By becoming a major shareholder group, employees can help to improve the governance of their company, by helping to mitigate conflicts of interest and reduce the asymmetry of information experienced by other shareholders (Cardoni, 2020). It is assumed that significant employee shareholding and the resulting representation on the board of directors affect the overall performance of the company's governance system.

Analysis of a sample of companies listed on the SBF 120 stock market index between 2012 and 2021 shows that significant employee shareholding has a positive effect on corporate governance. To control for the potential endogeneity problems that most econometric studies on corporate governance suffer from (Guery and Stevenot, 2017), the generalized method of moments (GMM) estimator was employed in our regression analyses (Blundell and Bond, 1998). The results were confirmed by checking the endogeneity of the models tested. In parallel with the analysis of the influence of significant employee ownership on corporate governance, we analyzed the threshold effect linked to employee ownership. We find that an employee shareholding exceeding 3% of the capital in voting rights improves corporate governance, while an employee shareholding of less than 3% of the capital has no significant effect on corporate governance. The results also show that levels of employee share ownership between 3% and 10% and exceeding 15% of the capital in terms of voting rights have positive and significant effects on the overall performance of the company's system of governance. This supports the French legislator's ambition to achieve a 10% employee shareholding in company capital by 2030. The absence of a significant relationship below 3% of the capital can be explained by the relatively low levels of employee shareholding compared to the ownership structure of large companies. Of course, if the proportion held by employees is very low, employee shareholders find themselves powerless in the face of controlling shareholders who exert a decisive influence on the company's direction.

We also studied the effects of employee shareholding representation on the board of directors. French legislation requires the presence of at least one employee shareholder representative on the board of directors once employees collectively hold more than 3% of their company's share capital. The results show that employee shareholding representation on the board negatively affects the overall performance of the company's governance system. To this end, employee shareholder representatives are often identified as natural allies of managers (Hollandts et *al.*, 2018). According to Desbrières (1997a), collusion may exist between managers and employee shareholder representatives on the board of directors aimed at making the exercise of control within the board of directors less effective.

The conclusion to be drawn from this research is that significant employee ownership improves corporate governance. Thus, companies should understand that it is in their governance interest to favor the development of employee share ownership. This implies that significant employee ownership can be seen by the company's external partners, and in particular investors, as a sign of more responsible and long-term governance. One of the major contributions of this research is that it focuses on the particular case of significant employee ownership, which is rarely studied in the literature. In addition, this research suggests a number of recommendations that could help companies in their choice of ownership structure and could enlighten regulators on the issue of good governance practices. In addition, this research highlights the fact that employee shareholder representation on the board of directors has negative effects in terms of governance. Regulators could consider measures to better supervise the practice of employee shareholder representation on boards of directors, focusing on the influence of managers. Beyond these implications, this research has certain limitations that open up avenues for future research. The main limitation of this work is the purely quantitative method adopted. Other research could therefore strengthen and extend our results by using qualitative methods. Furthermore, the fact that employee shareholder representation on the board of directors negatively affects corporate governance merits further investigation. Another extension of this research would be to extend the analysis to other contexts.

REFERENCES

Abdelnour, J. A., Aubert, N., and Campa, D. (2022), "Does employee ownership decrease agency costs? Evidence from French listed companies", *Finance Contrôle Stratégie*, n° 25-3/4.

Alchian, A. A., & Demsetz, H. (1972). Production, information costs, and economic organization. *The American Economic Review*, 62(5), 777–795.

Arellano, M., & Bond, S. (1991). Some tests of specification for panel data: Monte Carlo evidence and an application to employment equations. *The Review of Economic Studies*, 58(2), 277–297. DOI: 10.2307/2297968

Aubert, N., Chassagnon, V., & Hollandts, X. (2016). Employee ownership, governance and firm performance: An econometric case study of a listed French group. *Revue d'Economie Industrielle*, (154), 151–176. DOI: 10.4000/rei.6365

Aubert, N., Garnotel, G., Lapied, A., & Rousseau, P. (2014). Employee ownership: A theoretical and empirical investigation of management entrenchment vs. reward management. *Economic Modelling*, 40(2), 423–434. DOI: 10.1016/j.econmod.2013.12.011

Aubert, N., Kern, A., & Hollandts, X. (2017). Employee stock ownership and the cost of capital. *Research in International Business and Finance*, 41(16), 67–78. DOI: 10.1016/j.ribaf.2017.04.007

Barnea, A., & Rubin, A. (2010). Corporate social responsibility as a conflict between shareholders. *Journal of Business Ethics*, 97(1), 71–86. DOI: 10.1007/s10551-010-0496-z

Berle, A., & Means, G. (1932). *The Modern Corporation and the Private Property*. Mc Millan.

Blair, M. (1999). Firm-Specific Human Capital and Theories of the Firm. In Blair, M., & Roe, M. (Eds.), *Employees & Corporate Governance* (pp. 58–90). Brooking Institution Press.

Blair, M., Kruse, D., & Blasi, J. (2000). Is employee ownership an unstable form or a stabilizing force? In Kochan, T., & Blair, M. (Eds.), *The new relationship: Human capital in the American Corporation* (pp. 241–288). The Brookings Institution. DOI: 10.2139/ssrn.142146

Blundell, R., & Bond, S. (1998). Initial conditions and moment restrictions in dynamic panel data models. *Journal of Econometrics*, 87(1), 115–143. DOI: 10.1016/S0304-4076(98)00009-8

Boubaker, S., & Sami, H. (2011). Multiple large shareholders and earnings informativeness. *Review of Accounting and Finance*, 10(3), 246–266. DOI: 10.1108/14757701111155789

Bova, F., Kolev, K., Thomas, J. K., & Zhang, X. F. (2015). Non-executive employee ownership and corporate risk. *The Accounting Review*, 90(1), 115–145. DOI: 10.2308/accr-50860

Cardoni, H. (2020), "Contribution à la connaissance de l'impact de l'actionnariat salarié sur la gouvernance des entreprises", *Entreprise & société*, no. 5, pp. 147-176.

Cardoni, H. (2021), "Le rôle de l'administrateur actionnaire salarié dans la gouvernance de l'entreprise: entre dualité et légitimité", *Finance Contrôle Stratégie*, ns° 24-4.

Charreaux, G. (1997). *Le Gouvernement Des Entreprises – Corporate Governance: Theories Et faits*. Economica.

Charreaux, G. (2002). "L'actionnaire comme apporteur de ressources cognitives". *Revue française de gestion*, n° 5, p. 77-107.

Charreaux, G. (2005). "Pour une gouvernance d'entreprise "comportementale" Une réflexion exploratoire..." *Revue française de gestion*, vol. 157, n°4, pp. 215-238.

Charreaux, G. (2011), "Quelle théorie pour la gouvernance? De la gouvernance actionnariale à la gouvernance cognitive et comportementale", Working Paper FARGO n° 1110402.

Crifo, P., & Rebérioux, A. (2019). *La participation des salariés. Du partage d'information à la codétermination*. Presses de Sciences Po.

Desbrières, P. (1997a). Le rôle de l'actionnariat des salariés non-dirigeants dans le système de gouvernement de l'entreprise. In *Le GE*. Economica.

Desbrières, P. (2002). Les actionnaires salariés. *Revue Française de Gestion*, (5), 255–281.

Dondi, J. (1992). *Contribution à la connaissance de l'actionnariat des salariés dans les entreprises françaises*. Diss.

Elage, A., & Dardour, A. (2021). *Rémunérations incitatives des dirigeants et gestion réelle des résultats: quel impact de la structure de l'actionnariat? Le cas des sociétés cotées au SBF 120*. Finance Contrôle Stratégie.

Faleye, O., Mehrotra, V., & Morck, R. (2006). When labor has a voice in corporate governance. *Journal of Financial and Quantitative Analysis*, 41(3), 489–510. DOI: 10.1017/S0022109000002519

Fama, E. F. (1980). Agency problems and the theory of the firm. *Journal of Political Economy*, 88(2), 288–307. DOI: 10.1086/260866

Freeman, R. E. (1984, 2010), *Strategic management: A stakeholder approach*, Cambridge University Press.

Garfatta, R., & Zorgati, I. (2021). Employee stock ownership and value creation: Evidence from system GMM estimates. *Managerial Finance*, 47(9), 1270–1285. DOI: 10.1108/MF-10-2020-0517

Gharbi, H., & Lepers, X. (2008). Actionnariat salarié et enracinement des dirigeants: Un essai de compréhension. *Innovations (Paris)*, (1), 121–146. DOI: 10.3917/inno.027.0121

Gillet-Monjarret, C., & Martinez, I. (2012). La vérification sociétale des entreprises du SBF 120: L'impact de la structure de propriété et du conseil d'administration. *Comptabilité Contrôle Audit*, 18(3), 43–66. DOI: 10.3917/cca.183.0043

Ginglinger, E., Megginson, W., & Waxin, T. (2011). Employee ownership, board representation, and corporate financial policies. *Journal of Corporate Finance*, 17(4), 868–887. DOI: 10.1016/j.jcorpfin.2011.03.005

Guedri, Z., & Hollandts, X. (2008). Beyond dichotomy: The curvilinear impact of employee ownership on firm performance. *Corporate Governance*, 16(5), 460–474. DOI: 10.1111/j.1467-8683.2008.00703.x

Guery, L., and Stévenot, A. (2017), "Does employee share ownership promote the dissemination of information to employees and their participation in strategic decisions? Une question de gouvernance d'entreprise", *Management international*, vol. 21, No. 4, pp. 61-75.

Guney, Y., Hernandez-Perdomo, E., & Rocco, C. M. (2020). Does relative strength in corporate governance improve corporate performance? Empirical evidence using MCDA approach. *The Journal of the Operational Research Society*, 71(10), 1593–1618. DOI: 10.1080/01605682.2019.1621216

Hansmann, H. (2000). *The ownership of enterprise*. Harvard University Press.

Hollandts, X. (2018). Friend or foe? Employee ownership and CEO dismissal. *MDE. Managerial and Decision Economics*, 39(4), 377–388. DOI: 10.1002/mde.2911

Hollandts, X., and Guedri, Z. (2008), “Les salariés capitalistes et la performance de l'entreprise”, *Revue française de gestion*, n° 3, p. 35-50.

Hollandts, X., Guedri, Z., and Aubert, N. (2011), “Les déterminants de la représentation des actionnaires salariés au conseil d'administration ou de surveillance”, *Management international*, vol. 15, No. 4, pp. 69-82.

Jahmane, A., Hofaidhllaoui, M., & Ali, A. B. (2021), “La gouvernance responsable, moyen d’assurer une performance financière en période de crises et post-crise?”, *Management & Sciences Sociales*, vol. 31, n° 4-21.

Jensen, M. C., & Meckling, W. H. (1976). Theory of the firm: Managerial behavior, agency costs and ownership structure. *Journal of Financial Economics*, 3(4), 305–360. DOI: 10.1016/0304-405X(76)90026-X

Jensen, M. C., & Meckling, W. H. (1979). Rights and production functions: An application to labor-managed firms and codetermination. *The Journal of Business*, 52(4), 469–506. DOI: 10.1086/296060

Kaswan, M. J. (2022). Property, ownership and employee ownership: Employee control in ESOPs. *Journal of Participation and Employee Ownership*, 5(1), 14–31. DOI: 10.1108/JPEO-11-2020-0028

Kim, E. H., & Ouimet, P. (2014). Broad-based employee stock ownership: Motives and outcomes. *The Journal of Finance*, 69(3), 1273–1319. DOI: 10.1111/jofi.12150

Klein, K. J. (1987). Employee stock ownership and employee attitudes: A test of three models. *The Journal of Applied Psychology*, 72(2), 319–332. DOI: 10.1037/0021-9010.72.2.319 PMID: 3583982

Krause, R., Semadeni, M., & Cannella, A. A.Jr. (2014). CEO duality: A review and research agenda. *Journal of Management*, 40(1), 256–286. DOI: 10.1177/0149206313503013

Kruse, D. (2022). Does employee ownership improve performance? *IZA World of Labor: Evidence-Based Policy Making*. Advance online publication. DOI: 10.15185/izawol.311.v2

Mard, Y., Marsat, S., & Roux, F. (2014). *Structure de l’actionnariat et performance financière de l’entreprise: le cas français*. Finance Contrôle Stratégie.

Mygind, N., & Poulsen, T. (2021). Employee ownership-pros and cons-a review. *Journal of Participation and Employee Ownership*, 4(2), 136–173. DOI: 10.1108/JPEO-08-2021-0003

Nekhili, M., Boukadhaba, A., & Nagati, H. (2021). The ESG-financial performance relationship: Does the type of employee board representation matter? *Corporate Governance*, 29(2), 134–161. DOI: 10.1111/corg.12345

Park, R., Kruse, D., & Sesil, J. (2004). Does employee ownership enhance firm survival? In *Employee participation, firm performance and survival*. Emerald Group Publishing Limited. DOI: 10.1016/S0885-3339(04)08001-9

Poulain-Rehm, T., & Lepers, X. (2013). Does employee ownership benefit value creation? The case of France (2001-2005). *Journal of Business Ethics*, 112(2), 325–340. DOI: 10.1007/s10551-012-1255-0

Pugh, W. N., Jahera, J. S., & Oswald, S. (1999). ESOPs, takeover protection, and corporate decision-making. *Journal of Economics and Finance*, 23(2), 170–183. DOI: 10.1007/BF02745951

Rajan, R. G., & Zingales, L. (1998). Power in a Theory of the Firm. *The Quarterly Journal of Economics*, 113(2), 387–432. DOI: 10.1162/003355398555630

Semadeni, M., Withers, M. C., & Trevis Certo, S. (2014). The perils of endogeneity and instrumental variables in strategy research: Understanding through simulations. *Strategic Management Journal*, 35(7), 1070–1079. DOI: 10.1002/smj.2136

St-Pierre, J., Gagnon, J. M., & Saint-Pierre, J. (1996). Concentration of voting rights and board resistance to takeover bids. *Journal of Corporate Finance*, 3(1), 25–54. DOI: 10.1016/S0929-1199(96)00008-9

Tangjitprom, N. (2013). The role of corporate governance in reducing the negative effect of earnings management. *International Journal of Economics and Finance*, 5(3), •••. DOI: 10.5539/ijef.v5n3p213

Toe, S. D., Hollandts, X., & Valiorgue, B. (2017). *The "dark side" of employee ownership: An empirical study on the SBF 120 index (2000-2014)* (Vol. 20). Finance Contrôle Stratégie.

Trébucq, S. (2002). L'actionnariat salarié dans les entreprises familiales du SBF250: Un outil de création de valeur. *Finance Contrôle Stratégie*, 5(4), 107–135.

Winkler, A. L. P., Brown, J. A., & Finegold, D. L. (2019). Employees as conduits for effective stakeholder engagement: An example from B corporations. *Journal of Business Ethics*, 160(4), 913–936. DOI: 10.1007/s10551-018-3924-0

Wirtz, P. (2011). The cognitive dimension of corporate governance in fast growing entrepreneurial firms. *European Management Journal*, 29(6), 431–447. DOI: 10.1016/j.emj.2011.06.004

Wooldridge, J. M. (2010). *Econometric analysis of cross section and panel data.* MIT press.

Wu, F., Cao, J., & Zhang, X. (2023). Do non-executive employees matter in curbing corporate financial fraud? *Journal of Business Research*, 163, 1–17. DOI: 10.1016/j.jbusres.2023.113922

ENDNOTES

1 Source: https://www.amundi-ee.com/entr/Local-Content/News/Barometre-2020-de-l-actionnariat-salarie-succes-du-dispositif-notamment-chez-les-ETI?xtmc=barom%C3%A8tre&xtcr=7&xtnp=1

2 Where the managers are not the owners.

Chapter 9
Comparing Employee Ownership Models in Iran and Western Economies:
Bridging Perspectives

Amirhossein Nozari
ICN Business School, France

ABSTRACT

From agency theory perspective, employee ownership is a decisive factor in reducing agency problem and it can improve firms' performance. In recent years many countries especially western countries implement certain employees' ownership plans, for example, Employee Stock Ownership Plan (ESOP) in the U.S. Iran also introduced Preferred shares plan. According to this plan, the companies' shares are able to be sold in the form of Preferred shares to the employees. This chapter investigated the differences of employees' ownership plans in Iran and western countries including USA, France, Spain and the UK. The findings indicated that there are many differences between employees' ownership plans of Iran and western countries; such as the plans of the western countries which were reviewed are in both private and state-owned companies; however, the plan of Iran is only for state-owned companies.

1. INTRODUCTION

The defective performance of state-owned enterprises in the 1970s led to the popularity of privatization in the early 1980s. Afterward, privatization was supported by most developed countries. For example, United Kingdom began to privatize state-

DOI: 10.4018/979-8-3693-7031-5.ch009

owned enterprises. Furthermore, due to the economic challenges and inefficiencies faced by public sectors, emerging countries have paid special attention to privatization as an important economic reform program. One prominent characteristic of privatization across numerous nations is the implementation of various kinds of modalities of employee share ownership plans. As an emerging country, Iran has introduced an employee ownership plan. However, challenges associated with privatization in Iran—such as the continued control of many privatized companies by the government and quasi-government institutions, resulting in widespread inefficiency—have limited the plan to publicly owned companies. Unlike in Western countries, where such plans are implemented in both public and private sectors, Iran's approach reflects its unique context. This distinct situation offers a fresh perspective on the issue.

Employee ownership is crucial to strategic human capital by the lens of agency theory. Agency theory focuses on incentive and monitoring costs resulting from a misalignment of purposes between principals and agents. In the context of employee ownership, employees often have purposes, which are not in accordance with those of the principals. Owing to the discretion that employees have in their work, employees' (agents') behaviors are self-serving at times and are not essential in contract with business owners' (principals') purposes as agreed upon in their arrangements (Kim & Patel, 2017). In other words, employee ownership is posited to synchronize the objectives of employees with those of other shareholders (Kong et al. 2024). In fact, there are two interconnected mechanisms through which employee ownership facilitates this synchronization, resulting in enhancements in corporate performance. First, employee ownership mitigates agency problems between shareholders and employees by enabling the latter to derive financial advantages from the collective prosperity of the organization. This incentivizes employees to perceive themselves as sharing common interests with the shareholders (Adwan et al, 2022). Second, a significant advantage associated with employee ownership is its favorable influence on employee retention (Chen et al. 2020). Therefore, it has positive effects on corporate social performance; since one of the dimensions of corporate social performance is job security.

Moreover, Employee ownership is increasingly common in industrialized countries. There has been an important improvement in employee ownership plans across countries including North America, the United Kingdom, Japan, and the European Union. However, the prevalence of employee ownership varies in a variety of countries. For instance, in Italy, France, and Spain, employee ownership is widespread, but in Scandinavian countries, fewer companies have active employee ownership plans (Kim & Patel, 2017). With regard to employee control and participation, various institutional settings vary in acceptable levels of employee control and participation. For instance, in Scandinavia and in countries with a Germanic governance tradition, employees usually own a fixed number of seats on the board, whereas in the UK, unions, by representation, make employee owners a moderate amount of control and governance. In France, employee ownership programs are essential for companies employing more than a definite number of employees and in Spain, Sociedades Laborales, or employee-owned firms, are an emerging form of organization (Roelants, et al, 2012).

Regarding employee stock ownership, different kinds of plans are usual in most industrial and developing countries. Several countries have for a great number of years had special legislation promoting different types of employee ownership by direct subsidies, tax benefits or other benefits. For instance, in the US ESOPs (Employee Stock Ownership Plans) the shares are owned by an employee fund, which in the beginning often are hold by loans with collateral in the firm. The shares are then cautiously shifted to the employees often in the form of profit sharing. (Mygind, 2012). Additionally, in the UK the Employee-ownership Trust (EOT) was presented in the year of 2014. A key factor in the EOT model is the role and powers of the trustees that is set out in the trust deed. The major responsibility of the trustees is to protect the interests of the employees as owners of the organization (Mygind, 2023a).

With regard to Iran after revolution in 1979, the circle of governmental economic units was remarkably improved. Nevertheless, after this period, since the early of 1990s, privatization has been on the program. It became one of the most significant axes of economic adoption policies and with the compliance of the general policies of Article 44 of the Constitution improved. Hence, in accordance with the implementation of Article 44 of Iran's Constitution Law and with the purpose of privatizing state-owned firms, due to Article 61 of the Fifth Development Plan Law, in 2011-2015, Preferred shares were identified, that owing to the law, a maximum of 5% of the company's shares is able to be sold in the form of Preferred shares to the employees of the firm.

Objective and contribution of the chapter

This chapter seeks to address a critical question: *What are the differences between employee ownership plans in Iran and Western countries?* By filling this research gap, the chapter highlights the strengths and weaknesses of Iran's Preferred Shares Plan, ultimately assessing whether a more specific legal framework is needed. The contribution lies in providing actionable insights for policymakers, stakeholders, and scholars exploring governance mechanisms in diverse economic contexts.

Methodology

This chapter adopts a mixed-method approach combining a systematic literature review (SLR), legal analysis, and qualitative interviews to explore the differences between employee ownership plans in Iran and Western countries. In summary, the analysis is based on the following:

- The Systematic Literature Review (SLR) technique for searching the articles published in Web of Science (WOS), Scopus and Google Scholar to identify the concept of employees' ownership, employees' ownership plans and the relationship of employees' ownership and firm performance.
- the investigation of the Trade law, Fifth Development Plan and Article 44 of the Constitution Law of Iran
- the interviews' analysis of officials of Iranian Privatization Organization with website news

The remainder of this paper is structured as follows. Section 2 provides the theoretical and conceptual framework. Section 3 explains the comparative analysis of employee shareholding models. Finally, the conclusion is given in section 4.

2. THEORETICAL AND CONCEPTUAL FRAMEWORK

2.1. Definition of employee ownership

- **Employee ownership and its structure**

Employee ownership can be explained as the percentage of firm stocks owned by employees in their firms (Kim & Patel, 2017). Employee ownership gives the probability to divide the wealth sharing features of investment among employee groups (Mackin, 2024). Employee ownership is a concept that covers various forms. Due to employees stock ownership that is the subject of this chapter, two significant dimensions of employee ownership has been considered:

1. The proportion of ownership held within the firm by employees;

The first dimension is the proportion of ownership held within the firm by employees. Three forms of ownership care able to be characterized related to the proportion of ownership owned by employees: minority employee ownership, controlling employee ownership and significant employee ownership. The first one which is minority employee ownership takes place when employees have fewer than 5% of the total shares. The second is significance of employee ownership, which is distinguished as the proponent of ownership exceeding 5% of the total market value of the equity. The last form is controlling ownership; at the time of all owning 51% of the total shares or more by employees together; controlling employee ownership is spoken (Roeterdink, 2018).

2. The high positions and rights that ownership offers upon employees

The second dimension focuses on the method whether ownership is direct or indirect. Direct is defined that employees are able to purchase and sell shares of the firm whenever they are interested and registered as individual shareholders. Consequently, employees own the rights of a shareholder, financial award and voting rights themselves. Nevertheless, this method is less common because employees often held liquidity constraints. Indirect ownership is characterized by the shares owned by an employee trust or a cooperative, such as an employee stock ownership plan (ESOP). An ESOP is a procedure by which employees are able to achieve shares by a confident functioning in place of the employees (Roeterdink, 2018).

In addition, with regard to the types of employee ownership, the usual types of employee ownership consist: (i) worker cooperatives, where all or almost all workers share in ownership and generally prefer to decide owing to one-person/one-vote instead of the number of shares owned; (ii) US Employee Stock Ownership Plans (ESOPs), that employees own accounts in a collective pension trust, and the trust may borrow money with the aim of finance stock purchases (returned through the firm) therefore it is nonessential for employees to put up their own money; (iii) employer stock in other retirement targets, that firms may match pre-tax employee contributions with firm stock or workers purchase the stock themselves; (iv) targets of employee stock purchase, that permit employees to purchase company stock at a discount; (v) stock owned after the exercise of granted stock alternatives (Kruse, 2022).

2.2. Underlying theories of employee ownership

To understand the reasons behind companies adopting employee ownership, several theories have been developed to explain this concept. The existing literature highlights three primary theories: agency theory, resource-based theory, and stakeholder theory. Among these, agency theory is the most frequently referenced framework in employee ownership research (Moustabchir et al., 2024). Consequently, agency theory serves as the central theoretical foundation for this chapter.

- **Employee ownership and agency theory**

One theory to describe employee ownership is the agency theory. Jensen and Meckling (1976) claim that the agency theory is an agreement in which one or more individuals, principals, engage another individual, the agent, to do several services on their behalf which consists of delegating several decision-making authorities to the agent. The agency theory opines that when the purposes of principals and agents are not properly adjusted, agency issues may exist at the employee level, where monitoring is more challenging and monitoring costs are higher (O'Boyle et al, 2016). Hence, employee ownership is able to help alleviate agency problems as it aids in the alignment of employees and shareholders' interests that decreases the requirement for external monitoring (Kishk, 2023).

According to agency theory, employee ownership is regarded as an effective mechanism for mitigating agency issues and managing employee behavior. Since a misalignment of interests often exists between shareholders and employees, enabling employees to become co-owners helps reduce this conflict by aligning their income directly with the company's success (Kim & Patel, 2021). Additionally, employee ownership fosters motivation by encouraging a long-term perspective, shifting employees' focus from short-term financial objectives to the sustained performance of the firm (Kishk, 2023).

- **Employee ownership and Resource based theory**

Another theory which analyzes employee ownership is resource based theory. This theory shows that an enterprise's competitiveness and economic rent is in accordance with the collection of beneficial, scarce, unique and non-replaceable resources. These special resources are able to result in competitive benefit which is related to firm performance. Human capital is one of the key resources that can generate a sustainable competitive advantage. Employee ownership plays a vital role in cultivating complex human resources that are difficult to replicate, thereby contributing to this advantage. It grants employees greater control over their tasks, involves them in decision-making processes, fosters positive attitudes, promotes desirable behaviors, and cultivates psychological ownership. Employees who feel a stronger sense of ownership are more invested in the company's long-term goals and plans, motivating them to improve their job performance (Roeterdink, 2018).

- **Employee ownership and Stakeholder theory**

Stakeholder theory asserts that companies have a responsibility not only to pursue profits but also to address the interests of various stakeholders, such as employees, investors, customers, local communities, and governments. According to this theory, all stakeholders contribute significantly to a firm's long-term success (Roeterdink,

2018). However, employees, as the stakeholders most closely connected to the firm, hold a particularly pivotal role (Abdelnour et al., 2023).

A company that fails to inspire its employees is unlikely to achieve long-term success. Employee ownership is an effective strategy for empowering employees. This approach enhances employee engagement, boosts productivity, and motivates individuals to showcase their own efforts as well as support the contributions of their colleagues, ultimately benefiting the firm as a whole (Roeterdink, 2018).

After discussing theoretical aspect of employees' ownership, the chapter will present its respective advantages and disadvantages.

2.3. Advantages and disadvantages of employee shareholding

Employee ownership has positive effects on firm performance, CSR performance, firm survival, and economic stability.

- **Employee ownership and firm performance**

Owing to the alignment of interests which nurtures within the organization, employee ownership is able to function as a conduit for the exchange of information that is likely to enhance decision-making processes within the organization. By capitalizing on their dual status and the resulting amalgamation of various informational sources, employee shareholders are able to contribute to the reduction of information asymmetry and the enhancement of transparency within the organization, particularly during general meetings. From the perspective of agency theory, if employee ownership facilitates the alignment of interests between employees and shareholders and ensures improved information flow within the organization, it should effectively minimize sources of conflict and enhance organizational performance. (Moustabchir et al, 2024). The relationship between employee ownership and firm performance is surveyed empirically through a great number of researchers:

A meta-analysis of 102 studies from 56,984 companies reveals that employee ownership has a modest yet significant positive correlation with firm performance on average. This finding aligns with earlier reviews and meta-analyses, including one that concluded two-thirds of 129 analyses reported positive relationships between employee ownership and either firm performance or employee perspectives, while only one-tenth identified negative relationships (Kruse, 2022). In China, Ren, et al (2019) said that organizations having employee ownership have better performance than those without employee ownership (Kishk, 2023). Additionally, a study conducted by the UK Treasury analyzed data from confidential tax records of more than 16,000 UK companies with tax-advantaged share plans. The study found that broad-based employee ownership was associated with improved firm performance metrics, such as value-added and turnover. Furthermore, research on French cooperatives demonstrated that employee-owned firms were at least as productive as traditional firms (Kruse, 2022).

- **Employee ownership and CSR performance**

According to agency theory, employee shareholders are inclined to diminish the overall degree of information asymmetry, as they possess greater access to information (in their capacity as employees) compared to external shareholders (Abdelnour et al., 2023). Due to their informational superiority, employee shareholders are positioned to facilitate a more effective dissemination of information regarding corporate social responsibility (CSR), particularly by providing external shareholders at general meetings with the specific insights they possess concerning the execution of their organization's CSR strategy (Moustabchir et al., 2024). To achieve a more profound comprehension of the relationships between employee ownership and CSR, and to maintain coherence within this chapter, this analysis will exclusively investigate the practice's influence with respect to social performance.

o **Employee ownership and social performanc**

Corporate social performance encompasses various dimensions, including the adherence to human rights, the combat against corruption and discrimination, the alleviation of social inequalities and unemployment, ethical trade practices, and effective social dialogue, in addition to considerations related to working conditions such as employee health and safety, the prevailing social climate, access to training opportunities, and the rights to freedom of association and trade union membership, among other factors. The concept of employee ownership can enhance the propensity of employees to exert social pressure on their organization (Winkler et al., 2019). In this scholarly discourse, the research conducted by Farooq et al. (2019) elucidates that firms which actively engage their workforce in the decision-making frameworks manifest enhanced social performance. More contemporaneously, Bonelli et al. (2022) claim that employees display an increased vigilance regarding their organization's working conditions and safety protocols following their decision to participate in employee stock ownership plans (ESO) (Moustabchir et al, 2024). Moreover, research illustrated that employee owners appear to own better job security (Kruse, 2022). This is indicated by smaller employment drops among employee ownership firms compared to similar firms without employee ownership during the 2001–2002 and 2007–2009 downtrend and by lower layoff rates among employee ownership firms in the early stages of the 2020 pandemic collapse. According to the perspective that employee-owned firms reduce layoffs during downturns, their relative productivity advantage tends to diminish during recessions. This may be linked to efforts to retain workers who undergo new training or engage in activities that contribute to long-term productivity (Kurtulus & Kruse, 2017; Kruse, 2022).

- **Employee ownership and firm survival**

Employee ownership companies also seem to comprise higher survival rates (Kurtulus & Kruse, 2017). Is it more possible that publicly traded US firms that their employee ownership is around 20% to survive than closely matched comparable companies during a 12-year period, and closely held companies with employee ownership plans are only half as likely as comparable firms to go bankrupt or close down during a 12-year period. Additionally, researches of worker cooperatives showed high survival rates compared to conventional companies in France, Uruguay, the UK and other countries (Kruse, 2022).

- **Employee ownership and economic stability**

The reasons for more stability and survival among employee ownership companies have not been investigated sufficiently. It can be said that it is more possible that more stable companies to adopt employee ownership or that other factors are responsible. If employee ownership is responsible, this may happen by: (i) raised productivity from better cooperation, information-sharing, and commitment; (ii) decreased dysfunctional workplace conflict; (iii) enhanced employee investments in valuable firm-specific skills; and/or (iv) making and keeping of a workplace culture that instills a sense of ownership, with a corresponding commitment to save employee jobs whenever possible (Kruse, 2022).

A number of advantages about employee ownership have been generally pointed by the above evidence. But, what about disadvantages of employee ownership? The following section will answer this question.

- **What are the cons of employee ownership?**

There are some disadvantages for employee ownership. For example, the free-rider problem, managerial entrenchment, the difficulty in configuring policies for effective performance, and financial risk are four cons that are often raised about employee ownership.

Free-riding is a definite potentially significant part in all group incentives (Kruse, 2022). Employee ownership promotes free riding among employees that would negatively impact the motivation of several opportunistic employees (Abdelnour et al, 2022). Nevertheless, Free-riding may be decreased or overcome through supportive policies with the purpose of creating team spirit, loyalty, and high work standards (Kruse, 2022).

Following Rauh (2006), since employees can be seen as management's natural allies against takeover, with managers potentially implementing employee stock ownership to keep shares in "friendly hands", employee stock ownership favors managerial entrenchment. Hence, with management entrenchment, employee stock ownership may grow agency costs. (Abdelnour et al, 2022).

Difficulty in implementing employee ownership for effective performance can be seen as a third con. To know how supportive policies should be combined with various types and levels of employee ownership, no simple formula has been found until now. Several research results opine that simply being an owner is able to impact standpoints and behavior, while other results indicate that the measurement of the financial stake is significant.

The forth con is financial risk can be significant for a great number of employee-owners. Stock values is able to fluctuate, and own a considerable share of one's capital in only one asset—comprising of the stock of one's employer—means that one can face financial risk through not being correctly varied. The financial risk may be raised under employee ownership because if the company does not succeed, the employee is able to lose both his or her profession and the firm stock value (Kruse, 2022).

3. COMPARATIVE ANALYSIS OF EMPLOYEE SHAREHOLDING MODELS

Employee share ownership takes various forms. In the following section, the chapter analyzes the employee share ownership plans of various western countries and Iran.

3.1. Employee stock ownership plan (ESOP) in the US

The most popular employee ownership plan in the U.S is ESOP. In 1974, the Employee Stock Ownership Plan (ESOP) framework was formalized via the Employee Retirement Income Security Act (ERISA) that delineated the pre-existing retirement legislation, thereby allowing the retirement plan to invest in and retain up to 100% of the equity shares of the associated corporation for the advantages of the plan's participants, who are the employees of the firm. (Gonza, 2024).

3.1.1. Main characteristics of ESOP

ESOP is a model for employee buyouts, which is in accordance with the leveraged financial mechanism by a disjointed legal vehicle that holds shares of the underlying business company in the name of the employees in the firm. In a nutshell, an ESOP is a retirement trust with individual accounts which collects company shares tax-free until the worker retires or leaves the company, typically without the employee having to pay for the shares by salaries or benefit deductions (Blasi et al, 2024). The purpose of ESOP is simply to enhance the equity holdings of ordinary workers. ESOPs are able to have any percentage of company stock. ESOPs are provided in both public and private companies. In regard to entry and exit of employee members for the ESOP, the principles for employee entry and exit are very simple. There is a theory for all employees. Nevertheless, before participation, an employee must be 21 years or older and have worked in the firm for at least 1000 hours a year. After resignation, the value of the individual shares can be paid out over a period of more than six years, although this typically occurs more quickly (Mygind, 2023a).

3.1.2. Advantages and disadvantages of ESOP

There are several positive attributions of ESOP:

- **Broad-based employee ownership model**

The Employee Retirement Income Security Act (ERISA) requires that all permanent employees participate in the ESOP employee ownership program, provided they risk none of their own savings or assets. Since all permanent employees are included in this model, the U.S. ESOP creates a firm of owners, which helps foster a positive workplace culture. In fact, ESOPs, on average, tend to experience better business performance, growth, and resilience compared to similarly situated conventionally owned companies (Gonza, 2024).

- **Leveraged buyout mechanism**

As the ESOP buyout is leveraged through bank or seller-supplied credit, a large number of shares may be bought at one time from a retiring owner. Regarding the debt leverage through an external financier, the firm guarantees the loan through securing a note promising regular ESOP contributions on a monthly or annual basis. In the case of ESOP, the underlying company guarantees for the loan, that is eventually repaid by changing of retained net income channeled through the ESOP to the seller (seller's credit) or the external creditor (loan leverage). The seller's credit option is generally cheaper and less complicated; nevertheless, it needs the owner to agree on being paid out after a period of several years, owing to cash flow to the ESOP trust (Gonza, 2024).

- **Tax incentives**

There are three primary tax incentives designed to stimulate the economy by motivating shareholders to sell their company shares to employees through an ESOP:

The first tax incentive was the tax-free rollover operation as per Section 1042 (IRA) of the US tax code, that permits the owner of C-corporation shares to hold up the payment of capital income tax indefinitely in the situations of the ESOP trust becomes the owner of at least 30% of the shares, The ESOP represents ownership for all employees, and the owner reinvests the financial capital back into the U.S. economy within 12 months of selling the shares. This tax breaks inspired great shareholders, especially in closely held corporations, to plan for ownership succession, and to avoid the worthless closure of these firms. The second incentive was about creditors of debt-leveraged ESOP buyouts. The provision assigned a 50% tax break on income from interest on the loan to the ESOP utilized to buy corporate shares. This incentive was purposed at sellers who chose the sellers' credit; however, it also helped provide a market for ESOP loans in the private financial sector that further facilitated the conversion to ECEs by the ESOP structure. The third tax provision was verifiable dividends that permitted a firm to deduct a limited amount of dividends on company shares held by an ESOP if the dividends were passed through to employees or utilized to pay for the corporate stock. The aim behind this provision was to decrease the cost of capital utilized to buy corporate shares by the ESOP trust. The recent version of deductible dividends is the ESOP contribution that is a tax-deductible expense of the operating company utilized to finance ESOP leverage, such as paying off shares from sellers, achieving loans, or paying off the shares of departing beneficiaries (Gonza, 2024).

- **Other benefits of ESOP**

With regards to the control rights and the role of trustees, ESOPs have some benefits: 1) Probability for a democratic governance structure in ESOPs; 2) Opportunity for the previous owners to shape the model in accordance with their preferences within the given framework. It is able to be presumed, that this likelihood makes the previous owners more favorable to the model and this encourages more transformations to ESOPs. With regards to membership entry and exit ESOPs own some benefits: 1) The easy entry and exit of employee-members is a powerful benefit for ESOPs. In the ESOP when the employees are employed in the firm, they are automatically members. Nevertheless, if the trust deed opens for employees voting for trustees or directly for members of the company board several employment conditions for obtaining the tax-free bonus and possible control rights will be made. 2) ESOPs are broad all-employee models that do not get entry fee which leads to an easy entry. As regards to Finance, ESOPs have some benefits: for example, there are no contributions from the employees in the ESOP model; because the payment for the takeover of the firm is a significant problem for ESOP model. This could be a combination of gifts/contributions from the firm, vendor loan from the previous owner and external bank loans with collateral in the firm (Mygind, 2023b).

While ESOPs offer numerous advantages for companies and their employees, it is important to consider some of the potential drawbacks and limitations associated with this model.

- **Buying liability again**

As the US ESOP was done as a specific kind of retirement plan, it does not require to buyback the share until the employee remains or retires. Shares could be bought after the beneficiary becomes 55 years old. But there exist individual and distinctive cases where employees are able to access Internal Capital Account (ICA) liquidity before retirement. There are several issues associated with the fact that the ESOP buys back the collective value of ICAs only upon exit. One of the biggest concerns is the potential problem of incurring buyback liabilities, which can be exacerbated if a large number of "large accounts" choose to exit the plan within a short period. In such cases, the buyback liability can become significant, and the ESOP may sometimes struggle to fulfill its financial obligations to retiring or exiting members (Ellerman et al., 2022).

- **Higher risk for older accounts compared to younger accounts**

The next issue with the combination of the ICA value is that older accounts tolerate higher risk unevenly to younger accounts—the division of risk in the case of insolvency is much enormous for workers who have been with the firm more and own much higher account value on their ICAs (Ellerman et al, 2022).

- **Presenting an unattractive motivated structure to workers**

Another issue with the ICA value structure is that older accounts bear a disproportionately higher risk compared to younger accounts. In the event of insolvency, the risk distribution is much greater for employees who have been with the company longer and have higher account values in their ICAs (Ellerman et al., 2022).

- **Non-participatory valid design**

In the US ESOP, the ESOP is a trust, and the only "beneficiaries" are employees; in such a way that they were minors. The issue with this is that member of employee owners is main part to healthy organizational culture and the productivity impacts that are totally linked with the successful employee ownership companies. Early studies on employee ownership opine that the positive productivity influences are "largely contingent on the presence of programs of workers membership" (Ellerman et al, 2022). Current studies support these results—the most significant complementary factor to ownership for obtaining raised productivity, growth, and business resilience is meaningful effect of workers Researches showed that the most salient correlation is between performance and participation of workers; a very early research already illustrates that ESOP firms which instituted participation plans rose at a rate three to four times faster than ESOP firms which did not (Ellerman et al, 2022).

- **Other downsides of ESOP**

As regards to the control rights and the role of trustees, ESOPs own one drawback: Long distance from the employee to the controlling top of the enterprise. With regard to membership entry and exit ESOPs own one downside: There is an administrative burden for the ESOP to administer the individual shares comprising of the pay back of the fair market value of the individual shares to leaving participants. Hence, the ESOP is not proper for small firms. With regards to Finance and tax benefits, ESOPs own one negative effect: Making the group wide for tax-exempt conveys lower tax-revenue in the short run. Nevertheless, in the ESOP model, after the employee cash out the asset, the capital gains are taxed. With regards to Startups and takeovers ESOPs hold one drawback: The ESOP model are scarcely utilized for starting new firms (Mygind, 2023b)

Case study of ESOP

Ringland-Johnson is one of the prosperous instances of an ESOP business. Ringland-Johnson is one of the leading commercial and industrial construction companies in the United States. Established in 1946 in Des Moines, Iowa, the business became employee-owned in 2019. The company's CEO, Brent Johnson says: "Our ESOP has significantly enhanced the company's stability and performance. Increased productivity, profit, creativity, and a greater dedication to quality have all resulted from bringing employees' interests into line with the company's long-term objectives. Because employees are inspired by the chance to personally profit from the company's success, the shared ownership model has also helped us draw in and keep great talent". The ESOP has given the employee owners a feeling of pride and responsibility for their work. It has produced a more welcoming and cooperative work environment where everyone takes pride in the accomplishments of the business. Furthermore, the ESOP has provided a significant retirement benefit and enhancing the employees' long-term financial stability.

In terms of social impact, the company's ESOP benefits the community at large in addition to the business. Since the company is locally owned, the stability and financial success it attains through its ESOP result in more local investment and the creation of jobs. Furthermore, the firm's employees are more involved in local activities and philanthropy because they are stakeholders in the community, which strengthens links within the community. Last but not least, the corporation intends to assist neighbourhood initiatives, foster economic growth, and deepen its relationships with neighbourhood organisations. By succeeding as an employee-owned firm, the company hopes to inspire other companies and promote wider ESOP model adoption, which will strengthen the local economy and make it more inclusive and resilient (MENKE, 2024).

The features, benefits, and drawbacks of ESOP were covered above. However, what types of employee share ownership exist in other western nations? The number of European companies with employee share plans has been steadily rising over the past few years. In 2020, around 88% of major European corporations had employee share plans, up from roughly 57% in 2006 (Adwan & Ahamed, 2024). Therefore, this chapter will comprehensively examine the leading European countries in the field of employee shares ownership in the section 3.2, 3.3, 3.4, including France, Spain and the UK.

3.2. Employee ownership plan in France

Since the nineteenth century, French firms have offered shares to their employees; however privatization has been a main driver of employee share ownership (ESO). ESO was developed through vending French government shares in car manufacturer Renault and in some public banks and insurance firms to the organizations' employees in 1970 and 1973. in the year of 1973, a legal framework for ESO permitted firms to sell shares to their employees by employee stock purchase plans (ESPP) with not more than 10% for discount (this later rose to 20%). After the second half of the twentieth century, France has improved and combined some techniques of employee participation and gain-sharing with three main purposes: 1) to offer employees a share of company profits; 2) motivate employee savings by company savings plans

(CSP or Plan d'Épargne Entreprise – PEE) and 3) to raise employee share ownership in the CSP framework (Aubert, & Bernheim, 2021).

Main sources of employee savings are the Profit-sharing bonuses. These bonuses can be reduced from corporate tax and are therefore appealing to employers; meanwhile, their income tax reduction boosts employees to save this money that they would otherwise have to involve in their taxable income. Identified in 1967, profit-sharing schemes (participation) are mandatory in companies employing 50 or more employees in France, however they stay optional for firms with smaller number than 50 members of staff. Every employee working in a firm for over than three months is able to have advantages from a profit-sharing bonus. The total amount of profit shared is scattered between all the firm's employees in France, either equally or proportionally to their wages with the possibility of mixing the bonus conditions. The amount paid out to employees is able to be reduced from corporate taxable income, even though it is subject to a social tax of 20%. The new PACTE law (action plan for the growth and transformation of companies) has decreased this rate for small firms (in this case, those with less than 50 employees) (Aubert, & Bernheim, 2021).

3.2.1. Main characteristics of PEE

In 1967, the company savings plan (CSP, or plan d'épargne entreprise – PEE) was improved. Before that, profit-sharing bonuses had to be invested either in securities issued by the employer or in a locked, fixed interest account. The CSP became the major savings scheme for profit-sharing bonuses. Also, employees are able to create voluntary contributions to CSPs; these are often matched by the employer. The main benefit of the CSP is its tax exempt status. To have profit from this status, the money invested must stay in the scheme during five years. After investing in a CSP, 9.7% of money for social tax can be paid on the amount invested. Neither the firm nor the employee is needed to pay income tax or social charges on the bonuses granted. A social tax must be paid after withdrawing of money on capital increase gains (17.2% in 2020), nevertheless no income tax is payable. The same conditions apply to any voluntary contributions made by the employee. A CSP must give some types of funds with variety of risk levels including short-term monetary funds, obligations, or diversified assets. One or more investment possibility can be employee share ownership. The employee selects the firm savings funds (CSF or fonds commun de placement entreprise – FCPEs) they want to invest in, even though they can shift their assets from one CSF to another in several conditions (Aubert, & Bernheim, 2021).

- **Tax incentives**

The taxation of the PEE is not similar over the life of the plan and the release. Over the life of the plan the taxation varies due to the nature of the sums paid into the PEE:

- The contribution paid by the firm is exempt from income tax for the employee, up to a limit of € 3,290.88. This limit is increased to € 5,923.58 in the event of an investment in shares or investment certificates issued through your firm.
- Up to € 30,852, the profit-sharing that the company pays and deposits on the PEE is free from income tax.
- The income from the plan's securities
    - Income from securities reinvested in the plan: When you reinvest interest generated on securities kept in the plan, it is not subject to income tax. They must make contributions to social security.
    - Income from securities not reinvested in the plan: If you do not reinvest interest earned by securities you own in the plan, you will be liable for income tax and social security contributions.
    - Gains made in the plan: The profits from the sale of stocks under the PEE are not subject to income tax, but they are liable for social security contributions.

However, the amounts taken out of the plan at the end of the plan or during early release, match the employer and employee payments as well as the plan's profits that the employee has reinvested. These sums are subject to social security contributions but are not liable to income tax at the time of withdrawal (CIDIF capital, 2024).

3.2.2. Benefits and downsides of PEE

The PEE savings plan permits employee and manager beneficiaries to make financial savings under favorable tax and social situations. For the employee, the contribution, if it exists, performs an attractive help from the employer in growing his asset (Rozade, 2021).

Nevertheless, In exchange for tax and social advantages, PEE has the drawback of locking the amounts invested into it during of 5 years. In spite of being quite a few cases of early release (10 in total) they stayed limited. Furthermore, PEE can be seen as a portfolio of securities. The plan beneficiary must select between several financial investment vehicles. Several are risky and may cause capital losses since they invest in the stock market. As a result, it is important to control your investments in PEE and conduct arbitrage that is not always easy without the assistance of experts (Rozade, 2021).

In accordance with a research conducted by OpinionWay on behalf of the organisations that arrange Employee Savings Week; a greater proportion of French workers have at least one employee savings plan, including PEE. In January and February of 2023, 1,004 employees participated in this survey. According to the findings, about two-thirds of the recipients invested their profit-sharing bonuses in these programs because they felt they were satisfactory. The PEE employee savings plan is at the top of the list at 31%, ahead of the other plans. In the 12 months before the study, more over half of the employees received profit sharing bonuses. 64% of respondents said they put this money into their employee savings scheme, up from 60% in 2020. Their reasons for doing this are the tax exemption and the employer's increased payment.

These schemes are well-evaluted. Nine out of ten holders believe that building a nest egg without any financial effort is attainable with an employee savings scheme. 78% of them claim they are generally or very satisfied, and 71% refer to such programs as good investments. Regarding the lack of an employee savings plan, 76% of workers believe that its implementation could affect their loyalty to the company and 72% their motivation for it (AMF, 2023).

3.3. Employee ownership plan in Spain

Worker-owned firms in Spain have a long history. The two most identified models are worker cooperatives and worker-owned companies, or Sociedades Laborales (SL). For alignment of this chapter, worker-owned or (SL) model is investigated.

The growth of the SL occurred at the end of the 1970s in Spain. Coinciding with the worst years of the economic crisis, public aid was made to alleviate the lack of employment, mainly in industry, in such a way that the workers in these industries were made co-responsible for the crisis, therefore in the condition that they were forced into unemployment, they got on the dual role of employers and workers, purchasing the assets of the firms and initiating the essential modernization processes. They did so, as far as possible, with decreased aid and investment. The important reply of workers to the closure of their firms led to the first rule on SL (Law 15/1986 of 25 April 1986) being passed in the 1980s (Marcuello, 2023).

3.3.1. Main characteristics of Sociedades Laborales (SL)

Sociedades Laborales (SLs) are trading companies. A SL is dependent on shared ownership and is allowed to utilize non-employee capital. This creates it an ideal instrument for business progression in partnership or micro-enterprises where retiring owners are able to regularly cash out and for transition period remain shareholders in the SL while controlling over the management to the new employee owners. In

SL the workers' share capital is equally scattered among themselves, hence they are distinguished by the existence of democratic decision-making processes and equitable profit distribution (Marcuello, 2023).

The requirements for SL are as follows:

- The majority of share capital must be owned by workers, who create paid services under an employment relationship for an undefined period of time.
- No shareholder may hold shares showing more than one-third of the share capital, unless:
    - o The workforce-owned company is initially built through two worker shareholders (each with 50% of the share capital and voting rights) with the obligation to adapt the organization during 36 months to meet all the legal needs.
- The number of hours/year worked by workers hired for an undefined period of time who are not members may not be more than 49% of the total number of hours/year worked by all worker-members.
- Two partners are required for building the Sociedades Laborales which both of them must be employees (Marcuello, 2023).

The entry and exit of shareholders may occur through the transfer of shares or holdings. The shares and holdings may be freely shifted to worker-members and non-member employees with an undefined term contract. When a worker-owner leaves the firm, his or her shares must be suggested for sale internally, with non-shareholding employees having priority. There are two outlines: Sociedad Limitada Laboral (SLL) with minimum equity capital of Euro 3,000 and Sociedad Anonima Laboral (SAL) with minimum equity capital of Euro 60,000 (Lowitzsch et al, 2024).

- **Tax Incentives**

Sociedades Laborales are eligible to obtain the following tax benefits which states that they must transfer 25% of their net profit to a Special Reserve Fund by the end of the relevant tax year in order to maintain their position as Sociedadlaboral. 1) Tax exemption for capital growth, the creation of an SL, and the conversion of an SLL to a SAL or vice versa (in addition to a tax credit of 99% of taxes related to the transfer of shares to employees); 2) Exclusion from notarial documents on transfers to the business, bond obligations, and debenture bonds; additionally, 99% of transfer taxes are reimbursed when the SL purchases assets or rights from a firm where the majority of its employees were formerly employed; (Lowitzsch et al, 2017).

Nevertheless, in corporation tax, worker-owned firms are free to reduce tangible and intangible fixed assets utilized to perform their activities, achieved over the first five years from the date on which they are classified as such. With the purpose of receiving tax benefits, it is essential to follow a twofold requirement related to classification as a workforce-owned company and with the special reserve (Marcuello, 2023).

3.3.2. Advantages and limitations of SL

The first advantage is that workers themselves who exercise monitor the society. It is easier to build well-blended structure. Furthermore, workers are more inspired to work. Because the more profit the firm makes, the higher its proponent of profits. The second privilege is that workers are able to select a series of social benefits that the rest of the firms do not have access to. The most substantial is the capitalization for unemployment, which permits you to collect the advantages in case of unemployment in one go. The third profit is that SLs make a set of tax exemption and advantages (Economia Desde Casa, 2020)

Nevertheless, the SLs own several drawbacks, the first one being the requirement of establishing special reserve fund of 10%: the firm is not able to enhance so fast or to invest all their profits. The second negative effect is that the number of worker partners must be at least two instead of one, as happens in public restricted firms and restricted liability firms. (Economia Desde Casa, 2020).

Case Study

A limited liability firm, Hirunox Calderería Inoxidable specialised in boiler construction and related engineering services. After their former employer's insolvency, three partners capitalised their unemployment benefits to start it in 2012. Due to problems with one of their primary clients, Hirunox had an especially challenging fiscal year in 2018 that would account for the negative numbers. That year, their financial performance fell short of the industry average. Since 2012, the firm has maintained its microbusiness status, and since 2013, the number of employees and worker-owners has been constant. Management has also voiced worries regarding the SL legislation's restrictions on non-partner working hours. Additionally, the business is concerned that adding partners from the current workforce may hinder their ability to make quick decisions (Scocozza 2020).

Taking into account the constraints and examining the presence of issues that SLs enterprises face, their number has declined. The Ministry of Labour and Social Economy reports that in 2020, there were 7,801 firms of SL employing 54,954 clerks. Nonetheless, it is important to draw attention to the on-going decline in SL over the previous ten years. Among the explanations offered for this decrease are (1) the absence of advantageous tax treatment for worker-owned companies. 2) The implementation of more advantageous policies for capitalist firms, like lowering the corporation tax rate for them (Marcuello, 2023).

Employees ownership plan of Spain (SL) were discussed above. It was found that the number of SLs has been decreased in the last years. However, the number of companies using the UK model is increasing. In the following section the chapter will examine that why is the employees' ownership plan of the UK more successful?

3.4. Employee ownership plan in UK

Employee ownership is an increasingly significant form of business ownership and company in the UK. An employee trust meeting definite demands is now identified by regulation of an employee ownership trust (EOT). The EOT, that is now the main form of employee ownership in the UK has become a role model for employee ownership, and there is noticeable interest around the globe in reflecting this form of employee ownership. It has become the paramount format of employee ownership for medium sized and large firms (Pendleton et al., 2023).

3.4.1. Main characteristics of EOT

The EOT model depends on indirect ownership by a trust, and the EOT trustees exercise this handling on behalf of the employees. The actual impact of employees is based on the statutes of the EOT. The principles for selecting the EOT trustees may give employees handle like in a worker cooperative; however, it is also feasible to own trustees with far employees and with important control by the previous owner (Mygind, 2023a).

In the case of an EOT (Employee Ownership Trust), ownership rights to benefits and wealth are straightforward. The rights align with the EOT's share of ownership, operating under a permanent rule that individual employees do not have personal claims to the wealth or the ability to withdraw an individual share of the accumulated capital. In contrast, the ESOP (Employee Stock Ownership Plan) allocates funds to individual accounts, allowing employees to accumulate a share of the company's wealth during their employment. Upon exiting the firm, employees can realize this share at market value. However, the UK model includes an optional tax-free reward for employees, which may take the form of profit-sharing up to a specified maximum value, as in the UK, or as a percentage of salaries (Mygind, 2023b).

With regards to entry and exit, the easy entry and exit of employee-members is a great benefit for EOTs like ESOPs. In the EOT the employees are automatically members when they are employed in the firm. There is no entry fee; nevertheless if the trust deed opens for employees voting for trustees or directly for members of the firm board, there are several employment situations for taking the tax-free rewards and possible control rights. Regarding exit, the EOT is much simpler than the ESOP since the EOT does not oblige to the leaving employees. To prevent a fast drain of capital, there is maximum six years payback period. The length of this period has to harmonize the two considerations: not to provide the payback period too short to cause the stress to the firm and not to create it too long for employees who must wait for a long time for their money after resigning the organization. Six years sounds to be a well-proven and reasonable maximum. The firm is able to pay back faster if preferred. Nonetheless, because of no personal capital to pay back in the EOT, exit seems just exit from the occupation. When the employee withdraws from the organization, the accumulated capital value is based on the value of the shares at that time. Employees require to work for a period to take the right to their shares (Mygind, 2023b).

The EOT also alleviates a great number of the traditional hinders to employee ownership, such as the long-standing lack of awareness of employee ownership among professional advisers and (un)availability of finance. The ordinary financing mechanisms of EOT shifts, whereby owners are able to get deferred consideration (i.e. the owner achieved the sale price in installments over time) due to future profit streams, avoids or limits dependence on external sources of finance to attain the ownership transfer. Taking prolonged consideration from an EOT dependent on future advantage streams rather than selling to an external shopper also makes greater certainty and simplicity in the valuation and selling process. This shape of transaction can also simplify preferably a staged, than cliff-edge, exit by retiring owners (Pendleton et al., 2023).

- **Tax incentives**

The share of ownership to be suitable for tax-relief is a significant choice. In UK, the EOT shall buyout over 50% to open up for tax-relief. Owners who sell a controlling interest including necessarily more than 50% of a firm's ordinary share capital to the trustee of an EOT achieve a capital gains tax exemption on the improvement in value in accordance with an excluding from inheritance tax liabilities (in addition, employee beneficiaries indirectly benefit from this) if the shares are changed below market value (Mygind, 2023b). The beneficial value of the capital receives tax exemption has grown since 2020 since the lifetime limit for Business Assets Disposal Relief (previously identified as Entrepreneur's Relief) on capital gains from business assets was decreased from £10 million to £1 million. In the EOT case, there are no capital gains to the employees when the money entered collective reserves. As a result, the firms which are handled by an EOT are able to pay the employees a tax-free reward of up to £3,600 per year. This is a broad all-employee plan. The trust must "serve" all employees on a similar basis or different from this only through reason of their reward, length of service, or hours worked. The employees are able to have decisive effects, therefore the model permits for full employee control (Pendleton et al., 2023).

Globally,, EOT offers the following tax advantages to the owner, staff, and business: 1) Owners can save up to 20% by making disposals into the trust without incurring capital gains tax. For inheritance tax goals, a donation of shares to an EOT is an exempt transfer; 2) For employees: The EOT is able to offer bonuses to employees of up to £3,600 per year without paying income tax; 3) For organizations: The firm will be able to deduct the value of the incentives from its corporation tax (PWC, 2020).

3.4.2. Benefits and drawbacks of EOT

Employee Ownership Trusts (EOTs) present several benefits and drawbacks, which are worth considering for their implementation in organizational structures.

- Benefits of EOT

EOTs offer significant advantages for both employees and corporations. Firms co-owned by EOTs can provide tax-free cash rewards to employees, up to £3,600 per year per employee. Additionally, payments to an EOT are eligible for corporation tax relief, making this model financially advantageous (Jordan, 2022).

EOTs also facilitate faster and easier sales compared to third-party transactions. Many shareholders prefer selling to EOTs because such sales involve smoother and quicker processes, reducing the complexity of negotiations (Jordan, 2022).

Other benefits align closely with those of Employee Stock Ownership Plans (ESOPs), including:

1. The potential for democratic governance structures.
2. Flexibility for previous owners to customize the model according to their preferences, promoting further adoption of EOTs.
3. Simple entry and exit for employee-members, as participation is automatic upon employment, with no capital repayment required upon exit.
4. Broad accessibility due to the absence of entry fees.
5. Ease of exit processes, which resemble leaving a job (Jordan, 2022).
    - Drawbacks of EOT

Despite their advantages, EOTs come with certain limitations. Shareholders face delayed payment for the sale, receiving funds gradually rather than upfront. This introduces additional risks, particularly if business profits are insufficient to pay off the sale cost in a reasonable timeframe. Moreover, the total value received by shareholders may be less than what could be obtained through an open market sale (Jordan, 2022).

Valuing the business can also be challenging. Employees may overestimate the firm's worth, leading to increased costs and risks. Furthermore, EOTs operate under complex regulations that are difficult to navigate. Declines in firm performance can extend the repayment period for selling shareholders, and transactions often occur over several years (Jordan, 2022).

1. EOTs share some drawbacks with ESOPs, including:

2. Limited proximity between employees and the decision-making leadership of the company.
3. Reduced short-term tax revenue due to the broader tax-exempt status, although no capital gains are distributed to employees since funds go into collective reserves.
4. Limited use of the EOT model for establishing new enterprises (Mygind, 2023b).

- Case study of EOT

Mediascape is an audio-visual company that its positive effect on employee engagement, recruitment, and retention, has been an employee ownership trust (EOT) for the past five years.

Niall MacDonald, managing director of the company states that, “Becoming an employee ownership trust was the perfect solution. A traditional trade sale wouldn’t necessarily secure the employment of the individuals working at Mediascape”. The new framework has allowed employees to engage with the business more than ever before.

Employers in the UK have faced numerous challenges over the past five years due to Brexit, COVID, and the cost of living issue. However, it was simpler to develop long-term solutions for these issues thanks to Mediascape's EOT paradigm. For instance, having an EOT aided the company in overcoming the most external obstacles throughout this transformation. Additionally, the company was able to provide its employees with one-time monthly payments from November to February by using the employee ownership model in light of the cost of living problem. Furthermore, choices will always consider the welfare of the employees since they are the company's beneficiaries.

In terms of cultural changes, the culture of organization has undergone the largest transformation since going EOT. Because they have greater accountability and responsibility than they may have had in the past, employees value the company far more. Additionally, the managers of the firm meet with all employees once a month to provide an update on our financial situation and what is doing well and what needs improvement. Additionally, Mediascape has established employee improvement teams that promote particular causes, such as environmental or worker health. Moreover, recruitment has enhanced, but retention has grown more significantly. People are definitely drawn to the team when they learn about the employee ownership model. Actually, the reason for the company's extremely effective hiring practices is that its employees are happy with their jobs (Machell, 2023).

Advantages and disadvantages of employees' ownership plans in different countries is provided in Table 1.

Table 1. Advantages and disadvantages of employees' ownership plans (model) in different countries

Country	Model	Advantage	Disadvantage
USA	ESOP	• Possibility for democratic model • Providing tax exemption • Broad-based employee ownership model • Leveraged buyout mechanism • ESOP capital values gains to employee individual accounts • Automatic membership and no entry fee • Individual employee stock accounts	• Often long distance from employees to trustees • Repurchase liability • Higher risk for older accounts compared to younger accounts • Presenting an unappealing incentive structure to workers • Non participatory legal design • Not proper for small firms • ESOPs rarely used for new startups
France	PEE	• Providing tax exemption **• The employer's contribution**	• Locking the amounts invested into it for a period of 5 years. • PEE is a portfolio of securities
Spain	Sociedades Laborales (SL)	• Creating well-blended structure • Workers can opt for a series of social benefits • Providing tax exemption	• Need of establish of special reserve fund of 10% • Two partners are needed for creating Sociedades Laborales (SL)
UK	EOT	• Possibility for democratic model • Providing tax exemption • Quicker and smoother sales • Automatic membership and no entry fee	• Often long distance from employees to trustees • No capital gains to employees • No employee accounts • Shareholders will not receive the money immediately • Not easy to determine the value of the business • Complex rules • EOTs rarely used for new startups

Source(s): Author's own work

In the previous sections, the employee shares ownership plans of western countries were investigated. In order to answer the main question of this chapter, employee shares ownership plan of Iran will be investigated in the next section.

3.5. Employee ownership plan in Iran

3.5.1. Historical and economic context

Regarding employees stock ownership of Iran, in 1975, The thirteen principal of the White Revolution (The Shah and People Revolution) was approved, according to which private and state-owned industrial and production firms (except for parent industries such as ironworks, petrochemicals and some others that will remain in the hands of the government) that have been established for five years must be convert it into a public company and sell up to 49% of the shares of private companies first to the workers and employees of the same companies and then to other people. State-owned industrial firms also pledged to sell 99% of their shares. After revolution of Iran in 1979, the circle of governmental economic units was notably expanded. However, after this period, since the early of 1990s, privatization has been on the agenda. It became one of the most important axes of economic adjustment policies and with the approval of the general policies of Article 44 of the Constitution improved. An executive order for privatization envisaged by Article 44 of the Constitution Law of Iran was issued in July 2006. According to the plan of action, the government is assigned to cede 80 percent of the shares of major state-owned enterprises to the people. Therefore, in line with the implementation of Article 44 of Iran's Constitution Law and with the aim of privatizing state-owned companies, according to Article 61 of the Fifth Development Plan Law, in 2011-2015, Preferred shares were introduced.

3.5.2. Current legal framework (Preferred shares)

According to the law, a maximum of 5% of the company's shares can be sold in the form of Preferred shares to the employees of the company. Considering the audit requirements that exist in state-owned companies and these requirements always make it difficult to grant stock options, and this has been the reason why the title of Preferred shares has been given to the employees of the state-owned company's shares. In general, the state of a company has always been an obstacle for granting stock options or implementing support plans, because there are always concerns about the protection of government property. However, the existence of regulations such as Article 40 of the law amending the articles of the law of the Fourth Economic, Social and Cultural Development Plan of Iran and the implementation of the general policies of the Article 44 of the constitution and the regulations on the transfer of Preferred shares provide easier conditions for granting part of the shares of state-owned companies to employees (Beheshti et al, 2018).

Preferred shares differ from stock options in several ways. Stock options are typically granted to incentivize key employees, offering tax advantages and fostering loyalty, ownership participation, and contributions to the company's growth and performance. The primary distinction lies in their usage: Preferred shares are specific to state-owned companies, whereas stock options are commonly issued by private companies and startups (Beheshti et al, 2018). Additionally, there is no specific law regarding stock options in public, private companies and in startups. However, some of private companies independently grant their shares to their employees to increase the company's productivity and performance. Regarding the tax of stock options, the employee who owns these shares is not required to pay the share tax. Since the payment of share tax is specific to the main shares and the stock options are not considered among the main shares of the company (Hamed, 2022).

Regarding conditions of allocating Preferred shares, Article 1 and Article 4 of the bylaw on How to Grant Preferred shares approved in 2006 specify the conditions and ceiling for granting Preferred shares. Based on Article 1 of this bylaw, the limit for the transfer of these shares has been determined in relation to the maximum capital of the company, and it cannot be transferred more than this amount. This is the reason why some people, such as managers and employees, have a special right to buy preferred shares compared to the retirees of the company.

According to Article 1 of the bylaw, preferential sale and installment a maximum of 5% of the shares of the companies subject to transfer at the proposal of the privatization of organization and the approval of the board of transfer to the managers, employees and retirees of the same company, as well as the sale of a maximum of 5% of the shares of the mentioned companies in installments other experienced, expert and efficient managers are allowed based on the rules of this bylaw. In fact, the volume of Preferred shares is always the same compared to other company shares, and a maximum of 5% of the company's total shares can have the title of Preferred shares. It seems that although the second 5% (shares that are given to experienced, expert and efficient managers), is given the title of Preferred shares, it is essentially stock options. Because of the mentioned shares are given only to certain people.

Some of the articles related to the regulations of the premium shares state that:

- In the sale of shares of companies, Preferred shares have priority, and their sale to managers, employees and retirees of the same company depends on the submission of a written request by the applicants collectively.
- Transferring shares to managers and employees has a higher priority compared to retirees, and if there are still transferable shares of the company after

the transfer to these people, the remained shares will be given to the retirees of the same company.

- Managers and employees, who have at least one year of work experience at the time of the transfer of shares are eligible to purchase Preferred shares
- According to Article 4 of the bylaw, the amount of Preferred shares that can be allocated to each qualified person is up to 10 times the average of the last six months of the salary and benefits received.

Additionally, according to the interview of the head of the Privatization Organization of Iran, transfer of preferred shares is done in 100% installments with a period of 10 years, and the price of the transferred shares is paid from the dividend of the transferred shares. Moreover, the government is considering giving the price of the Preferred shares of transferable companies to the employees with discounts (Mehr, 2024a). Until May 2024, more than 5 billion shares have been transferred to employees)Ana, 2024); and to about 400,000 employees of the companies have been given Preferred shares, of which 35,000 belong to Iran Telecommunication Company and 1,500 belong to Shazand Oil Refinery (Mehr, 2024b).

3.5.3. Comparison Preferred shares with Western models

As it was mentioned, in Preferred shares plan of Iran, companies are only allowed to transfer 5% of their shares to their managers, employees and retirees, as well as another 5% to experienced managers under certain conditions. However, in the employees stock ownership plans of the countries that reviewed in this chapter there is no limit for granting shares to employees. Additionally, the tax benefits in the laws of western countries in order to encourage more companies to transfer shares to their employees is another difference between these countries and Iran because in Iran there is no specific law regarding tax exemption for transferring company shares to their employees. Another difference between employees' stock plans of Iran and western countries is that managers and employees who have at least one year of work experience at the time of the transfer of shares are eligible to purchase Preferred shares. However, in western countries such as USA, employees must be in the firm for minimum 1000 hours a year before participation and with the age of 21 years or older. Furthermore, in western countries such as France companies sell shares to their employees with a maximum discount of 20%. On the contrary, the government of Iran is considering giving the price of the Preferred shares of transferable companies to the employees with discounts the exact amount is not determined. Moreover, employee ownership plan of Iran which profit from Preferred shares depends on the submission of a written request by the applicants collectively. However, in the USA or UK, employees are automatically members of the plan when they are employed in the company.

3.5.4. Strengths and weaknesses of the Iranian system

Although employees' ownership plans in western countries are very different, Preferred shares have some advantages such as: 1) There is an opportunity for corporate retirees to benefit from preference shares. 2) Transfer of Preferred shares is done in 100% installments with a period of 10 years, and the price of the transferred shares is paid from the dividend of the transferred shares

Nevertheless, there are several disadvantages of Preferred shares plan such as: 1) This type of shares is provided only to employees, managers, and retirees of public and not for private companies. 2) There is no specific law regarding tax exemption for transferring company Preferred shares to their employees. 3) In the laws related to the Preferred shares, there is no mention of whether the company can limit the non-financial rights of the recipients of Preferred shares, such as the right to vote, the right to attend company meetings. 4) Benefit from Preferred shares depends on the submission of a written request by the applicants collectively and it can bring about problems for employees.

Advantages and disadvantages of Preferred shares is provided in Table 2.

Table 2. Advantages and disadvantages of employees ownership plan (Preferred shares) in Iran

Model	Advantage	Disadvantage
Preferred shares	• The possibility of benefiting from preferred shares for retirees • Transfer of Preferred shares is done in 100% installments	• It is only for public companies • No specific tax exemption • Uncertainty of non-financial rights of recipients of preferred shares • Benefit from Preferred shares depends on the submission of a written request by the applicants collectively

Source(s): Author's own work

3.6. Discussion and recommendations

3.6.1. Summary of the main differences between Iran and Western countries plans

The studies conducted in this chapter related to the employees ownership plans in Western countries and Iran showed that there are main differences between the plan of Iran and Western countries, that are in western countries plans but not considered in Iran plan including: tax incentive; covering all sectors (public and private) and no limit for granting shares to employees.

3.6.2. Lessons to be learned from international models

By examining international employee ownership plans, many lessons can be learned from their strengths and weaknesses, such as: all of them have this advantage that tax exemptions are provided for employees and companies; also their plans provided for public and private companies. However, they also have some weaknesses such as: ESOP and EOT rarely used for new startups. Additionally, it is a bit difficult to setting up SL companies in Spain; and two partners are needed. It was found that the number of SLs has been decreased in the last years. The main reason of this reduction is the lack of effective favorable tax treatment for worker-owned companies compared to capitalist companies in Spain. Moreover, in France, there is a need of guidance from experts because there are several financial investment vehicles and some of them are risky.

In fact, it can be concluded that the role of tax incentive is very important; due to having suitable tax exemption plans, more companies tend to become ESOP, PEE and EOT. However, because of the lack of suitable tax treatment, the number of SLs firms has been decreased.

3.6.3. Recommendations for improving the Iranian system

In this section, the chapter provided some recommendations in order to improve the current employee ownership plan of Iran. First, it is better the Preferred shares plan is also be applied to private companies. Second, if possible and with considering the economic and financial conditions of the companies, it is better to give a higher percentage of the company's shares to the employees as preferred shares because it can lead to employees to benefit more from the company's shares and finally higher performance. Third, in the laws related to the Preferred shares, there is no mention of whether the company can limit the non-financial rights of the recipients of Preferred shares, such as the right to vote, the right to attend company meetings. Although the mentioned shares will become ordinary shares after the payment of installments is completed, the question that arises here is whether the owners of Preferred shares have the right to attend and vote in the company's general meetings during the ten-year period of payment of installments. Therefore, for more transparency, it is suggested to the policymakers to add a note to the bylaw of how transfer of Preferred shares. Finally, since benefit from Preferred shares depends on the submission of a written request by the applicants collectively and it can have some difficulties for employees, it is suggested that like the US and UK plans, employees would be automatically members of the Preferred shares plan when they are employed in the company.

4. CONCLUSION

According to agency theory, employees' ownership has a positive impact on reducing agency conflicts and can reduce information asymmetry, which ultimately increases company performance and employee satisfaction. Moreover, employee ownership can increase employees' willingness to exert pressure on their company from a social point of view. Therefore, choosing a suitable employee share ownership plan is important for companies. This chapter investigated the employees' ownership plans in Iran and western countries including USA, France, Spain and the UK. In Iran, with the aim of privatization of state-owned companies, a new kind of shares that called Preferred shares were introduced by the government of Iran. According to this plan, state-owned companies' shares can be sold in the form of Preferred shares to the employees of the companies. This type of shares is different from stock options and also different from western countries employees' ownership plans such as ESOP in the U.S.

By answering the question "What are the differences between employees' ownership plans in Iran and western countries?" this chapter exhibited several differences among systems. Despite the importance and impact of employee ownership on the companies' performance and giving of Preferred shares to employees of state-owned companies, there is no mention of stock options in Iran's Trade law and other related laws. Moreover, the attribution of these shares is a private agreement and is valid according to Article 10 of the Civil Law. Hence, the lack of a specific related law to encourage companies, especially private companies, to sell shares to their employees is evident.

Theoretically, an examination of employee ownership plans in Western countries, along with an analysis of their advantages and disadvantages and the significance of tax exemptions, reveals important insights. Based on agency theory, it can be concluded that enhancing employee share ownership helps mitigate agency conflicts and reduce information asymmetry. This, in turn, can improve a firm's financial and social performance while also increasing employee satisfaction. Moreover, the comparison of advantages and disadvantages of employee ownership plan of Iran among Western countries, leads to diverse managerial implications. Iran could be incited to adopt International Practices: Private companies should adopt successful employee ownership plans from other countries by selling a portion of shares to employees, enhancing motivation, productivity, and overall company performance. Since employees with stock options are not required to pay share taxes, companies could be encouraged to grant stock options to boost employee motivation.

As regards prudential rules, policymakers should require companies, particularly private ones, to sell a certain portion of shares to employees, potentially offering options like discounts to facilitate ownership. To improve company performance and productivity, laws should be enacted similar to those in Western countries, introducing Preferred shares with benefits like tax exemptions. Last but not least, the government should offer special discounts for employee purchases and clearly specify the discount amounts.

Beyond its contribution this chapter is not free from limitations. Our results could be deepened through a quantitative analysis on employees' ownership. Quantitative research facilitates a significant degree of generalizability and provides accurate outcomes which are independent of interpretative subjectivity. Therefore, it is suggested that in order to better understand the efficiency of Preferred shares on Iranian companies, the effect of employee ownership (Preferred shares) on the performance and productivity of these companies be examined. It is also possible to check the extent of this impact in different industries. The second limitation of this chapter is that, there is no study on the impact of Preferred shares in the lives of employees and society. Therefore, for addressing this limitation, future research could use interviews; since interviews facilitate the identification of profound insights from respondents regarding their social contexts.

REFERENCES

Abdelnour, J., Aubert, N., & Ben-Amar, W. (2023). Employee stock ownership and voluntary carbon disclosure. *Bankers Markets & Investors: an academic & professional review*. ⟨halshs-04094880⟩

Abdelnour, J., Aubert, N., & Campa, D. (2022). Does employee ownership reduce agency costs? Evidence from French listed companies. *Finance Contrôle Stratégie*, 25-3/4

Adwan, S., & Ahamed, M. M. (2024). Employee ownership and corporate investment efficiency in Europe. *Review of Quantitative Finance and Accounting*, 0(0). Advance online publication. DOI: 10.1007/s11156-024-01300-5

Adwan, S., Alhaj-Ismail, A., & Jelic, R. (2022). Non-executive employee ownership and financial reporting quality: Evidence from Europe. *Review of Quantitative Finance and Accounting*, 59(2), 793–823. DOI: 10.1007/s11156-022-01058-8

Ahmad, N., Harun, A., Khizar, H. M. U., Khalid, J., & Khan, S. (2022). Drivers and barriers of travel behaviors during and post COVID-19 pandemic: A systematic literature review and future agenda. *Journal of Tourism Futures*, 0(0). Advance online publication. DOI: 10.1108/JTF-01-2022-0023

AMF. (2023, March 23). Employee savings: a sharp increase in awareness and ownership of employee savings schemes; support for employees and company managers should be reinforced. https://www.amf-france.org/en/news-publications/news-releases/amf-news-releases/employee-savings-sharp-increase-awareness-and-ownership-employee-savings-schemes-support-employees

Ana, (2024, May 6). Head of the Privatization Organization: 5 billion preferred shares were given to the workers. *Ana News*. https://ana.ir

AON. (2020). How Common are Employee Stock Purchase Plans? It Varies Widely by Demographics. https://rewards.aon.com/en-us/insights/articles/2020/how-common-are-employee-stockpurchase-plans-it-varies-widely-by-demographic

Aubert, N., & Bernheim, P. (2021). *What the PACTE law changes for employee savings and participation? Post-Print hal-02532708*. HAL.

Beheshti, S., Eskini, R., Pasban, M., & Zare, A. (2018). Company Employees' Incentive Plan: Incentive Shares and Preferred Shares with a Study in the Legal Systems of England and Iran. *International Legal Investigations*, 11(40), 39–70.

Blasi, J. (2017). *Tech Companies Are Shutting Employees Out of the Stock Market's Boom*. Fortune.

Blasi, J., Kruse, D., & Weltmann, D. (2021). The response of majority employee-owned firms during the pandemic compared to other firms. *Journal of Participation and Employee Ownership*, 4(2), 92–101. DOI: 10.1108/JPEO-09-2021-0014

Blasi, J., Scharf, A., & Kruse, D. (2024). Employee ownership in the US: Some issues on ESOPs – overcoming the barriers to further development. *Journal of Participation and Employee Ownership*, 7(1), 26–45. DOI: 10.1108/JPEO-11-2022-0028

Bonelli, M., Brière, M., & Derrien, F. (2022). *Altruism or Self-Interest? ESG and Participation in Employee Share Plans*. ESG and Participation in Employee Share Plans. DOI: 10.2139/ssrn.4164062

CDIF capital, (2024). Employee saving: Retain your employees & build up common capital while reducing taxes! *CDIF capital website*. https://www.cidif-capital.fr/en/plan-%C3%A9pargne-entreprise-pee

Chen, J., King, T.-H. D., & Wen, M.-M. (2020). Non-executive ownership and private loan pricing. *Journal of Corporate Finance*, 64, 101638. DOI: 10.1016/j.jcorpfin.2020.101638

Economia Desde Casa. (2020). Sociedad Laboral | Business Economics 23#. You Tube. https://www.youtube.com/watch?app=desktop&v=ylpPnJ6Yd7o

Ellerman, D., Gonza, T., & Berkopec, G. (2022). European Employee Stock Ownership Plan (ESOP): The main structural features and pilot implementation in Slovenia. *SN Business & Economics*, 2(186), 186. DOI: 10.1007/s43546-022-00363-7

Farooq, O., Farooq, M., & Reynaud, E. (2019). Does employees' participation in decision making increase the level of corporate social and environmental sustainability? An investigation in South Asia. *Sustainability (Basel)*, 11(2), 511. DOI: 10.3390/su11020511

Fernández-Guadaño, J., & López-Millán, M. (2019). Assessing employee-owned firms: An examination of the Spanish economic model. *Ekonomska Istrazivanja*, 32(1), 1994–2008. DOI: 10.1080/1331677X.2019.1642781

Freeman, R. (1984). *Strategic management: A stakeholder approach*. Pitman Publishing Inc.

Gonza, T. (2024). *Comparative Analysis of Organizational Structures of Employee Centred Enterprises*. PhD thesis, University of Ljubljana.

Hamed, Z. (2022). Sample contract for awarding incentive shares and legal challenges of assigning shares to employees. Lawmingo website. https://lawmingo.com/mag/sample-contract-for-awarding-incentive-shares-and-legal-challenges-of-assigning-shares-to-employees/

Jensen, M. C., & Meckling, W. H. (1976). Theory of the firm: Managerial behavior, agency costs and ownership structure. *Journal of Financial Economics*, 3(4), 305–360. DOI: 10.1016/0304-405X(76)90026-X

Jordan, A. (2022, December 8). Pros and cons of employee ownership trusts (EOTs), *Small Business website*. https://smallbusiness.co.uk/pros-and-cons-of-employee-ownership-trusts-eots-2552031/

Kim, K. Y., & Patel, P. C. (2017). Employee ownership and firm performance: A variance decomposition analysis of European firms. *Journal of Business Research*, 70, 248–254. DOI: 10.1016/j.jbusres.2016.08.014

Kim, K. Y., & Patel, P. C. (2021). A multilevel contingency model of employee ownership and firm productivity: The moderating roles of industry growth and instability. *Organization Science*, 32(3), 625–648. DOI: 10.1287/orsc.2020.1404

Kishk, I. (2023). *The impact of Ownership Structure on Firm Performance: A Comparative Multi-Country Analysis*. PhD thesis, University of Essex.

Kong, D., Liu, J., Wang, Y., & Zhu, L. (2024). Employee stock ownership plans and corporate environmental engagement. *Journal of Business Ethics*, 189(1), 177–199. DOI: 10.1007/s10551-023-05334-y

Kruse, D. (2022). Does employee ownership improve performance? *IZA World of Labor: Evidence-Based Policy Making*, 311. Advance online publication. DOI: 10.15185/izawol.311.v2

Kurtulus, F., & Kruse, D. (2017). *How Did Employee Ownership Firms Weather the Last Two Recessions?* W.E. Upjohn Institute for Employment Research.

Lowitzsch, J., Dunsch, S., & Hashi, I. (2017). *Spanish Sociedades Laborales—Activating the Unemployed*. Palgrave Macmillan. DOI: 10.1007/978-3-319-54870-8

. Lowitzsch, j; Menke, J.D; Suarsana, D; Nuttall, G; Gonza, T & Mirabel, T. (2024). Toward a european employee stock ownership plan (European ESOP), Kellogg College.

Machell, M. (2023, May 22). Lessons from an employee ownership trust: a HR case study. *HR Magazine*. https://www.hrmagazine.co.uk/content/news/lessons-from-an-employee-ownership-trust-a-hr-case-study/

Mackin, C. (2024). Defining employee ownership: Four meanings and two models. *Journal of Participation and Employee Ownership*, 7(1), 1–25. DOI: 10.1108/JPEO-10-2022-0019

Marcuello, C. (2023). Employee ownership in Spain: Worker cooperatives and sociedades laborales. *Journal of Participation and Employee Ownership*, 6(2), 149–165. DOI: 10.1108/JPEO-10-2022-0022

Mehr, (2024a, May 5). The preferred shares of 64,000 workers were given to their names. *Mehr News*. https://www.mehrnews.com/

Mehr, (2024b, July 17). 400,000 people became shareholders by handing over preferred shares. *Mehr News*. https://www.mehrnews.com/

MENKE. (2024, November, 1). A Fireside Chat with Ringland-Johnson. MENKE website.https://www.menke.com/esop-archives/a-fireside-chat-with-ringland johnson/

Moustabchir, O., Khenissi, M., & Juban, J. (2024). *The influence of employee share ownership on CSR performance. The case of SBF 120 listed companies*. Finance Contrôle Stratégie.

Mygind, N. (2012). Trends in Employee Ownership in Eastern Europe. *International Journal of Human Resource Management*, 23(8), 1611–1642. DOI: 10.1080/09585192.2012.661992

Mygind, N. (2023a). Overcoming barriers of employee ownership in France, Italy, Spain, the UK and the US. *Journal of Participation and Employee Ownership*, 6(3), 230–263. DOI: 10.1108/JPEO-10-2022-0026

Mygind, N. (2023b). Three models of employee ownership: Worker cooperative, EOT and ESOP – overcoming barriers – important choices – pros and cons. *Journal of Participation and Employee Ownership*, 6(3), 264–280. DOI: 10.1108/JPEO-10-2022-0027

O'Boyle, E., Patel, P., & Gonzalez, E. (2016). Employee ownership and firm performance: A meta-analysis. *Human Resource Management Journal*, 26(4), 425–448. DOI: 10.1111/1748-8583.12115

Pendleton, A., Robinson, A., & Nuttall, G. (2023). Employee ownership in the UK. *Journal of Participation and Employee Ownership*, 6(3), 194–214. DOI: 10.1108/JPEO-11-2022-0030

PWC. (2020). Tax incentives for business owners and employees. *PWC website*. https://www.pwc.co.uk/tax/assets/pdf/employee-ownership-trusts.pdf

Rauh, J. D. (2006). Own company stock in defined contribution pension plans: A takeover defense? *Journal of Financial Economics*, 81(2), 379–410. DOI: 10.1016/j.jfineco.2005.07.004

Ren, T., Xiao, Y., Yang, H., & Liu, S. (2019). Employee ownership heterogeneity and firm performance in China. *Human Resource Management*, 58(6), 621–639. DOI: 10.1002/hrm.21995

. Roelants, B., Dovgan, D., Eum, Hyungsik, & Terrasi, E. (2012). The resilience of the cooperative model. CECOP.

Roeterdink, M. (2018). *The influence of employee ownership and employee board representation on firm performance: Evidence from French listed firms*. PhD thesis, University of Twente

Rosen, C. (2023). Employee ownership in the USA: Lessons to consider in creating more inclusive capitalism. *Journal of Participation and Employee Ownership*, 6(3), 215–229. DOI: 10.1108/JPEO-11-2022-0029

. Rouzade, O, (2021, December 24). PEE Collective Savings Plan, *Cabinet ROUZADE website*. Подробная информация о коллективном плане сбережений PEE

Scocozza, G. N. (2020). *Growth of sociedades laborales (worker-owned companies) in Spain and the Basque Country*. Master Thesis, Universidad Católica de Córdoba

Winkler, A. L. P., Brown, J. A., & Finegold, D. L. (2019). Employees as conduits for effective stakeholder engagement: An example from B corporations. *Journal of Business Ethics*, 160(4), 913–936. DOI: 10.1007/s10551-018-3924-0

KEY TERMS

Agency Theory: Agency theory is a contract in which one or more persons, principals, engage another person, the agent, to do several services on their behalf which consists of delegating several decision-making authorities to the agent. The agency theory opines that when the purposes of principals and agents are misaligned, agency problems may exist at the employee level, where monitoring is more difficult and monitoring costs are higher.

Employees Ownership: Employee ownership can be explained as the percentage of firm stocks owned by employees in their firms

Employee Stock Ownership Plan (ESOP): An ESOP handouts firm shares to employees based on the period of their employment.

Preferred Shares Plan: Preferred shares plan is a plan, that owing to the law, a maximum of 5% of the company's shares is able to be sold in the form of Preferred shares to the employees of the firm.

Chapter 10
Does Employee Ownership Enhance Financial Performance of Moroccan Companies Listed on the Casablanca Stock Exchange?

Houssam Errommani
https://orcid.org/0009-0007-6073-6342
Hassan II University of Casablanca, Morocco

Sara Elouadi
https://orcid.org/0000-0001-5412-2714
Hassan II University of Casablanca, Morocco

ABSTRACT

Employee Share Ownership (ESO) is a practice that is beginning to emerge in the managerial practices of Moroccan companies listed on the Casablanca Stock Exchange. This study examines the impact of ESO on the financial performance of these firms, focusing on employees' contribution to financial value creation. An empirical analysis was conducted using panel data and Estimated Generalized Least Squares (EGLS) via Eviews software. Financial data for the period of 2017–2023 were sourced from company reports, the Casablanca Stock Exchange website, and AMMC annual reports. The results indicate that ESO has a non-significant effect on Return on Assets (ROA) but a significant positive effect on Return on Equity (ROE) at the 10% threshold. This means that companies with employee share ownership

DOI: 10.4018/979-8-3693-7031-5.ch010

plans (ESOPs) outperform their counterparts in terms of ROE but have no impact on ROA.

1. INTRODUCTION

Employee share ownership (ESO) is an internationally widespread phenomenon, which has attracted growing interest in recent decades from academics, professionals and policymakers because of its effects on company performance. According to the latest statistics from the European Federation of Employee Share Ownership (EFES, 2023), 35 million employees own shares in their company in Europe, and there are 14.7 million employee-shareholders in the USA (NCEO, 2024). In Morocco, ESO was introduced alongside the 2013 finance law (Errommani and Elbouanani, 2022), which developed a regulatory framework accompanied by tax incentives, as well as the introduction of the company savings plan. However, its adoption remains modest in the sense that only 35 out of 76 companies listed on the Casablanca Stock Exchange have conducted at least one ESO operation since their listing. Indeed, the majority of these 35 companies have done so only once.

This study examines the evolution of ESO in Morocco and seeks to address a central question: What is the impact of ESO on the financial performance of Moroccan companies listed on the Casablanca Stock Exchange? It holds both academic and managerial significance by contributing to the expanding body of research on ESO in emerging economies while offering actionable insights for business leaders aiming to enhance financial performance through innovative employee engagement strategies.

The main hypothesis of the study is that ESO positively influences corporate financial performance, as measured by two indicators widely recognized in the literature: return on equity (ROE) and return on assets (ROA). Methodologically, the variable of interest, ESO, is operationalized through a binary variable. The study's sample was categorized into two comparative groups: those that practice ESO and those that have never practiced it. The empirical investigation encompasses 76 listed companies, employing multiple regression via the EGLS method using EVIEWS software to assess this impact. Data for the analysis were comprehensively sourced from the annual reports of the Moroccan Capital Markets Authority, data from the CDG Capital Brokerage website, information available from the Casablanca Stock Exchange, and the annual reports of companies since their IPO.

To address the research question, the study is structured in three key phases. Firstly, a theoretical analysis of ESO is performed and enriched by a combination of previous empirical work examining the relationship between corporate financial performance and ESO. Secondly, the research methodology adopted in this study is outlined, followed by a presentation and discussion of the results. Finally, the conclusion synthesizes the study's objectives and key findings, while critically reflecting on its theoretical, methodological, and managerial contributions, as well as identifying its limitations and potential avenues for future research.

2. LITERATURE REVIEW AND HYPOTHESES DEVELOPMENT

ESO has its origins essentially in agency theory, which examines the relationship established between the agent (management-employees) and the principal (shareholders). This theory identifies a potential conflict of interest between these parties, with agents tending to favor their own interests to the detriment of those of shareholders, particularly due to divergent interests and incomplete contracts (Jensen and Meckling, 2019). To remedy these divergences, the implementation of mechanisms aimed at aligning interests becomes essential. With this in mind, ESO has emerged as a major strategic lever (Cardoni and Poulain-Rehm, 2023).

O'Boyle et al. (2016) show that in an organizational environment characterized by flatter structures and greater difficulty in exercising control, ESOPs play a key role in strengthening organizational cohesion and cooperation. By linking employees' financial performance to that of the company, these schemes foster collective responsibility and establish a culture of shared interests. In a similar vein, Richter and Schrader (2017) point out that ESOPs solve agency problems by aligning employees' interests with those of shareholders, thereby reducing agency costs. This mechanism relies on performance-based incentive contracts and reinforces employees' sense of belonging as well as responsibility. Finally, Kundić et al. (2020) highlight that employee shareholding improves productivity, profitability, and business organization, while mitigating conflicts between managers and owners, which also helps reduce supervisory costs.

In another framework, stakeholder theory, developed by Freeman (1984), defines a stakeholder as any individual or group that can influence or be influenced by an organization's objectives. This theory stresses the importance of reconciling the interests of all stakeholders to ensure the success of the company. Within this perspective, ESO is presented as a strategic lever promoting the harmonization of internal and external interests (Elouadi, 2015). In this sense, it constitutes an incentive mechanism with positive effects on employee attitudes and behavior. In fact, recent studies have highlighted that ESO serves as a crucial component of stakeholder remuneration models, promoting equitable wealth distribution and enhancing collaboration within organizations. For instance, Aubert and Hollandts (2023) discuss how ESO aligns the interests of employees and shareholders, fostering a more inclusive approach to corporate governance.

According to Aubert and Cordova (2022), ESOPs have the potential to ensure the financial liquidity of companies while promoting social inclusion and empowerment of employees, directly linking their efforts to the organization's performance and orienting the economic system towards a sharing capitalism. The same authors assert that the sharing of risk and power represents a major shift in the spirit of traditional capitalism towards a more inclusive and participatory model. This new configuration transforms traditionally hegemonic structures into more diversified and inclusive management systems (Naim, 2015).

In the French context, ESOPs have been shown to strengthen employees' organizational commitment and significantly reduce their intention to leave the company (Elouadi, 2020). These positive effects are amplified by incentive variables such as the presence of employee shareholder directors and the existence of employee shareholder associations (Elouadi, 2020). Furthermore, Elouadi and Ben Noamene (2017) show that ESO improves employee satisfaction and develops their sense of belonging in the organization. Similarly, Degbey et al. (2020) demonstrate that during mergers and acquisitions operations, ESO plays a decisive role in employee retention, boosting their emotional involvement and organizational commitment.

These results reveal the transformative potential of ESO to foster employee organizational loyalty, improve corporate financial resilience, and promote a more equitable distribution of power and value among stakeholders.

Regarding the theoretical framework exploring the relationship between ESO and financial performance, the literature identifies four main hypothetical models.

2.1 The Null Hypothesis: Absence of Significant Correlation between Employee Share Ownership (ESO) and Financial Performance

This hypothesis posits an absence of a significant correlation between ESO implementation and corporate financial performance. In a study conducted by Bangun et Al. (2017) analyzed the effects of financial leverage, firm size, and ESOP on the performance of Indonesian listed manufacturing firms over the period 2013-2015. The results reveal that the effect of financial leverage and firm size have a significant impact on ROA and ROE. However, ESO has no effect on ROA and ROE. In the same context, Handayani and Yurniwati (2020) find that the ESO program has no effect on the company's financial performance (ROE) and that there are no differences in the company's financial performance when it issues ESOPs and when it does not. Kang and Kim (2019) highlight in their study the existence of contextual influences that modify the effectiveness of ESOPs based on a sample of 1,741 companies from 21 European countries. They take into account the contextual and cultural aspects of European countries and the distinction between managerial and non-managerial employee ownership. In fact, Kang and Kim (2019) conclude that managerial employee ownership has a direct positive effect on ROE, while non-managerial employee ownership has no significant effect on ROA.

Furthermore, in the same European context, over the period between 2006 and 2014, Kim and Patel (2017) maintain that ESO per se cannot lead to significant results on financial performance measured by ROA. The study underlines the importance of other variables linked to the context of the country, sector of activity, and the company itself. Hamdani and Gumanti (2019) assert in their study of 12 companies listed on the Indonesian Stock Exchange (IDX) that there is no difference between the three variables studied, namely ROA, ROE, and net profit margin, before and after the company's implementation of ESO. In addition, based on a sample of 163 French companies over a five-year period (from 2001 to 2005), a study conducted by Poulain-Rehm and Lepers (2013) indicates that ESO has no effect on either shareholder or stakeholder value creation. Similarly, Guery (2015) states that employee ownership has no influence on either financial performance or productivity for similar companies measured via propensity score matching methods.

2.2 The Negative Correlation Hypothesis: ESO Potentially Deteriorating Financial Performance

This perspective advocates that ESO may potentially deteriorate financial performance. Based on a sample of Chinese companies listed between 2012 and 2019. Feng et al. (2022) find that the implementation of ESOPs reduces management agency costs and improves internal control. However, the mechanism has a significant inhibiting effect on corporate financialization. The results are most pronounced in companies with higher financing constraints, low external audit quality, and higher shares held by management. Furthermore, Livingston and Henry (1980) find a negative effect of ESO on profitability ratios, Tobin's Q, and economic profitability (Park and Song, 1995). Faleye et al. (2006) show that companies with significant levels of employee shareholding (over 5% of capital) perform less well than companies with employee shareholding of less than 5% of capital.

2.3 The Positive Linear Relationship Hypothesis: ESO Directly Enhancing Financial Performance

This configuration suggests that ESO directly and proportionally enhances financial performance. These studies show that employee ownership will have a positive impact on financial performance measured by ROE (Fang et al, 2015) on productivity (Fang et al, 2021) ROA, and tobin Q (Ismiyanti, and Mahadwartha, 2017). Similarly, Cézanne and Hollandts (2022) conclude in their empirical work on a sample of listed companies in France over the period 2000-2014 that ESO increases corporate profitability. Kaarsemaker et al. (2010) also show that ESO increases employee productivity and company performance.

In the Chinese context, Ren et al. (2019) report that based on a total of 3,396 companies and 36,559 business-year observations, SA-adopting companies perform better than non-ESOP-adopting companies matched before and after adoption. Le and Nguyen (2023) reveal a positive effect between ESOP mechanisms and the financial performance of listed commercial banks in Ho Chi Minh and Hanoi, Vietnam, from 2015 to 2019. The authors call on Vietnamese banks and companies to be aware of the benefits of ESOP mechanisms for employees, companies, and shareholders alike. In the European context, Richter and Schrader (2017) show on the basis of a panel of 1115 companies from Europe's five largest countries that companies with ESO achieve significantly higher levels of capital market performance and accounting performance than companies that do not adopt ESO. However, the marginal effect of ESO decreases when its levels increase.

In the United States, Kim and Ouimet (2014) observe that small-scale ESO programs (below 5%) have a positive impact on company shareholder value, while large-scale programs have more mixed effects. Moreover, O'Boyle et al. (2016) prove through a meta-analysis that ESO was likely to have a slightly positive influence on performance, while Kim and Patel (2017) show in their analysis the preponderant effect of context (country, sector, company, time) on the relationship studied. In the Moroccan context, Tajer et al. (2021) show as part of their research studying the relationship between shareholding structure and financial performance measured by ROA and ROE of 31 listed Moroccan companies, over the period 2014-2018 that the presence of employee, and industrial shareholding has a positive and significant impact on financial performance. Thus, ESO can be a means of improving company performance thanks to the positive effects it can have on employee attitudes and behavior, particularly in terms of greater involvement, higher job satisfaction, increased motivation, reduced staff turnover and absenteeism. It can also serve to stabilize capital, and even combat takeover bids, particularly in listed companies (Benhamou, 2010).

As highlighted by Garfatta (2010), Kaarsemaker et al. (2010), and Ngongang (2013), the majority of empirical studies (over two-thirds) have demonstrated a positive correlation between the implementation of ESO programs and employee attitudes and behaviors. These positive attitudes and behaviors could in turn enhance the company's economic and financial performance. Indeed, O'Boyle et al. (2016) show through a meta-analysis of 102 samples representing nearly 56,984 companies aiming to synthesize results and direction for future theoretical developments, that ESO has a weak, but positive and statistically significant relationship with company performance. The positive impact is generally observed for studies with different sample designs (samples assessing the change in performance before and after ESO adoption, or samples of companies with ESO programs), different operationalization of performance (efficiency or growth), and different company categories (public or private). According to the same authors, the effect of ESO on performance has evolved in the literature over time, and studies based on samples outside the context of the U.S. show stronger effects than those carried out in the U.S. In the French context, Garfatta (2023) reveals that it is very important for investors to be aware that companies with significant employee shareholding programs tend to manage their earnings upwards.

2.4 The Non-Linear Relationship Hypothesis: Complex Interaction between ESO and Financial Metrics

This hypothesis indicates a more nuanced perspective proposing a complex, potentially nuanced interaction between ESO and financial metrics where the relationship is neither uniformly negative nor strictly linear: The idea underlying this category is that ESO is positively related to company performance at limited levels and that the relationship between ESO and company performance takes the form of an inverted U. Indeed, based on the data provided, the relationship between ESO and company performance is curvilinear.

Indeed, based on data published by the China Securities Regulatory Commission on employee and managerial ownership of 620 listed Chinese companies between 2014 and 2020, Dasilas, (2024) unveils an inverted-U-shaped relationship between employee ownership and company performance. However, this inverted-U relationship only applies to non-state-owned Chinese companies. Finally, an inverted-U relationship between managerial shareholding and company performance has been proven. Thus, studies carried out in the French context by Poulain-Rehm (2007) and Poulain-Rehm and Lepers (2013) conclude that companies with significant employee shareholding (which are included in the French Employee Shareholding Index) do not create more value or distribute more wealth to employees, whether in the form of dividends, stock market value or book value. In the same vein, Belanès and Saihi (2014) indicate that there is a significant non-linear effect of ESO on company performance, which increases when it is average but decreases when employee shareholding is low or high.

Furthermore, Ben Abdelhamid (2021) demonstrates that ESO can also strengthen the position of incumbent managers, making it more difficult to replace them even in the event of underperformance. The results indicate an inverted-U relationship between ESO and CEO entrenchment, suggesting that at moderate levels, ESO can protect executives from market pressures and layoff risks. Similarly, Toe et Al. (2017) have highlighted that the impact of significant ESO on corporate economic performance can sometimes lead to organizational inefficiencies, notably due to entrenched management and free rider behavior (Elouadi, 2015).

2.5 Proposed Research Hypotheses

In the light of previous studies and based on the results of the above-mentioned research, we propose to test the following hypotheses:

H_0: Employee share ownership would have no effect on CFP

H_1: ESO has a positive effect on CFP

3. RESEARCH DESIGN

This research is embedded within a longitudinal framework and adopts a positivist paradigm, utilizing a hypothetico-deductive approach where theoretical foundations precede practical application (Charreire and Durieux, 2003). The subsequent sections outline the study's dataset, describe the variables along with their respective measurement methods, and present carefully chosen statistical models employed for hypothesis testing.

3.1 Sample

To test the research hypotheses, we used the annual reports of the Moroccan capital markets authority, data from the CDG Capital Bourse website, information available from the Casablanca Stock Exchange, and the annual reports of companies listed on the Casablanca Stock Exchange since their IPO, to update our database and determine which companies practice ESO in Morocco. All these sources were examined in detail to gather relevant information.

To date, the Casablanca Stock Exchange has 76 listed companies, and more than 35 of them have already carried out and publicized at least one employee shareholding operation since their listing on the stock exchange. The first step was to expose all the operations carried out by these companies, by sector of activity; number of ESO operations carried out; date of operation, and any other details relevant to our analysis.

After that, we extracted the financial data needed for our study for the period from 2017 to 2023. We then established our data in the form of an Excel panel, where each line corresponds to an observation for each company in a specific year.

In fact, our database includes a list that we have drawn up of companies practicing ESO in Morocco, as well as those that do not practice it and their affiliation to different sectors of activity. In this respect, we opted for the binary variable to measure ESO. Therefore, the financial data of these companies was expressed via financial ratios including ROA, ROE, total sales, debt level, and company size. The characteristics of these variables are described in the following section.

It is worth noting that all the data taken into account in this study are quantitative. In this respect, to guarantee a fair analysis of all variables, we have standardized them by integrating the natural logarithm (Ln).

3.2 Measures

3.2.1 Corporate financial performance

Referring to previous studies, several variables have been recommended to measure the financial performance of companies: ROA, ROE, Return on Investment (ROI), value added (VA), tobin Q, etc (Ngongang, 2013; Bangun et al., 2017; Handayani and Yurniwati, 2020; Kang and Kim, 2019; Ismiyanti and Mahadwartha, 2017).

In this respect, we opted for the following rigorous financial ratios in our study: ROA and ROE. The choice of these two ratios is justified by their purely accounting measure of financial performance. Indeed, ROE measures a company's ability to generate profits based on a certain level of equity (Ismiyanti and Mahadwartha, 2017).

ROE = Net Income / Total Equity

ROA measures the company's ability to create net income based on a certain level of assets (Ismiyanti and Mahadwartha, 2017).

ROA = Net Income / Total Assets

3.2.2 Employee share ownership

ESO is generally measured in the literature with the percentage held by employees in the capital, or by the binary variable (Ismiyanti and Mahadwartha, 2017; Kim and Ouimet, 2014).

Within the framework of this empirical work, we opted for the binary variable used by Ismiyanti and Mahadwartha (2017), namely the binary variable (0; 1):

- 1 = Companies that have already carried out employee shareholding operations.
- 0 = Companies that have never carried out ESO schemes.

This variable takes into account the specificities of the Moroccan context, in particular the absence of the percentage of capital held by employees for all the companies in our sample, due to the non-disclosure of this information by companies. Thus, ESO gives an idea of the effect of the regularity of employee shareholding operations carried out by listed Moroccan companies.

3.2.3 Control variables

Our database includes four control variables that enable us to better capture and characterize the influence of the independent variables. According to Thiétard (1999), the inclusion of control variables helps to strengthen the external validity of the results.

The inclusion of these variables enables us to control the characteristics of companies likely to influence the dependent variable of our model, namely financial performance. The various control variables used in our model are presented below:

- Debt: it is measured by the ratio of financial debt to equity. This measure has been adopted by several authors, including Ngongang (2013), Arcimoles and Trébucq (2003) and Poulain-Rehm (2006).
- Level of activity: given that Rappaport (1986) and Copeland et al. (1994) recommend considering the level of activity as a determining variable of financial performance, the variation in sales was included in our analysis. This measure has also been adopted by Ngongang, (2013), Trébucq (2002), and Poulain-Rehm (2006).
- Company size: the effect of company size is essential for a meaningful comparison of financial performance between companies. The literature shows that the "size" variable is measured in different ways. Three measures are commonly used: number of employees, sales volume, and total assets. In this study, following the example of Trébucq (2002), Poulain-Rehm (2006), and Gharbi and Lepers (2008), the natural logarithm of total assets is used as a measure of company size.
- Sector of activity: the financial performance of companies must be assessed in relation to the performance of their sector. In our study, we considered three main sectors: financial, industrial and services. We sought to assess the specific effects of the financial sector, which includes banking companies on companies' financial performance. To achieve this goal, we integrated binary variables to capture these effects. The first variable takes value 1 if the company belongs to the financial sector and 0 otherwise, while similar variables have been defined for the industrial and other sectors. This approach enables us to isolate the impact of each sector in our analysis.

3.3 Models Estimation

Financial performance was analyzed using Generalized Least Squares (GLS) multiple regression using Eviews software (Alim and Victor, 2019; Ngongang, 2013).

Based on the assumptions made and the associated explanatory and control variables, the models used are as follows:

$$ROA_{it}=\alpha+\beta_1 ESO_{it}+\beta_2 SIZE_{it}+\beta_3 DEBT_{it}+\beta_4 SECT_{it}+\beta_5 SALES_{it}+_{\varepsilon it}\ \textbf{(Model1)}$$

$$ROE_{it}=\alpha+\beta_1 ESO_{it}+\beta_2 SIZE_{it}+\beta_3 DEBT_{it}+\beta_4 SECT_{it}+\beta_5 SALES_{it}+_{\varepsilon it}\ \textbf{(Model2)}$$

We have structured our study around two rigorously chosen methods of analysis:

The first method (Model 1) consists of an empirical analysis using multiple regression to assess the effect of ESO (binary variable) on ROA of companies that practice ESO and those that have never practiced it.

The second method (Model 2) consists of assessing the effect of ESO (binary variable) on the ROE of companies that practice ESO and those that have never practiced it.

This regression aims to examine the hypothesis that companies that practice ESOP in Morocco have a sustained financial performance compared to those that do not.

4. EMPIRICAL RESULTS

In this section, we present the various statistics obtained and the results of our analyses and estimates.

4.1 Descriptive Statistics

Our study covers a sample of 76 listed companies between 2017-2023, 35 of which practice ESO. The following table presents the descriptive statistics for our sample and the study variables (expressed in % for some variables and in M MAD for others).

Table 1. Descriptive statistics

	Descriptive statistics				
Variable	*Obs*	*Mean*	*Stand-dev*	*Min*	*Max*
ROE	516	11,8%	41,8%	-4,2%	333,3%
ROA	516	3,2%	8,0%	-62,6%	22,2%
SALES	516	3533,6	6014,4	4	36786
DEBT	516	124,2%	414,4%	-3842,9%	5180,0%
SIZE	516	27177,9	91340,6	24,7	659005

4.2. Effect of ESO on ROA

In order to analyze the effect of ESO on ROA, we proceed by verifying the presence or absence of heteroscedasticity in the panel data using the Breusch-Pagan test:

Table 2. Breusch-Pagan test

Lagrange Multiplier Tests for Random Effects			
Null hypotheses: No effects			
Alternative hypotheses: Two-sided (Breusch-Pagan) and one-sided (all others) alternatives			
	Test Hypothesis		
	Cross-section	Time	Both
Breusch-Pagan	299,3519	0,4271	299,7790
	0,0000	-0,5134	0,0000
Honda	17,3018	0,6535	12,6963
	0,0000	-0,2567	0,0000
King-Wu	17,3018	0,6535	5,3372
	0,0000	-0,2567	0,0000
Standardized Honda	18,3869	0,9709	7,7386
	0,0000	-0,1658	0,0000
Standardized King-Wu	18,3869	0,9709	2,2706
	0,0000	-0,1658	-0,0116
Gourieroux, et al.	--	--	299,7790
			0,0000

The Breusch-Pagan test verifies the existence of random effects in the data.

Table 2 reveals the existence of random effects between companies (cross-section), but no effects with regard to the time dimension. In this respect, we opted for a random-effects model to take account of variability between companies. The results of the Breusch-Pagan test were validated by the other tests.

Afterward, we performed the Hausman test to determine the appropriate model to use (a random-effects or fixed-effects model).

Table 3. The Hausman test

Correlated Random Effects - Hausman Test			
Equation: MODELE_ROA			
Test cross-section random effects			
Test Summary	Chi-Sq. Statistic	Chi-Sq. d.f.	Prob.
Cross-section random	30.92040906616431	3	0.3883

Table 3 indicates a p-value of 0.3883, which is well above the 5% threshold, so we do not reject the null hypothesis. This means that the random effects model is more appropriate than the fixed effects model, as there is no significant correlation between the random effects and the explanatory variables.

Then, we performed modeling using the EGLS method, which addresses issues of heteroscedasticity and correlation. This method accounts for the variance-covariance structure specific to panel data, allowing us to obtain more efficient estimators.

Table 4. Regression results

Dependent Variable: ROA				
Method: Panel EGLS (Cross-section random effects)				
Sample: 2017-2023				
Periods included: 7				
Cross-sections included: 76				
Total panel (unbalanced) observations: 516				
Swamy and Arora estimator of component variances				
Variable	**Coefficient**	**Std. Error**	**t-Statistic**	**Prob.**
C	-0,030430	0,038224	-0,796101	0,4263
ESOP	-0,016706	0,014330	-1,165797	0,2442
DEBT	-0,000265	0,000682	-0,388679	0,6977
SALES	0,046928	0,006197	7,572954	0,000

continued on following page

Table 4. Continued

Dependent Variable: ROA				
SIZE	-0,030143	0,006381	-4,724140	0,000
FINANCIAL SECTOR	0,015276	0,027771	0,550083	0,5825
INDUSTRY SECTOR	-0,000968	0,023901	-0,040492	0,9677
SERVICES SECTOR	-0,024558	0,026609	-0,922926	0,3565
Effects Specification				
			S.D.	Rho
Cross-section random			0,053862	0,5305
Idiosyncratic random			0,050673	0,4695
Weighted Statistics				
	0,117329	Mean dependent var		0,010564
Adjusted R-squared	0,105167	S.D. dependent var		0,055142
S.E. of regression	0,052221	Sum squared resid		1,385350
F-statistic	9,646589	Durbin-Watson stat		1,709185
Prob(F-statistic)	0,000000			
Unweighted Statistics				
R-squared	0,112397	Mean dependent var		0,032049
Sum squared resid	2,942245	Durbin-Watson stat		0,804767

As presented in Table 4, several indicators were checked to analyze its overall significance and statistical properties.

F statistic: The value of 9.646589 obtained for the F statistic reveals that the model is globally significant. This statistic measures the model's ability to explain variations in the data, compared to a model with no relationship between variables. A high value, as in our case, suggests that the explanatory variables contribute significantly to the prediction of the dependent variable.

Probability of the F-statistic: The P-value of the F-statistic is 0.000000, well below the 5% threshold. This value indicates that the null hypothesis, according to which all coefficients of the explanatory variables are equal to zero, is rejected at a very high confidence level. In other words, the model's explanatory variables have a statistically significant impact on the dependent variable.

Durbin-Watson statistic: The value of 1.709185 obtained for the Durbin-Watson test is close to 2, suggesting a notable absence of autocorrelation in the residuals.

Table 4 shows that ESO has an effect close to 0 (-0.016706) on ROA, and not significant ($p=0.2442>0.05$). This means that companies practicing ESO in Morocco do not benefit from the potential advantages of ESO as approved in the majority of previous studies, and do not outperform companies without ESO in terms of ROA.

This result corroborates the findings of the study by Kang and Kim (2019) on a sample of 1,741 companies in 21 European countries, which concluded that ESO had no significant effect on ROA. Thus, the study highlights the existence of contextual influences that modify the effectiveness of employee share ownership programs.

In the same European context, Kim and Patel (2017) conclude that ESO per se cannot lead to significant results on financial performance measured by ROA. The study highlights the importance of other variables linked to the context of the country, business sector and company itself.

The non-significance of the results may be due to the entrenchment of managers, as well as to the absence of other proxy variables linked to tax incentives, a well-crafted legal and legislative framework, the quality of Moroccan managers, and corporate governance. Furthermore, through the effects it induces, ESO can be used as an instrument of confidence to limit the uncertainty and mistrust of borrowers and providers of funds (Elouadi, 2017). In this respect, a major issue is the management aspect of this mechanism within Moroccan companies, as well as the place of Moroccan employee-shareholders in decision-making and the degree of their involvement in their company's management and development projects.

Furthermore, concerning our control variables, the results indicate that indebtedness has an almost null (-0.000265) and insignificant (0.6977p > 0.05) effect on ROA, indicating the non-existence of a solid relationship between return on assets and indebtedness. Company size had a negative (0.030143) and significant (0.000< 0.05) effect on ROA, meaning that the larger the company's total assets, the lower its profitability in terms of ROA. On the other hand, sales reflect a positive (0.046928) and highly significant (0.000<5%) effect on ROA. This means that for each unit of variation in sales, ROA varies in the same direction by 0.04 (units of measurement). Thus, the financial sector has a positive (0.015276) and insignificant (0.5825p > 0.05) impact on ROA. The industrial sector shows an effect (-0.000968) close to 0 and insignificant (0.9677), meaning that there is no observable link between the industrial sector and ROA. Thus, the effect of other sectors (notably services) shows a negative correlation (-0.024558) but not significant at the 5% threshold (P=0.3565) on ROA.

4.3 Effect of ESO on ROE

In the same way, we carried out the Breusch-Pagan Test to verify the existence or otherwise of heteroscedasticity in the panel data (Table 5).

Test Breusch-Pagan

Table 5. Breusch-Pagan test

Lagrange Multiplier Tests for Random Effects			
Null hypotheses: No effects			
Alternative hypotheses: Two-sided (Breusch-Pagan) and one-sided (all others) alternatives			
	Test Hypothesis		
	Cross-section	Time	Both
Breusch-Pagan	56,1062	0,1159	56,2221
	0,0000	-0,7335	0,0000
Honda	7,4904	-0,3405	5,0557
	0,0000	-0,6333	0,0000
King-Wu	7,4904	-0,3405	1,7107
	0,0000	-0,6333	-0,0436
Standardized Honda	8,2688	-0,0936	-0,4599
	0,0000	-0,5373	-0,6772
Standardized King-Wu	8,2688	-0,0936	-1,6461
	0,0000	-0,5373	-0,9501
Gourieroux, et al.	--	--	56,1062
			0,0000

Subsequently, the Hausman Test is conducted to determine the suitability of either a random-effects or fixed-effects model.

Table 6. Hausman test

Correlated Random Effects - Hausman Test			
Equation: MODELE_ROE			
Test cross-section random effects			
Test Summary	Chi-Sq. Statistic	Chi-Sq. d.f.	Prob.
Cross-section random	14.931048	3	0.1942

The Hausman specification test, as presented in Table 6, yields a p-value of 0.1942, which substantially exceeds the conventional statistical significance threshold of 0.05. Consequently, we fail to reject the null hypothesis, thereby providing statistical justification for employing the random-effects model in our econometric analysis.

Accordingly, we proceed with the modeling:

Table 7. Regression results

Dependent Variable: ROE				
Method: Panel EGLS (Cross-section random effects)				
Sample: 2017-2023				
Periods included: 7				
Cross-sections included: 76				
Total panel (unbalanced) observations: 516				
Swamy and Arora estimator of component variances				
Variable	**Coefficient**	**Std, Error**	**t-Statistic**	**Prob,**
C	-0,23524	0,13814	-1,70292	0,08919
ESOP	0,09123	0,05079	1,79616	0,07306
DEBT	-0,06771	0,00400	-16,93190	0,00000
SALES	0,02817	0,02477	1,13752	0,25586
SIZE	0,00608	0,02507	0,24261	0,80841
FINANCIAL SECTOR	0,25514	0,09942	2,56628	0,01057
INDUSTRY SECTOR	0,00748	0,08407	0,08897	0,92914
SERVICES SECTOR	-0,02481	0,09377	-0,26460	0,79142
Effects Specification				
			S,D,	Rho
Cross-section random			0,16264	0,22008
Idiosyncratic random			0,30617	0,77992
Weighted Statistics				
R-squared	0,3566	Mean dependent var		0,06924
Adjusted R-squared	0,3478	S,D, dependent var		0,38452
S,E, of regression	0,3105	Sum squared resid		48,98977
F-statistic	40,2287	Durbin-Watson stat		1,91716
Prob(F-statistic)	0,0000			
Unweighted Statistics				
R-squared	0,30396	Mean dependent var		0,11841
Sum squared resid	62,50167	Durbin-Watson stat		1,50270

As presented in Table 7, the F statistic reveals a value of 40.2287 is relatively high, indicating that the model explains the variance of the dependent variable well compared to a null hypothesis of no effect. This suggests that the explanatory variables have a significant impact on the dependent variable.

Prob(F-statistic) = 0.0000, below the 5% threshold: The p-value of the F-statistic of 0.0000 shows that the probability of rejecting the null hypothesis is extremely low. This means that the model is highly significant and that the independent variables have a statistically significant effect on the dependent variable.

In addition, the Durbin-Watson stat detects autocorrelation in the model's residuals. The value of 1.91716 is close to 2, revealing that there is no serious autocorrelation in the residuals. This is generally a good sign.

Table 7 shows that ESO has a positive effect (0.09123) on ROE and is significant at the 10% threshold (p= 0.07306<10%). This means that companies practicing ESO in Morocco show some outperformance to those that do not practice it. This means that shareholders and fund providers of companies with ESOP benefit in terms of productivity and results generated via their equity investment.

These findings are in line with much of the work that has focused on the link between ESO and firm performance, which has inferred a positive effect (Ngongang, 2013; Garfatta, 2010) and corroborates the results of the study by Fang et al. (2015) in the Chinese context. Le and Nguyen (2023) reveal a positive effect between ESOP mechanisms and the financial performance of listed commercial banks in Ho Chi Minh and Hanoi in Vietnam from 2015 to 2019.

Concerning our control variables, the results indicate that the level of indebtedness has a negative (-0.06771) and highly significant (0.00000<0.05) effect on ROE, indicating the existence of a negative relationship between ROE and indebtedness. Company size, on the one hand, shows an almost nil (0.00608) and insignificant (0.80841> 0.05) effect on ROE, indicating that there is no strong relationship between company size and ROE. On the other hand, sales reflect a positive (0.02817) and insignificant (0.25586>5%) effect on ROE. Thus, the financial sector has a positive (0.25514) and highly significant (0.01057<0.05) impact on ROE. The industrial sector shows an effect (0.00748) close to 0 and not significant (0.92914), meaning that there is no observable link between the industrial sector and ROE. Thus, the effect of other sectors (notably services) shows a negative correlation (-0.02481) but not significant at the 5% threshold (P=0.79142) on ROE.

5. CONCLUSION

This study aimed to assess the impact of ESO on the financial performance of Moroccan companies listed on the Casablanca Stock Exchange. Accordingly, we carried out a multiple regression using the EGLS method, establishing the link between ESO and the financial performance of companies, as well as the control variables of our study using Eviews software. ESO was measured by the binary variable, which divided Moroccan companies listed on the Casablanca Stock Exchange into two groups: those that had already published and publicized at least one ESO operation, and those that had never practiced it. In addition, the financial performance of the companies was expressed by two rigorously selected financial ratios: ROE and ROA. The study's control variables are debt level, sales, company size and sector of activity. The results tend to favor ESO companies in terms of ROE and reveal that ESO companies outperform non-ESO companies in terms of ROE but show no difference in terms of ROA.

In ROA assessment made in the present study, these results corroborate the findings of Kang and Kim (2019) on a sample of 1,741 companies in 21 European countries, which concluded that ESO has no significant effect on ROA. Thus, the study highlights the existence of contextual influences that modify the effectiveness of ESO programs.

In addition, our second investigation is in line with most of the work that has focused on the link between ESO and corporate performance and inferred a positive effect (Ngongang, 2013) as well as corroborates the results of the study by Fang et Al (2015) in the Chinese context. Additionally, Le and Nguyen (2023) reveal a positive effect between ESOP mechanisms and the financial performance of listed commercial banks in Ho Chi Minh and Hanoi in Vietnam from 2015 to 2019.

The results obtained which are insignificant for ROA and positive and significant at the 10% threshold for ROE, reflect a promising future for this practice in the Moroccan context. In this respect, several efforts should be made to promote this beneficial practice within Moroccan companies, and to address the underdevelopment and nascent state of ESO in Morocco, particularly as the majority of companies practicing ESO in Morocco have generally carried it out only once since their IPO (Errommani & Elbouanani, 2022). Therefore, companies should be aware of the need to involve employees in the company's development projects.

In this perspective, the ESO, through the effects it promotes on the attitudinal and behavioral aspect developed by a heightened sense of belonging (Elouadi, 2015) can affect employee productivity, and can consequently serve not only the company itself but also the national economy in terms of its gross domestic product as highlighted by the precursor of financial participation in the United States Louis Kelso in binary theory.

In this respect, several efforts need to be made, particularly with regard to tax incentives and a well-crafted legal framework, as well as good management and communication of the mechanism within companies.

Beyond the results obtained, our study presents three contributions to research:

Scientific and methodological: This research adopts a longitudinal approach, focusing specifically on the relationship between ESO and the financial performance of listed Moroccan companies, measured through ROA and ROE. By providing statistics and empirical results adapted to the Moroccan context, it enriches the existing literature and opens prospects for future studies of corporate governance mechanisms in Morocco. This analysis also explores the temporal effects of ESO, highlighting how its effectiveness can vary according to the length of implementation.

Managerial: From a practical point of view, our study provides important answers for Moroccan executives and managers, making them aware of the virtuous benefits of ESO on the financial performance of their companies. It also proposes guidelines that could encourage them to adopt ESO practices to boost employee commitment, improve corporate governance, and strengthen the competitiveness of their companies. Our results can also serve as a reference for policymakers, suggesting that ESO could be an effective policy for improving the competitiveness and stability of Moroccan companies, by strengthening the alignment of employee and shareholder interests.

Policy implications: Our study also provides concrete evidence for public decision-makers, encouraging them to consider tax incentives and an attractive regulatory and legal framework that would facilitate the adoption of ESO by Moroccan companies. Such an approach could have positive repercussions on the overall economic climate, notably by promoting a more equitable distribution of the wealth created, as well as strengthening social cohesion within companies.

However, our study has certain limitations, and it would have been wise to use the percentage of capital held by employees, a variable that proved to be unavailable to us due to the non-disclosure of this data by certain Moroccan companies, which led us to rely on the binary variable.

In this study, we chose to include the banking and financial sectors. This choice is justified by the small and unstable number of companies listed on the Casablanca Stock Exchange, which is made up of 76 companies, with one company delisting and another joining each time. ESO is therefore particularly popular in this sector, where the majority of companies in the financial sector declare their employee shareholding, the number of ESO operations carried out, and all other ESO-related information, unlike the majority of other companies in different sectors.

Finally, the subject of ESO offers a vast field of research for researchers, by looking at the obstacles to the spread of the ESO in Morocco via semi-directive interviews, and by examining the place and role of Moroccan employee-shareholders within the governance bodies of Moroccan companies listed on the Casablanca Stock Exchange. Other avenues of research could focus on assessing the contribution of this practice to the business sector, particularly as ESO is more popular in some sectors than in others.

REFERENCES

Abdelhamid, A. B. (2021). Corporate governance and employee ownership: evidence from France (Doctoral dissertation, Université Clermont Auvergne).

Achour, Z. (2024). Impact Of Employee Stock Ownership On Firm Financial Performance: Does Corporate Social Responsibility Matter? *International Journal of Management and Enterprise Development*, 23(2), 155–170. DOI: 10.1504/IJMED.2024.139275

Aubert, N., & Cordova, M. (2022). Dealing With COVID-19 Through Employee Stock Ownership Plans: Saving Money and Losing Power to Live an Extra Day. In Employee Share Ownership and Impacts on Organizational Value and Behavior (pp. 1-17). IGI Global.

Aubert, N., & Hollandts, X. (2023). La codétermination sera-t-elle la grande Réforme de notre siècle? (No. hal-04501083).

Bangun, N., Tjakrawala, F. K., Andani, K. W., & Santioso, L. (2017). The effect of financial leverage, employee stock ownership program and firm size on firm performance of companies listed in Indonesia Stock Exchange. *International Business and Accounting Research Journal*, 1(2), 82–98. DOI: 10.15294/ibarj.v1i2.7

Belanès, A., & Saihi, M. (2014). Does Employee Ownership Really Boost Performance? Bankers. *Markets & Investors*, (130), 55–68.

Caramelli, M. (2011). *Employee ownership and corporate performance: Toward unlocking the black box. Employee ownership and shared capitalism: New directions in research.* Labor and Employment Relations Association.

Cardoni, H., & Poulain-Rehm, T. (2023). The impact of employee shareholding on corporate governance: The employee shareholder director in France. *The Journal of Management and Governance*, 27(4), 1073–1114. DOI: 10.1007/s10997-022-09634-9

Cézanne, C., & Hollandts, X. (2022). Employee Participation in Corporate Governance: What Impact Does It Have on Performance and Cash Distribution Policy in the SBF 120 (2000-2014)?[La participation des salariés à la gouvernance d'entreprise: quel impact sur la performance et la politique de distribution des liquidités dans le SBF120 (2000-2014)?] (No. hal-04135429).

Dasilas, A. (2024). The nonlinear relationship between employee stock ownership plans and firm performance: Evidence from China. *Journal of Business Research*, 173, 114470. DOI: 10.1016/j.jbusres.2023.114470

Degbey, W. Y., Rodgers, P., Kromah, M. D., & Weber, Y. (2021). The impact of psychological ownership on employee retention in mergers and acquisitions. *Human Resource Management Review*, 31(3), 100745. DOI: 10.1016/j.hrmr.2020.100745

Elouadi, S. (2015). Les effets attitudinaux de l'actionnariat salarié: une étude empirique dans le contexte des entreprises françaises du SBF 250. Question (s) de management, (3), 11-24.

Elouadi, S. (2020). L'influence des variables incitatives sur la satisfaction des actionnaires salariés: une modélisation par équations structurelles. Question (s) de management, (2), 35-49.

Elouadi, S., & El Kerbani, M. (2022). Exploratory Study of the Attitudinal Effects of Employee Shareholding in Morocco. In Employee Share Ownership and Impacts on Organizational Value and Behavior (pp. 123-145). IGI Global. DOI: 10.4018/978-1-7998-8557-3.ch007

Elouadi, S., & Errommani, H. E. (2021). Analyse des effets de l'actionnariat salarié sur la création de valeur financière des entreprises marocaines cotées en bourse. Revue du contrôle, de la comptabilité et de l'audit, 5(1).

Elouadi, S., & Noamene, T. B. (2017). Does Employee Ownership Reduce the Intention to Leave? In Handbook of Research on Human Resources Strategies for the New Millennial Workforce (pp. 111-127). IGI Global.

Errommani, H., & Elbouanani, H. (2022). Analysis of the Effects of Employee Share Ownership on the Creation of Financial Value of Moroccan Companies Listed on the Stock Exchange. In *Employee Share Ownership and Impacts on Organizational Value and Behavior* (pp. 103–122). IGI Global. DOI: 10.4018/978-1-7998-8557-3.ch006

Fang, H., Nofsinger, J. R., & Quan, J. (2015). The effects of employee stock option plans on operating performance in Chinese firms. *Journal of Banking & Finance*, 54, 141–159. DOI: 10.1016/j.jbankfin.2015.01.010

Feng, Y., Yu, Q., Nan, X., & Cai, Y. (2022). Can employee stock ownership plans reduce corporate financialization? Evidence from China. *Economic Analysis and Policy*, 73, 140–151. DOI: 10.1016/j.eap.2021.11.002

Garfatta, R. (2010). Actionnariat salarié et création de valeur dans le cadre d'une gouvernance actionnariale et partenariale: application au contexte français (Doctoral dissertation, Université de Bourgogne).

Garfatta, R. (2023). Employee stock ownership and earnings management: Evidence from France. *International Journal of Management Practice*, 16(2), 249–265. DOI: 10.1504/IJMP.2023.129210

Guery, L. (2015, July). L'actionnariat salarié en période de crise: performance économique, performance sociale, et questions de gouvernance. In Preuves empiriques françaises et éclairage britannique, Convention de recherche avec l'IRES pour le compte de la CFECGC.

Hamdani, A. M., & Gumanti, T. A. (2019, October). Company Profitability Before and After Employee Stock Ownership Program in 2011-2014. In *2019 International Conference on Organizational Innovation (ICOI 2019)* (pp. 553-556). Atlantis Press.

Handayani, F., & Yurniwati, Y. (2020). Analysis of the influence of employee stock ownership program (ESOP) application of company financial performance. *Jurnal Ilmiah Universitas Batanghari Jambi*, 20(2), 616–625. DOI: 10.33087/jiubj.v20i2.978

Ismiyanti, F., & Mahadwartha, P. A. (2017). Does employee stock ownership plan matter? An empirical note. Investment management and financial innovations, (14,N° 3 (contin. 2)), 381-388.

Jensen, M. C., & Meckling, W. H. (2019). Theory of the firm: Managerial behavior, agency costs and ownership structure. In *Corporate governance* (pp. 77–132). Gower.

Kang, S., & Kim, A. (2019). Employee stock ownership and financial performance in European countries: The moderating effects of uncertainty avoidance and social trust. *Human Resource Management*, 58(6), 641–655. DOI: 10.1002/hrm.21942

Kim, K. Y., & Patel, P. C. (2017). Employee ownership and firm performance: A variance decomposition analysis of European firms. *Journal of Business Research*, 70, 248–254. DOI: 10.1016/j.jbusres.2016.08.014

Kundić, M., Smajla, N., & Cibulka, M. (2020). *Employee Stock Ownership and Agency Theory Problem. In 16th Interdisciplinary Management Research* (Vol. 1). IMR.

Le, p. L., & Nguyen, h. T. T. (2023). Effects Of Employee Stock Ownership Plans On Firm Performance–Evidence From Listed Commercial Banks Of Vietnam.

Mard, Y., Marsat, S., & Roux, F. (2014). Structure de l'actionnariat et performance financière de l'entreprise: le cas français. Finance Contrôle Stratégie, (17-4).

Moroccan capital market authority website (AMMC, 2013): https://www.ammc.ma/sites/default/files/PEE_20130227.pdf

Naím, M. (2015). *The End of Power*. Basic Books.

National Center For Employee Ownership Website. (NCEO, 2024):_Https://Www.Nceo.Org/What-Is-Employee-Ownership

Ngongang, D. (2013). Actionnariat salarié comme levier de création de valeur ajoutée et de productivité dans les entreprises camerounaises. *La Revue Gestion et Organisation*, 5(1), 1–8. DOI: 10.1016/j.rgo.2013.10.001

O'Boyle, E. H., Patel, P. C., & Gonzalez-Mulé, E. (2016). Employee ownership and firm performance: A meta-analysis. *Human Resource Management Journal*, 26(4), 425–448. DOI: 10.1111/1748-8583.12115

Pendleton, A. D., Poutsma, F., Van Ommeren, J. W., & Brewster, C. (2001). Employee share ownership and profit-sharing in the European Union. Luxembourg: Office for official publications of the European Communities.

Poulain-Rehm, T., & Lepers, X. (2013). Does employee ownership benefit value creation? The case of France (2001–2005). *Journal of Business Ethics*, 112(2), 325–340. DOI: 10.1007/s10551-012-1255-0

Ren, T., Xiao, Y., Yang, H., & Liu, S. (2019). Employee ownership heterogeneity and firm performance in China. *Human Resource Management*, 58(6), 621–639. DOI: 10.1002/hrm.21995

Richter, A., & Schrader, S. (2017). Levels of employee share ownership and the performance of listed companies in Europe. *British Journal of Industrial Relations*, 55(2), 396–420. DOI: 10.1111/bjir.12169

Statistics of the federation europeenne de l'actionnariat salarie (FEAS, 2023)- Https://Www.Efesonline.Org/Annual%20Economic%20Survey/2023/Recensement%20 2023.Pdf

Tajer, A. (2021). Contribution à l'étude de l'impact des mécanismes de la gouvernance et des caractéristiques du dirigeant sur la performance financière des PME familiales* (Thèse de doctorat, Université Cadi Ayyad, 2020/2021).

Tajer, A., Ouberka, B., & Rigar, S. M. (2021). Structure de l'actionnariat et performance financière des entreprises marocaines cotées en bourse. *Revue Française d'Economie et de Gestion*, 2(8).

Chapter 11
The Impact of Employee Share Ownership on Governance and Company Performance:
A Psychological Mediation Analysis

Telelaz Galaa Esposito
University of Carthage, Tunisia

ABSTRACT

This study investigates the impact of employee share ownership (ESO) on company performance and governance, focusing on the mediating role of psychological factors. Using SOMFY Tunisia as a case study, we analyzed data from 50 employees participating in an ESO plan. Results indicate that ESO significantly positively influences employee engagement, job satisfaction, and perceptions of governance. These psychological factors, in turn, mediate the relationship between ESO and company performance. Employee-shareholders demonstrate higher commitment, leading to improved individual performance and active participation in company projects. Furthermore, ESO positively impacts overall employee satisfaction, fostering a more participatory corporate culture. These findings suggest that ESO is a strategic tool for enhancing organizational performance by positively influencing employee attitudes and behaviors. However, limitations due to sample size and context should be considered, and further research is needed to generalize these results.

DOI: 10.4018/979-8-3693-7031-5.ch011

1. INTRODUCTION

Employee share ownership has emerged as a prominent strategy in contemporary organizations, offering the potential to align employee and organizational goals. While the concept has been widely studied, the underlying mechanisms linking employee share ownership to firm performance remain relatively under-explored. This study seeks to address this gap by examining the mediating role of psychological factors.

Specifically, we investigate how psychological factors, such as perceived ownership, job satisfaction, engagement, and involvement, mediate the relationship between employee share ownership and organizational performance. By operationalizing these psychological constructs, we aim to develop a more nuanced understanding of how ownership structures psychologically transform employee behaviors and organizational dynamics. Granting employees a stake in the company, employee share ownership can foster a more participatory governance structure, influencing decision-making processes and potentially improving organizational outcomes. This transformative potential extends beyond mere financial participation, suggesting a profound reshaping of organizational culture and employee-organization relationships.

This research contributes to the literature by providing a comprehensive understanding of the complex interplay between employee share ownership, psychological factors, and organizational performance, offering valuable insights for both researchers and practitioners. Theremainder of this chapter is structured as follows:

This chapter is structured as follows: Section 2 provides a comprehensive literature review, critically examining the theoretical foundations of employee share ownership and situating our research within the broader academic discourse. Section 3 details the methodological approach, offering a rigorous exposition of our research design, including data collection strategies, variable operationalization, and analytical frameworks. In Section 4, we present a detailed analysis of empirical results, critically interpreting our findings and comparing them with existing scholarship. Section 5 concludes the chapter by synthesizing key insights, highlighting theoretical contributions, and discussing potential practical implications for organizational research and management practice.

2. BACKGROUND AND CONTEXT

Employee share ownership (ESO) has emerged as a prominent tool in contemporary corporate governance, experiencing a surge in popularity in recent years. This practice, once considered marginal, has now established itself as a rapidly expanding global phenomenon, becoming an essential element in the growth models of many developed countries (Baker & Kahn, 2020). ESO involves granting employees shares or ownership stakes in the capital of the company they work for. This practice has witnessed remarkable growth, gaining traction in both large listed companies and small and medium-sized enterprises (SMEs) (Baker & Kahn, 2020).

The prevalence of ESO varies geographically. The United States boasts the highest rate, with one in four employees holding shares in their company (NCEO, 2005). In Europe, the figure is slightly lower, with one in five employees participating in ESO schemes (Pérotin & Robinson, 2002).

While ESO is well-established in many European countries, the experience in Tunisia remains limited, primarily confined to foreign-owned subsidiaries. Tunisia has sought to adapt employee share ownership to its economic and social realities, as shown by the TESOP model proposed by Trabelsi in 2021. The author proposedthis model to broaden capital ownership across public companies, offering a strategic alternative to traditional privatization approaches.

In this context, Trabelsi (2021) has proposed the concept of citizen shareholding, materialized through the Tunisian Employee Stock Ownership Plan (TESOP) model. This model aims to open up the capital of public companies to a broader range of stakeholders, including employees, consumers, and Tunisian citizens. Trabelsi suggests that the TESOP model could be applied to approximately 200 companies across various sectors in Tunisia, ranging from livestock to olive oil production. These companies are often small or medium-sized, making information on their practices more challenging to access. Inspired by Western models, the TESOP approach seeks to foster a sense of belonging among stakeholders and ultimately enhance company performance.

Although promising initiatives such as the TESOP (Employee Share Ownership Plan) exist, there are still doubts about the real impact of employee share ownership, especially in contexts where governance structures and organisational practices are very different from those in developed countries.

The significant growth of ESO can be attributed to the combined support of successive governments and businesses who recognize its potential benefits (Kruse, 2002). There is now a growing consensus that ESO mechanisms can serve to align the interests of employees and shareholders, leading to increased employee motivation and engagement within organizations (Desbrières, 2002).

However, the actual impact of employee share ownership on firm performance remains a subject of debate. While some studies have highlighted significant positive effects, such as increased productivity and profitability, others have found no clear link or even negative consequences (Klein & Kauffman, 2019; Whitfield et al., 2017).

This disparity underscores the complexity of the phenomenon, where numerous factors come into play, including the structure of share ownership plans, employee characteristics, and the broader economic and social context (Corfe & Kirkup, 2020).

Despite its widespread adoption, the real impact of employee share ownership on organizational performance continues to be debated among researchers and practitioners. While some studies have demonstrated significant positive effects, such as increased productivity, profitability, and employee satisfaction, others have failed to find a clear relationship or have even suggested potential negative effects (Klein & Kauffman, 2019).

The structure of the share ownership plan, employee and firm characteristics, as well as the economic and social context, are all factors that can play a significant role (Baker & Kahn, 2020). To better understand the mechanisms through which employee share ownership influences organizational performance, it is essential to explore the psychological variables underlying employee behavior.

Beyond the mixed results on the effectiveness of employee share ownership, it is crucial to examine the internal mechanisms, in particular the psychological dimensions that influence employee behaviour and organisational dynamics. The psychological factors studied by Pierce & Jussila (2019), such as the sense of ownership individuals develop towards their company, appear particularly relevant. Other researchers (Gomez-Mejia, 2018; Avey et al., 2009; Mayhew et al., 2007) have highlighted psychological factors like job satisfaction, motivation, engagement, and job commitment.

Furthermore, share ownership contributes to enhancing employee motivation and satisfaction by giving them a sense of participating in the company's success and sharing in its rewards. Moreover, employee motivation is seen as a means of improving alignment between managers and employees, encouraging the latter to become more involved in the company's performance (Gomez-Mejia, 2018). This sentiment can translate into increased employee commitment, a sense of responsibility, and more active participation in decision-making processes (Van Dyne & Pierce, 2004).

Job satisfaction, defined as the extent to which employees are satisfied with their role and work environment, is another important outcome of psychological ownership. According to Avey et al. (2009), employees who experience psychological ownership are more likely to report higher levels of job satisfaction. Indeed, feelings of ownership satisfy their psychological need for control and personal efficacy, leading to positive evaluations of their work conditions and experiences. High levels of job satisfaction can, in turn, reduce turnover intentions and promote workforce stability.

Employee engagement, characterized by vigor, dedication, and absorption in one's work, is closely linked to psychological ownership. When employees feel a sense of ownership, they are more likely to invest themselves in their roles and responsibilities, as they perceive their success as tied to that of the organization (Mayhew et al., 2007). Engaged employees are more likely to be emotionally and cognitively invested in their work, which can enhance organizational effectiveness and performance.

When an employee really cares about their company, that's professional commitment. If they feel like the company is theirs, they're more likely to be committed (Van Dyne & Pierce, 2004). Committed employees are less likely to leave the organization and are more willing to contribute to its long-term success. This commitment can manifest in various forms, including affective commitment, continuance commitment, and normative commitment, all of which are positively influenced by the sense of belonging.

Several studies have shown that the psychological factors of employee satisfaction, engagement, and involvement can positively impact individual and collective performance, thus enhancing overall organizational performance (Kahn, 1990; Albrecht & al, 2023).

To summarize, employee share ownership is a rapidly expanding trend that has garnered growing attention from scholars and practitioners. Although its actual effect on firm performance is still under debate, psychological factors provide a promising avenue for a deeper understanding of the underlying mechanisms of this phenomenon.

Beyond its psychological effects on employees, employee share ownership plays a crucial role in corporate governance by enhancing employee participation in decision-making processes and improving transparency and accountability within the organization. According to Gomez-Mejia (2018), employee share ownership promotes better governance by aligning the interests of employees and shareholders, while mitigating information asymmetries between the parties involved. Furthermore, share ownership can strengthen internal controls and improve the quality of strategic decisions, as employee-shareholders are often more inclined to advocate for policies that support the long-term sustainability of the company (Kruse, 2002). By facilitating open dialogue and collaboration between management and employees, participative governance not only improves employee morale but also enhances organizational stability by clarifying tensions between different stakeholders. This, in turn, contributes to improved overall company performance.

Given the increasing prevalence of employee share ownership, our general research question is as follows:

To what extent does employee share ownership influence corporate performance, both at the individual level (satisfaction, engagement, involvement) and at the organizational level (governance and overall performance), and what are the underlying mechanisms?

Following our theoretical analysis, we will formulate a general research hypothesis stated as follows: Employee share ownership acts as a catalyst for organizational change by strengthening participatory governance and fostering a closer alignment of employee interests with those of the company, significantly improving overall company performance by leveraging multiple factors such as employee satisfaction, engagement, quality of strategic decisions, and innovation. To further explore this hypothesis, we have also developed a set of operational hypotheses to test the influence of employee share ownership on various dimensions of psychological factors. Reformulated operational hypotheses:

H_1: Transitioning to shareholder status significantly improves both intrinsic and extrinsic job satisfaction, reinforcing employees' sense of belonging and their participation in governance processes.

H_2:Transitioning to shareholder status significantly enhances employee engagement, with increases in absorption, dedication, and vigor.

H_3: Employee share ownership significantly enhances employees' involvement in decision-making by strengthening their affective, calculative, and normative commitment, improving strategic decision quality and governance.

H_4:The adoption of employee share ownership introduces governance characteristics, such as employee representation in decision-making bodies, that improve organizational performance and decision-making processes

These hypotheses aim to explore the potential effects of employee share ownership on employees' attitudes and behaviors, focusing on dimensions of satisfaction, engagement, and organizational involvement.

3. METHODOLOGY

3.1. Research Design

To examine the issue of comparing results before and after the implementation of Employee Share Ownership as perceived by participants, we conducted a study using a quasi-experimental design. We conduct a quasi-experimental design is a research plan that allows for the evaluation of the effect of an intervention or program without resorting to complete randomization. This type of design is often used when strict experimental conditions cannot be met, but where it is still essential to observe potential changes.

We propose a two-pronged approach:

Retrospective Pretest: Participants were asked to retrospectively assess their pre-ESO perceptions of individual psychological factors (satisfaction, engagement, and commitment) and organizational factors (governance and performance) using a questionnaire.

Post-implementation measurement: The same participants provided post-ESO assessments of the same factors. This design allowed for a comparison of perceptions before and after the implementation of ESO.

3.2. Population and Sampling Method

Population: This study focused on Tunisian employees of SOMFY Tunisia, a French multinational subsidiary with employee share ownership plan. This specific context offers a valuable opportunity to delve into the implications of employee ownership.

Sampling method: 50 Participants were selected using a convenience sampling approach, focusing on employees directly involved in the ESO program to ensure relevant insights into its impact

Sample characteristics: Our sample of 50 participants presents a diverse profile. It comprises a majority of males (60%) and 40% females. Regarding age, the majority of participants are between 35 and 44 years old (40%), followed by the 25-34 age group (32%). In terms of marital status, 44% of participants are single, while 42% are married. Concerning educational level, 54% of participants hold a bachelor's degree, followed by those with a master's degree (22%). Regarding professional occupations, the distribution shows that 24% of participants work in the production sector, while 20% are engaged in marketing and sales. Finally, in terms of services, the accounting and finance sector represents the largest share (20%), followed by production (16%) and transportation and delivery (14%). This diversity within the sample enriches the analysis of the results and conclusions of the study.

3.3. Measurement Instruments

The selected measurement instruments were aligned with the research hypotheses to ensure precise evaluation of psychological and organizational constructs.

3.3.1. Minnesota Satisfaction Questionnaire (MSQ)

Assessing Job Satisfaction with the Minnesota Satisfaction Questionnaire (MSQ)

The Minnesota Satisfaction Questionnaire (MSQ) is a well-established tool used to measure job satisfaction. A short version of the MSQ, consisting of 20 items, was employed in this study. The original English version of the questionnaire was translated into French by Patrice Roussel (1993) to better suit our population.

Each item on the MSQ explores a specific facet of job satisfaction, such as skill utilization, achievement, or relationships with colleagues. Participants rate each item on a 5-point Likert scale, ranging from "very dissatisfied" to "very satisfied." These responses are then numerically coded for analysis.

The MSQ allows for the calculation of three types of scores:

Overall Satisfaction: This score reflects general job satisfaction and is obtained by summing the scores of all 20 items.

Intrinsic Satisfaction: This score measures satisfaction related to the intrinsic aspects of work, such as personal achievement and recognition. It is calculated by summing the scores of 15 specific items.

Extrinsic Satisfaction: This score evaluates satisfaction related to extrinsic factors, such as salary and working conditions. It is calculated by summing the scores of 5 specific items.

The interpretative thresholds for each type of score are as follows (Roussel, cited in Billion, 2010):

- Dissatisfaction (Score < 20): Employees with scores below 20 on the overall satisfaction scale are generally dissatisfied with their jobs.

- Neutrality (Score 20-59): Employees with scores in this range have a neutral attitude towards their jobs.

- Satisfaction (Score > 70 overall, > 60 intrinsic, > 20 extrinsic): Employees with scores in this range are generally satisfied with their jobs.

3.3.2. Utrecht Work Engagement Scale (UWES)

The Utrecht Work Engagement Scale (UWES) is a widely used tool for measuring work engagement, a positive mental state characterized by vigor, dedication, and absorption. Developed by Schaufeli & Bakker (1999), the UWES consists of 17 items divided into three dimensions:

1. **Absorption:** This dimension assesses the extent to which individuals are focused and immersed in their work.
2. **Dedication:** This dimension measures the sense of significance and importance that individuals attach to their work.
3. **Vigor:** This dimension evaluates the level of energy and perseverance that individuals exhibit in their work.

Respondents rate each item on a 7-point Likert scale, ranging from "never" to "daily," to indicate the frequency with which they experience the described feelings.

3.3.3. Organizational Commitment Scale (adapted from Meyer, Allen, and Smith)

To measure the organizational commitment of trainee accountants, we used the scale developed by Meyer, Allen, and Smith (1993), adapted into French by Durrieu and Roussel (2002). This instrument, composed of 18 items, assesses three dimensions of commitment: affective, calculative, and normative. The items were slightly modified to better fit the context of accounting firms.

The Meyer, Allen, and Smith scale is a 10-point Likert scale, where 0 corresponds to "strongly disagree" and 10 to "strongly agree". Participants are asked to express their level of agreement with each item, based on their feelings towards the firm.

- Affective Commitment Scale Items (1,4,7,9,12,15)

This dimension reflects emotional attachment to the organization. Items measure feelings of loyalty, identification, and pride.

- Continuance commitment scale items (2,5,8,10,13,16)

This dimension concerns the bonds of interest that link the individual to the organization. The items assess the perceived costs associated with a potential departure and the benefits of staying.

- Normative commitment scale items (3,6,11,14,17,18)

This dimension measures the individual's sense of moral obligation towards the organization. The items assess the social norms and personal values that influence the individual's continued membership in the organization.

3.3.4. Designing a Questionnaire to Assess the Impact of ESO on Governance

The design of a questionnaire to measure the impact of employee share ownership (ESO) on governance and performance requires a methodical and rigorous approach.

The primary objective of this questionnaire is to assess the impact of employee share ownership (ESO) on corporate governance through several dimensions related to employee participation, representation in decision-making bodies, formalization of decision-making processes, and perceptions of transparency and equity. The questionnaire aims to gather employees' perceptions regarding their involvement in decision-making processes since the implementation of ESO, as well as their feelings about the company's performance, internal communication, and sense of belonging.

The questionnaire is structured around seven key dimensions:

1. **Employee Participation in Decision-Making:** This dimension measures the extent to which employees are involved in strategic decision-making and can share their ideas.
2. **Employee Representation in Decision-Making Bodies:** This dimension assesses the effectiveness of employee representatives in defending employee interests and addressing concerns.
3. **Formalization of Decision-Making Processes:** This dimension examines the clarity, transparency, and fairness of decision-making processes.
4. **Perception of Transparency and Equity:** This dimension measures employees' perceptions of the transparency and fairness of company decisions.
5. **Overall Governance:** This dimension assesses employees' overall satisfaction with the governance practices of the company.
6. **Company Performance:** This dimension evaluates the perceived impact of ESO on the company's overall performance.
7. **Stakeholder Perception:** This dimension measures employees' sense of belonging and the quality of internal communication.

To collect quantitative data, a 5-point Likert scale is utilized. Respondents indicate their level of agreement with each statement on a scale ranging from 1 (strongly disagree) to 5 (strongly agree).

The scale is designed to capture both polar responses and more moderate, neutral viewpoints, thus offering a granular understanding of employee perceptions.

the dimensions of the questionnaire on governance characteristics, which is designed to assess various aspects of employee involvement and organizational performance.

The scores of the dimensions included in the questionnaire are calculated as follows:

- **Employee Participation in Decisions**: This dimension consists of 3 questions, with a possible score ranging from 3 to 15. The normalized score is calculated using the formula: (Score Obtained−3)/(15−3)×100.
- **Employee Representation in Decision-Making Bodies**: This dimension includes 2 questions, allowing for a possible score between 2 and 10. The normalized score is derived from the formula: (Score Obtained−2)/(10−2)×100.

- **Formalization of Decision-Making Processes**: Comprising 2 questions, this dimension has a possible score of 2 to 10, with the normalized score calculated as follows: (Score Obtained−2)/(10−2)×100.
- **Perception of Transparency and Fairness**: This dimension consists of 2 questions, with a possible score ranging from 2 to 10. The normalized score formula is: (Score Obtained−2)/(10−2)×100.
- **Overall Governance**: This dimension includes 3 questions, allowing for a possible score between 3 and 15. The normalized score is calculated using the formula: (Score Obtained−3)/(15−3)×100.
- **Company Performance**: This dimension consists of 2 questions, with a possible score ranging from 2 to 10. The normalized score is derived from the formula: (Score Obtained−2)/(10−2)×100.
- **Stakeholder Perception**: Comprising 2 questions, this dimension has a possible score between 2 and 10, with the normalized score calculated as follows: (Score Obtained−2)/(10−2)×100.
- **Total Score**: The total of all dimensions comprises a total of 16 questions, with a possible cumulative score ranging from 16 to 80. The normalized total score is calculated using the formula: (Score Obtained−16)/(80−16)×100.

The total possible score is bounded by a minimum of 0 (achieved when all dimensions are at their minimum values) and a maximum of 80 (achieved when all dimensions are at their maximum values).

- Scores between 0% and 25%: Low perceived impact of ESO on governance.
- Scores between 26% and 50%: Moderate perceived impact.
- Scores between 51% and 75%: High perceived impact.
- Scores between 76% and 100%: Very high perceived impact.

This questionnaire is designed to provide valuable insights into the impact of employee share ownership (ESO) on various aspects of corporate governance. The results obtained will contribute to a better understanding of the benefits and challenges associated with ESO, particularly in terms of employee involvement in decision-making processes, representation, and perceptions of transparency and fairness. These data will be useful for assessing the benefits of ESO and informing future organizational decisions.

3.3.5. The internal consistency of the items in the various scale

This section presents the results of the internal consistency analysis for each measurement instrument. as follows:

- **MSQ Scale:** The internal consistency of the MSQ scale increased from 0.800 to 0.967, indicating a substantial improvement in the reliability of the scale.
- **UWES Scale:** The reliability of the UWES scale also increased significantly, from 0.753 to 0.969, suggesting a more robust and reliable measure of employee engagement.
- **Professional Commitment Scale:** This scale experienced a dramatic improvement in reliability, with Cronbach's alpha increasing from 0.696 to 0.982. This indicates a strong internal consistency among the items and a more accurate measure of commitment.

The psychometric properties of the questionnaire demonstrated notable enhancement, as evidenced by the substantial improvement in Cronbach's alpha from 0.749 to 0.846, thereby indicating a more robust and statistically sound instrument for assessing participatory governance practices (refer to Table 1).

These improvements in reliability suggest that the introduction of employee share ownership has had a positive impact on the measurement of various constructs related to employee attitudes and behaviors. This, in turn, strengthens the validity and reliability of the research findings.

Table 1. Test score reliability analysis

Scale	*Reliability Statistics Before AS*	*Reliability Statistics After AS*	*Number of Items*
MSQ Scale			
Cronbach's Alpha	0.800	0.965	20
Cronbach's Alpha (Standardized Items)	0.812	0.967	20
Engagement Scale			
Cronbach's Alpha	0.753	0.969	17
Cronbach's Alpha (Standardized Items)	0.752	0.970	17
Professional Commitment Scale			
Cronbach's Alpha	0.696	0.982	18
Cronbach's Alpha (Standardized Items)	0.697	0.982	18
Participatory Governance Questionnaire			
Cronbach's Alpha	0.749	0.846	16
Cronbach's Alpha (Standardized Items)	0.761	0.843	16

4. RESULTS AND DISCUSSION

4.1. Impact on Employee Satisfaction (H_1)

For the first hypothesis paired samples t-tests show that employee share ownership significantly increased both intrinsic and extrinsic employee satisfaction. The mean difference in intrinsic satisfaction was -23.000 ($t = -12.678$, $p < .001$), indicating a substantial increase in job satisfaction. Similarly, the mean difference in extrinsic satisfaction was -5.880 ($t = -8.818$, $p < .001$), demonstrating a significant positive impact on satisfaction related to pay, working conditions, and job security.

The mean difference in overall satisfaction was -24.780 ($t = -9.357$, $p < .001$), indicating a substantial increase in overall employee satisfaction. In summary, employee share ownership significantly improved both intrinsic, extrinsic, and overall employee satisfaction, suggesting increased well-being, accomplishment, and engagement.

Table 2 highlights the significant increase in intrinsic and extrinsic satisfaction following ESO implementation, with mean differences indicating marked improvements in both dimensions

Table 2. Paired samples t-test results comparing satisfaction before and after employee share ownership implementation

Pairs (Before/ After)	Mean Before ESO	Mean after ESO	Mean Difference	t-student	Sig. (2-tailed)	Cohen's *d*
Intrinsic Satisfaction	31.06	54,06	-23	-12.678	<0.001	-1,793
Extrinsic Satisfaction	11.54	17,42	-5.88	-8.818	<0.001	-1,247
Overall Satisfaction	46.7	71,48	-24.78	-9.357	<0.001	-1,323

4.2. Impact on Employee Engagement (H_2)

The paired samples t-test analysis indicates a significant positive impact of implementing employee share ownership on job engagement across these dimensions. The results are as follows:

- **Absorption**: The average difference between pre- and post-employee share ownership is -9.300, with a standard deviation of 6.964. The 95% confidence interval ranges from -11.279 to -7.321, excluding zero ($p < 0.001$), indicating a substantial increase in employees' absorption in their work post-implementation.

- **Dedication**: The average difference for dedication to the organization is -7.460, with a standard deviation of 5.563. The confidence interval spans from -9.041 to -5.879, also excluding zero ($p < 0.001$), demonstrating an increased level of dedication among employees following the introduction of employee share ownership.
- **Vigor**: The average difference for vigor is -6.420, with a standard deviation of 6.315. The confidence interval ranges from -8.215 to -4.625 ($p < 0.001$), indicating that employees experienced enhanced vigor and energy in their work as a result of employee share ownership.
- **Overall Engagement**: The mean difference in overall engagement scores is -23.180, with a standard deviation of 16.196. The confidence interval ranges from -27.783 to -18.577 ($p < 0.001$), highlighting a significant improvement in overall employee engagement levels after the implementation of employee share ownership.

The consistently large Cohen's d values (> 1) indicate and significant positive impact of employee share ownership on all dimensions of employee engagement, including absorption, dedication, and overall engagement. (as shown in Table 3)

These findings collectively suggest that the introduction of employee share ownership has significantly enhanced employee engagement, leading to greater emotional and cognitive investment in their work, which may ultimately result in improved performance and well-being within the workplace.

Table 3. Paired samples t-tests engagement scale

Pairs (Before/After)	Mean Before ESO	Mean after ESO	Mean Difference	t-student	Sig. (2-tailed)	Cohen's *d*
Pair 1: Absorption	14,14	23,44	9.30	-9,443	<0.001	-1,335
Pair 2: Dedication to the organization	13,14	20,6	-7,46	-9,482	<0.001	-1,341
Pair 3: Vigor	18,5	24,92	-6,42	-7,188	<0.001	-1,017
Overall Engagement	45,78	68,96	-23,18	-10,12	<0.001	-1,431

(df=49/n=50)

4.3. Impact on Employee Decision-Making Commitment (H_3)

Regarding Affective Commitment, the results show a significant increase in employees' affective commitment after the introduction of employee share ownership. Before ESO, the average affective commitment score was 17.06, while it increased to 28.7 after ESO, with a mean difference of -11.64. This change indicates that employee shareholders feel a stronger emotional connection to the company. In other words, employee share ownership stimulates employees' affective commitment by strengthening their emotional attachment to the organization. Employees develop a stronger bond with the company, feeling more invested and committed to its success. This affective dimension is crucial for motivation and talent retention. Our findings align with those of other empirical studies on the subject, such as the one conducted among French SBF 250 companies, which revealed a strong positive correlation between employee share ownership and job satisfaction, as well as organizational commitment. The results indicate that holding shares in one's company creates a sense of intrinsic satisfaction among employee-shareholders (Tannenbaum, 1983). Moreover, Long's research (1978a and 1978b) demonstrates a link between equity participation and a sense of identification with the company. Rhodes and Steers' research (1981) also indicates that equity participation contributes to reducing turnover intention, reinforcing the idea that employees who feel emotionally attached to their organization are more likely to invest their efforts and become involved in the company's activities. Tucker et al.'s studies (1989) further confirm the link between employee share ownership and job satisfaction as well as organizational commitment.

Furthermore, the research by Buchko (1992, 1993) and Frohlich et al. (1998) reinforces the idea that employee share ownership is associated with increased work commitment, highlighting the importance of this emotional commitment in creating a positive and productive work environment. In summary, employee shareholders who feel emotionally attached to their organization are more likely to invest their efforts and engage in the company's activities, thereby creating a positive and productive work environment.

Regarding Calculated commitment, the results also show a significant improvement, with an average increasing from 15.22 before employee share ownership (ESO) to 29.38 after, resulting in a mean difference of -14.16. This increase suggests that employees perceive more benefits associated with their commitment, particularly due to their participation in the company's capital. Employees who positively evaluate the costs and benefits of their engagement are more likely to remain in the organization and contribute to its success. This dimension is crucial, as it encourages employees to reflect on the repercussions of their commitment, thereby enhancing their long-term motivation. Previous studies support this observation. For example, Vaughan-Whitehead's (1992) study revealed that employee share ownership contributes to an increase in employee motivation and commitment, which is directly related to their perception of the benefits of their commitment.

Similarly, the research by Poutsma et al. (2012) indicates that employee shareholders are more likely to positively evaluate their commitment, as they directly benefit from the company's performance. Furthermore, the work of Long (1978a and 1978b) shows that participation in capital strengthens employees' perception of the long-term benefits of their commitment, which encourages them to remain in the organization. The studies by Buchko (1992, 1993) and Frohlich et al. (1998) also reinforce the idea that employee share ownership is associated with increased work commitment, highlighting the importance of this calculated dimension in creating a positive and productive work environment. In summary, employee share ownership enhances employees' calculated commitment by encouraging them to evaluate the costs and benefits of their commitment. By becoming shareholders, employees better perceive the benefits related to their personal investment in the company, which strengthens their long-term commitment.

Regarding normative commitment, it also experienced a significant increase, rising from 14.78 to 28.8, with an average difference of -14.02. This indicates that employees feel a heightened sense of obligation towards the company, considering it their duty to contribute to its success. This sense of responsibility can foster a strong company culture, where employees support each other and work together towards common goals. Studies show that this type of normative commitment is often linked to higher levels of job satisfaction and a decrease in turnover intention. Employee share ownership fosters a sense of obligation among employees towards the company. By becoming shareholders, employees feel a duty to contribute to the success of the organization that has made them part of its capital. This shared sense of responsibility can foster a more collaborative work environment and a positive company culture. Previous studies support this observation, such as the one conducted by Vaughan-Whitehead (1992), which showed that employee share ownership generates positive effects, including increased employee motivation and commitment, as well as improved organizational dynamics.

Moreover, Degbey et al. (2020) assert that, within the context of mergers and acquisitions, employee share ownership plays a pivotal role in retaining employees by enhancing their psychological ownership. Building upon Allen and Meyer's (1990) work, normative commitment is evident when employees align their behaviors with organizational expectations out of a sense of duty. This obligation can be reinforced through mechanisms like employee share ownership, which aligns employees' interests with those of the organization, thereby fostering greater commitment in decision-making processes. In essence, employee share ownership transcends mere capital participation; it cultivates an environment where employees feel accountable and committed, contributing to a positive organizational culture and strengthened collaboration.

Furthermore, the overall score for decision-making commitment exhibited a substantial increase, rising from 52.88 to 86.88, reflecting an average difference of -34. This underscores that employee share ownership has engendered heightened employee participation in decision-making processes. Additionally, extending beyond these three dimensions, employee share ownership fosters active employee participation in decision-making processes (Overall Decision-Making Commitment) across all organizational levels. As shareholders, employees feel more invested in the strategic choices that shape their work environment. This enhanced commitment in decision-making is conducive to innovation and the company's agility in responding to market challenges. Prior research supports these findings. For example, Poutsma et al. (2012) demonstrated that employee share ownership facilitates information dissemination and fosters employee participation in strategic decision-making, thereby enhancing their commitment. Additionally, Vaughan-Whitehead (1992) revealed that employee share ownership yields positive outcomes, including increased employee motivation and commitment, as well as decreased absenteeism and turnover. Blasi et al. (1996) further emphasize that employee share ownership can mitigate conflicts of interest between managers and employees by aligning their interests, thereby promoting greater collaboration in decision-making. Moreover, D'Arcimolès and Trébucq's (2003) research indicated a positive correlation between employee share ownership and organizational performance, reinforcing the concept that employee commitment in strategic decisions can contribute to improved business performance.

Paired samples t-tests demonstrate a significant mean difference in decision-making commitment scores, signifying that the implementation of employee share ownership has positively influenced employee participation. This dynamic is noteworthy as it reflects a transformation in organizational culture, whereby employees feel valued and their opinions are considered. In fact, employees who actively engage in strategic decision-making are more inclined to be engaged in their daily work, potentially leading to enhanced productivity and job satisfaction.

The large Cohen's d values (> 1) for all pairs indicate a substantial increase in absorption, dedication to the organization, vigor, and overall engagement following the introduction of employee share ownership. (as shown in Table 4)

Table 4. Paired samples t-tests commitment scale

Pairs (Before/After)	Mean Before ESO	Mean after ESO	Mean Difference	t-student	Sig. (2-tailed)	Cohen's *d*
Affective commitment	17,06	28,7	-11,64	-8,972	0	-1,27
Continuance commitment	15,22	29,38	-14,16	-11,742	0	-1,66
Normative commitment	14,78	28,8	-14,02	-11,577	0	-1,64
Commitment	52,88	86,88	-34	-9,053	0	-1,28

4.4. The impact on corporate governance (H_4)

Hypothesis is strongly supported by the results presented in the table below. Indeed, all p-values are less than 0.001, indicating that the observed differences between the "before" and "after" measurements of employee share ownership implementation are statistically significant.

More specifically, the results show that:

- Employee participation in decision-making has significantly increased following the implementation of employee share ownership.
- Employee representation within decision-making bodies has strengthened.
- Decision-making processes have become more formalized.
- Perceptions of transparency and fairness have improved.
- Overall governance is perceived as more effective.
- Company performance appears to have improved.
- Perceptions of the various stakeholders involved in governance have evolved positively.

The Cohen's d values for all pairs exceed 1, signifying very large effect sizes. This suggests that ESO has led to significant improvements in employee participation in decision-making, perceptions of transparency and fairness, and overall governance. (as shown in Table 5)

These results all converge towards the same conclusion: the implementation of employee share ownership has led to a profound transformation of governance practices, fostering increased employee participation in decision-making, better representation of their interests, and a more positive perception of transparency and fairness.

Table 5. Paired samples t-tests of the questionnaire on governance characteristics

Pair	Dimension	Mean Difference before-after	Standard Deviation	t	Sig.	Cohen's *d*
1	Employee participation in decision-making	-6.6	2.857	-16.334	<0.001	-2,31
2	Employee representation in decision-making bodies	-4.52	1.992	-16.043	<0.001	-2,27
3	Formalization of decision-making processes	-4.02	2.114	-13.446	<0.001	-1,90
4	Perception of transparency and fairness	-4.96	1.989	-17.63	<0.001	-2,49
5	Overall governance	-6.32	2.599	-17.197	<0.001	-2,43
6	Company performance	-4.6	2.185	-14.884	<0.001	-2,11
7	Perception of actors	-2.82	1.395	-14.292	<0.001	-2,02
	Impact of ESOP on governance	-33.84	9.438	-25.353	<0.001	-3,59

4.5. Pre-ESOP Correlation Analysis and Interpretation

Figure 1 illustrates the methodological approach to constructing a decision tree through a comprehensive analysis of the intricate correlational relationships among the measured variables. This process entails a systematic examination of the underlying statistical interconnections to inform the strategic development of the predictive decision tree model.

Figure 1. The correlations between the variables before the implementation of employee share ownership

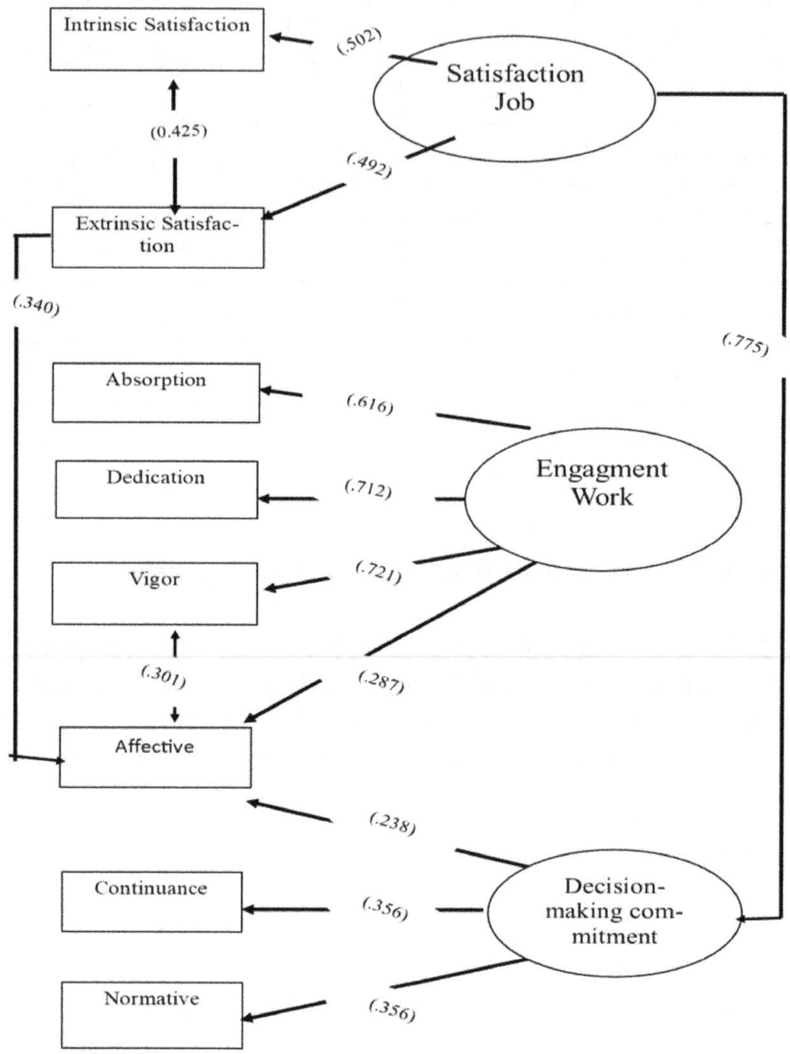

4.6. Discussion

The study results provide a crucial snapshot of the situation before the implementation of employee share ownership. They reveal a strong correlation between intrinsic satisfaction and affective commitment, highlighting the importance employees place on the content of their work. In contrast, the relationship between calculated commitment and decisional involvement appears less pronounced, suggesting a potential need to improve communication regarding the financial benefits associated with employment. Notably, it was observed that decisional involvement is not significantly correlated with affective commitment, suggesting that employee participation in company decision-making processes is not necessarily linked to their emotional attachment or identification with the company. In other words, even if employees feel emotionally engaged and committed to their work (affective commitment), this does not automatically translate into a greater willingness to actively participate in company decisions (decisional involvement).

This lack of correlation indicates that other factors, such as the perceived influence of decisions, the transparency of decision-making processes, or perceived opportunities for involvement, play a more significant role in motivating employees to engage in company decisions. This also implies a need to strengthen employee integration into decision-making processes so that they feel more involved and committed to the company's strategy and direction.

The study reveals that extrinsic satisfaction and affective commitment are the dominant dimensions, distinguished by their strong correlations with other variables. Extrinsic satisfaction, which includes elements such as remuneration and tangible benefits, is closely linked to intrinsic satisfaction (which concerns interest and fulfillment at work), overall satisfaction, and affective commitment, which reflects employees' emotional attachment to the company.

Moreover, affective commitment is not only strongly associated with extrinsic satisfaction; it is also correlated with vigor, representing energy and enthusiasm at work, as well as decisional involvement, which refers to employees' willingness to participate in company decisions. This correlation highlights the importance of emotional well-being and tangible recognition in strengthening employee engagement and their motivation to actively contribute to the organization's success.

These results explain that employee share ownership can have a more significant impact if companies pay particular attention to two key aspects: financial incentives and involvement in decisions. On the one hand, employees seem to react positively to tangible financial benefits (extrinsic satisfaction), suggesting that an improvement or better communication of the financial advantages associated with share ownership could strengthen their commitment.

Moreover, although affective commitment is already strong, it could be further leveraged to encourage employee participation in decision-making processes. This would involve creating an environment where employees not only feel emotionally invested in the company but also feel recognized and commitment in the decisions that affect their work and their future.

By strengthening both of these dimensions—financial and decision-making—while maintaining a focus on enriching and engaging work, companies can maximize the benefits of employee share ownership, cultivating a deeper and more lasting commitment from their employees.

The study results provide valuable insights into the relationships between various psychological factors related to employee engagement, decision involvement, and satisfaction following the implementation of employee share ownership.

After the introduction of employee share ownership, the observed correlations reveal significant trends. For instance, absorption shows high correlations with devotion (0.902), vigor (0.858), and commitment (0.966). This indicates that employees who feel deeply absorbed in their work also exhibit high levels of devotion, vigor, and commitment. These results reinforce the notion that these dimensions are interconnected and represent different but complementary aspects of employee engagement.

Table 5 delineates a noteworthy empirical observation revealing a robust statistical correlation of 0.887 between intrinsic and extrinsic job satisfaction dimensions. This substantial correlation coefficient substantiates the interconnected nature of employees' psychological engagement with work content and their perception of external compensatory and environmental workplace factors.

This implies that these two types of satisfaction reinforce each other: an employee satisfied with the nature of their work is more likely to perceive positively the external benefits they receive, and vice versa.

Both types of satisfaction also show a strong correlation with overall employee satisfaction following the introduction of employee share ownership. This means that employees' overall perception of satisfaction is largely determined by their satisfaction with both intrinsic and extrinsic aspects. Together, these dimensions constitute key factors for assessing employees' overall well-being and satisfaction within the organization.

The strong correlation between extrinsic satisfaction and affective commitment indicates that employees who are emotionally attached to their work are also sensitive to the extrinsic benefits offered by the company. This suggests that employee share ownership has reinforced the idea that financial or material benefits are not only rewards for work done, but also elements that strengthen their affective commitment to the organization.

Affective commitment also shows significant correlations with vigor, decision-making involvement, overall satisfaction, and extrinsic satisfaction. This indicates that employees who feel emotionally connected to their work after the introduction of employee share ownership are also more energetic, more involved in decisions, and experience high overall satisfaction. Employee share ownership thus seems to have strengthened these links, making affective commitment a central element of employee well-being and motivation.

Furthermore, regarding the impact of employee share ownership on participatory governance, our results align with a majority of studies that show a positive impact of ESOPs on corporate governance and performance. Indeed, several studies corroborate the findings of this analysis. Blasi et al. (1996) have shown that ESOPs can improve the performance of public companies by fostering greater employee involvement in strategic decisions. This aligns with the results observed where employee participation and representation were significantly improved after the introduction of ESOPs.

Employee ownership promotes alignment of interests and improved communication among stakeholders. By becoming shareholders, employees are incentivized to engage more in decision-making processes, leading to a better understanding of the company's strategic challenges and greater motivation to contribute to its success (Cézanne & Hollandts, 2021). This dynamic is reinforced by the fact that employees, as shareholders, not only share the financial risks but also the benefits of the company's performance.

However, our results also provide nuances compared to some studies that have highlighted more nuanced or even negative effects of employee share ownership. For example, Caramelli (2011) points out that while ESOPs can increase participation, there are cases where this has not led to a measurable improvement in performance. This observation highlights the fact that the effects may vary depending on the organizational context and industry. Agency theory (Jensen & Meckling, 1976) is often used to explain how ESOPs can align the interests of employees and shareholders, which could explain the positive results observed in this study.

Furthermore, a qualitative study conducted by Cardoni (2020) suggests that the presence of an employee shareholder representative on the governance board can strengthen the legitimacy and effectiveness of decisions made within the company.

Table 6(a). Correlational analysis of variables post-employee ownership implementation

	Absorption	Devotion	Vigor	Engagement	Intrinsic Satisfaction
Dedication	**,902****				
	0,000				
Vigor	,858**	,847**			
	0,000	0,000			
Engagement	,966**	,957**	,943**		
	0,000	0,000	0,000		
Intrinsic Satisfaction	,524**	,387**	,635**	,541**	
	0,000	0,006	0,000	0	
Extrinsic Satisfaction	,639**	,552**	,649**	,644**	,887**
	0,000	0,000	0,000	0	0,000
	,564**	,437**	,652**	,579**	,993**
	0,000	0,001	0,000	0	0,000
Affective commitment	,683**	,655**	,822**	,753**	,662**
	0,000	0,000	0,000	0	0,000
Continuance commitment	,480**	,514**	,676**	,580**	,569**
	0,000	0,000	0,000	0	0,000
Normative Commitment	,573**	,592**	,783**	,678**	,633**
	0,000	0,000	0,000	0	0,000
Commitment	,595**	,605**	,785**	,691**	,642**
	0,000	0,000	0,000	0,000	0,000

Table 6(b). Correlational analysis of variables post-employee ownership implementation

Extrinsic Satisfaction	Satisfaction	Affective Commitment	Continuance Commitment	Normative Commitment

continued on following page

Table 6(b). Continued

Extrinsic Satisfaction	Satisfaction	Affective Commitment	Continuance Commitment	Normative Commitment
,935**				
0,000				
,674**	,679**			
0,000	0,000			
,626**	,596**	,875**		
0,000	0,000	0,000		
,632**	,647**	,888**	,925**	
0,000	0,000	0,000	0,000	
,666**	,662**	,952**	,970**	,972**
0,000	0,000	0,000	0,000	0,000

4.7. Analyzing correlations between governance and employee share ownership

Results showed a significant positive correlation between employee representation and both calculated and general involvement. This suggests that when employees are more represented, they are more engaged in their work.

Greater employee representation in decision-making fosters a sense of belonging and autonomy, thereby stimulating engagement.

Table 6 reveals a statistically significant positive correlation between the procedural formalization of decision-making mechanisms and multidimensional organizational commitment, encompassing affective, calculative, normative, and aggregate involvement constructs. This empirical finding underscores the intricate relationship between organizational structural processes and employee psychological engagement.

This explains why clear and structured decision-making processes enhance employee involvement at various levels. This can be attributed to a better understanding of expectations, reduced uncertainty, and a greater sense of control.

Furthermore, a significant positive correlation was found between company performance and both calculated and general involvement. Higher employee involvement appears to be linked to better company performance. This could be explained by greater motivation, higher quality work, and a greater ability to adapt to change.

Regarding the Perception of Actors, results demonstrated a significant positive correlation with various dimensions of engagement (absorption, dedication, vigor, etc.) as well as satisfaction. This indicates that a positive perception of the work environment and management practices is associated with higher levels of engagement. Employees who perceive their environment positively are more likely to feel invested in their work and in the company.

Finally, for the overall results of the governance questionnaire, a significant positive correlation was found with the various dimensions of involvement. This explains why effective, transparent, and participatory governance fosters employee involvement. This suggests that the way a company is managed has a direct impact on employee engagement.

Table 7. Correlation analysis of governance dimensions and psychological factors Post-Eso

Variable	Correlation with	Significance (sig)
Representation of employees in decision-making	Continuance commitment	0.026
	General commitment	0.047
Formalization of decision-making processes	Affective commitment post	0.016
	Calculated commitment	0.002
	Normative commitment	0.011
	Overall commitment	0.005
Company performance	Continuance commitment	0.051
	General commitment	0.056
Perception of actors	Absorption	0.039
	Vigor	0.008
	Engagement	0,031
	Intrinsic satisfaction	0.019
	Extrinsic satisfaction	0.060
	Overall satisfaction	0.023
	Affective commitment	0.018
Overall governance results	Affective commitment	0.056
	Calculated commitment	0.031
	Normative commitment	0.059
	Overall commitment	0.039

4.8. Interpretation of the mediation effect

To summarize, the study highlights that the implementation of employee share ownership has a positive impact on governance and employee engagement. This is evidenced by several key findings:

Employee representation and engagement: The results show a significant positive correlation between employee representation in decision-making processes and calculated and general involvement. This indicates that greater representation fosters increased engagement at work. Psychologically, this reinforces a sense of belonging and autonomy, thereby stimulating engagement.

Formalization of decision-making processes: A clear structure in decision-making processes is positively correlated with affective, calculated, normative, and general involvement. This highlights that well-defined decision-making processes reduce uncertainty and provide employees with a better understanding of expectations, thereby increasing their level of engagement.

Link to company performance: Results reveal a significant positive correlation between company performance and calculated and general involvement. Higher employee involvement appears to be linked to better company performance, likely due to increased motivation, higher quality work, and a greater ability to adapt to change.

Perception of the work environment: A positive perception of the work environment is significantly correlated with various dimensions of engagement (absorption, dedication, vigor) and satisfaction. Employees who perceive their environment favorably are more likely to feel invested in their work and in the company and satisfied with their job.

Overall governance results: The study shows a significant positive correlation between overall governance results and various dimensions of involvement. Effective, transparent, and participatory governance practices foster employee involvement, suggesting that the way a company is managed has a direct impact on employee engagement.

The results support the idea that psychological factors such as satisfaction, engagement, and involvement play a mediating role in the relationship between employee share ownership and both company performance and governance. This aligns with the study's overall hypothesis that seeks to understand how these psychological elements function as mediators to improve organizational outcomes following the introduction of employee share ownership.

5. CONCLUSION

In conclusion, this study highlights the mediating role of psychological factors in the relationship between employee share ownership (ESO) and employee performance, as well as corporate governance. Our research reveals that ESO is a complex socio-economic mechanism transcending mere financial redistribution, fundamentally reshaping organizational dynamics. The findings suggest that the introduction of ESO is not merely a redistribution of profits, but also plays a crucial role in influencing psychological dimensions that, in turn, affect overall employee performance and governance quality.

The data indicates that ESO promotes increased affective commitment, dedication, and vigor among employees. Specifically, our findings demonstrate that:

- Psychological ownership significantly transforms employee perceptions
- Emotional engagement correlates directly with performance improvement
- Decision-making participation increases with financial stake

Moreover, the psychological mechanisms underlying ESO can be conceptualized through three key transformation pathways:

1. Cognitive transformation: Reshaping employees' perception of organizational belonging
2. Emotional transformation: Enhancing intrinsic motivation and commitment
3. Behavioral transformation: Encouraging proactive participation in organizational processes

These psychological dimensions' act as mediators in the relationship between ESO and performance. In other words, when employees feel more engaged and emotionally connected to their work, their performance improves, as does their participation in the company's decision-making processes. This dynamic underscores the importance of a work environment where employees feel valued and involved in decision-making.

Furthermore, the observed correlations between employees' intrinsic and extrinsic satisfaction reinforce the notion that these factors are interconnected and contribute to overall high satisfaction. This interdependence suggests a virtuous cycle where psychological investment generates tangible organizational benefits.

Ultimately, employee share ownership emerges as a strategic lever to enhance not only employee satisfaction and engagement, but also their performance and the quality of corporate governance. By incorporating mechanisms that foster psychological involvement and employee participation in decision-making, companies can create an environment conducive to sustainable performance and more transparent, democratic governance. The study therefore emphasizes the importance of considering psychological dimensions and governance as key elements in the implementation of employee share ownership, to ensure a positive transformation within organizations.

The study therefore offers a nuanced framework for understanding ESO, positioning it not as a static financial instrument, but as a dynamic organizational intervention with profound psychological and strategic implications.

While the research provides valuable insights into Employee Share Ownership programs, it is essential to recognize certain methodological constraints. The study's relatively limited sample size and potential recall bias inherent in the retrospective pretest design underscore the need for more comprehensive research methodologies. Future academic investigations should prioritize expanding sample diversity and implementing longitudinal research approaches to enhance the robustness of findings.

Future research trajectories should focus on exploring the nuanced, long-term implications of ESO programs across varied cultural and economic contexts. Scholars are encouraged to delve deeper into understanding how different ESO structural configurations influence psychological outcomes and governance mechanisms, thereby enriching our comprehensive understanding of these complex organizational interventions.

REFERENCES

Albrecht, S. L., Furlong, S., & Leiter, M. P. (2023). The psychological conditions for employee engagement in organizational change: Test of a change engagement model. *Frontiers in Psychology*, 14, 1071924. DOI: 10.3389/fpsyg.2023.1071924 PMID: 36743243

Allen, N. J., & Meyer, J. P. (1990). The Measurement and Antecedents of Affective, Continuance, and Normative Commitment to the Organization. *Journal of Occupational Psychology*, 63(1), 1–18. DOI: 10.1111/j.2044-8325.1990.tb00506.x

Avey, J. B., Luthans, F., & Jensen, S. M. (2009). Psychological capital: A positive resource for combating employee stress and turnover. *Human Resource Management*, 48(5), 677–693. DOI: 10.1002/hrm.20294

Baker, G. P., & Kahn, A. (2020). Employee Ownership and Corporate Governance. *Journal of Corporate Finance*, 65, 101–115.

Blasi, J., Kruse, D., & Bernstein, A. (1996). *Incentive Effects of Employee Ownership: A Review of the Evidence*. Industrial Relations Research Association.

Buchko, A. (1992). Employee Ownership, Attitudes and Turnover: An Empirical Assessment. *Human Relations*, 45(7), 711–733. DOI: 10.1177/001872679204500704

Buchko, A. (1993). The effects of employee ownership on employee attitudes: An integrated causal model and path analysis. *Journal of Management Studies*, 30(4), 633–657. DOI: 10.1111/j.1467-6486.1993.tb00319.x

Corfe, S. (2021). A stake in success: Employee share ownership and the post-COVID economy. Kindly supported by https://www.smf.co.uk/wp-content/uploads/2021/05/A-stake-in-success-May-21.pdf

Corfe, S., & Kirkup, J. (2020). *Strengthening employee share ownership in the UK*. Social Market Foundation.

D'Arcimolès, C., & Trébucq, S. (2003). Employee ownership and performance: Evidence from French firms. *International Journal of Human Resource Management*, 14(2), 284–300.

Degbey, W. K., Karam, C., & Mazzola, J. (2020). Employee Ownership and Retention: The Role of Psychological Ownership in Mergers and Acquisitions. *Journal of Business Research*, 112, 230–241.

Durrieu, F., & Roussel, P. (2002). *« L'implication organisationnelle dans les réseaux de franchise: un concept pertinent pour les entreprises en réseau », Revue de Gestion des Ressources Humaines, N°44, 2ème trimestre*. Avril – Mai-Juin.

Frohlich, N., Godard, J., Oppenheimer, J. A., & Starke, F. A. (1998). Employee versus conventionally-owned and controlled firms: An experimental analysis. *MDE. Managerial and Decision Economics*, 19(4-5), 311–326. DOI: 10.1002/(SICI)1099-1468(199806/08)19:4/5<311::AID-MDE893>3.0.CO;2-I

Gomez-Mejia, L. R. (2018). The Role of Employee Ownership in Corporate Governance. *The Academy of Management Perspectives*, 32(2), 145–158.

Kahn, W. A. (1990). Psychological Conditions of Personal Engagement and Disengagement at Work. *Academy of Management Journal*, 33(4), 692–724. DOI: 10.2307/256287

Klein, K. J., & Kauffman, C. (2019). The Effects of Employee Ownership on Organizational Performance: A Meta-Analysis. *Journal of Business Research*, 98, 1–10.

. Kruse D., (2002), Recherche sur la prévalence et les effets de l'actionnariat salarié, Revue de l'actionnariat salarié, droit et finance, vol. 14, n°4, pp 65- 90.

Long, R. J. (1978a). The effects of employee ownership on organizational identification, employee attitudes, and organizational performance: A tentative framework and empirical findings. *Human Relations*, 31(1), 29–38. DOI: 10.1177/001872677803100102

Long, R. J. (1978b). The relative effects of share ownership vs. control on job attitudes in an employee owned company. *Human Relations*, 31(9), 753–763. DOI: 10.1177/001872677803100901

Mayhew, M., Ashkanasy, N., Bramble, T., & Gardner, J. (2007). A Study of the Antecedents and Consequences of Psychological Ownership in Organizational Settings. *The Journal of Social Psychology*, 147(5), 477–500. DOI: 10.3200/SOCP.147.5.477-500 PMID: 18225830

Meyer, J. P., Allen, N. J., & Smith, C. A. (1993). Commitment to organizations and occupations: Extension and test of a three-component conceptualization. *The Journal of Applied Psychology*, 78(4), 538–551. DOI: 10.1037/0021-9010.78.4.538

National center for employee ownership (NCEO) (2005), données disponible sur: https://www.nceo.org/what-is-employee-ownership

. Pérotin V & Robinson A, (2002). Employee participation in profit and ownership: A review of the issues and evidence. Report for the European parliament, novembre, social affairs services, SOCI109 EN.

Pierce, J. L., & Jussila, I. (2011). *Psychological ownership and the organizational context: Theory, research evidence, and application.* Edward Elgar. DOI: 10.4337/9780857934451

Pierce, J. L., & Jussila, L. (2019). The Psychology of Ownership: The Role of Psychological Ownership in Employee Engagement. *Journal of Organizational Behavior*, 40(7), 787–803.

Poutsma, E., Huitema, H., & de Lange, R. (2012). Employee ownership and participation: A review of the literature. *Journal of Employee Ownership Law and Studies*, 4(1), 1–25.

Rhodes, S. R., & Steers, R. M. (1981). Conventional vs. worker-owned organizations. *Human Relations*, 34(12), 1013–1035. DOI: 10.1177/001872678103401201

Schaufeli, W., & Bakker, A. (2004). *Work Engagement Scale: Preliminary Manual (Version 1.1). Occupational Health Psychology Unit.* Utrecht University.

Schaufeli, W. B., Bakker, A. B., & Salanova, M. (2006). The Measurement of Work Engagement With a Short Questionnaire: A Cross-National Study. *Educational and Psychological Measurement*, 66(4), 701–716. DOI: 10.1177/0013164405282471

Tannenbaum, A. S. (1983). Employee-owned companies. *Research in Organizational Behavior*, 5, 235–265.

Trabelsi, S. (2021, Février). L'actionnariat citoyen en Tunisie: Pensez-y! Leaders. https://www.leaders.com.tn/article/31395-l-actionnariat-citoyen-en-tunisie-pensez-y

Tucker, J., Nock, S., & Toscano, D. (1989). Employee ownership and perceptions of work: The effect of an employee stock ownership plan. *Work and Occupations*, 16(1), 26–42. DOI: 10.1177/0730888489016001002

Van Dyne, L., & Pierce, J. L. (2004). Psychological Ownership and Feelings of Possession: Three Field Studies Predicting Employee Attitudes and Organizational Citizenship Behavior. *Journal of Organizational Behavior*, 25(4), 439–459. DOI: 10.1002/job.249

Vaughan-Whitehead, D. (1992). Employee Ownership: A New Approach to Industrial Relations. *International Labour Review*, 131(4), 421–446.

Weiss, D. J., Dawis, R. V., England, G. W., & Lofquist, L. H. (1967) Manual for the Minnesota Satisfaction Questionnaire. University of Minnesota, Minneapolis. Patrice Roussel (1993)

Whitfield, K., Pendleton, A., Sengupta, S., & Huxley, K. (2017). Employee share ownership and organizational performance: A tentative opening of the black box. *Personnel Review*, 46(7), 128. DOI: 10.1108/PR-09-2016-0243

Chapter 12
Challenges and Opportunities for Sharing the Ownership in Peru

Miguel Cordova
https://orcid.org/0000-0002-1010-8803
Tecnologico de Monterrey, Mexico

Hellen López-Valladares
Pontificia Universidad Católica del Perú, Peru

ABSTRACT

The world has been living its processes so fast that when it looks back over its shoulder, it realizes that there are many changes needed to fix the flaws and tensions created due to speeding, to include everyone in the promise of progressive growth and prosperity within the current economic system. This issue is more evident in emerging markets, where institutional weaknesses, informal economies, and insufficient resources are considerable. Hence, our chapter explores how feasible the implementation of mechanisms of shared capitalism, specifically Employee Ownership initiatives, could be achieved in Peru. The result of our discussion proposes that traditional companies would suffer from an enormous inertia towards more inclusive and participatory business models because of what they have been doing to overcome the local institutional voids, contrary to new social businesses that could represent the start point of the diffusion of Employee Ownership practices in the Peruvian business community.

DOI: 10.4018/979-8-3693-7031-5.ch012

INTRODUCTION

"The only true and sustainable prosperity is shared prosperity"
(Joseph E. Stiglitz)

The capitalist system that we have been developing for decades needs important adjustments to truly become an inclusive free trade as well as collaborative mechanism to promote the wellbeing for all. Big companies have raised industry entry barriers, reduced the competition, took over emerging entrepreneurs, and concentrated economic and political power, becoming highly diversified and extended profit-driven machines (Stiglitz, 2019; Tepper & Hearn, 2023). However, besides the already-known traditional schemes and mainly economically driven orientations in the current global economic system, the trend of Shared Capitalism has stated new avenues for a fairer economic development worldwide. Among those new alternatives, Employee Ownership (EO) mechanisms provide a comprehensive and fresh proposal on how firms could include their employees into their profit structure as well as into their governance one, giving them part of the ownership that they would naturally deserve by their work and affiliation (Blasi et al., 2013) while these companies would be perceiving the benefits of a more motivated and productive workforce at the same time (O'Boyle et al., 2016).

Nevertheless, following those novel paths would demand not only new resources and the abandonment of traditional hierarchies from companies (Aubert & Cordova, 2020), but also important structural changes in the local business environments they operate in. Hence, how nations shape their domestic regulations, institutional contexts, and local economic advantages for firms would determine how companies can adopt and adapt those Shared Capitalism's initiatives (Peng et al., 2009). Moreover, this would be particularly tough for companies located in emerging markets, where institutional voids are prevalent, outlining specific conditions for firms' survival (Gao et al., 2017).

Latin America has been the focus of vast research due to its socioeconomic characteristics for doing business and for its turbulent business context (Ugaz, 2020; Vassolo et al., 2011), as well as for its hierarchical governance structures (Schneider, 2013). Furthermore, each Latin American country has its own peculiarities in terms of business culture, institutional strength, and trust among economic actors (Khanna, 2018) and companies in the region must find a way to work around those institutional constraints to thrive and grow (Dávila, 2013; Khana & Palepu, 2011). Hence, even though some Latin American countries have experienced successful cases in using specific EO mechanisms such as the implementation of Employee Stock Purchase Plans (ESPP) led by multinationals' subsidiaries (Aubert et al., 2024), aiming for a comprehensive inclusion in the ownership structure and control of firms through other EO options such as Employee Stock Ownership Plans (ESOP) would still be challenging in the region (Hernandez & Zuloaga, 2023). This chapter focuses on Peru, highlighting the country's patterns towards a specific business culture and institutional licenses (Cordova et al, 2022; Durand, 2017; Ganoza & Stiglich, 2015; Vergara, 2018), which would craft together an environment that would be potentially reluctant to EO implementations (Aubert & Cordova, 2022).

Therefore, the main goal of this chapter is to discuss how the development of the institutional theory (DiMaggio & Powell, 1983; Peng et al., 2009) could set the basis for an infertile ground (Wolf & Gonzalez-Perez, 2024) for the implementation of EO initiatives in Peru and how the lack of trust as a meta resource (Khanna, 2018) would increase the reluctance of managers and owners in the country to adopt them. We argue that institutional forces, the current business elite, the absence of the State, the lack of trust among organizations, and the ongoing business culture have created a business environment in Peru that would be naturally reluctant to some of the Shared Capitalism initiatives such as EO. However, to cover the institutional voids in the business environment, new business models can adapt and develop EO initiatives to improve the human capital market, enhance financial skills, increase productivity, and accomplish a minimum of conditions that allow them to continue producing and generating value.

Following this, our chapter organizes as follows. The second section briefly explains about the EO concept and two well-known mechanisms derived from it, ESPP and ESOP. It also discusses the benefits and drawbacks of EO implementations found in the literature. Then, the third part provides an overview of the institutional context in the country, identifying the key forces that underlie the business culture that would be preventing EO mechanisms to be appraised and implemented. The following section includes a brief revision on the antecedents of EO in the country, describing some first attempts and how local stakeholders went toward EO efforts. The fifth section discusses the opportunities for an emerging economy such as Peru to overcome the local institutional voids to prepare the ground for a potential EO implementation. Finally, the chapter presents final thoughts and insights on the potential EO adoption by Peruvian companies and concludes the analysis providing final remarks for policymakers and practitioners, as well as future research alternatives for researchers.

Employee Ownership

Employee ownership is one of the concepts developed within the Shared Capitalism that aims to assist to traditional capitalism with an alternative mechanism that would be more participatory and inclusive than other current economic initiatives, getting back to the original meaning of capital, labor, and property ownership, and revisiting the discourse of distribution of wealth (Blasi et al., 2013; Freeman et al.,

2010). EO initiatives occur when firms decide to implement a business strategy to shift its governance and control structures, sharing part of the ownership and the decision-making process with their employees. Following this, Mackin (2023) describes four different reasons or drivers for companies to use EO for their employees: (i) as a compensation strategy in the form of options and broad-based equity grants, (ii) as an investment through equity to obtain capital appreciation over time, (iii) as a retirement benefit by a relationship of long-term investment, and (iv) as a membership through the affiliation to companies' governance structure at different levels.

Traditionally, there are two well-known formats under which EO is implemented in firms. The first one is the Employee Stock Ownership Plans (ESOP), which is characterized by the grant of property and control to the employees who will not directly pay for these but the company, using its future profits and utilizing an instrument called a special purpose vehicle to facilitate the buyout for the employees. The second one is the Employee Stock Purchase Plans (ESPP), which consist in companies selling a controlled portion of the ownership to their employees in the form of stocks who would need to use their own cash or salary to buy them, providing liquidity to the firms. Multinational companies (MNCs) have usually developed ESPP programs in a successful way, selling stock options to their employees all over the world through a coordinated effort through their subsidiaries. Nevertheless, as the employees must pay for those shares, the main benefit normally goes to those who earn more or hold top levels in the organization.

There are different reported benefits in the literature for firms that decide on EO implementations, either related to financial benefits, managerial practices, or employee's wellbeing. According to O'Boyle et al. (2016), EO plans in general have a positive relationship with firms' financial performance. Companies can get several benefits in terms of profitability, productivity, and compensation outcomes after implementing EO initiatives, and these advantages are especially evidenced in small firms (Blasi et al., 1996). Firms' stakeholders perceive benefits as well, as companies that have implemented EO plans are more willing for disclosure practices, reflecting responsibility and transparency towards the market and the society (Bova et al., 2014). Also, Wagner et al. (2006) found that the sense of affiliation as well as the ownership beliefs in workers promote ownership attitudes on them, which in turn derive on a positive financial performance for companies. Empirical evidence suggests that employee shareholders can appoint executives to be part of the board of directors who might increase company valuation and profitability (Ginglinger et al., 2011). Moreover, the incorporation of EO plans in companies promotes positive motivation, sense of belongingness and inclusion, increased financial and technological skills, a long-term saving perspective, and new financial assets for the employees (Aubert & Cordova, 2022). Thus, EO plans would have positive effects on firms' performance and outcomes, as well as positive impacts for the employees' behavior.

On the other hand, there are also some drawbacks highlighted due to the implementation of EO initiatives, which usually undermine building a generalized intention towards EO from companies. Ben-Ner and Jones (1995) stated that organizational performance and employee ownership strategies may have a negative relationship under specific combinations of control granted and financial return perceived. In addition, unfulfilled beliefs about what being a shareholder means can produce breaches in the psychological contract between employees and employers, which would undermine workers' behavior towards the achievement of organizational goals (Paul et al., 2000). Hence, potential negative impacts of EO are also really interesting to consider, especially for emerging markets in which new business models could find an inadequate as well as reluctant business community where to implement it.

Nevertheless, providing a fertile ground for EO implementation it's not only a matter of internal factors but of external ones too. External factors shape organizational perceptions and attitudes towards EO, promoting or constraining the opportunities for companies on exploring and adapting new business models of Shared Capitalism such as EO. Some of these external drivers could be allocated in the competition in the market, local labor regulations, strength of institutions, local business culture, and other firms' expansion strategies. For instance, willingness and attitudes towards the implementation of compensation practices such as EO plans are contingent on the local business environment in which companies are developing (Schuler & Rogovsky, 1998). Furthermore, some EO initiatives are driven by firms' strategies against hostile takeovers scenarios (Chaplinsky & Niehaus, 1994) or are shielding them by strategic restructuring while dealing with intensive global competition (Domadenik et al., 2008). Hence, despite the reported benefits and drawbacks of EO in firms, the local business environment as well as its institutional voids can fertilize or not the local ground to be able to host an EO initiative to be planted, grow, and survive over time.

The Institutional Context in Peru

The institutional context in which organizations operate in emerging markets such as Peru presents the absence of a strong rule of law or institutional voids, as it began to be called a few decades ago. These voids refer to the absence or poor functioning of economic agents to bring together buyers and sellers in markets, preventing companies from entering a new market or having poor performance or even failure (Khanna y Palepu, 2010). Among the most present formal and informal institutional voids in Peru are the lack of contract execution mechanisms, control systems, the government structure, infrastructure, property rights, rules and regulatory system, and/or intermediary experts (López et al., 2023). These are conditions that hinder the normal functioning of markets, excluding, for example, people in poverty from being able to participate in market activities, impeding economic and social development.

According to Grompone and Tanaka (2009), the inefficient and insufficient assistance from the Peruvian government to the needs of the population in different areas of the country has promoted a generalized negative perception towards national institutions, which has triggered several social unrest situations. Tensions between extractive industries and local communities in Peru due to the increased global demand for commodities and their subsequent expansion have caused significant social conflicts that could be prevented by incorporating trust-based relationships (Ventura & Jauregui, 2017). Furthermore, the centralization phenomenon, the absence of the state, and social and economic inequalities have created an uncertain and turbulent scenario for doing business in Peru (Cordova et al., 2022). In addition, a growing informal market, corruption scandals, and inadequate local regulation constantly undermine the managerial efforts of entrepreneurs, organizations from civil society, and businesses (Briolo & Cordova, 2022; Borda et al., 2022).

Moreover, corporations in Perú face mainly two formal institutional voids: product & information market and labor market (López et al., 2023). The first is based on the scarcity of information that exists both in supply and demand, as well as in the entire value chain in various industries. Since the information is difficult to access, the cost will be higher, increasing transaction costs for the actors in the environment. In addition to lacking information, continuous regulation changes generate a complex legal scenario discouraging investors (IGCB, 2023). The second is the labor market void, based on the shortage of well-trained people that the economy needs. It manifests itself when missing or inadequately trained human capital increases search and training costs for companies. Liedong et al. (2020) claim this might happen because of gaps in a country's education systems, which can create skills or capacity gaps for businesses. This lack of job skills makes it difficult for the company to adjust to changing economic conditions.

Among the informal institutions voids, in Peru, the loss of credibility and trust towards institutions and formal processes is the most significant barrier among businesses (De Soto, 2006). Among the factors that most affect corporations highlight corruption in its various facets, which can generate distrust in the transactions or dealing with specific actors (Webb et al., 2020). On the other hand, electoral promises that benefit one social sector over another and perpetuate inequality demonstrate that individual interest takes precedence over the common good, achieving that society and its formal institutions create their mechanisms of action and stop believing in the common good that elected authorities should create. Due to the low trust that exists between people and institutions, there arises the risk aversion gap, which creates a barrier for companies to invest in projects since, as Khanna and Palepu (2000) mention, a high degree of aversion risk and low trust in society could hinder such developments, as commonly observed in emerging and transition economies. According to López-Concepción et al. (2023), empirical evidence from Peru, together with other Latin American countries has emphasized the trust in institutions as instrumental for having a positive perception of science and technology for well-being by people. In addition, trust is a reliable resource for businesses that can enhance Peruvian entrepreneurs' international relationships to achieve local economic resilience (Henn et al., 2022).

Furthermore, informal institutions raised by the business elites in Peru have concentrated economic and political power, increasing the social and economic inequalities in the country over time and weakening the presence and cohesiveness of formal institutions in the country (Pazos & Cordova, 2024; Rivas et al., 2023). Consequently, the institutional void of social exclusion or marginalization has been reinforced in Peruvian society. This arises from norms and beliefs established in society that specific individuals, based on their gender, ethnicity, age, or other demographic attributes, lack the status to participate in the market, own property, and/or be part of certain types of exchange relational (Khoury & Prasad, 2016). This gap shows that, due to these social norms, companies exclude certain human groups from their market strategy or along its value chain for various reasons, such as a high cost of investment, individual biases or collective patterns on the performance of these groups, among others (López et al., 2023).

The First Attempts at Shared Capitalism in Peru

Many of the models similar to ESOP that began to be established in the Latin American region and in Peru mainly since the 70s responded to the need to improve the economic equality of workers versus owners or employers. Thus, mechanisms began to be proposed within Latin American labor legislation so that workers receive the benefits obtained by the company in a certain period. It should be noted that national governments imposed all these initiatives on companies or through collective agreements with the workers themselves (Morgado, 1991).

In Peru, with the reform promoted by Juan Velasco Alvarado, shareholding models for workers were established in several state and private companies. Since the 1930s, some of the first were introduced in the 1931 Constitution, in article 45: "The State will favor a system of participation of employees and workers in the profits of companies and will legislate on other aspects of the relations between them, and/or on the defense of employees and workers in general." Later, between 1950 and 1968, according to Neffa (2020), some political parties continued to promote participatory ideas, for example, that companies should be self-managed after having gone through co-management. This implied that the integration of capital and labor could occur through: "the distribution of profits, participation in management and access to its ownership, with its integration having to be adapted, progressively, to the economic possibilities of each company." (p. 45).

In the government of Velasco Alvarado, the Socially Owned Enterprises Law (EPS) is created, and they are defined as legal companies of social law made up exclusively of workers, established within the principle of solidarity to carry out economic activities and confirm the Social Property Sector. It is pointed out that ongoing training is necessary to prepare workers for their participation in the various levels of decision-making. To this end, it is specified that there must be a Training Committee that formulates training plans for job and technical improvement, has funds for this, and continues to spread the principles of social property. Since the law's implementation, 62 socially owned companies have been created, bringing together approximately 7,500 workers.

Other associative forms of business management were the companies self-managed by workers (EAT), which had a number quite similar to those of social participation (EPS). These were created after moments of high labor conflict that led to the mandatory creation of industrial communities and, subsequently, bankruptcies of the capitalist owners (Salas, 1982). Industrial communities were created in different production and service sectors, the first being mining, fishing, and telecommunications. The community had to be constituted by any industrial company with six or more stable workers or with a gross annual income greater than the equivalent of 25,000 dollars. Participation in the company's capital was carried out through the community, which received 15% of the net income annually (Morgado, 1991).

Some reflections on the functioning of industrial communities show that although it helped increase productivity, the conflict between workers also increased. Although the workers participated in the board through the community rather than individually, reaching agreements on the decisions that would be taken to the board was a challenging task. Instead of having more significant ties of cooperation, disputes were generated. Therefore, given that the communities did not last long, it was not seen that the proposed system had improved the distribution of income and improved the quality of life of the workers.

Another element discussed was the structural design problems required by this type of company, where there are more communities. In the case of the EPS, although there were bodies with various functions, such as the general assembly, the steering committee, the management, the honor committee, the training committee, the specialized committees, and the electoral committee, the political origin was filtered in all instances instead of making sure the model works at a technical level.

In the 1990s, new forms of employee shareholding appeared as a result of the privatization processes that were generated. Among the first steps of this privatization process was the transfer to a strategic operator of a majority set of shares so that it would have more control over the management of the company. Secondly, a group of shares became part of the organizations' workers, and the remaining balance was opened to citizens; that is, the general public could buy shares (CEPAL, 2002). These operations were carried out through the Citizen Participation System (SPC) created in 1994. According to Copri data, in net terms – that is, discounting buyers of more than one offer – 410,000 people became owners of actions, which constituted the most important experience of this type in Latin America (Ruiz, 2007).

In total, there were around 15 companies that made offers for their workers, but only in the case of 3 of them the workers were encouraged to buy more than 50% of the shares offered since, in most of the other companies, it was only reached 10%. However, in an investigation carried out by Salinas (1996), it was found that workers began to quickly sell their shares, which benefited private investors who had no employment relationship with the company. On the other hand, it is believed that the motivations for which the State, through Legislative Decree 674, created the modality of shareholding were mainly to reduce workers' resistance to the privatization processes of state companies added to the political clientelism of the time. On the other hand, this system was not very attractive to the people who managed the businesses since it involved high governance costs; that is, they had to negotiate with the various interests of workers and shareholders (Salinas, 1996).

The business community has not been skeptical of the sharing ownership model, given this historical background. Nowadays, no Peruvian company has implemented the ownership model within the companies that have B certification - those that carry out actions to contribute socially and environmentally in their business environment and within the company itself. In Latin America, only three companies have adopted the model: Brazil and Colombia. Beyond the history that can demonstrate a specific resistance among entrepreneurs, business models and types of companies have been found that are seeking to overcome institutional voids and that could be configured as good candidates to apply the ownership model.

Overcoming institutional Voids in Emerging Markets: Opportunities in Peru towards Employee Ownership Initiatives

The Peruvian State has not guaranteed the institutional conditions that allow equal opportunities for market participation, which, consequently, increased the probability of opportunism and informality, thus limiting the integral involvement and power of the market. Without a strong State, various actors emerge with different roles, such as multinational companies that transmit knowledge, capital, ideas, and value through borders, promoting economic development and well-being in certain nations (Meyer, 2004). Multinational companies in Peru are one of the primary sources of formal employment; however, they face high staff turnover and difficulties finding and retaining talent. In recent years, Peru has been one of the countries with the highest labor turnover rate in Latin America. An average of 20% is above the region's average (10.9%) (ESAN, 2020), which can also create an opportunity when looking for strategies for increasing brand employer.

Another actor who appears on stage is the family businesses, which have proven to be a primary alternative in emerging countries. This type of organization that has an identity capable of building closer relationships between employees and forming relevant connections with interest groups external to the organizations (López et al., 2023) tends to form small communities in which their principal social capital is the cohesion and synergy of their members in the face of the potential lack of capital, products or infrastructure. It is stated that family businesses penalize internal selfishness and promote the generosity of its members in such a way that they generate a sustainable organizational culture across generations that can address the potential institutional voids of a given country (Miller et al., 2009).

According to EY (2019), nearly 80% of companies in Peru are family-owned, and their participation in employment reaches between 60% and 70%. These types of companies focus more on talent as a facilitator of growth over their peers. To do this, they seek to maintain scarce talent by motivating staff in the long term through a more participatory approach to their decision-making. However, they face the risks of generational change in management since only 15% have a defined succession plan. Given this, using the employee ownership model is presented as an opportunity to avoid disruption in the business. A business family should not assume that the next generation will be willing to take over the company since the interests of different family members are only sometimes aligned with the interests of the family business (EY, 2019).

Although companies like family businesses and multinationals have indeed tried to operate in a context of institutional voids, the presence of these voids, as already mentioned, generates barriers to development since it does not guarantee a fair and equitable market for citizens. Given this, a new actor emerges to fill the voids, the social enterprises. With a mission and social purpose aimed at solving users' social needs instead of just generating profits (Defourny & Nyssens, 2017), these organizations have a business model and use social innovation to achieve their social purpose. Social enterprises display their qualities and strategies to develop ventures that involve a change in the rules, the flow of resources, cultural beliefs, and power relations of an entire social system (López et al., 2024).

In this sense, social entrepreneurs develop innovative business models or systems that tend to reorganize, deconstruct, or renew existing institutional arrangements to create jobs and opportunities for different societal actors. Likewise, these companies not only deal with market deficiencies regarding the structures of formal institutional gaps, such as gaps in the labor market, the product market, or the capital market, but also with informal institutional voids, such as those related to trust, support, and social acceptance (Ebrashi & Darrag, 2017).

Social enterprises create and operate with new business models that provide high levels of trust among stakeholders. For instance, in the labor market, they are offering decent employment to groups traditionally at risk of being excluded and marginalized in the current labor market. In this model, vulnerable groups join the enterprise as workers for producing goods or services that are subsequently sold in the market, thus generating a flow of financial resources in the organization that are seen as beneficial. Through training and workshops, social enterprises improve human capital, which is beneficial not only for the organization and the vulnerable population but also for companies in the sector that can hire more specialized talent later.

Other business models act as a bridge between clients and producers. The purpose of this type of entrepreneurship is that communities that have a product or service with high potential value can generate better income through a fair price that is not diluted by the presence of intermediate companies, which usually take a large part of the profits. Several bridge-type social enterprises in Peru have been created because the geographical distance does not allow producers such as farmers, artisans, and fishermen to take the merchandise to the final consumer. Besides providing training, social enterprises engage in government activism to promote laws that give more power to invisible workers in specific sectors and companies.

Market failures, such as exclusion and the absence of a State with education and health services in remote areas of Peru, have not allowed adequate human capital development and ventures in other regions. Social enterprises use the power of the market to close institutional gaps since they develop capacities in vulnerable people, workers, and organizations to find and advance innovative solutions. On the one hand, in the void of the product market, they provide information along the chain of value through traceability and transparency. Thus, they increase the power of suppliers and customers, who can make more informed decisions. On the other hand, in the labor market void, they increase the employability of people neglected by the market and allow them to be and do what they want. Likewise, they decentralize human talent so that they can work to develop localities and regions outside Lima.

As has been seen, in emerging markets such as Peru, many institutional voids can come together. These gaps are so established in the economy and in the way of interactions between citizens living and enterprises that different mechanisms and ways of operating to overcome them have been created, preventing the implementation of EO initiatives. However, business models such as social enterprises might contribute to the construction of institutions, mainly trust, laying the foundations for integrating workers into more accessible and fair pre-distribution mechanisms.

CONCLUSIONS ON THE IMPLEMENTATION OF EMPLOYEE OWNERSHIP IN PERU

The main objective of this chapter was to highlight how the institutional context has shaped specific conditions that add to the business environment in order for it to become an infertile ground for the implementation of shared capitalism mechanisms, specifically, EO initiatives. Indeed, the information we have gathered and analyzed in this chapter as well as our previous discussion evidence that EO plans would find several operational constraints as well as a reluctant attitude to be approached or even incorporated in companies' strategies. Deep and structural patterns in the Peruvian business community have rooted a particular type of capitalism which would not leave enough room for a diversity-oriented and including governance.

Institutional weakness in the country forces organizations that operate locally to find shortcuts or turnarounds to thrive within the business context, relying more on informal institutions and concentration of resources. Therefore, business elites gain prominence in the local business landscape, reinforcing the importance and value of informal mechanisms for market strategies and corporate governance. This business elite in Peru would be reluctant to share the ownership as most of the governance structures respond to a more traditional managerial and/or family capitalism, which is strongly hierarchical and less accountable.

Moreover, lack of trust in the business environment among economic agents would severely constrain the dialogue and undermine collaboration efforts between employers and employees, as well as with other stakeholders that could be related to the EO initiatives. Historical patterns in the country about failures, delays and/or insufficiently implemented share-profit plans would exacerbate trust issues between government and businesses. Hence, overcoming the barrier of trust would be instrumental for going forward with EO initiatives in the country. This would require a multi-stakeholder action to create successful synergies and shared value actions among government, academe, civil society, and businesses, to reflect how trust can be mobilized across disciplines and local projects towards society's wellbeing. In this way, the government would be a key player by providing the adequate local regulation to promote and incentive joint initiatives, alliances, partnerships, and synergies across economic sectors, different stakeholders, and disciplines.

Furthermore, social, and economic inequalities in Peru would set improper conditions for employees to have a base of standard financial and managerial skills. This lack of knowledge would not only increase mistrust between stakeholders but also would undermine the communication and convincing efforts from companies willing to adapt and implement EO initiatives on their workforce. Thus, upgrading basic financial skills as well as managerial knowledge in employees would strongly support EO implementations, having the employees as true partners of their own economic prosperity and social inclusion. Consequently, policy-makers can propose changes in the labor regulations oriented to the enhancing of these skills as part of firms' responsibility towards their employees.

Finally, our chapter has underlined that traditional business actors, namely family business groups or multinational corporations would suffer from a natural inertia to change their current business strategies to adopt shared capitalism mechanisms such as EO plans, considering the infertile ground for EO in which they operate. Nevertheless, we argue that social businesses in the country would be more willing to incorporate EO into their strategies and business operations, and this could be a proper beginning for the introduction of EO mechanisms in the country. In addition, these new business models and leaders can address institutional gaps by providing good employment conditions to scarce talent in the environment. At sum, local stakeholders would be responsible to create together a fertile business environment that could be able to gently receive new business models that promote a comprehensive inclusiveness and prosperity in the country, through the multiple options that the shared capitalism offers.

REFERENCES

Aubert, N., & Cordova, M. (2020). Sharing the risk at expense of power: Paying wages in equity to face the COVID-19. Repositorio institucional PUCP. https://repositorio.pucp.edu.pe/index/handle/123456789/173261

Aubert, N., & Cordova, M. (2022). How society's constraints would undermine ESPP adaption in Latin America: The Case of Peru. In Hernandez, G., & Zuloaga, R. (Eds.), *Employee Ownership in the Americas: A Path to Shared Prosperity.*

Aubert, N., Cordova, M., & Hernandez, G. (2024). Sharing the ownership in Peru and Mexico: The case of a French MNE prompting the SDGs achievement. *Critical Perspectives on International Business*, 20(2), 246–271. DOI: 10.1108/cpoib-12-2022-0133

Ben-Ner, A., & Jones, D. C. (1995). Employee Participation, Ownership, and Productivity: A Theoretical Framework. *Industrial Relations*, 34(4), 532–554. DOI: 10.1111/j.1468-232X.1995.tb00387.x

Blasi, J. R., Conte, M., & Kruse, D. (1996). Employee Stock Ownership and Corporate Performance among Public Companies. *Industrial & Labor Relations Review*, 50(1), 60–79. DOI: 10.1177/001979399605000104

Blasi, J. R., Freeman, R. B., & Kruse, D. L. (2013). *The Citizen's Share: Reducing Inequality in the 21st Century*. Yale University Press.

Borda, A., Cordova, M., & Narro, L. (2022). Entrepreneurship in Peru. In Dana, L. P., Keen, C., & Ramadani, V. (Eds.), *Entrepreneurship in South America. Springer Texts in Business and Economics*. Springer., DOI: 10.1007/978-3-030-97060-4_11

Bova, F., Dou, Y., & Hope, O.-K. (2014). Employee Ownership and Firm Disclosure. *Contemporary Accounting Research*, 32(2), 639–673. DOI: 10.1111/1911-3846.12084

Briolo, C., & Cordova, M. (2022). A Cracked Public Administration in Peru: How "Vacunagate" Has Shaken the Foundations of an Already Damaged Society. *AD-Minister*, (41), 91–114. DOI: 10.17230/Ad-minister.41.4

CEPAL. (2002). *El proceso de privatizaciones en el Perú durante el período 1991-2002*. Series Gestión Pública.

Chaplinsky, S., & Niehaus, G. (1994). The Role of ESOPs in Takeover Contests. *The Journal of Finance*, 49(4), 1451–1470. DOI: 10.1111/j.1540-6261.1994.tb02461.x

Cordova, M., Huamán, F., Liñan, T., & Powosino, R. (2022). Regenerative Futures for Peru. In Gonzalez-Perez, M. A. (Ed.), *Regenerative and Sustainable Futures for Latin America and the Caribbean* (pp. 235–254). Emerald Publishing Limited., DOI: 10.1108/978-1-80117-864-820221011

Dávila, C. (2013). The current state of business history in Latin America. *Australian Economic History Review*, 53(2), 109–120. DOI: 10.1111/aehr.12006

De Soto, H. (2006). *Realizing property rights*. Ruffer & Rub Sachbuchverlag.

DiMaggio, P. J., & Powell, W. W. (1983). The iron cage revisited: Institutional isomorphism and collective rationality in organizational fields. *American Sociological Review*, 48(2), 147–160. DOI: 10.2307/2095101

Domadenik, P., Prašnikar, J., & Svejnar, J. (2008). Restructuring of firms in transition: Ownership, institutions and openness to trade. *Journal of International Business Studies*, 39(4), 725–746. DOI: 10.1057/palgrave.jibs.8400379

Durand, F. (2017). *Los doce apóstoles de la economía peruana: Una mirada social a los grupos de poder limeños y provincianos*. Fondo Editorial PUCP.

Ebrashi, R. E., & Darrag, M. (2017). Social entrepreneurs' strategies for addressing institutional voids in developing markets. *European Journal of International Management*, 11(3), 325–346. DOI: 10.1504/EJIM.2017.083876

Ernest & Young (2019). ¿Cuál es el impacto de las familias empresarias? Resultados de la 1era Encuesta de Familias empresarias en Perú. Asociación de empresas familiares del Perú.

ESAN. (2020). *Rotación laboral en el Perú: ¿qué hacer para disminuirla?* Conexiones ESAN.

Freeman, R., Blasi, J. R., & Kruse, D. (2010). Introduction to "Shared Capitalism at Work: Employee Ownership, Profit and Gain Sharing, and Broad-based Stock Options". In Kruse, D., Freeman, R., & Blasi, J. R. (Eds.), *Shared Capitalism at Work: Employee Ownership, Profit and Gain Sharing, and Broad-based Stock Options, 2010* (pp. 1–37). DOI: 10.7208/chicago/9780226056968.003.0001

Ganoza, C., & Stiglich, A. (2015). *El Perú está calato. El falso milagro de la economía peruana y las trampas que amenazan nuestro progreso* (1st ed.). Editorial Planeta.

Gao, C., Zuzul, T., Jones, G., & Khanna, T. (2017). Overcoming Institutional Voids: A Reputation-Based View of Long-Run Survival. *Strategic Management Journal*, 38(11), 2147–2167. DOI: 10.1002/smj.2649

Ginglinger, E., Megginson, W., & Waxin, T. (2011). Employee ownership, board representation, and corporate financial policies. *Journal of Corporate Finance*, 17(4), 868–887. DOI: 10.1016/j.jcorpfin.2011.03.005

Grompone, R., & Tanaka, M. (2009). Entre el crecimiento económico y la insatisfacción social. Las protestas sociales en el Perú actual. 1st ed. Lima: Instituto de Estudios Peruanos (IEP).

Henn, R., Terzidis, O., Kuschel, K., Leiva, J. C., & Alsua, C. (2022). One step back, two steps forward: Internationalization strategies and the resilient growth of entrepreneurial ecosystems. *Small Enterprise Research*, 29(3), 273–307. DOI: 10.1080/13215906.2022.2134191

Hernandez, G., & Zuloaga, R. (2023). *Employee Ownership in the Americas: A Path to Shared Prosperity*. ITESO, Universidad Jesuita de Guadalajara. DOI: 10.31391/JDTD1733

Índice Global de Competitividad Corporativa. (2023). *Niveles de complejidad: los desafíos del cumplimiento corporativo internacional*. TMF Group.

Khanna, T. (2018). *Trust: Creating the Foundation for Entrepreneurship in Developing Countries. Harvard Business School*. Berrett-Koehler Publishers.

Khanna, T., & Palepu, K. (2000). The Future of Business Groups in Emerging Markets: Long Run Evidence from Chile. *Academy of Management Journal*, 43(3), 268–285. https://www.hbs.edu/faculty/Pages/item.aspx?num=12431. DOI: 10.2307/1556395

Khanna, T., & Palepu, K. (2010). *Winning in Emerging Markets*. Harvard Business Press.

Khanna, T., & Palepu, K. (2011). *Winning in Emerging Markets: Spotting and Responding to Institutional Voids, World Financial Review*. Harvard Business School.

Khoury, T. A., & Prasad, A. (2016). Entrepreneurship amid concurrent institutional constraints in less developed countries. *Business & Society*, 55(7), 934–969. DOI: 10.1177/0007650314567641

Liedong, T. A., Peprah, A. A., Amartey, A. O., & Rajwani, T. (2020). Institutional voids and firms' resource commitment in emerging markets: A review and future research agenda. *Journal of International Management*, 26(3), 100–756. DOI: 10.1016/j.intman.2020.100756

López, H., Huamani, J., Arroyo, G., & Díaz, M. (2024). Estrategias de emprendedores sociales peruanos desde lo cognitivo y el entorno. *Estudios Gerenciales*, 40(171), 162–176. DOI: 10.18046/j.estger.2024.171.6290

López, H., Vega, A., Robles, V & Arroyo, G. (2023). Vacíos institucionales en las organizaciones: una mirada a cómo los emprendimientos sociales. Serie de Ciencias de la Gestión N° 11.

López-Concepción, A., Gil-Lacruz, A., Saz-Gil, I., & Bazán-Monasterio, V. (2023). Social Well-Being for a Sustainable Future: The Influence of Trust in Big Business and Banks on Perceptions of Technological Development from a Life Satisfaction Perspective in Latin America. *Sustainability (Basel)*, 15(1), 628. DOI: 10.3390/su15010628

Mackin, C. (2024). Defining employee ownership: Four meanings and two models. *Journal of Participation and Employee Ownership*, 7(1), 1–25. DOI: 10.1108/JPEO-10-2022-0019

Meyer, K. E. (2004). Perspectives on multinational enterprises in emerging economies. *Journal of International Business Studies*, 35(4), 259–276. DOI: 10.1057/palgrave.jibs.8400084

Morgado, E. (1991). *América Latina. Participación de los trabajadores en la empresa*. Laborem.

Neffa, J. (2020). *La participación de los trabajadores en la gestión de las empresas*. Universidad Nacional de Moreno. UNM Editora.

O'Boyle, E. H., Patel, P. C., & Gonzalez-Mulé, E. (2016). Employee ownership and firm performance: A meta-analysis. *Human Resource Management Journal*, 26(4), 425–448. DOI: 10.1111/1748-8583.12115

Paul, R. J., Niehoff, B. P., & Turnley, W. H. (2000). Empowerment, expectations, and the psychological contract—Managing the dilemmas and gaining the advantages. *Journal of Socio-Economics*, 29(5), 471–485. DOI: 10.1016/S1053-5357(00)00083-4

Pazos, J., & Cordova, M. (2024). Legal gaps in the peruvian corporate network: Negative practices in boards of directors. *Pensamiento Americano*, 17(33), e-481. DOI: 10.21803/penamer.17.33.481

Peng, M. W., Sun, S. L., Pinkham, B., & Chen, H. (2009). The Institution-Based View as a Third Leg for a Strategy Tripod. *The Academy of Management Perspectives*, 23(3), 63–81. DOI: 10.5465/amp.2009.43479264

Rivas, J. L., Salvaj, E., & Cordova, M. (2023). Family vs non family networks: Chile, Mexico and Peru. *Management Research*, 21(3), 217–236. DOI: 10.1108/MRJIAM-12-2022-1369

Ruiz, A. (2007). Las privatizaciones en Perú: un proceso con luces y sombras. *Nueva Sociedad.* 207.

Salas, M. (1982). *Participación Laboral y la autogestión en el Perú.* Pontificia Universidad Católica del Perú.

Schneider, B. R. (2013). *Hierarchical capitalism in Latin America. Business, labor, and the challenges of equitable development* (1st ed.). Cambridge University Press., DOI: 10.1017/CBO9781107300446

Schuler, R. S., & Rogovsky, N. (1998). Understanding Compensation Practice Variations Across Firms: The Impact of National Culture. *Journal of International Business Studies*, 29(1), 159–177. DOI: 10.1057/palgrave.jibs.8490030

Stiglitz, J. (2019). *People, Power, and Profits: Progressive Capitalism for an Age of Discontent* (1st ed.). W.W. Norton & Company.

Tepper, J., & Hearn, D. (2023). *The Myth of Capitalism: Monopolies and the Death of Competition* (1st ed.). Wiley.

Ugaz, J. (2020). *La Gran Corrupción.* Planeta.

Vassolo, R., De Castro, J., & Gomez-Mejia, L. (2011). Managing in Latin America. Common issues and a research agenda. *The Academy of Management Perspectives*, 25(4), 22–34. DOI: 10.5465/amp.2011.0129

Ventura, J., & Jauregui, K. (2017). Business-Community Relationships for Extractive Industries: A Case Study in Peru. Brazilian Administration Review, 14(2), e160114. https://doi.org/DOI: 10.1590/1807-7692bar2017160114

Vergara, A. (2018). *Ciudadanos sin república. De la precariedad institucional al descalabro político* (2nd ed.). Editorial Planeta.

Wagner, S. H., Parker, C. P., & Christiansen, N. D. (2006). Employees that think and act like owners: Effects of Ownership Beliefs and Behaviors on Organizational Effectiveness. *Personnel Psychology*, 56(4), 847–871. DOI: 10.1111/j.1744-6570.2003.tb00242.x

Webb, J. W., Khoury, T. A., & Hitt, M. A. (2020). The influence of formal and informal institutional voids on entrepreneurship. *Entrepreneurship Theory and Practice*, 44(3), 504–526. DOI: 10.1177/1042258719830310

Wolf, R., & Gonzalez-Perez, M. A. (2024). (Forthcoming). A Tale of Soft Power: How the United States Used Business Administration Schools to Promote its Interests and Values in Latin America. *Palgrave Macmillan.*

Compilation of References

Kruse D., (2002), Recherche sur la prévalence et les effets de l'actionnariat salarié, Revue de l'actionnariat salarié, droit et finance, vol. 14, n°4, pp 65- 90.

Lewis, J. (2019). John Lewis Partnership Annual Report.

Lowitzsch, j; Menke, J.D; Suarsana, D; Nuttall, G; Gonza, T & Mirabel, T. (2024). Toward a european employee stock ownership plan (European ESOP), Kellogg College.

National Center for Employee Ownership. (2023). Employee Ownership in Canada.

Pérotin V & Robinson A, (2002). Employee participation in profit and ownership: A review of the issues and evidence. Report for the European parliament, novembre, social affairs services, SOCI109 EN.

Roelants, B., Dovgan, D., Eum, Hyungsik, & Terrasi, E. (2012). The resilience of the cooperative model. CECOP.

Rouzade, O, (2021, December 24). PEE Collective Savings Plan, *Cabinet ROUZADE website*. Подробная информация о коллективном плане сбережений PEE

Abdelhamid, A. B. (2021). *Corporate governance and employee ownership: evidence from France* (Doctoral dissertation, Université Clermont Auvergne).

Abdelnour, J. A., Aubert, N., and Campa, D. (2022), "Does employee ownership decrease agency costs? Evidence from French listed companies", *Finance Contrôle Stratégie*, n° 25-3/4.

Abdelnour, J., Aubert, N., & Ben-Amar, W. (2023). Employee stock ownership and voluntary carbon disclosure. *Bankers Markets & Investors: an academic & professional review*. ⟨halshs-04094880⟩

Abdelnour, J., Aubert, N., & Campa, D. (2022). Does employee ownership reduce agency costs? Evidence from French listed companies. *Finance Contrôle Stratégie*, 25-3/4

Abhilasha, A., Sreenivasulu, A., & Manimozhi, T. Satheesh kumar P., Selvakumar P. and Singh P.,(2022). "The Model of Smart Sensing Device For Sensitive Nano-clusters Modification in Sensing Properties," 2022 2nd International Conference on Advance Computing and Innovative Technologies in Engineering (ICACITE), Greater Noida, India, 2022, pp. 1043-1047, DOI: 10.1109/ICACITE53722.2022.9823846

Acemoglu, D., & Robinson, J. A. (2013). Economics versus politics: Pitfalls of policy advice. *The Journal of Economic Perspectives*, 27(2), 173–192. DOI: 10.1257/jep.27.2.173

Achour, Z. (2024). Impact of employee stock ownership on firm financial performance: Does corporate social responsibility matter? *International Journal of Management and Enterprise Development*, 23(2), 155–170. DOI: 10.1504/IJMED.2024.139275

Acquah, I. S. K., Issau, K., Dei Mensah, R., & Vanderpuye, F. (2023, September 21). When stakeholder orientations matter: Modelling employee orientation, shareholder orientation and supply chain orientation as necessary and sufficient conditions for firm performance. *Heliyon*, 9(10), e20359. DOI: 10.1016/j.heliyon.2023.e20359 PMID: 37771530

Adwan, S., & Ahamed, M. M. (2024). Employee ownership and corporate investment efficiency in Europe. *Review of Quantitative Finance and Accounting*. Advance online publication. DOI: 10.1007/s11156-024-01300-5

Adwan, S., Alhaj-Ismail, A., & Jelic, R. (2022). Non-executive employee ownership and financial reporting quality: Evidence from Europe. *Review of Quantitative Finance and Accounting*, 59(2), 793–823. DOI: 10.1007/s11156-022-01058-8

Agrawal, A., & Knoeber, C. R. (1996). Firm performance and mechanisms to control agency problems between managers and shareholders. *Journal of Financial and Quantitative Analysis*, 31(3), 377–397. DOI: 10.2307/2331397

Ahlquist, J. S. (2017). Labor unions, political representation, and economic inequality. *Annual Review of Political Science*, 20(1), 409–432. DOI: 10.1146/annurev-polisci-051215-023225

Ahmad, N., Harun, A., Khizar, H. M. U., Khalid, J., & Khan, S. (2022). Drivers and barriers of travel behaviors during and post COVID-19 pandemic: A systematic literature review and future agenda. *Journal of Tourism Futures*, 0(0). Advance online publication. DOI: 10.1108/JTF-01-2022-0023

Al-Ahdal, A. A., & Hashim, H. A. (2022). The impact of audit reputation on firm performance: Evidence from Indian non-financial firms. *Journal of Financial Reporting and Accounting*, 20(5), 866–896. DOI: 10.1108/JFRA-12-2020-0361

Albrecht, S. L., Furlong, S., & Leiter, M. P. (2023). The psychological conditions for employee engagement in organizational change: Test of a change engagement model. *Frontiers in Psychology*, 14, 1071924. DOI: 10.3389/fpsyg.2023.1071924 PMID: 36743243

Alchian, A. A., & Demsetz, H. (1972). Production, information costs, and economic organization. *The American Economic Review*, 62(5), 777–795.

Aleissa, S., Alakkas, M., Albugeaey, Z., Alshelaly, H., Alotaibi, S., & Alzubaidi, T. (2024). Leveraging Parallel Computing for Enhanced Stock Movement Forecasting Using Machine Learning. *2024 Seventh International Women in Data Science Conference at Prince Sultan University (WiDS PSU)*, 67–72. DOI: 10.1109/WiDS-PSU61003.2024.00028

Al-Gamrh, B., Farooq, U., & Ahsan, T. (2024). Beyond the balance sheet: Assessing corporate governance through the Lens of debtholders. *International Review of Financial Analysis*, 96, 103625. Advance online publication. DOI: 10.1016/j.irfa.2024.103625

Alhydary, T., Qashqary, L., Alotaibi, S., Jaha, R., & Alansari, S. (2024a). Smart Trader: Towards an Advisory Chatbot Service for Saudi Stock Market Investment. *2024 Seventh International Women in Data Science Conference at Prince Sultan University (WiDS PSU)*, 32–35. DOI: 10.1109/WiDS-PSU61003.2024.00021

Allen, N. J., & Meyer, J. P. (1990). The Measurement and Antecedents of Affective, Continuance, and Normative Commitment to the Organization. *Journal of Occupational Psychology*, 63(1), 1–18. DOI: 10.1111/j.2044-8325.1990.tb00506.x

Almond, G. A., & Verba, S. (2015). *The civic culture: Political attitudes and democracy in five nations*. Princeton university press. and International Perspectives. Washington: Brookings.

Alperovitz, G. (2011). *America Beyond Capitalism: Reclaiming Our Wealth, Our Liberty, & Our Democracy* (2nd ed.). Democracy Collaborative Press.

AMF. (2023, March 23). Employee savings: a sharp increase in awareness and ownership of employee savings schemes; support for employees and company managers should be reinforced. https://www.amf-france.org/en/news-publications/news-releases/amf-news-releases/employee-savings-sharp-increase-awareness-and-ownership-employee-savings-schemes-support-employees

Amin, A., Ali, R., Rehman, R., Naseem, M. A., & Ahmad, M. I. (2022). Female presence in corporate governance, firm performance, and the moderating role of family ownership. *Ekonomska Istrazivanja*, 35(1), 929–948. DOI: 10.1080/1331677X.2021.1952086

Ammirato, P. (2018). *The growth of italian cooperatives: innovation, resilience and social responsibility*. Routledge. DOI: 10.4324/9781315158785

Ana, (2024, May 6). Head of the Privatization Organization: 5 billion preferred shares were given to the workers. *Ana News*. https://ana.ir

Andersen, R. (2012). Support for democracy in cross-national perspective: The detrimental effect of economic inequality. *Research in Social Stratification and Mobility*, 30(4), 389–402. DOI: 10.1016/j.rssm.2012.04.002

Anderson, R. C., & Reeb, D. M. (2003). Founding-family ownership and firm performance: Evidence from the S&P 500. *The Journal of Finance*, 58(3), 1301–1328. DOI: 10.1111/1540-6261.00567

AON. (2020). How Common are Employee Stock Purchase Plans? It Varies Widely by Demographics. https://rewards.aon.com/en-us/insights/articles/2020/how-common-are-employee-stockpurchase-plans-it-varies-widely-by-demographic

Appelbaum, E., & Berg, P. (2001). High-Performance Work Systems and Labor Market Structures. In Berg, I., & Kalleberg, A. L. (Eds.), *Sourcebook of Labor Markets. Plenum Studies in Work and Industry*. Springer., DOI: 10.1007/978-1-4615-1225-7_11

Arando, S., Gago, M., Kato, T., Jones, D., & Freundlich, F. (2010). Assessing Mondragon: Stability & Managed Change in the Face of Globalization. William Davidson Institute Working Paper No. 1003, Available at *SSRN*: https://ssrn.com/abstract=1726449 or http://dx.doi.org/DOI: 10.2139/ssrn.1726449

Arellano, M., & Bond, S. (1991). Some tests of specification for panel data: Monte Carlo evidence and an application to employment equations. *The Review of Economic Studies*, 58(2), 277–297. DOI: 10.2307/2297968

Arora, A., & Sharma, C. (2016). Corporate governance and firm performance in developing countries: Evidence from India. *Corporate Governance (Bradford)*, 16(2), 420–436. DOI: 10.1108/CG-01-2016-0018

Arrighi, B. A., & Maume, D. J. (1994). Workplace control and political participation. *Sociological Focus*, 27(2), 147–159. DOI: 10.1080/00380237.1994.10571016

Atkinson, A. (2015). *Inequality: What Can Be Done?* Harvard University Press. DOI: 10.4159/9780674287013

Attanasio, G., Preghenella, N., De Toni, A. F., & Battistella, C. (2022). Stakeholder engagement in business models for sustainability: The stakeholder value flow model for sustainable development. *Business Strategy and the Environment*, 31(3), 860–874. DOI: 10.1002/bse.2922

Aubert, N., & Cordova, M. (2020). Sharing the risk at expense of power: Paying wages in equity to face the COVID-19. Repositorio institucional PUCP. https://repositorio.pucp.edu.pe/index/handle/123456789/173261

Aubert, N., & Cordova, M. (2022). Dealing With COVID-19 Through Employee Stock Ownership Plans: Saving Money and Losing Power to Live an Extra Day. In Employee Share Ownership and Impacts on Organizational Value and Behavior (pp. 1-17). IGI Global.

Aubert, N., & Hollandts, X. (2023). La codétermination sera-t-elle la grande Réforme de notre siècle? (No. hal-04501083).

Aubert, N., & Bernheim, P. (2021). *What the PACTE law changes for employee savings and participation? Post-Print hal-02532708*. HAL.

Aubert, N., Chassagnon, V., & Hollandts, X. (2016). Employee ownership, governance and firm performance: An econometric case study of a listed French group. *Revue d'Economie Industrielle*, (154), 151–176. DOI: 10.4000/rei.6365

Aubert, N., & Cordova, M. (2022). How society's constraints would undermine ESPP adaption in Latin America: The Case of Peru. In Hernandez, G., & Zuloaga, R. (Eds.), *Employee Ownership in the Americas: A Path to Shared Prosperity.*

Aubert, N., Cordova, M., & Hernandez, G. (2024). Sharing the ownership in Peru and Mexico: The case of a French MNE prompting the SDGs achievement. *Critical Perspectives on International Business*, 20(2), 246–271. DOI: 10.1108/cpoib-12-2022-0133

Aubert, N., Garnotel, G., Lapied, A., & Rousseau, P. (2014). Employee ownership: A theoretical and empirical investigation of management entrenchment vs. reward management. *Economic Modelling*, 40, 423–434. DOI: 10.1016/j.econmod.2013.12.011

Aubert, N., Kern, A., & Hollandts, X. (2017). Employee stock ownership and the cost of capital. *Research in International Business and Finance*, 41, 67–78. DOI: 10.1016/j.ribaf.2017.04.007

Auer, P., & Cazes, S. (2000). The resilience of the long-term employment relationship: Evidence from the industrialized countries. *International Labour Review*, 139(4), 379–408. DOI: 10.1111/j.1564-913X.2000.tb00525.x

Autor, D., Dorn, D., Hanson, G., & Majlesi, K. (2020). Importing political polarization? The electoral consequences of rising trade exposure. *The American Economic Review*, 110(10), 3139–3183.

Avey, J. B., Luthans, F., & Jensen, S. M. (2009). Psychological capital: A positive resource for combating employee stress and turnover. *Human Resource Management*, 48(5), 677–693. DOI: 10.1002/hrm.20294

Avey, J. B., Wernsing, T. S., & Palanski, M. E. (2012). Exploring the process of ethical leadership: The mediating role of employee voice and psychological ownership. *Journal of Business Ethics*, 107(1), 21–34. DOI: 10.1007/s10551-012-1298-2

Baker, G. P., & Kahn, A. (2020). Employee Ownership and Corporate Governance. *Journal of Corporate Finance*, 65, 101–115.

Ballard-Rosa, C., Jensen, A., & Scheve, K. (2022). Economic decline, social identity, and authoritarian values in the United States. *International Studies Quarterly*, 66(1), sqab027. DOI: 10.1093/isq/sqab027

Bangun, N., Tjakrawala, F. K., Andani, K. W., & Santioso, L. (2017). The effect of financial leverage, employee stock ownership program and firm size on firm performance of companies listed in Indonesia Stock Exchange. *International Business and Accounting Research Journal*, 1(2), 82–98. DOI: 10.15294/ibarj.v1i2.7

Bao, X., Sadiq, M., Tye, W., & Zhang, J. (2024). *The impact of environmental, social, and governance (ESG) rating disparities on corporate risk: The mediating role of financing constraints*. DOI: 10.1016/j.jenvman.2024.123113

Bao, Y., Li, C., & Zhao, H. (2020). Servant leadership and employee ownership behavior: A moderated mediation model. *International Journal of Human Resource Management*, 31(17), 2155–2183.

Barnea, A., & Rubin, A. (2010). Corporate social responsibility as a conflict between shareholders. *Journal of Business Ethics*, 97(1), 71–86. DOI: 10.1007/s10551-010-0496-z

Bartels, L. M. (2017). "Political Inequality in Affluent Democracies: The Social Welfare Deficit." CSDI Working Paper 5-2017. Vanderbilt University.https://www.vanderbilt.edu/csdi/includes/Working_Paper_5_2017.pdf

Bartels, L. M. (2008). *Unequal Democracy: The Political Economy of the New Gilded Age*. Russell Sage Foundation.

Bartlett, C. A., & Ghoshal, S. (1994). Changing the role of top management: Beyond strategy to purpose. *Harvard Business Review*, 72(6), 79–88.

Barzuza, M., Curtis, Q., & Webber, D. H. (2020). Shareholder Value(s): Index Fund ESG Activism and the New Millennial Corporate Governance. *Southern California Law Review*, 93(6), 1243–1322.

Basterretxea, I., & Storey, J. (2018). Do employee-owned firms produce more positive employee behavioural outcomes? If not, why not? A British-Spanish comparative analysis. *British Journal of Industrial Relations*, 56(2), 292–319. DOI: 10.1111/bjir.12247

Bauer, R., Derwall, J., & Tissen, C. (2023). Private shareholder engagements on material ESG issues. *Financial Analysts Journal*, 79(4), 64–95. DOI: 10.1080/0015198X.2023.2220648

Becher, M., & Stegmueller, D. (2020). Reducing unequal representation: The impact of labor unions on legislative responsiveness in the U.S. Congress. *Perspectives on Politics*, 19(1), 92–109. DOI: 10.1017/S153759272000208X

Becker, C. (2021). Environmental performance boosts market value, but a firm's collective reputation may sink it. Wisconsin School of Business. https://business.wisc.edu/news/environmental-performance-boosts-market-value-but-a-firms-collective-reputation-may-sink-it/

Becker, G. S. (1964). *Human capital theory*.

Beheshti, S., Eskini, R., Pasban, M., & Zare, A. (2018). Company Employees' Incentive Plan: Incentive Shares and Preferred Shares with a Study in the Legal Systems of England and Iran. *International Legal Investigations*, 11(40), 39–70.

Belanès, A., & Saihi, M. (2014). Does Employee Ownership Really Boost Performance? Bankers. *Markets & Investors*, (130), 55–68.

Benach, J., Vives, A., Tarafa, G., Delclos, C., & Muntaner, C. (2016). What should we know about precarious employment and health in 2025? Framing the agenda for the next decade of research. *International Journal of Epidemiology*, 45(1), 232–238. DOI: 10.1093/ije/dyv342 PMID: 26744486

Ben-Ner, A., & Jones, D. C. (1995). Employee participation, ownership, and productivity: A theoretical framework. *Industrial Relations*, 34(4), 532–554. DOI: 10.1111/j.1468-232X.1995.tb00387.x

Berle, A., & Means, G. (1932). *The Modern Corporation and the Private Property*. Mc Millan.

Bernstein, J. (2016, January). *Employee Ownership, ESOPs, Wealth and Wages*. Employee-Owned S Corporations of America. http://esca.us/wp-content/uploads/2016/01/ESOP-Study-Final.pdf

Bhattacharya, A., & Ray, T. (2021). Precarious work, job stress, and health-related quality of life. *American Journal of Industrial Medicine*, 64(4), 310–319. DOI: 10.1002/ajim.23223 PMID: 33543533

Bhattacharya, C. B., Sen, S., Edinger-Schons, L. M., & Neureiter, M. (2023). Corporate purpose and employee sustainability behaviors. *Journal of Business Ethics*, 183(3), 963–981. DOI: 10.1007/s10551-022-05090-5

Bhatti, Y., Dahlgaard, J. O., Hansen, J. H., & Hansen, K. M. (2019). Is door-to-door canvassing effective in Europe? Evidence from a meta-study across six European countries. *British Journal of Political Science*, 49(1), 279–290. DOI: 10.1017/S0007123416000521

Bivens, J., Engdahl, L., Gould, E., Kroeger, T., McNicholas, C., Mishel, L., ... & Zipperer, B. (2017). How today's unions help working people: Giving workers the power to improve their jobs and unrig the economy.

Bjørnskov, C. (2008). Social trust and fractionalization: A possible reinterpretation. *European Sociological Review*, 24(3), 271–283. DOI: 10.1093/esr/jcn004

Blair, M. (1999). Firm-Specific Human Capital and Theories of the Firm. In Blair, M., & Roe, M. (Eds.), *Employees & Corporate Governance* (pp. 58–90). Brooking Institution Press.

Blair, M., Kruse, D., & Blasi, J. (2000). Is employee ownership an unstable form or a stabilizing force? In Kochan, T., & Blair, M. (Eds.), *The new relationship: Human capital in the American Corporation* (pp. 241–288). The Brookings Institution. DOI: 10.2139/ssrn.142146

Blasi, J. R., Kruse, D. L., & Weltmann, D. (2013). "Firm Survival and Performance in Privately Held ESOP Companies." In Sharing Ownership, Profits, and Decision-Making in the 21st Century, Douglas L. Kruse, ed. Vol. 14 in the series Advances in the Economic Analysis of Participatory and Labor-Managed Firms, Takao Kato, ed. Bingley, UK: Emerald Group Publishing, pp. 109-124. DOI: 10.1108/S0885-3339(2013)0000014006

Blasi, J. (2017). *Tech Companies Are Shutting Employees Out of the Stock Market's Boom*. Fortune.

Blasi, J. R. (2016). *Employee ownership through ESOPs: Implications for the public corporation*. Elsevier.

Blasi, J. R., Conte, M., & Kruse, D. (1996). Employee Stock Ownership and Corporate Performance among Public Companies. *Industrial & Labor Relations Review*, 50(1), 60–79. DOI: 10.1177/001979399605000104

Blasi, J. R., Freeman, R. B., & Kruse, D. (2014). *The Citizen's Share: Reducing Inequality in the 21st Century*. Yale University Press.

Blasi, J. R., Freeman, R. B., & Kruse, D. L. (2018). Evidence and perspectives on broad-based employee stock ownership and profit sharing. *Journal of Participation and Employee Ownership*, 1(1), 38–60. DOI: 10.1108/JPEO-02-2018-0001

Blasi, J. R., & Kruse, D. L. (2019). *Building the Assets of Low and Moderate Income Workers and their Families: The Role of Employee Ownership*. Institute for the Study of Employee Ownership and Profit Sharing, Rutgers University.

Blasi, J. R., Kruse, D. L., & Weltman, D. (2022). (forthcoming). Employee Share Ownership in the U.S. *Statistics, Research, and Lessons Learned.*

Blasi, J., Freeman, R., & Kruse, D. (2016). Do broad-based employee ownership, profit sharing and stock options help the best firms do even better? *British Journal of Industrial Relations*, 54(1), 55–82. DOI: 10.1111/bjir.12135

Blasi, J., Kruse, D., & Bernstein, A. (1996). *Incentive Effects of Employee Ownership: A Review of the Evidence*. Industrial Relations Research Association.

Blasi, J., Kruse, D., & Freeman, R. B. (2006). Shared capitalism at work: Impacts and policy options. In *America at work: Choices and challenges* (pp. 275–295). Palgrave Macmillan US. DOI: 10.1057/9781403983596_16

Blasi, J., Kruse, D., & Weltmann, D. (2021). The response of majority employee-owned firms during the pandemic compared to other firms. *Journal of Participation and Employee Ownership*, 4(2), 92–101. DOI: 10.1108/JPEO-09-2021-0014

Blasi, J., Scharf, A., & Kruse, D. (2024). Employee ownership in the US: Some issues on ESOPs – overcoming the barriers to further development. *Journal of Participation and Employee Ownership*, 7(1), 26–45. DOI: 10.1108/JPEO-11-2022-0028

Blau, P. M. (1964). *Exchange and power in social life*. Wiley.

Blundell, R., & Bond, S. (1998). Initial conditions and moment restrictions in dynamic panel data models. *Journal of Econometrics*, 87(1), 115–143. DOI: 10.1016/S0304-4076(98)00009-8

Bocken, N. M. P., Short, S., Rana, P., & Evans, S. (2013). A value mapping tool for sustainable business modelling. *Corporate Governance (Bradford)*, 13(5), 482–497. DOI: 10.1108/CG-06-2013-0078

Boguslaw, J., & Schur, L. (2019). Building the Assets of Low and Moderate Income Workers and their Families: The Role of Employee Ownership. Institute for the Study of Employee Ownership and Profit Sharing, Rutgers University School of Management and Labor Relations. https://smlr.rutgers.edu/sites/default/files/Documents/Centers/Institute_Employee_Ownership/rutgerskelloggreport_april2019.pdf

Boiral, O., Heras-Saizarbitoria, I., & Testa, F. (2021). Improving CSR performance through employee participation and engagement. *Journal of Business Ethics*, 170(2), 325–346.

Bonal, X., & Cooper, D. (2008). The cooperative advantage: A comparative study of the performance of worker cooperatives and conventional firms. *International Journal of Cooperative Studies*, 22, 1–26.

Bonelli, M., Brière, M., & Derrien, F. (2022). *Altruism or Self-Interest? ESG and Participation in Employee Share Plans*. ESG and Participation in Employee Share Plans. DOI: 10.2139/ssrn.4164062

Borda, A., Cordova, M., & Narro, L. (2022). Entrepreneurship in Peru. In Dana, L. P., Keen, C., & Ramadani, V. (Eds.), *Entrepreneurship in South America. Springer Texts in Business and Economics*. Springer., DOI: 10.1007/978-3-030-97060-4_11

Boubaker, S., & Nguyen, P. (2021). Does employee stock ownership mitigate information asymmetry? Evidence from Australia. *Pacific-Basin Finance Journal*, 66, 101508.

Boubaker, S., & Sami, H. (2011). Multiple large shareholders and earnings informativeness. *Review of Accounting and Finance*, 10(3), 246–266. DOI: 10.1108/14757701111155789

Bova, F., Dou, Y., & Hope, O.-K. (2014). Employee Ownership and Firm Disclosure. *Contemporary Accounting Research*, 32(2), 639–673. DOI: 10.1111/1911-3846.12084

Bova, F., Kolev, K., Thomas, J. K., & Zhang, X. F. (2015). Non-executive employee ownership and corporate risk. *The Accounting Review*, 90(1), 115–145. DOI: 10.2308/accr-50860

Brady, H. E., Verba, S., & Schlozman, K. L. (1995). Beyond SES: A resource model of political participation. *The American Political Science Review*, 89(2), 271–294. DOI: 10.2307/2082425

Briolo, C., & Cordova, M. (2022). A Cracked Public Administration in Peru: How "Vacunagate" Has Shaken the Foundations of an Already Damaged Society. *AD-Minister*, (41), 91–114. DOI: 10.17230/Ad-minister.41.4

Brolis, O. (2018). Do social enterprises attract workers who are more pro-socially motivated than their counterparts in for-profit organizations to perform low-skilled jobs? *International Journal of Human Resource Management*, 29(20), 2861–2879. DOI: 10.1080/09585192.2017.1328611

Brown, R., McQuaid, R., Raeside, R., Dutton, M., Egdell, V., & Canduela, J. (2019). Buying into capitalism? Employee ownership in a disconnected era. *British Journal of Industrial Relations*, 57(1), 62–85. DOI: 10.1111/bjir.12309

Bryson, A., Clark, A. E., Freeman, R. B., & Green, C. P. (2019). Share capitalism and worker wellbeing. *Labour Economics*, 61, 101754. PMID: 28725118

Buchko, A. (1992). Employee Ownership, Attitudes and Turnover: An Empirical Assessment. *Human Relations*, 45(7), 711–733. DOI: 10.1177/001872679204500704

Buchko, A. (1993). The effects of employee ownership on employee attitudes: An integrated causal model and path analysis. *Journal of Management Studies*, 30(4), 633–657. DOI: 10.1111/j.1467-6486.1993.tb00319.x

Budd, J., Lamare, J. R., & Timming, A. R. (2018). Learning about democracy at work: Cross-national evidence on individual employee voice influencing political participation in civil society. *Industrial & Labor Relations Review*, 71(4), 956–985. DOI: 10.1177/0019793917746619

Buhl, A., Blazejewski, S., & Dittmer, F. (2016). The More, the Merrier: Why and How Employee-Driven Eco-Innovation Enhances Environmental and Competitive Advantage. *Sustainability (Basel)*, 8(9), 946. DOI: 10.3390/su8090946

Burn, S. M., & Konrad, A. M. (1987). Political participation: A matter of community, stress, job autonomy, and contact by political organizations. *Political Psychology*, 8(1), 125–138. DOI: 10.2307/3790989

Caramelli, M. (2011). *Employee ownership and corporate performance: Toward unlocking the black box. Employee ownership and shared capitalism: New directions in research*. Labor and Employment Relations Association.

Carberry, E. J., & Meyers, J. S. (2022). Employee Ownership and the Future of Work. In The Cambridge Handbook of the Changing Nature of Work (pp. 415-432). Cambridge University Press.

Carberry, E. J. (2021). *Employee ownership and shared capitalism: New directions in research*. Cornell University Press.

Carberry, E. J. (2022). Making Sense of Employee Ownership: A Typology of Broad-Based Employee Stock Ownership Plans. *Industrial & Labor Relations Review*, 75(5), 1172–1204.

Card, D. (1996). The effect of unions on the structure of wages: A longitudinal analysis. *Econometrica*, 64(4), 957–979. DOI: 10.2307/2171852

Cardoni, H. (2020), "Contribution à la connaissance de l'impact de l'actionnariat salarié sur la gouvernance des entreprises", *Entreprise & société*, no. 5, pp. 147-176.

Cardoni, H. (2021), "Le rôle de l'administrateur actionnaire salarié dans la gouvernance de l'entreprise: entre dualité et légitimité", *Finance Contrôle Stratégie*, ns° 24-4.

Cardoni, H., & Poulain-Rehm, T. (2023). The impact of employee shareholding on corporate governance: The employee shareholder director in France. *The Journal of Management and Governance*, 27(4), 1073–1114. DOI: 10.1007/s10997-022-09634-9

Carnes, N., & Hansen, E. (2016). Does paying politicians more promote economic diversity in legislatures? *The American Political Science Review*, 110(4), 699–716. DOI: 10.1017/S000305541600054X

Carter, N. (2006). Political participation and the workplace: The spillover thesis revisited. *The British Journal of Politics and International Relations, 8*(3), 410-426.

CDIF capital, (2024). Employee saving: Retain your employees & build up common capital while reducing taxes! *CDIF capital website*. https://www.cidif-capital.fr/en/plan-%C3%A9pargne-entreprise-pee

CEPAL. (2002). *El proceso de privatizaciones en el Perú durante el período 1991-2002*. Series Gestión Pública.

Cézanne, C., & Hollandts, X. (2022). Employee Participation in Corporate Governance: What Impact Does It Have on Performance and Cash Distribution Policy in the SBF 120 (2000-2014)?[La participation des salariés à la gouvernance d'entreprise: quel impact sur la performance et la politique de distribution des liquidités dans le SBF120 (2000-2014)?] (No. hal-04135429).

Chan, K. W., & Lam, W. (2011). The trade-off of servicing empowerment on employees' service performance: Examining the underlying motivation and workload mechanisms. *Journal of the Academy of Marketing Science*, 39(4), 609–628. DOI: 10.1007/s11747-011-0250-9

Chaplinsky, S., & Niehaus, G. (1994). The Role of ESOPs in Takeover Contests. *The Journal of Finance*, 49(4), 1451–1470. DOI: 10.1111/j.1540-6261.1994.tb02461.x

Charreaux, G. (2002). "L'actionnaire comme apporteur de ressources cognitives". *Revue française de gestion*, n° 5, p. 77-107.

Charreaux, G. (2005). "Pour une gouvernance d'entreprise "comportementale" Une réflexion exploratoire..." *Revue française de gestion*, vol. 157, n°4, pp. 215-238.

Charreaux, G. (2011), "Quelle théorie pour la gouvernance? De la gouvernance actionnariale à la gouvernance cognitive et comportementale", Working Paper FARGO n° 1110402.

Charreaux, G. (1997). *Le Gouvernement Des Entreprises – Corporate Governance: Theories Et faits*. Economica.

Chartered Management Institute. The MoralDNA of Employee-Owned Companies. (2019). https://moraldna.org/wp-content/uploads/2019/06/CMI-Managers-and-Their-MoralDNA.pdf

Cha, T. (2014). *Two Essays on Corporate Policy and Corporate Governance*. The George Washington University.

Chen, J., King, T.-H. D., & Wen, M.-M. (2020). Non-executive ownership and private loan pricing. *Journal of Corporate Finance*, 64, 101638. DOI: 10.1016/j.jcorpfin.2020.101638

Chen, Y. J., Hong, L. H., & Chen, Y. C. (2024a). Social Media Analytic-Based Corporate Credit Rating Forecasting. *6th International Conference on Artificial Intelligence in Information and Communication, ICAIIC 2024*, 1–6. DOI: 10.1109/ICAIIC60209.2024.10463454

Cingano, F. (2014), "Trends in Income Inequality and Its Impact on Economic Growth", OECD SEM Working Paper No. 163, www.oecd.org/els/workingpapers

Cooperative Development Foundation. (2020). The Power of Employee Ownership: A Guide to Cooperative Business Models. Cooperative Development Foundation. Retrieved from https://www.cdf.coop/3. Comparative Analysis of Different Employee Ownership Models

Cooper, D., & Bidelman, P. (2014). *The Mondragon experience: Lessons from a cooperative enterprise*. Routledge.

Cordova, M., Huamán, F., Liñan, T., & Powosino, R. (2022). Regenerative Futures for Peru. In Gonzalez-Perez, M. A. (Ed.), *Regenerative and Sustainable Futures for Latin America and the Caribbean* (pp. 235–254). Emerald Publishing Limited., DOI: 10.1108/978-1-80117-864-820221011

Corfe, S. (2021). A stake in success: Employee share ownership and the post-COVID economy. Kindly supported by https://www.smf.co.uk/wp-content/uploads/2021/05/A-stake-in-success-May-21.pdf

Corfe, S., & Kirkup, J. (2020). *Strengthening employee share ownership in the UK*. Social Market Foundation.

Crane, A., Matten, D., Glozer, S., & Spence, L. J. (2019). *Business ethics: Managing corporate citizenship and sustainability in the age of globalization*. Oxford University Press. DOI: 10.1093/hebz/9780198810070.001.0001

Crifo, P., & Rebérioux, A. (2019). *La participation des salariés. Du partage d'information à la codétermination*. Presses de Sciences Po.

Culpepper, P. D. (2021). Quiet politics in tumultuous times: Business power, populism, and democracy. *Politics & Society*, 49(1), 133–143. DOI: 10.1177/0032329220985725

D'Arcimolès, C., & Trébucq, S. (2003). Employee ownership and performance: Evidence from French firms. *International Journal of Human Resource Management*, 14(2), 284–300.

Dadush, U., Dervis, K., Milsom, S. P., & Stancil, B. 2012. Inequality in America: Facts, Trends, Democracy at Work Institute. (2022). *2021 State of the Sector: Worker Cooperatives in the U.S.*https://institute.coop/resources/2021-worker-cooperative-state-sector-report

Dahl, R. (1985). *A preface to economic democracy*. Polity. DOI: 10.1525/9780520341166

Darko, A.. (2016). The impact of audit committee characteristics on firm performance: Evidence from Ghana. *International Journal of Accounting and Financial Reporting*, 6(1), 1–20.

Dasilas, A. (2024). The nonlinear relationship between employee stock ownership plans and firm performance: Evidence from China. *Journal of Business Research*, 173, 114470. DOI: 10.1016/j.jbusres.2023.114470

Dávila, C. (2013). The current state of business history in Latin America. *Australian Economic History Review*, 53(2), 109–120. DOI: 10.1111/aehr.12006

Davis, J. H., Schoorman, F. D., & Donaldson, L. (1997). Toward a stewardship theory of management. *Academy of Management Review*, 22(1), 20–47. DOI: 10.2307/259223

De Angelis, M. (2021). *The Commons: Social Sharing for a Sustainable Future*. Zed Books Ltd.

De Soto, H. (2006). *Realizing property rights*. Ruffer & Rub Sachbuchverlag.

Degbey, W. K., Karam, C., & Mazzola, J. (2020). Employee Ownership and Retention: The Role of Psychological Ownership in Mergers and Acquisitions. *Journal of Business Research*, 112, 230–241.

Degbey, W. Y., Rodgers, P., Kromah, M. D., & Weber, Y. (2021). The impact of psychological ownership on employee retention in mergers and acquisitions. *Human Resource Management Review*, 31(3), 100745. DOI: 10.1016/j.hrmr.2020.100745

Desbrières, P. (1997a). Le rôle de l'actionnariat des salariés non-dirigeants dans le système de gouvernement de l'entreprise. In *Le GE*. Economica.

Desbrières, P. (2002). Les actionnaires salariés. *Revue Française de Gestion*, (5), 255–281.

Detthamrong, A.. (2017). The impact of audit committee characteristics on financial performance: Evidence from Thailand. *International Journal of Business and Management*, 12(3), 1–12.

DiMaggio, P. J., & Powell, W. W. (1983). The iron cage revisited: Institutional isomorphism and collective rationality in organizational fields. *American Sociological Review*, 48(2), 147–160. DOI: 10.2307/2095101

Domadenik, P., Prašnikar, J., & Svejnar, J. (2008). Restructuring of firms in transition: Ownership, institutions and openness to trade. *Journal of International Business Studies*, 39(4), 725–746. DOI: 10.1057/palgrave.jibs.8400379

Donaldson, L., & Davis, J. H. (1991). Stewardship theory or agency theory: CEO governance and shareholder returns. *Australian Journal of Management*, 16(1), 49–64. DOI: 10.1177/031289629101600103

Dondi, J. (1992), Contribution to the knowledge of employee ownership: theoretical and empirical approach, PhD Thesis, University of Bordeaux IV.

Dondi, J. (1992). *Contribution à la connaissance de l'actionnariat des salariés dans les entreprises françaises*. Diss.

Dow, G. K. (2003). *Governing the firm: workers' control in theory and practice.* Cambridge University Press. DOI: 10.1017/CBO9780511615849

Dudley, T., & Rouen, E. (2021, July 12). The big benefits of employee ownership. *Harvard Business Review.*

Durand, F. (2017). *Los doce apóstoles de la economía peruana: Una mirada social a los grupos de poder limeños y provincianos.* Fondo Editorial PUCP.

Durrieu, F., & Roussel, P. (2002). *« L'implication organisationnelle dans les réseaux de franchise: un concept pertinent pour les entreprises en réseau », Revue de Gestion des Ressources Humaines, N°44, 2ème trimestre.* Avril – Mai-Juin.

Dutton, J. E., Dukerich, J. M., & Harquail, C. V. (1994). Organizational images and member identification. *Administrative Science Quarterly*, 39(2), 239–263. DOI: 10.2307/2393235

Ebrashi, R. E., & Darrag, M. (2017). Social entrepreneurs' strategies for addressing institutional voids in developing markets. *European Journal of International Management*, 11(3), 325–346. DOI: 10.1504/EJIM.2017.083876

Eccles, R. G., Ioannou, I., & Serafeim, G. (2014). The impact of corporate sustainability on organizational processes and performance. *Management Science*, 60(11), 2835–2857. DOI: 10.1287/mnsc.2014.1984

Economia Desde Casa. (2020). Sociedad Laboral | Business Economics 23#. You Tube. https://www.youtube.com/watch?app=desktop&v=ylpPnJ6Yd7o

Edinger, J., Edinger-Schons, L. M., Schäfer, D., Stelmaszczyk, A., & Becker, C. (2019). Of money and morals—The contingent effect of monetary incentives in peer-to-peer volunteer computing. *Proceedings of the 52nd Hawaii International Conference on System Sciences.* DOI: 10.24251/HICSS.2019.115

Edmans, A. (2020). *Grow the Pie: How Great Companies Deliver Both Purpose and Profit.* Cambridge University Press. DOI: 10.1017/9781108860093

Elage, A., & Dardour, A. (2021). *Rémunérations incitatives des dirigeants et gestion réelle des résultats: quel impact de la structure de l'actionnariat? Le cas des sociétés cotées au SBF 120.* Finance Contrôle Stratégie.

Elden, J. M. (1981). Political efficacy at work: The connection between more autonomous forms of workplace organization and a more participatory politics. *The American Political Science Review*, 75(1), 43–58. DOI: 10.2307/1962158

Elkington, J. (1997). *Cannibals with forks: The triple bottom line of 21st century business.* Capstone.

Elkjær, M. A., & Klitgaard, M. B. (2021). Economic inequality and political responsiveness: A systematic review. *Perspectives on Politics*, •••, 1–20.

Ellerman, D. (1992). *Property and Contract in Economics: The Case for Economic Democracy*. Basil Blackwell.

Ellerman, D., Gonza, T., & Berkopec, G. (2022). European Employee Stock Ownership Plan (ESOP): The main structural features and pilot implementation in Slovenia. *SN Business & Economics*, 2(186), 186. DOI: 10.1007/s43546-022-00363-7

Elouadi, S. (2015). Les effets attitudinaux de l'actionnariat salarié: une étude empirique dans le contexte des entreprises françaises du SBF 250. Question (s) de management, (3), 11-24.

Elouadi, S. (2020). L'influence des variables incitatives sur la satisfaction des actionnaires salariés: une modélisation par équations structurelles. Question (s) de management, (2), 35-49.

Elouadi, S., & El Kerbani, M. (2022). Exploratory Study of the Attitudinal Effects of Employee Shareholding in Morocco. In Employee Share Ownership and Impacts on Organizational Value and Behavior (pp. 123-145). IGI Global. DOI: 10.4018/978-1-7998-8557-3.ch007

Elouadi, S., & Errommani, H. E. (2021). Analyse des effets de l'actionnariat salarié sur la création de valeur financière des entreprises marocaines cotées en bourse. Revue du contrôle, de la comptabilité et de l'audit, 5(1).

Elouadi, S., & Noamene, T. B. (2017). Does Employee Ownership Reduce the Intention to Leave? In Handbook of Research on Human Resources Strategies for the New Millennial Workforce (pp. 111-127). IGI Global.

Employee Ownership Foundation. (2020). COVID-19 and employee-owned companies: Research findings. Employee Ownership Foundation, https://assets-eof.s3.us-east-2.amazonaws.com/assets/public/2020-10/EOF_CovidResearch_Oct23b.pdf

EOA. (2022). John Lewis partnership. https://employeeownership.co.uk/case-studies/john-lewis-partnership

Ernest & Young (2019). ¿Cuál es el impacto de las familias empresarias? Resultados de la 1era Encuesta de Familias empresarias en Perú. Asociación de empresas familiares del Perú.

Errommani, H., & Elbouanani, H. (2022). Analysis of the Effects of Employee Share Ownership on the Creation of Financial Value of Moroccan Companies Listed on the Stock Exchange. In *Employee Share Ownership and Impacts on Organizational Value and Behavior* (pp. 103–122). IGI Global. DOI: 10.4018/978-1-7998-8557-3.ch006

ESAN. (2020). *Rotación laboral en el Perú: ¿qué hacer para disminuirla?* Conexiones ESAN.

Faleye, O., Mehrotra, V., & Morck, R. (2006). When labor has a voice in corporate governance. *Journal of Financial and Quantitative Analysis*, 41(3), 489–510. DOI: 10.1017/S0022109000002519

Fama, E. F. (1980). Agency problems and the theory of the firm. *Journal of Political Economy*, 88(2), 288–307. DOI: 10.1086/260866

Fandos, N. (2021, March 10). House passes labor rights expansion, but Senate chances are slim. *The New York Times*. https://www.nytimes.com/2021/03/09/us/politics/house-labor-rights-bill.html

Fang, H., Nofsinger, J. R., & Quan, J. (2015). The effects of employee stock option plans on operating performance in Chinese firms. *Journal of Banking & Finance*, 54, 141–159. DOI: 10.1016/j.jbankfin.2015.01.010

Farber, H. S., Herbst, D., Kuziemko, I., & Naidu, S. (2021). Unions and inequality over the twentieth century: New evidence from survey data. *The Quarterly Journal of Economics*, 136(3), 1325–1385. DOI: 10.1093/qje/qjab012

Farooq, O., Farooq, M., & Reynaud, E. (2019). Does employees' participation in decision making increase the level of corporate social and environmental sustainability? An investigation in South Asia. *Sustainability (Basel)*, 11(2), 511. DOI: 10.3390/su11020511

FasterCapital (N.D). Choosing the Right ESOP Structure for Your Business. https://fastercapital.com/keyword/esop-structure.html

Fatemi, A., Glaum, M., & Kaiser, S. (2018). ESG performance and firm value: The moderating role of disclosure. *Global Finance Journal*, 38, 45–64. DOI: 10.1016/j.gfj.2017.03.001

FCLTGlobal. (2023). The Long-term Payoff of Employee Ownership. FCLTGlobal. Retrieved from https://hbr.org/2021/05/the-big-benefits-of-employee-ownership

Feigenbaum, J., Hertel-Fernandez, A., & Williamson, V. (2018). *From the bargaining table to the ballot box: Political effects of right to work laws* (No. w24259). National Bureau of Economic Research.

Feng, Y., Yu, Q., Nan, X., & Cai, Y. (2022). Can employee stock ownership plans reduce corporate financialization? Evidence from China. *Economic Analysis and Policy*, 73, 140–151. DOI: 10.1016/j.eap.2021.11.002

Fernández-Guadaño, J., & López-Millán, M. (2019). Assessing employee-owned firms: An examination of the Spanish economic model. *Ekonomska Istrazivanja*, 32(1), 1994–2008. DOI: 10.1080/1331677X.2019.1642781

Ferreras, I. (2017). *Firms as Political Entities: Saving Democracy through Economic Bicameralism*. Cambridge University Press. DOI: 10.1017/9781108235495

Ferreras, I. (2021). *Democratizing Firms: A Cornerstone of Shared and Sustainable Prosperity*. University of Chicago Press Economics Books.

Ferreras, I. (2022). From the Politically Impossible to the Politically Inevitable: Taking Action. In *Democratize Work: The Case for Reorganizing the Economy*. University of Chicago Press. DOI: 10.7208/chicago/9780226819631.001.0001

Fieldfisher: Ethics matters more to managers in employee-owned companies, new research reveals. (n.d.). https://www.fieldfisher.com/en/services/employee-ownership-solutions

Fieveson, L. (2023) August 28. Labor Unions and the US Economy. US Department of the Treasury. Featrued Stories. https://home.treasury.gov/news/featured-stories/labor-unions-and-the-us-economy#ftn6

Flanders, A., Pomeranz, R., & Woodward, J. (1968). *Experiment in Industrial Democracy: A Study of the John Lewis Partnership*. Faber and Faber.

Fortin, N. M., Lemieux, T., & Lloyd, N. (2021). Labor market institutions and the distribution of wages: The role of spillover effects. *Journal of Labor Economics*, 39(S2), S369–S412. DOI: 10.1086/712923

Freedman, R. B., & Medoff, J. (1984). *What do unions do?* Basic Books.

Freeman, R. B. (2003) What do unions do… to voting? National Bureau of Economic Research. Working paper no. 9992.

Freeman, R. B., Blasi, J. R., & Kruse, D. L. (2010). Introduction to" Shared Capitalism at Work: Employee Ownership, Profit and Gain Sharing, and Broad-based Stock Options". In *Shared capitalism at work: Employee ownership, profit and gain sharing, and broad-based stock options* (pp. 1-37). University of Chicago Press.

Freeman, R. E. (1984, 2010), *Strategic management: A stakeholder approach*, Cambridge University Press.

Freeman, R. E. (1984). *Stakeholder management: a strategic approach*. Pitman.

Freeman, R. E. (1984). *Strategic management: A stakeholder approach*. Pitman.

Freeman, R., Blasi, J. R., & Kruse, D. (2010). Introduction to "Shared Capitalism at Work: Employee Ownership, Profit and Gain Sharing, and Broad-based Stock Options". In Kruse, D., Freeman, R., & Blasi, J. R. (Eds.), *Shared Capitalism at Work: Employee Ownership, Profit and Gain Sharing, and Broad-based Stock Options, 2010* (pp. 1–37). DOI: 10.7208/chicago/9780226056968.003.0001

Freudenreich, B., Lüdeke-Freund, F., & Schaltegger, S. (2020). A stakeholder theory perspective on business models: Value creation for sustainability. *Journal of Business Ethics*, 166(1), 3–18. DOI: 10.1007/s10551-019-04112-z

Friant, M. C., Vermeulen, W. J. V., & Salomone, R. (2020). A typology of circular economy discourses: Navigating the diverse visions of a contested paradigm. *Resources, Conservation and Recycling*, 161, 104917. DOI: 10.1016/j.resconrec.2020.104917

Friant, M. C., Vermeulen, W. J. V., & Salomone, R. (2024). Transition to a sustainable circular society: More than just resource efficiency. *Circular Economy and Sustainability*, 4(1), 23–42. DOI: 10.1007/s43615-023-00272-3

Frohlich, N., Godard, J., Oppenheimer, J. A., & Starke, F. A. (1998). Employee versus conventionally-owned and controlled firms: An experimental analysis. *MDE. Managerial and Decision Economics*, 19(4-5), 311–326. DOI: 10.1002/(SICI)1099-1468(199806/08)19:4/5<311::AID-MDE893>3.0.CO;2-I

Gallego, A. (2016). Inequality and the erosion of trust among the Poor: Experimental evidence. *Socio-economic Review*, 14(3), 443–460. DOI: 10.1093/ser/mww010

Ganoza, C., & Stiglich, A. (2015). *El Perú está calato. El falso milagro de la economía peruana y las trampas que amenazan nuestro progreso* (1st ed.). Editorial Planeta.

Gao, C., Zuzul, T., Jones, G., & Khanna, T. (2017). Overcoming Institutional Voids: A Reputation-Based View of Long-Run Survival. *Strategic Management Journal*, 38(11), 2147–2167. DOI: 10.1002/smj.2649

Garfatta, R. (2010). Actionnariat salarié et création de valeur dans le cadre d'une gouvernance actionnariale et partenariale: application au contexte français (Doctoral dissertation, Université de Bourgogne).

Garfatta, R. (2023). Employee stock ownership and earnings management: Evidence from France. *International Journal of Management Practice*, 16(2), 249–265. DOI: 10.1504/IJMP.2023.129210

Garfatta, R., & Zorgati, I. (2021). Employee stock ownership and value creation: Evidence from system GMM estimates. *Managerial Finance*, 47(9), 1270–1285. DOI: 10.1108/MF-10-2020-0517

Gartenberg, C., Prat, A., & Serafeim, G. (2019). Corporate purpose and financial performance. *Organization Science*, 30(1), 1–18. DOI: 10.1287/orsc.2018.1230

Gatti, L., Seele, P., & Rademacher, L. (2019). Grey zone in – greenwash out. A review of greenwashing research and implications for the voluntary-mandatory transition of CSR. *International Journal of Corporate Social Responsibility*, 4(1), 1–15. DOI: 10.1186/s40991-019-0044-9

Geurkink, B., Akkerman, A., & Sluiter, R. (2022). Political participation and workplace voice: The spillover of suppression by supervisors. *Political Studies*, 70(2), 327–347. DOI: 10.1177/0032321720960969

Gharbi, H., & Lepers, X. (2008). Actionnariat salarié et enracinement des dirigeants: Un essai de compréhension. *Innovations (Paris)*, (1), 121–146. DOI: 10.3917/inno.027.0121

Ghoshal, S. (2005). Bad management theories are destroying good management practices. *Academy of Management Learning & Education*, 4(1), 75–91. DOI: 10.5465/amle.2005.16132558

Gilens, M. (2005). Inequality and Democratic Responsiveness. *Public Opinion Quarterly*, 69(5), 778–796. DOI: 10.1093/poq/nfi058

Gilens, M. (2012). *Affluence and Influence: Economic Inequality and Political Power in America*. Russell Sage Foundation.

Gilens, M., & Page, B. I. (2014). Testing Theories of American Politics: Elites, Interest Groups, and Average Citizens. *Perspectives on Politics*, 12(3), 564–581. DOI: 10.1017/S1537592714001595

Gillet-Monjarret, C., & Martinez, I. (2012). La vérification sociétale des entreprises du SBF 120: L'impact de la structure de propriété et du conseil d'administration. *Comptabilité Contrôle Audit*, 18(3), 43–66. DOI: 10.3917/cca.183.0043

Ginglinger, E., Megginson, W., & Waxin, T. (2011). Employee ownership, board representation, and corporate financial policies. *Journal of Corporate Finance*, 17(4), 868–887. DOI: 10.1016/j.jcorpfin.2011.03.005

Gittleman, M., & Kleiner, M. M. (2016). Wage effects of unionization and occupational licensing coverage in the United States. *Industrial & Labor Relations Review*, 69(1), 142–172. DOI: 10.1177/0019793915601632

Glass, A., Weller, C. E., & Madland, D. (2023, May 3). Unions build wealth for the American working class. *Center for American Progress*. https://www.americanprogress.org/article/unions-build-wealth-for-the-american-working-class/

Glavin, P., Bierman, A., & Schieman, S. (2021). Über-Alienated: Powerless and alone in the gig economy. *Work and Occupations*, 48(4), 399–431. DOI: 10.1177/07308884211024711

Global Reporting Initiative. (2021). GRI Standards. https://www.globalreporting.org/standards/

Gomez-Mejia, L. R. (2018). The Role of Employee Ownership in Corporate Governance. *The Academy of Management Perspectives*, 32(2), 145–158.

Gonza, T. (2024). *Comparative Analysis of Organizational Structures of Employee Centred Enterprises*. PhD thesis, University of Ljubljana.

Gostu, H., Parmar, M., Naik, T., & Jagtap, N. (2024). Risk Navigation in Finance: A Deep Dive into Silicon Valley Bank and Credit Suisse Strategies. *2024 3rd International Conference for Innovation in Technology, INOCON 2024*. DOI: 10.1109/INOCON60754.2024.10511378

Government Accountability Office. Contingent workforce: Size, characteristics, earnings, and benefits. GAO-15-168R. Retrieved from: https://www.gao.gov/products/GAO-15-168R

Gramlich, J. (2021) September 3. Majorities of Americans say unions have a positive effect on U.S. and that decline in union membership is bad. Pew Research Center. https://www.pewresearch.org/short-reads/2021/09/03/majorities-of-americans-say-unions-have-a-positive-effect-on-u-s-and-that-decline-in-union-membership-is-bad/

Greenberg, E. S. (2008). Spillovers from cooperative and democratic workplaces: Have the benefits been oversold. *Cooperation: The political psychology of effective human interaction*, 219-239. Edited by Snyder, M., Sullivan, B., & Sullivan, J - Mark Snyder, Brandon Sullivan, and John Sullivan

Greenberg, E. S., Snyder, M., Sullivan, B., & Sullivan, J. (2008). Spillovers from cooperative and democratic workplaces: Have the benefits been oversold. *Cooperation: The political psychology of effective human interaction*, 219-239

Greenberg, E. S. (1981). Industrial democracy and the democratic citizen. *The Journal of Politics*, 43(4), 964–981. DOI: 10.2307/2130183

Greenberg, E. S. (1986). *Workplace democracy: The political effects of participation*. Cornell University Press.

Greenberg, E. S., Grunberg, L., & Daniel, K. (1996). Industrial Work and Political Participation: Beyond "Simple Spillover". *Political Research Quarterly*, 49(2), 305–330. DOI: 10.1177/106591299604900204

Gregorič, A., & Poulsen, T. (2020). The power of non-controlling stakes: Minority ownership and board representation. *Journal of Corporate Finance*, 64, 101660.

Grigoli, F. (2017). *A New Twist in the Link Between Inequality and Economic Development. May 11th 2017*. IMF Blog.

Grompone, R., & Tanaka, M. (2009). Entre el crecimiento económico y la insatisfacción social. Las protestas sociales en el Perú actual. 1st ed. Lima: Instituto de Estudios Peruanos (IEP).

Guedri, Z., & Hollandts, X. (2008). Beyond dichotomy: The curvilinear impact of employee ownership on firm performance. *Corporate Governance*, 16(5), 460–474. DOI: 10.1111/j.1467-8683.2008.00703.x

Guery, L. (2015, July). L'actionnariat salarié en période de crise: performance économique, performance sociale, et questions de gouvernance. In Preuves empiriques françaises et éclairage britannique, Convention de recherche avec l'IRES pour le compte de la CFECGC.

Guery, L., and Stévenot, A. (2017), "Does employee share ownership promote the dissemination of information to employees and their participation in strategic decisions? Une question de gouvernance d'entreprise", *Management international*, vol. 21, No. 4, pp. 61-75.

Guney, Y., Hernandez-Perdomo, E., & Rocco, C. M. (2020). Does relative strength in corporate governance improve corporate performance? Empirical evidence using MCDA approach. *The Journal of the Operational Research Society*, 71(10), 1593–1618. DOI: 10.1080/01605682.2019.1621216

Hacker, J. (2006). *The Great Risk Shift: The Assault on American Jobs, Families, Health Care and Retirement and How You Can Fight Back*. Oxford University Press.

Hacker, J., & Pierson, P. (2010). Winner-Take-All Politics: Public Policy, Political Organization, and the Precipitous Rise of Top Incomes in the United States. *Politics & Society*, 38(2), 152–204. DOI: 10.1177/0032329210365042

Hamdani, A. M., & Gumanti, T. A. (2019, October). Company Profitability Before and After Employee Stock Ownership Program in 2011-2014. In *2019 International Conference on Organizational Innovation (ICOI 2019)* (pp. 553-556). Atlantis Press.

Hamed, Z. (2022). Sample contract for awarding incentive shares and legal challenges of assigning shares to employees. Lawmingo website. https://lawmingo.com/mag/sample-contract-for-awarding-incentive-shares-and-legal-challenges-of-assigning-shares-to-employees/

Handayani, F., & Yurniwati, Y. (2020). Analysis of the influence of employee stock ownership program (ESOP) application of company financial performance. *Jurnal Ilmiah Universitas Batanghari Jambi*, 20(2), 616–625. DOI: 10.33087/jiubj.v20i2.978

Hansmann, H. (2000). *The ownership of enterprise*. Harvard University Press.

Harjoto, M., Laksmana, I., & Lee, R. (2021). Employee ownership and corporate social responsibility. *Business Ethics (Oxford, England)*, 30(3), 383–397.

Harknett, K., Schneider, D., & Luhr, S. (2022). Who cares if parents have unpredictable work schedules?: Just-in-time work schedules and child care arrangements. *Social Problems*, 69(1), 164–183. DOI: 10.1093/socpro/spaa020 PMID: 37946720

Henn, R., Terzidis, O., Kuschel, K., Leiva, J. C., & Alsua, C. (2022). One step back, two steps forward: Internationalization strategies and the resilient growth of entrepreneurial ecosystems. *Small Enterprise Research*, 29(3), 273–307. DOI: 10.1080/13215906.2022.2134191

Henseler, J., Ringle, C. M., & Sarstedt, M. (2015). A new criterion for assessing discriminant validity in variance-based structural equation modeling. *Journal of the Academy of Marketing Science*, 43(1), 115–135. DOI: 10.1007/s11747-014-0403-8

Herath, S. K., & Herath, L. M. (2024). Accounting for Sustainability: The Measurements and Financial Reporting Disclosure. In Sun, L. (Ed.), *Contemporary Research and Practices for Promoting Financial Literacy and Sustainability* (pp. 50–91). IGI Global., DOI: 10.4018/979-8-3693-0863-9.ch003

Herath, S. K., & Kulathunga, H. G. E. R. (2024). Integrating ESG Metrics With Ecosystem Services Valuation: A Pathway to Sustainable Development. In Castanho, R. (Ed.), *ESG and Ecosystem Services for Sustainability* (pp. 143–170). IGI Global., DOI: 10.4018/979-8-3693-3771-4.ch006

Hertel-Fernandez, A. (2020) February 18. Aligning U.S. labor law with worker preferences for labor representation. Washington Center for Equitable Growth. https://equitablegrowth.org/aligning-u-s-labor-law-with-worker-preferences-for-labor-representation/

Hertel-Fernandez, A., & Gould-Werth, A. (2020). *Labor Organizations and Unemployment Insurance: A Virtuous Circle Supporting U.S. Workers' Voices and Reducing Disparities in Benefits*. Washington Center for Equitable Growth, October 2020.

Hill, C. W. L., & Jones, T. M. (1992). STAKEHOLDER-AGENCY THEORY. *Journal of Management Studies*, 29(2), 131–154. Advance online publication. DOI: 10.1111/j.1467-6486.1992.tb00657.x

Hirsch, B., Macpherson, D., Even, W. (2023). "Union Membership, Coverage, and Earnings from the CPS". Unionstats.com.

Hollandts, X., & Aubert, N. (2011). La représentation obligatoire des actionnaires salariés au conseil d'administration: un état des lieux. *Gestion 2000, 28*(6), 15-26.

Hollandts, X., and Guedri, Z. (2008), "Les salariés capitalistes et la performance de l'entreprise", *Revue française de gestion*, n° 3, p. 35-50.

Hollandts, X., Guedri, Z., and Aubert, N. (2011), "Les déterminants de la représentation des actionnaires salariés au conseil d'administration ou de surveillance", *Management international*, vol. 15, No. 4, pp. 69-82.

Hollandts, X. (2018). Friend or foe? Employee ownership and CEO dismissal. *MDE. Managerial and Decision Economics*, 39(4), 377–388. DOI: 10.1002/mde.2911

Hörisch, J., Freeman, E., & Schaltegger, S. (2014). Applying stakeholder theory in sustainability management: Links, similarities, and a conceptual framework. *Organization & Environment*, 27(4), 1–19. DOI: 10.1177/1086026614535786

Howell, D. R., & Kalleberg, A. L. (2019). Declining job quality in the United States: Explanations and evidence. *The Russell Sage Foundation Journal of the Social Sciences : RSF*, 5(4), 1–53. DOI: 10.7758/rsf.2019.5.4.01

https://cleartax.in/s/esop (Accessed in October 2024)

https://cleartax.in/s/long-term-capital-gains-on-shares (Accessed in October 2024)

https://cleartax.in/s/taxation-on-esop-rsu-stock-options (Accessed in October 2024)

https://cleartax.in/s/tax-deductibility-esop-expenses (Accessed in October 2024)

https://cleo.rutgers.edu/articles/largest-study-yet-shows-esops-improve-performance-and-employee-benefits/

https://economictimes.indiatimes.com/news/company/corporate-trends/esop-culture-making-india-inc-top-execs-richer/articleshow/113104554.cms?from=mdr (Accessed in October 2024)

https://eqvista.com/esop/employee-stock-ownership-plan-india/ (Accessed in October 2024) https://inc42.com/features/indian-startup-employees-made-at-least-inr-1250-cr-via-esop-buybacks-in-2024/# (Accessed in October 2024)

https://www.cnbctv18.com/business/esop-full-form-employee-stock-option-big-shareholders-dissent-17115661.htm (Accessed in October 2024)

Hu, C., Hu, Y., & Seo, S. (2019). A deep structural model for analyzing correlated multivariate time series. *Proceedings - 18th IEEE International Conference on Machine Learning and Applications, ICMLA 2019*, 69–74. DOI: 10.1109/ICMLA.2019.00020

Huang, R. (2019). Value investment in the semiconductor industry: A case study of three corporations. *Proceedings - 2019 International Conference on Economic Management and Model Engineering, ICEMME 2019*, 539–542. DOI: 10.1109/ICEMME49371.2019.00113

Huse, M. (2003). Renewing management and governance: New paradigms of governance? *The Journal of Management and Governance*, 7(3), 211–221. DOI: 10.1023/A:1025004111314

Hyman, J. (2021). *Employee Voice and Participation: Contested Past, Troubled Present, Uncertain Future*. Routledge.

Índice Global de Competitividad Corporativa. (2023). *Niveles de complejidad: los desafíos del cumplimiento corporativo internacional*. TMF Group.

Islam, G., & Greenwood, M. (2021). Reconnecting to the social in business ethics. *Journal of Business Ethics*, 170(1), 1–4. DOI: 10.1007/s10551-021-04775-7

Ismiyanti, F., & Mahadwartha, P. A. (2017). Does employee stock ownership plan matter? An empirical note. Investment management and financial innovations, (14,N° 3 (contin. 2)), 381-388.

Jahmane, A., Hofaidhllaoui, M., & Ali, A. B. (2021), "La gouvernance responsable, moyen d'assurer une performance financière en période de crises et post-crise?", *Management & Sciences Sociales*, vol. 31, n° 4-21.

Jensen, M. C., & Meckling, W. H. (1979). Rights and production functions: An application to labor-managed firms and codetermination. *The Journal of Business*, 52(4), 469–506. DOI: 10.1086/296060

Jensen, M. C., & Meckling, W. H. (2019). Theory of the firm: Managerial behavior, agency costs and ownership structure. In *Corporate governance* (pp. 77–132). Gower.

Jensen, M., & Meckling, W. (1976). The Theory of Firm: Managerial Behavior, Agency Costs and Ownership Structure. *Journal of Financial Economics*, 3(4), 305–360. DOI: 10.1016/0304-405X(76)90026-X

Jian, G., & Jeffres, L. (2008). Spanning the boundaries of work: Workplace participation, political efficacy, and political involvement. *Communication Studies*, 59(1), 35–50. DOI: 10.1080/10510970701849370

John Lewis Partnership. (2019). John Lewis Partnership Ethics & Sustainability Report 2019. John Lewis Partnership. Retrieved from https://www.johnlewispartnership.co.uk/content/dam/cws/pdfs/Juniper/ethics-and-sustainability/progress-report-2019-20.pdf

John Lewis Partnership. (2023).. . *Sustainability Report*, 2023, •••. https://www.johnlewispartnership.co.uk

Jordan, A. (2022, December 8). Pros and cons of employee ownership trusts (EOTs), *Small Business website*. https://smallbusiness.co.uk/pros-and-cons-of-employee-ownership-trusts-eots-2552031/

Julià, M., Vanroelen, C., Bosmans, K., Van Aerden, K., & Benach, J. (2017). Precarious Employment and Quality of Employment in Relation to Health and Well-being in Europe. [PubMed] [Google Scholar]. *International Journal of Health Services*, 47(3), 389–409. DOI: 10.1177/0020731417707491 PMID: 28449605

Kahn, W. A. (1990). Psychological Conditions of Personal Engagement and Disengagement at Work. *Academy of Management Journal*, 33(4), 692–724. DOI: 10.2307/256287

Kallas, J., Ritchie, K., & Friedman, E. (2022). Cornell-ILR Labor action tracker annual report. Accessed September 26 2023. https://www.ilr.cornell.edu/faculty-and-research/labor-action-tracker-2022?utm_source=npr_newsletter&utm_medium=email&utm_content=20230227&utm_term=8035455&utm_campaign=money&utm_id=208962&orgid=92&utm_att1=

Kalleberg, A. (2016). *December 21*. Institutions, Precarious Work, and Inequality. Russel Sage Foundation.

Kalleberg, A. L. (2011). *Good jobs, bad jobs: The rise of polarized and precarious employment systems in the United States*. Russell Sage Foundation.

Kalleberg, A. L., & Vallas, S. P. (2018). Probing precarious work: Theory, research, and politics. *Research in the Sociology of Work*, 31, 1–30. DOI: 10.1108/S0277-283320170000031017

Kang, N., & Moon, J. (2012). Institutional complementarity between corporate governance and corporate social responsibility: A comparative institutional analysis of three capitalisms. *Socio-economic Review*, 10(1), 85–108. DOI: 10.1093/ser/mwr025

Kang, S., & Kim, A. (2019). Employee stock ownership and financial performance in European countries: The moderating effects of uncertainty avoidance and social trust. *Human Resource Management*, 58(6), 641–655. DOI: 10.1002/hrm.21942

Kanitsar, G. (2022). The inequality-trust nexus revisited: At what level of aggregation does income inequality matter for social trust? *Social Indicators Research*, 163(1), 171–195. DOI: 10.1007/s11205-022-02894-w

Kaptein, M. (2008). Developing a measure of unethical behavior in the workplace: A stakeholder perspective. *Journal of Management*, 34(5), 978–1008. DOI: 10.1177/0149206308318614

Karasek, R. A.Jr. (1976). *The Impact of the Work Environment on Life Outside the Job. Ph.D. Disseration.* Massachusetts Institute of Technology.

Kardas, P., Scharf, A. L., & Keogh, J. (1998). Wealth and income consequences of ESOPs and employee ownership: a comparative study from Washington State. *Journal of Employee Ownership Law and Finance*,10(4), Keith, M. G., Harms, P. D., & Long, A. C. (2020). Worker health and well-being in the gig economy: A proposed framework and research agenda. In Perrewé, P. L., Harms, P. D., & Chang, C.-H. (Eds.), *Entrepreneurial and small business stressors, experienced stress, and well being* (pp. 1–33). Emerald Publishing., DOI: 10.1108/S1479-355520200000018002

Kasmir, S. (2016). The Mondragon cooperatives and global capitalism: A critical analysis. *New Labor Forum*, 25(1), 52–59. DOI: 10.1177/1095796015620424

Kaswan, M. (2014). *Happiness, Democracy, and the Cooperative Movement: The Radical Utilitarianism of William Thompson*. State University of New York Press.

Kaswan, M. (2022). Property, ownership and employee ownership: Employee control in ESOPs. *Journal of Participation and Employee Ownership*, 5(1), 14–31. DOI: 10.1108/JPEO-11-2020-0028

Kerrissey, J., & Schofer, E. (2013). Union membership and political participation in the United States. *Social Forces*, 91(3), 895–928. DOI: 10.1093/sf/sos187

Ketelaar, E., Beijaard, D., den Brok, P. J., & Boshuizen, H. P. A. (2013). Teachers' implementation of the coaching role: Do teachers' ownership, sensemaking, and agency make a difference? *European Journal of Psychology of Education*, 28(3), 991–1006. DOI: 10.1007/s10212-012-0150-5

Khanna, T. (2018). *Trust: Creating the Foundation for Entrepreneurship in Developing Countries. Harvard Business School.* Berrett-Koehler Publishers.

Khanna, T., & Palepu, K. (2000). The Future of Business Groups in Emerging Markets: Long Run Evidence from Chile. *Academy of Management Journal*, 43(3), 268–285. https://www.hbs.edu/faculty/Pages/item.aspx?num=12431. DOI: 10.2307/1556395

Khanna, T., & Palepu, K. (2010). *Winning in Emerging Markets.* Harvard Business Press.

Khanna, T., & Palepu, K. (2011). *Winning in Emerging Markets: Spotting and Responding to Institutional Voids, World Financial Review.* Harvard Business School.

Khoury, T. A., & Prasad, A. (2016). Entrepreneurship amid concurrent institutional constraints in less developed countries. *Business & Society*, 55(7), 934–969. DOI: 10.1177/0007650314567641

Kim, S. M., Krisher, T., & Megerian, C. (2023) September 26th Biden to show solidarity with striking UAW workers in historic move. Associated Press. https://www.pbs.org/newshour/politics/biden-to-show-solidarity-with-striking-uaw-workers-in-historic-move

Kim, E. H., & Ouimet, P. (2014). Broad-based employee stock ownership: Motives and outcomes. *The Journal of Finance*, 69(3), 1273–1319. DOI: 10.1111/jofi.12150

Kim, K. Y., & Patel, P. C. (2017). Employee ownership and firm performance: A variance decomposition analysis of European firms. *Journal of Business Research*, 70, 248–254. DOI: 10.1016/j.jbusres.2016.08.014

Kim, K. Y., & Patel, P. C. (2021). A multilevel contingency model of employee ownership and firm productivity: The moderating roles of industry growth and instability. *Organization Science*, 32(3), 625–648. DOI: 10.1287/orsc.2020.1404

Kishk, I. (2023). *The impact of Ownership Structure on Firm Performance: A Comparative Multi-Country Analysis*. PhD thesis, University of Essex.

Klein, K. J. (1987). Employee stock ownership and employee attitudes: A test of three models. *The Journal of Applied Psychology*, 72(2), 319–332. DOI: 10.1037/0021-9010.72.2.319 PMID: 3583982

Klein, K. J., & Kauffman, C. (2019). The Effects of Employee Ownership on Organizational Performance: A Meta-Analysis. *Journal of Business Research*, 98, 1–10.

Knepper, M. (2020). From the fringe to the fore: Labor unions and employee compensation. *The Review of Economics and Statistics*, 102(1), 98–112. DOI: 10.1162/rest_a_00803

Kochan, T. A., Yang, D., Kimball, W., & Kelly, E. (2018). Worker Voice in America: Is There a Gap between What Workers Expect and What They Experience? *Industrial & Labor Relations Review*, 72(1), 3–38. DOI: 10.1177/0019793918806250

Kolkowska, N. (2023, January 25). Employee engagement in sustainable business. Sustainable Review. https://sustainablereview.com/employee-engagement-in-sustainable-business/

Kong, D., Liu, J., Wang, Y., & Zhu, L. (2024). Employee stock ownership plans and corporate environmental engagement. *Journal of Business Ethics*, 189(1), 177–199. DOI: 10.1007/s10551-023-05334-y

Kotlar, M., & Milutinovic, V. (2018). Comparing Controlflow and Dataflow for Tensor Calculus: Speed, Power, Complexity, and MTBF. *Lecture Notes in Computer Science (Including Subseries Lecture Notes in Artificial Intelligence and Lecture Notes in Bioinformatics), 11203 LNCS*, 329–346. DOI: 10.1007/978-3-030-02465-9_22

Kramer, M. R. (2020). Coronavirus is putting corporate social responsibility to the test. *Harvard Business Review*, 1–13.

Krause, R., Semadeni, M., & Cannella, A. A.Jr. (2014). CEO duality: A review and research agenda. *Journal of Management*, 40(1), 256–286. DOI: 10.1177/0149206313503013

Krieckhaus, J., Son, B., Bellinger, N. M., & Wells, J. M. (2014). Economic inequality and democratic support. *The Journal of Politics*, 76(1), 139–151. DOI: 10.1017/S0022381613001229

Kruse, D. (2022). Does employee ownership improve performance? *IZA World of Labor: Evidence-Based Policy Making*. Advance online publication. DOI: 10.15185/izawol.311.v2

Kruse, D. L., & Blasi, J. R. (2019). Employee Ownership and Employee Stock Options in the US. In *Sharing in the Company* (pp. 257–292). Oxford University Press.

Kruse, D. L., Blasi, J. R., & Freeman, R. B. (2019). Broad-based employee stock ownership and profit sharing: History, evidence, and policy implications. *Journal of Participation and Employee Ownership*, 2(1), 38–61.

Kryzanowski, L., Li, M., Xu, S., & Zhang, J. (2024). Share pledging and corporate misconduct. *The British Accounting Review*, 101508. Advance online publication. DOI: 10.1016/j.bar.2024.101508

Kundić, M., Smajla, N., & Cibulka, M. (2020). *Employee Stock Ownership and Agency Theory Problem. In 16th Interdisciplinary Management Research* (Vol. 1). IMR.

Kurland, N. (2018). ESOP plus benefit corporation: Ownership culture with benefit accountability. *California Management Review*, 60(4), 51–73. DOI: 10.1177/0008125618778853

Kurtulus, F. A., & Kruse, D. L. (2017). *How Did Employee Ownership Firms Weather the Last Two Recessions?: Employee Ownership, Employment Stability, and Firm Survival: 1999-2011*. W.E. Upjohn Institute.

Kurtulus, F. A., & Kruse, D. L. (2018). An empirical analysis of the relationship between employee ownership and employment stability in the US: 1999–2011. *British Journal of Industrial Relations*, 56(2), 245–291. DOI: 10.1111/bjir.12254

Kurtulus, F., & Kruse, D. (2017). *How Did Employee Ownership Firms Weather the Last Two Recessions?* W.E. Upjohn Institute for Employment Research.

Kuvaas, B. (2003). Employee ownership and affective organizational commitment: Employees' perceptions of fairness and their preference for company shares over cash. *Scandinavian Journal of Management*, 19(2), 193–212. Advance online publication. DOI: 10.1016/S0956-5221(01)00044-6

Lafferty, W. (1985). Decision making involvement and socioeconomic resources in Norway: A normative–empirical analysis. *Scandinavian Political Studies*, 8(4), 1–32. DOI: 10.1111/j.1467-9477.1985.tb00325.x

Lafferty, W. M. (1989). Work as a source of political learning among wage-laborers and lower-level employees. *Political learning in adulthood*, 89-101. In Sigel, R. S. (Ed.), *Political Learning in Adulthood*. University of Chicago Press.

Lampel, J., Bhalla, A., & Jha, P. K. (2020). Reimagining Employee Ownership for the Digital Age. *International Review of Entrepreneurship*, 18(4), 473–490.

Landau, I., Mitchell, R., O'Connell, A., & Ramsay, I. (2020). Employee Share Ownership Schemes in Australia: A Survey of Key Issues and Themes. *Melbourne University Law Review*, 43(3), 1001–1041.

Le, p. L., & Nguyen, h. T. T. (2023). Effects Of Employee Stock Ownership Plans On Firm Performance–Evidence From Listed Commercial Banks Of Vietnam.

Lee, J., & Park, J. (2022). Employee ownership and corporate social responsibility: A meta-analysis. *Journal of Business Ethics*, 110(3), 599–614.

Leighley, J. E., & Nagler, J. (1992). Individual and systemic influences on turnout: Who votes? 1984. *The Journal of Politics*, 54(3), 718–740. DOI: 10.2307/2132308

Leighley, J. E., & Nagler, J. (2007). Unions, voter turnout, and class bias in the US electorate, 1964–2004. *The Journal of Politics*, 69(2), 430–441. DOI: 10.1111/j.1468-2508.2007.00541.x

Leighley, J. E., & Nagler, J. (2013). *Who votes now?: Demographics, issues, inequality, and turnout in the United States*. Princeton University Press. DOI: 10.23943/princeton/9780691159348.001.0001

Lewchuk, W., Clarke, M., & De Wolff, A. (2008). Working without commitments: Precarious employment and health. *Work, Employment and Society*, 22(3), 387–406. DOI: 10.1177/0950017008093477

Liedong, T. A., Peprah, A. A., Amartey, A. O., & Rajwani, T. (2020). Institutional voids and firms' resource commitment in emerging markets: A review and future research agenda. *Journal of International Management*, 26(3), 100–756. DOI: 10.1016/j.intman.2020.100756

Lim, S. (2017). "Bad jobs" for marriage: Precarious work and the transition to first marriage. *Research in the Sociology of Work*, 31, 399–427. DOI: 10.1108/S0277-283320170000031015

Liu, Z., & Huang, Q. (2019). Market competition and stock collapse risk. *Proceedings - 2019 International Conference on Economic Management and Model Engineering, ICEMME 2019*, 37–41. DOI: 10.1109/ICEMME49371.2019.00016

Liu, Y., Qu, Z., Meng, Z., & Kou, Y. (2022). Environmentally responsible behavior of residents in tourist destinations: The mediating role of psychological ownership. *Journal of Sustainable Tourism*, 30(4), 807–823. DOI: 10.1080/09669582.2021.1891238

Liu, Y., Xu, C., Hou, M., Liu, W., Bian, J., Liu, Q., & Liu, T.-Y. (2024, December). LiuMember, Q., & LiuFellow, T. Y. (2024). Digger-Guider: High-Frequency Factor Extraction for Stock Trend Prediction. *IEEE Transactions on Knowledge and Data Engineering*, 36(12), 7973–7985. Advance online publication. DOI: 10.1109/TKDE.2024.3424475

Long, R. J. (1978a). The effects of employee ownership on organizational identification, employee attitudes, and organizational performance: A tentative framework and empirical findings. *Human Relations*, 31(1), 29–38. DOI: 10.1177/001872677803100102

Long, R. J. (1978b). The relative effects of share ownership vs. control on job attitudes in an employee owned company. *Human Relations*, 31(9), 753–763. DOI: 10.1177/001872677803100901

Lopes, H., Lagoa, S., & Calapez, T. (2014). Declining autonomy at work in the EU and its effect on civic behavior. *Economic and Industrial Democracy*, 35(2), 341–366. DOI: 10.1177/0143831X13484606

López, H., Vega, A., Robles, V & Arroyo, G. (2023). Vacíos institucionales en las organizaciones: una mirada a cómo los emprendimientos sociales. Serie de Ciencias de la Gestión N° 11.

López-Concepción, A., Gil-Lacruz, A., Saz-Gil, I., & Bazán-Monasterio, V. (2023). Social Well-Being for a Sustainable Future: The Influence of Trust in Big Business and Banks on Perceptions of Technological Development from a Life Satisfaction Perspective in Latin America. *Sustainability (Basel)*, 15(1), 628. DOI: 10.3390/su15010628

López, H., Huamani, J., Arroyo, G., & Díaz, M. (2024). Estrategias de emprendedores sociales peruanos desde lo cognitivo y el entorno. *Estudios Gerenciales*, 40(171), 162–176. DOI: 10.18046/j.estger.2024.171.6290

Lowitzsch, J., Dunsch, S., & Hashi, I. (2017). *Spanish Sociedades Laborales—Activating the Unemployed.* Palgrave Macmillan. DOI: 10.1007/978-3-319-54870-8

Lozano, R. (2018). Sustainable business models: Providing a more holistic perspective. *Business Strategy and the Environment*, 27(8), 1159–1166. DOI: 10.1002/bse.2059

Lu, C. S., & Lin, C. C. (2014). The effects of ethical leadership and ethical climate on ethical behavior in the international port context. *Journal of Business Ethics*, 124(2), 209–223. DOI: 10.1007/s10551-013-1868-y

Machell, M. (2023, May 22). Lessons from an employee ownership trust: a HR case study. *HR Magazine*. https://www.hrmagazine.co.uk/content/news/lessons-from-an-employee-ownership-trust-a-hr-case-study/

Mackin, C. (2024). Defining employee ownership: Four meanings and two models. *Journal of Participation and Employee Ownership*, 7(1), 1–25. DOI: 10.1108/JPEO-10-2022-0019

Macmillan, R., & Shanahan, M. J. (2021). Why precarious work is bad for health: Social marginality as key mechanisms in a multi-national context. *Social Forces*, 100(2), 821–851. DOI: 10.1093/sf/soab006

Mahadev Madgule, N. (2023). Vinayaka, Yeshwant M. Sonkhaskar, Dhiren Ramanbhai Patel, R. Karthikeyan, P. Selvakumar,(2023). Mechanical properties and microstructure of activated TIG welded similar joints of Inconel alloys by desirability approaches. *Materials Today: Proceedings*, 77, 528–533. DOI: 10.1016/j.matpr.2022.12.250

Mao, Z., Zhang, S., & Li, X. (2021). Corporate social responsibility, employee stock ownership and sustainable supply chain management. *International Journal of Production Economics*, 235, 108078.

Marcuello, C. (2023). Employee ownership in Spain: Worker cooperatives and sociedades laborales. *Journal of Participation and Employee Ownership*, 6(2), 149–165. DOI: 10.1108/JPEO-10-2022-0022

Mard, Y., Marsat, S., & Roux, F. (2014). Structure de l'actionnariat et performance financière de l'entreprise: le cas français. Finance Contrôle Stratégie, (17-4).

Mard, Y., Marsat, S., & Roux, F. (2014). *Structure de l'actionnariat et performance financière de l'entreprise: le cas français*. Finance Contrôle Stratégie.

Martell, K., & Gielen, N. (2000). Employee ownership and firm performance: A meta-analysis. *International Journal of Management Reviews*, 2, 117–139.

Mason, R. M. (1982). *Participatory and workplace democracy: A theoretical development in critique of liberalism*. Southern Illinois University Press.

Mayer, C. (2020). The Future of the Corporation and the Economics of Purpose. *Journal of Management Studies*, 58(3), 887–901. DOI: 10.1111/joms.12660

Mayhew, M., Ashkanasy, N., Bramble, T., & Gardner, J. (2007). A Study of the Antecedents and Consequences of Psychological Ownership in Organizational Settings. *The Journal of Social Psychology*, 147(5), 477–500. DOI: 10.3200/SOCP.147.5.477-500 PMID: 18225830

Mazumder, S., & Yan, A. (2023). What Do Americans Want from (Private) Government? Experimental Evidence Demonstrates that Americans Want Workplace Democracy. *The American Political Science Review*, •••, 1–17. DOI: 10.1017/S0003055423000667

McCarthy, D., Reeves, E., & Turner, T. (2010). Can employee share-ownership improve employee attitudes and behaviour? *Employee Relations*, 32(4), 382–395. DOI: 10.1108/01425451011051604

McCarty, N., Poole, K. T., & Rosenthal, H. (2006). *Polarized America: the dance of ideology and unequal riches*. MIT Press.

Meckling, W. H., & Jensen, M. C. (1976). *Theory of the Firm*. Managerial Behavior, Agency Costs and Ownership Structure.

Mehak, S. S., & Batcha, H. M. (2024). Analyzing the influence of green human resource practices on organizational sustainability: The role of green attitudes and performance of employees. *Environment, Development and Sustainability*. Advance online publication. DOI: 10.1007/s10668-024-05157-5

Mehr, (2024a, May 5). The preferred shares of 64,000 workers were given to their names. *Mehr News*. https://www.mehrnews.com/

Mehr, (2024b, July 17). 400,000 people became shareholders by handing over preferred shares. *Mehr News*. https://www.mehrnews.com/

MENKE. (2024, November, 1). A Fireside Chat with Ringland-Johnson. MENKE website.https://www.menke.com/esop-archives/a-fireside-chat-with-ringland johnson/

Meyer, J. P., Allen, N. J., & Smith, C. A. (1993). Commitment to organizations and occupations: Extension and test of a three-component conceptualization. *The Journal of Applied Psychology*, 78(4), 538–551. DOI: 10.1037/0021-9010.78.4.538

Meyer, K. E. (2004). Perspectives on multinational enterprises in emerging economies. *Journal of International Business Studies*, 35(4), 259–276. DOI: 10.1057/palgrave.jibs.8400084

Mill, J. S. (1909). *Principles of Political Economy* (revised ed.). Longman's, Green & Co.

Moe, T. M. (2011). *Special interest: Teachers unions and America's public schools*. Brookings Institution Press.

Mondragon Corporation. (2024). Mondragon today annual report 2024. https://www.mondragon-corporation.com/en/

Moore, C., Mayer, D. M., Chiang, F. F. T., Crossley, C., Karlesky, M. J., & Birtch, T. A. (2019). Leaders matter morally: The role of ethical leadership in shaping employee moral cognition and misconduct. *The Journal of Applied Psychology*, 104(1), 123–145. DOI: 10.1037/apl0000341 PMID: 30221953

Morgado, E. (1991). *América Latina. Participación de los trabajadores en la empresa*. Laborem.

Moroccan capital market authority website (AMMC, 2013): https://www.ammc.ma/sites/default/files/PEE_20130227.pdf

Moustabchir, O., Khenissi, M., & Juban, J. (2024). *The influence of employee share ownership on CSR performance. The case of SBF 120 listed companies*. Finance Contrôle Stratégie.

Muslim, A. I., & Setiawan, D. (2024). *View of institutional ownership and value relevance in Indonesia: the nexus of accounting conservatism*. Rajagiri Management Journal.

Mygind, N. (2012). Trends in Employee Ownership in Eastern Europe. *International Journal of Human Resource Management*, 23(8), 1611–1642. DOI: 10.1080/09585192.2012.661992

Mygind, N. (2023a). Overcoming barriers of employee ownership in France, Italy, Spain, the UK and the US. *Journal of Participation and Employee Ownership*, 6(3), 230–263. DOI: 10.1108/JPEO-10-2022-0026

Mygind, N. (2023b). Three models of employee ownership: Worker cooperative, EOT and ESOP – overcoming barriers – important choices – pros and cons. *Journal of Participation and Employee Ownership*, 6(3), 264–280. DOI: 10.1108/JPEO-10-2022-0027

Mygind, N., & Poulsen, T. (2021). Employee ownership–pros and cons–a review. *Journal of Participation and Employee Ownership*, 4(2), 136–173. DOI: 10.1108/JPEO-08-2021-0003

Naím, M. (2015). *The End of Power*. Basic Books.

National center for employee ownership (NCEO) (2005), données disponible sur: https://www.nceo.org/what-is-employee-ownership

National Center For Employee Ownership Website. (NCEO, 2024): Https://Www.Nceo.Org/What-Is-Employee-Ownership

National Center for Employee Ownership. (n.d.). *ESOP (Employee Stock Ownership Plan) Facts*. https://www.esop.org/#:%7E:text=As%20of%202020%2C%20we%20at,in%20the%20number%20of%20participants

National Labor Relations Board (NLRB). (2022). "Election Petitions Up 53%, Board Continues to Reduce Case Processing Time in FY22" (news release). October 6, 2022 https://www.nlrb.gov/news-outreach/news-story/election-petitions-up-53-board-continues-to-reduce-case-processing-time-in

NCEO. (2017). Research on Employee Ownership. National Center for Employee Ownership. Retrieved from https://www.nceo.org/employee-ownership-data/academic-research

Neffa, J. (2020). *La participación de los trabajadores en la gestión de las empresas*. Universidad Nacional de Moreno. UNM Editora.

Nekhili, M., Boukadhaba, A., & Nagati, H. (2021). The ESG-financial performance relationship: Does the type of employee board representation matter? *Corporate Governance*, 29(2), 134–161. DOI: 10.1111/corg.12345

Ngongang, D. (2013). Actionnariat salarié comme levier de création de valeur ajoutée et de productivité dans les entreprises camerounaises. *La Revue Gestion et Organisation*, 5(1), 1–8. DOI: 10.1016/j.rgo.2013.10.001

Novkovic, S., & Webb, T. (2014). *Co-operatives in a post-growth era: Creating co-operative economics*. Zed Books Ltd. DOI: 10.5040/9781350219380

O'Boyle, E.H., Patel, P.C. and Gonzalez-Mulé, E. (2016) 'Employee ownership and firm performance: a meta-analysis'.Human Resource Management Journal 26: 4, 425–448doi: DOI: 10.1111/1748-8583.12115bs_bs_banner

O'Boyle, E. H., Patel, P. C., & Gonzalez-Mulé, E. (2016). Employee ownership and firm performance: A meta-analysis. *Human Resource Management Journal*, 26(4), 425–448. DOI: 10.1111/1748-8583.12115

OECD. (2014), "Focus on Inequality and Growth - December 2014" https://www.oecd.org/social/Focus-Inequality-and-Growth-2014.pdf

OECD. (2021). OECD Reviews of Labour Market and Social Policies: Germany 2021. OECD Publishing.

Olckers, C., & Du Plessis, Y. (2020). Psychological ownership as a requisite for talent retention: The voice of highly skilled employees. *SA Journal of Industrial Psychology*, 38(2), 995–1003.

Olson, D. G. (n.d.). Sustainable businesses, employee ownership & cooperatives. ESOP Law. https://www.esoplaw.com/sustainable-businesses-employee-ownership-cooperatives

Ones, D. S., & Dilchert, S. (2012). Employee green behaviors. In Jackson, S. E., Ones, D. S., & Dilchert, S. (Eds.), *Managing human resources for environmental sustainability* (pp. 85–116). Jossey-Bass.

Onkila, T., & Sarna, B. (2022). A systematic literature review on employee ownership and corporate sustainability. *Sustainability*, 14(1), 41.

Paille, P., Morelos, J. H. M., Raineri, N., & Stinglhamber, F. (2019). The influence of the immediate manager on the avoidance of non-green behaviors in the workplace: A three-wave moderated-mediation model. *Journal of Business Ethics*, 155(3), 723–740. DOI: 10.1007/s10551-017-3519-1

Palmieri, M. L. (2024). Retheorizing workplace spillover theory: Does an economic-based pathway exist? *International Review of Applied Economics*, •••, 1–23. DOI: 10.1080/02692171.2024.2406354

Palmieri, M., & Cooper, C. (2023). Employee Ownership: What it is and what it can achieve. In Hernandez Gutierrez, G., & Zuloaga Fernandez Del Valle, R. (Eds.), *Employee ownership in the Americas: A path to shared prosperity* (pp. 1–23). ITESO, Universidad Jesuita de Guadalajara. DOI: 10.31391/JDTD1733.6

Pan, H. ESOPs in the cycle of sustainability: Evidence of Chinese firms. *Book of Abstracts ARTEM OCC 2020 Edition*, 338.

Panda, B., & Leepsa, N. M. (2017). Agency theory: Review of theory and evidence on problems and perspectives. *Indian journal of corporate governance, 10*(1), 74-95.

Panda, K. (2024). Artificial Intelligence-based Analysis of Change in Public Finance between US and International Markets. *Proceedings - International Conference on Computing, Power, and Communication Technologies, IC2PCT 2024*, 1234–1238. DOI: 10.1109/IC2PCT60090.2024.10486276

Panwar, R., Vidal, N., & Holtmaat, E. A. (2024). From Neoliberal to Hybrid Corporate Social Responsibility. In *Sustainable Capitalism: Essential Work for the Anthropocene* (pp. 189–198). University of Utah Press. DOI: 10.2307/jj.19255101.16

Park, R., Kruse, D., & Sesil, J. (2004). Does employee ownership enhance firm survival? In *Employee participation, firm performance and survival*. Emerald Group Publishing Limited. DOI: 10.1016/S0885-3339(04)08001-9

Park, S., & Song, M. H. (1995). Employee stock ownership plans, firm performance, and monitoring by outside blockholders. *Financial Management*, 24(4), 52–65. DOI: 10.2307/3665950

Pateman, C. (1970). *Participation and democratic theory*. Cambridge University Press. DOI: 10.1017/CBO9780511720444

Paul, R. J., Niehoff, B. P., & Turnley, W. H. (2000). Empowerment, expectations, and the psychological contract—Managing the dilemmas and gaining the advantages. *Journal of Socio-Economics*, 29(5), 471–485. DOI: 10.1016/S1053-5357(00)00083-4

Pazos, J., & Cordova, M. (2024). Legal gaps in the peruvian corporate network: Negative practices in boards of directors. *Pensamiento Americano*, 17(33), e-481. DOI: 10.21803/penamer.17.33.481

Pellegrini, C., Rizzi, F., & Frey, M. (2018). The role of sustainable human resource practices in influencing employee behavior for corporate sustainability. *Business Strategy and the Environment*, 27(8), 1221–1232. DOI: 10.1002/bse.2064

Pendleton, A. D., Poutsma, F., Van Ommeren, J. W., & Brewster, C. (2001). Employee share ownership and profit-sharing in the European Union. Luxembourg: Office for official publications of the European Communities.

Pendleton, A., & Robinson, A. (2020). Employee ownership in Britain: Size, character and distribution. *Journal of Participation and Employee Ownership*, 3(1), 24–44.

Pendleton, A., Robinson, A., & Nuttall, G. (2023). Employee ownership in the UK. *Journal of Participation and Employee Ownership*, 6(3), 194–214. DOI: 10.1108/JPEO-11-2022-0030

Pendleton, A., Wilson, N., & Wright, M. (1998). The perception and effects of share ownership: Empirical evidence from employee buy-outs. *British Journal of Industrial Relations*, 36(1), 99–123. Advance online publication. DOI: 10.1111/1467-8543.00082

Peng, M. W., Sun, S. L., Pinkham, B., & Chen, H. (2009). The Institution-Based View as a Third Leg for a Strategy Tripod. *The Academy of Management Perspectives*, 23(3), 63–81. DOI: 10.5465/amp.2009.43479264

Peterson, S. A. (1992). Workplace politicization and its political spillovers: A research note. *Economic and Industrial Democracy*, 13(4), 511–524. DOI: 10.1177/0143831X92134004

Pfeffer, J., & Salancik, G. R. (1978). *The external control of organizations: A resource dependence perspective*. Harper & Row.

Pierce, J. L., & Jussila, I. (2011). *Psychological ownership and the organizational context: Theory, research evidence, and application*. Edward Elgar Publishing. DOI: 10.4337/9780857934451

Pierce, J. L., & Jussila, L. (2019). The Psychology of Ownership: The Role of Psychological Ownership in Employee Engagement. *Journal of Organizational Behavior*, 40(7), 787–803.

Pierce, J. L., Kostova, T., & Dirks, K. T. (2001). Toward a theory of psychological ownership in organizations. *Academy of Management Review*, 26(2), 298–310. DOI: 10.2307/259124

Polachek, S. W., & McCutcheon, E. P. (1983). Union effects on employment stability: A comparison of panel versus cross-sectional data. *Journal of Labor Research*, 4(3), 273–287. DOI: 10.1007/BF02685213

Poulain-Rehm, T., & Lepers, X. (2013). Does employee ownership benefit value creation? The case of France (2001-2005). *Journal of Business Ethics*, 112(2), 325–340. DOI: 10.1007/s10551-012-1255-0

Poutsma, E., Huitema, H., & de Lange, R. (2012). Employee ownership and participation: A review of the literature. *Journal of Employee Ownership Law and Studies*, 4(1), 1–25.

Poutsma, E., & Ligthart, P. E. (2017). Labor-management cooperation, employee ownership, and job stability in the European context. In *Advances in the Economic Analysis of Participatory & Labor-Managed Firms* (pp. 57–84). Emerald Publishing Limited.

Prasad, R. T., & Gupta, J. (2024). Recent Advances in the Application of Nanomaterials for Environmental Sustainability. In Verma, A., Gupta, H. S., & Sethi, S. K. (Eds.), *Hybrid Composite Materials*. Springer., DOI: 10.1007/978-981-97-2104-7_14

Pugh, W. N., Jahera, J. S., & Oswald, S. (1999). ESOPs, takeover protection, and corporate decision-making. *Journal of Economics and Finance*, 23(2), 170–183. DOI: 10.1007/BF02745951

Putnam, R. D. (2020). *The upswing: How America came together a century ago and how we can do it again*. Simon and Schuster.

PWC. (2020). Tax incentives for business owners and employees. *PWC website*. https://www.pwc.co.uk/tax/assets/pdf/employee-ownership-trusts.pdf

Qalati, S. A., Barbosa, B., & Iqbal, S. (2023). The effect of firms' environmentally sustainable practices on economic performance. *Ekonomska Istrazivanja*, 36(3), 2199822. Advance online publication. DOI: 10.1080/1331677X.2023.2199822

Rajan, R. G., & Zingales, L. (1998). Power in a Theory of the Firm. *The Quarterly Journal of Economics*, 113(2), 387–432. DOI: 10.1162/003355398555630

Ramakrishnan, T., Mohan Gift, M. D., Chitradevi, S., Jegan, R., & Subha Hency Jose, P. Nagaraja, Rajneesh Sharma H.N., Selvakumar P., Sintayehu Mekuria Hailegiorgis, (2022). "Study of Numerous Resins Used in Polymer Matrix Composite Materials", Advances in Materials Science and Engineering, vol. 2022, Article ID 1088926, 8 pages, 2022. DOI: 10.1155/2022/1088926

Raman, R., Kumar, V., Pillai, B. G., Rabadiya, D., Divekar, R., & Vachharajani, H. (2024). Forecasting Bitcoin Value with Hybrid LSTM-GRU Neural Networks. *2024 Second International Conference on Data Science and Information System (ICDSIS)*, 1–5. DOI: 10.1109/ICDSIS61070.2024.10594710

Rao, A. H. (2017). "You Don't Dare Plan Much": Contract work and personal life for international early-career professionals. *Research in the Sociology of Work*, 31, 429–453. DOI: 10.1108/S0277-283320170000031016

Rauh, J. D. (2006). Own company stock in defined contribution pension plans: A takeover defense? *Journal of Financial Economics*, 81(2), 379–410. DOI: 10.1016/j.jfineco.2005.07.004

Reddy, B. A., Kathiriya, H., Thapliyal, N., Vasuki, S., Sachdeva, M., & Shobana, A. (2024a). Predicting Financial Market Movements Through Time Series Analysis and Advanced Machine Learning Algorithms. *2024 International Conference on Advances in Modern Age Technologies for Health and Engineering Science (AMATHE)*, 1–6. DOI: 10.1109/AMATHE61652.2024.10582135

Rehman, Z. U., Khan, M. K., Ullah, N., Alam, S., Ullah, R., & Irshad, M. (2022). Corporate social responsibility and employee ownership: A systematic literature review. *Sustainability*, 14(14), 8793.

Ren, T., Xiao, Y., Yang, H., & Liu, S. (2019). Employee ownership heterogeneity and firm performance in China. *Human Resource Management*, 58(6), 621–639. DOI: 10.1002/hrm.21995

Rhodes, S. R., & Steers, R. M. (1981). Conventional vs. worker-owned organizations. *Human Relations*, 34(12), 1013–1035. DOI: 10.1177/001872678103401201

Richter, A., & Schrader, S. (2017). Levels of employee share ownership and the performance of listed companies in Europe. *British Journal of Industrial Relations*, 55(2), 396–420. DOI: 10.1111/bjir.12169

Rivas, J. L., Salvaj, E., & Cordova, M. (2023). Family vs non family networks: Chile, Mexico and Peru. *Management Research*, 21(3), 217–236. DOI: 10.1108/MRJIAM-12-2022-1369

Rochat, M. (2023). The determinants of growing economic inequality within advanced democracies. *International Review of Economics*, 70(4), 1–19. DOI: 10.1007/s12232-023-00427-6

Rodgers, L. (2019) "New Data on Employee Ownership from the General Social Survey". https://www.nceo.org/employee-ownership-blog/article/new-data-employee-ownership-general-social-survey

Roeterdink, M. (2018). *The influence of employee ownership and employee board representation on firm performance: Evidence from French listed firms*. PhD thesis, University of Twente

Rosalsky, G. (2023) February 28 2023. You may have heard of the 'union boom'. The numbers tell a different story. NPR. https://www.npr.org/sections/money/2023/02/28/1159663461/you-may-have-heard-of-the-union-boom-the-numbers-tell-a-different-story

Rosen, C. (2023). Employee ownership in the USA: Lessons to consider in creating more inclusive capitalism. *Journal of Participation and Employee Ownership*, 6(3), 215–229. DOI: 10.1108/JPEO-11-2022-0029

Rosen, C., Case, J., & Staubus, M. (2020). *Ownership culture: How employee ownership can drive inclusive growth and social responsibility*. Beyster Institute Press.

Rosenfeld, J. (2014). *What unions no longer do*. Harvard University Press. DOI: 10.4159/harvard.9780674726215

Rosenfeld, J., & Kleykamp, M. (2012). Organized labor and racial wage inequality in the United States. *American Journal of Sociology*, 117(5), 1460–1502. DOI: 10.1086/663673 PMID: 25620802

Ross, M., & Bateman, N. (2019, November). Meet the Low-Wage Workforce. Metropolitan Policy Program at Brookings. https://www.brookings.edu/wp-content/uploads/2019/11/201911_Brookings-Metro_low-wage-workforce_Ross-Bateman.pdf

Roztocki, N., & Weistroffer, H. R. (2007). *How Do Investments in Enter pr ise Application Integr ation Dr ive Stock Pr ices?* Shrieenidhi, A. M., Ruba Roshini, S., & Ranjana, P. (2024). Walmart Sales Forecasting Using Time Series Analysis. *2024 International Conference on Advances in Data Engineering and Intelligent Computing Systems, ADICS 2024*. DOI: 10.1109/ADICS58448.2024.10533547

Ruiz, A. (2007). Las privatizaciones en Perú: un proceso con luces y sombras. *Nueva Sociedad*. 207.

Saez, E., & Zucman, G. (2020). The rise of income and wealth inequality in America: Evidence from distributional macroeconomic accounts. *The Journal of Economic Perspectives*, 34(4), 3–26. DOI: 10.1257/jep.34.4.3

Salas, M. (1982). *Participación Laboral y la autogestión en el Perú*. Pontificia Universidad Católica del Perú.

Sarkar, A. (2024). *Common Good Capitalism: A new economic model for growth to benefit business and society*. Right Book Press.

Saylor, T. (2017) *Esops Help Some CPA Firms With Retention, Succession,* Journal Of Accountancy. https://tinyurl.com/pkv6e54t

Schaufeli, W. B., Bakker, A. B., & Salanova, M. (2006). The Measurement of Work Engagement With a Short Questionnaire: A Cross-National Study. *Educational and Psychological Measurement*, 66(4), 701–716. DOI: 10.1177/0013164405282471

Schaufeli, W. B., Salanova, M., Gonzalez-Roma, V., & Bakker, A. B. (2002). The measurement of engagement and burnout: A two sample confirmatory factor analytic approach. *Journal of Happiness Studies*, 3(1), 71–92. DOI: 10.1023/A:1015630930326

Schaufeli, W., & Bakker, A. (2004). *Work Engagement Scale: Preliminary Manual (Version 1.1). Occupational Health Psychology Unit.* Utrecht University.

Schlozman, K. L., Brady, H. E., & Verba, S. (2018). Unequal and Unrepresented. In *Unequal and Unrepresented.* Princeton University Press.

Schneider, B. R. (2013). *Hierarchical capitalism in Latin America. Business, labor, and the challenges of equitable development* (1st ed.). Cambridge University Press., DOI: 10.1017/CBO9781107300446

Schönherr, N., Findler, F., & Martinuzzi, A. (2017). Exploring the interface of CSR and the Sustainable Development Goals. *Transnational Corporations*, 24(3), 33–47. DOI: 10.18356/cfb5b8b6-en

Schuler, R. S., & Rogovsky, N. (1998). Understanding Compensation Practice Variations Across Firms: The Impact of National Culture. *Journal of International Business Studies*, 29(1), 159–177. DOI: 10.1057/palgrave.jibs.8490030

Scocozza, G. N. (2020). *Growth of sociedades laborales (worker-owned companies) in Spain and the Basque Country.* Master Thesis, Universidad Católica de Córdoba

Semadeni, M., Withers, M. C., & Trevis Certo, S. (2014). The perils of endogeneity and instrumental variables in strategy research: Understanding through simulations. *Strategic Management Journal*, 35(7), 1070–1079. DOI: 10.1002/smj.2136

Shierholz, H., Poydock, M., & McNicholas, C. (2023). January 19th. Unionization increased by 200,000 in 2022. Economic Policy Institute. https://www.epi.org/publication/unionization-2022/#:~:text=During%20fiscal%20year%202022%2C%20the,year%202016%20(NLRB%202022)

Shrivastav, A. (2022). Audit meeting frequency and firm performance: Evidence from Indian firms. *Journal of Business Research*, 112, 65–80. DOI: 10.1016/j.jbusres.2020.02.041

Sinkinson, C., & Hicks, A. (2013). Unraveling the research process: social bookmarking and collaborative learning. *The Plugged-In Professor: Tips and Techniques for Teaching with Social Media*, 49–60. DOI: 10.1016/B978-1-84334-694-4.50005-3

Smith, A. (1776). *The wealth of nations*. Methuen & Co., Ltd.

Smits, D., & Van Hillegersberg, J. (2018). The continuing mismatch between IT governance maturity theory and practice: A new approach. *Procedia Computer Science*, 138, 549–560. DOI: 10.1016/j.procs.2018.10.075

Sobel, R. (1993). From occupational involvement to political participation: An exploratory analysis. *Political Behavior*, 15(4), 339–353. DOI: 10.1007/BF00992102

Solaiman, S., Rahman, B. M. O., Arefin, M. F., Ahmed, C. F., Leung, C. K., & Madill, E. W. R. (2024). Unveiling Market Sentiments: A Comprehensive Analysis of Stock Market Responses to Diverse News Events Using Data Mining Techniques. *Proceedings of the 2024 18th International Conference on Ubiquitous Information Management and Communication, IMCOM 2024*. DOI: 10.1109/IMCOM60618.2024.10418389

Solar, N. (2021). 2021 Public Benefit Report. Retrieved from https://info.namastesolar.com/hubfs/2021_Namaste_Solar_Public_Benefit_Report_Final.pdf

Spreitzer, G. M. (1995). Psychological empowerment in the workplace: Dimensions, measurement, and validation. *Academy of Management Journal*, 38(5), 1442–1465. DOI: 10.2307/256865

Squillace, J. (2022). Examination of the Financial Relationship Between Overall Stock Market Value and Corporate Investments in Privacy. *Conference Proceedings - IEEE SOUTHEASTCON, 2022-March*, 339–347. DOI: 10.1109/SoutheastCon48659.2022.9764007

Standing, G. (2011). *The precariat: The new dangerous class* (p. 208). Bloomsbury academic.

Statistics of the federation europeenne de l'actionnariat salarie (FEAS, 2023)- Https://Www.Efesonline.Org/Annual%20Economic%20Survey/2023/Recensement%20 2023.Pdf

Steare, R., Stampoulidis, P., Lewis, P. N., & Woodman, P. (Sept 2015) The moraldna of employee-ownedcompanies. Available at https://www.eagatrust.com/wp-content/uploads/2017/01/The-MoralDNA-of-Employee-Owned-Companies.pdf

Stiglitz, J. (2019). *People, Power, and Profits: Progressive Capitalism for an Age of Discontent* (1st ed.). W.W. Norton & Company.

Stone, C., Trisi, D., Sherman, A., & Beltran, J. (2020, January). A Guide to Statistics on Historical Trends in Income Inequality. Center on Budget Policy Priorities. https://www.cbpp.org/research/poverty-and-inequality/a-guide-to-statistics-on-historical-trends-in-income-inequality

Stout, L. A. (2019). Stakeholder Governance and Employee Ownership. The Cambridge Handbook of Stakeholder Theory, 359-374.

Stout, L. A., & Blair, M. M. (2021). The Stakeholder Governance Model and Other Lessons from the Public Benefit Corporation Experiment. The Cambridge Handbook of Corporate Law, Corporate Governance and Sustainability, 307-321.

Stout, L. A. (2020). The Troubling Question of Corporate Purpose. Accounting, Economics, and Law. *Convivium*, 10(3), 20200021.

St-Pierre, J., Gagnon, J. M., & Saint-Pierre, J. (1996). Concentration of voting rights and board resistance to takeover bids. *Journal of Corporate Finance*, 3(1), 25–54. DOI: 10.1016/S0929-1199(96)00008-9

Stranahan, S., & Kelly, M. (n.d.). Ownership design for a sustainable economy. Fifty by Fifty. https://www.fiftybyfifty.org/2018/05/employee-ownership-and-ecological-sustainability/

Su, Y. L., & Liu, C. T. (2012). A study of the relationship of corporate governance and stock price of the marine industry in Taiwan: Using the Ohlson model. *Proceedings - 3rd International Conference on Innovations in Bio-Inspired Computing and Applications, IBICA 2012*, 177–180. DOI: 10.1109/IBICA.2012.40

Subramaniam, R. K., Samuel, S. D., Seera, M., & Alam, N. (2024). Utilising machine learning for corporate social responsibility (CSR) and environmental, social, and governance (ESG) evaluation: Transitioning from committees to climate. *Sustainable Futures : An Applied Journal of Technology, Environment and Society*, 8, 100329. Advance online publication. DOI: 10.1016/j.sftr.2024.100329

Sugumaran, K. M. D., Pandiyarajan V., Y. B S, Selvakumar P. and M. S, (2024). "Analysis of Electromyography Signals for Control of Mechanical Prosthesis using Machine Learning Techniques," 2024 2nd International Conference on Intelligent Data Communication Technologies and Internet of Things (IDCIoT), Bengaluru, India, 2024, pp. 1059-1067, DOI: 10.1109/IDCIoT59759.2024.10467707

Sullivan, L., Meschede, T., Shapiro, T., Kroeger, T., & Escobar, F. (2019, April). Occupational Segregation, Benefits, and the Racial Wealth Gap. Institute on Assets and Social Policy. http://www.appam.org/assets/1/7/occupational_segregation_report_40219.pdf

Sun, H., & Liu, C. (2023). Employee stock ownership plans and corporate environmental performance: Evidence from China. *International Journal of Environmental Research and Public Health*, 20(2), 1467. DOI: 10.3390/ijerph20021467 PMID: 36674233

Sun, Q., Xiao, Q., Jiang, J., & Huang, X. (2024). The loss of political connections and the fluctuation of corporate stock prices: Moderating effect based on media attention. *Heliyon*, 10(6), e27902. Advance online publication. DOI: 10.1016/j.heliyon.2024.e27902 PMID: 38509911

Syamlal, V. S. V. (2023). The impact of sustainable branding using big data and business analytics in the market research industry (Publication No. 31134975) [Doctoral dissertation, University of Wales Trinity Saint David]. ProQuest Dissertations & Theses.

Syariati, N. E., Subroto, B., & Andayani, W. (2017). The Role of Employee Stock Option Plan to Reduce Earnings Management Actions. Jurnal Keuangan dan Perbankan, 21(3), 425-435

Tajer, A. (2021). Contribution à l'étude de l'impact des mécanismes de la gouvernance et des caractéristiques du dirigeant sur la performance financière des PME familiales* (Thèse de doctorat, Université Cadi Ayyad, 2020/2021).

Tajer, A., Ouberka, B., & Rigar, S. M. (2021). Structure de l'actionnariat et performance financière des entreprises marocaines cotées en bourse. *Revue Française d'Economie et de Gestion*, 2(8).

Tajfel, H., & Turner, J. C. (1979). An integrative theory of intergroup conflict. In Austin, W. G., & Worchel, S. (Eds.), *The social psychology of intergroup relations* (pp. 33–75). Brooks/Cole.

Tangjitprom, N. (2013). The role of corporate governance in reducing the negative effect of earnings management. *International Journal of Economics and Finance*, 5(3), •••. DOI: 10.5539/ijef.v5n3p213

Tannenbaum, A. S. (1983). Employee-owned companies. *Research in Organizational Behavior*, 5, 235–265.

Taylor, S. (1992). Competitive Success through Participation: The John Lewis Partnership. In Bradley, K. (Ed.), *Human Resource Management* (pp. 133–140). Routledge.

Tepper, J., & Hearn, D. (2023). *The Myth of Capitalism: Monopolies and the Death of Competition* (1st ed.). Wiley.

The Hewison. K. (2016). Precarious work. *The SAGE handbook of the sociology of work and employment*, 428-443.

Thomas, H., Ornstein, J., & Woersdoerfer, M. (2021). The role of employee ownership in an era of economic insecurity. *Journal of Participation and Employee Ownership*, 4(1), 26–48.

Thompson, W. (1824). *Inquiry into the Principles for the Distribution of Wealth Most Conducive to Human Happiness*. Burt Franklin (1968 ed.)

Timming, A., & Summers, J. (2020). Is workplace democracy associated with wider pro-democracy affect? A structural equation model. *Economic and Industrial Democracy*, 41(3), 709–726. DOI: 10.1177/0143831X17744028

Tingle, K., & Wharton, E. S. G. Initiative. (2023). The power of shared ownership: How employee-owned businesses achieve sustainability goals. Retrieved from https://esg.wharton.upenn.edu/news/the-power-of-shared-ownership-how-employee-owned-businesses-achieve-esg-goals/

Toe, S. D., Hollandts, X., & Valiorgue, B. (2017). *The "dark side" of employee ownership: An empirical study on the SBF 120 index (2000-2014)* (Vol. 20). Finance Contrôle Stratégie.

Tollin, K., & Christensen, L. B. (2019). Sustainability marketing commitment: Empirical insights about its drivers at the corporate and functional level of marketing. *Journal of Business Ethics*, 156(4), 1165–1185. DOI: 10.1007/s10551-017-3591-6

Trabelsi, S. (2021, Février). L'actionnariat citoyen en Tunisie: Pensez-y! Leaders. https://www.leaders.com.tn/article/31395-l-actionnariat-citoyen-en-tunisie-pensez-y

Trébucq, S. (2002). L'actionnariat salarié dans les entreprises familiales du SBF250: Un outil de création de valeur. *Finance Contrôle Stratégie*, 5(4), 107–135.

Tucker, J., Nock, S., & Toscano, D. (1989). Employee ownership and perceptions of work: The effect of an employee stock ownership plan. *Work and Occupations*, 16(1), 26–42. DOI: 10.1177/0730888489016001002

Ugaz, J. (2020). *La Gran Corrupción*. Planeta.

Van Dyne, L., & Pierce, J. L. (2004). Psychological Ownership and Feelings of Possession: Three Field Studies Predicting Employee Attitudes and Organizational Citizenship Behavior. *Journal of Organizational Behavior*, 25(4), 439–459. DOI: 10.1002/job.249

Van Green, T. (2023) April 19th. Majorities of adults see decline of union membership as bad for the U.S. and working people. Pew Research Center. https://www.pewresearch.org/short-reads/2023/04/19/majorities-of-adults-see-decline-of-union-membership-as-bad-for-the-u-s-and-working-people/

Van Tuin, L., Schaufeli, W. B., Van den Broeck, A., & van Rhenen, W. (2020). A corporate purpose as an antecedent to employee motivation and work engagement. *Frontiers in Psychology*, 11, 572343. DOI: 10.3389/fpsyg.2020.572343 PMID: 33071907

Vassolo, R., De Castro, J., & Gomez-Mejia, L. (2011). Managing in Latin America. Common issues and a research agenda. *The Academy of Management Perspectives*, 25(4), 22–34. DOI: 10.5465/amp.2011.0129

Vaughan-Whitehead, D. (1992). Employee Ownership: A New Approach to Industrial Relations. *International Labour Review*, 131(4), 421–446.

Veldhuizen, M. (2022). Blockchain for corporate sustainability: Opportunities and challenges. *Business Strategy and the Environment*, 31(3), 698–713.

Ventura, J., & Jauregui, K. (2017). Business-Community Relationships for Extractive Industries: A Case Study in Peru. Brazilian Administration Review, 14(2), e160114. https://doi.org/DOI: 10.1590/1807-7692bar2017160114

Verba, S., & Almond, G. (1963). *The civic culture: Political attitudes and democracy in five nations*. Princeton University Press.

Verba, S., Schlozman, K. L., & Brady, H. E. (1995). *Voice and equality: Civic voluntarism in American politics*. Harvard University Press. DOI: 10.2307/j.ctv1pnc1k7

Vergara, A. (2018). *Ciudadanos sin república. De la precariedad institucional al descalabro político* (2nd ed.). Editorial Planeta.

Vijayakumar, G., Rajkumar, M., Rajiv Chandar, N., Selvakumar, P., & Duraisamy, R. (2024). Muniyandi Rajkumar, Rajiv Chandar N, Selvakumar P and Ramesh Duraisamy, (2024). Environmentally friendly TDS removal from waste water by electrochemical ion exchange batch-type recirculation (EIR) technique. *Environmental Science. Water Research & Technology*, 10(4), 826–835. DOI: 10.1039/D3EW00793F

Wagner, S. H., Parker, C. P., & Christiansen, N. D. (2006). Employees that think and act like owners: Effects of Ownership Beliefs and Behaviors on Organizational Effectiveness. *Personnel Psychology*, 56(4), 847–871. DOI: 10.1111/j.1744-6570.2003.tb00242.x

Walker, A. N. (2020). *Divided unions: The Wagner Act, federalism, and organized labor*. University of Pennsylvania Press. DOI: 10.9783/9780812296662

Wang, T. (2020). *Union Impact on Voter Participation–And How to Expand It*. Harvard Kennedy School Ash Center for Democratic Governance and Innovation.

Wang, Y., & Liu, Y. (2021). Does employee ownership enhance corporate social responsibility? Evidence from China. *Journal of Business Ethics*, 103(4), 753–776.

Wang, Y., & Wang, X. (2024). From ratings to action: The impact of ESG performance on corporate innovation. *Heliyon*, 10(4), e26683. Advance online publication. DOI: 10.1016/j.heliyon.2024.e26683 PMID: 38420449

Webb, J. W., Khoury, T. A., & Hitt, M. A. (2020). The influence of formal and informal institutional voids on entrepreneurship. *Entrepreneurship Theory and Practice*, 44(3), 504–526. DOI: 10.1177/1042258719830310

Weiss, D. J., Dawis, R. V., England, G. W., & Lofquist, L. H. (1967) Manual for the Minnesota Satisfaction Questionnaire. University of Minnesota, Minneapolis. Patrice Roussel (1993)

Weitzman, M., & Kruse, D. (1990). Profit sharing and productivity. In Blinder, A. (Ed.), *Paying for productivity: A look at the evidence* (pp. 95–140). Brookings Institution.

Welbourne, T. M., & Schlachter, S. (2022). Transforming Employee Share Ownership with Blockchain: Opportunities and Challenges. *Journal of Participation and Employee Ownership*, 5(1), 1–23.

Weller, C. E., & Karakilic, E. (2022). Wealth Inequality, Precariousness, Household Debt, and Macroeconomic Stability. *Journal of Economic Issues*, LVI(2), 599–606. DOI: 10.1080/00213624.2022.2065864

Wen, X., Li, Z., Zhang, Y., & Shen, S. (2021). ESOP and corporate sustainable growth. In *E3S Web of Conferences* (Vol. 253, p. 03039). EDP Sciences.

Whitfield, K., Pendleton, A., Sengupta, S., & Huxley, K. (2017). Employee share ownership and organizational performance: A tentative opening of the black box. *Personnel Review*, 46(7), 128. DOI: 10.1108/PR-09-2016-0243

Wilden, R., & Gudergan, S. P. (2015). The impact of dynamic capabilities on operational marketing and technological capabilities: Investigating the role of environmental turbulence. *Journal of the Academy of Marketing Science*, 43(2), 181–199. DOI: 10.1007/s11747-014-0380-y

Wilkinson, R. G., & Pickett, K. E. (2009). Income inequality and social dysfunction. *Annual Review of Sociology*, 35(1), 493–511. DOI: 10.1146/annurev-soc-070308-115926

Wilson, J., & Musick, M. A. (1997). Work and volunteering: The long arm of the job. *Social Forces*, 76(1), 251–272. DOI: 10.2307/2580325

Winkler, A. L. P., Brown, J. A., & Finegold, D. L. (2019). Employees as conduits for effective stakeholder engagement: An example from B corporations. *Journal of Business Ethics*, 160(4), 913–936. DOI: 10.1007/s10551-018-3924-0

Wirtz, P. (2011). The cognitive dimension of corporate governance in fast growing entrepreneurial firms. *European Management Journal*, 29(6), 431–447. DOI: 10.1016/j.emj.2011.06.004

Wolff, R. D. (2021). *The Sickness is the System: When Capitalism Fails to Save Us from Pandemics or Itself.* Democracy at Work.

Wolfinger, R. E., & Rosenstone, S. J. (1980). *Who votes?* Yale University Press.

Wolf, R., & Gonzalez-Perez, M. A. (2024). (Forthcoming). A Tale of Soft Power: How the United States Used Business Administration Schools to Promote its Interests and Values in Latin America. *Palgrave Macmillan.*

Wooldridge, J. M. (2010). *Econometric analysis of cross section and panel data.* MIT press.

World Business Council for Sustainable Development. (2019). WBCSD's 2019 Sustainability Leadership Report. https://www.wbcsd.org/

Wu, F., Cao, J., & Zhang, X. (2023). Do non-executive employees matter in curbing corporate financial fraud? *Journal of Business Research*, 163, 113922. DOI: 10.1016/j.jbusres.2023.113922

Xiao, J. (2024). Risk Assessment System for Digital Inclusive Finance Based on Convolutional Neural Network. *2024 Second International Conference on Data Science and Information System (ICDSIS)*, 1–5. DOI: 10.1109/ICDSIS61070.2024.10594199

Yermack, D. (2020). Corporate Governance and Blockchains. *Review of Finance*, 21(1), 7–31.

Yetim, M. A., & Gur, F. A. (2024). When they are more than just employees: Environmentally conscious decision-making in employee-owned organizations. *Business Strategy and the Environment*, 33(4), 2694–2711. Advance online publication. DOI: 10.1002/bse.3626

Yi, W., & Zhang, Y. (2021). Research of Equity Pledge on the Financial Performance of Real Estate Industry Listed Companies Based on SPSS 23.0. *Proceedings - 2nd International Conference on E-Commerce and Internet Technology, ECIT 2021*, 339–343. DOI: 10.1109/ECIT52743.2021.00077

Yu, X., & Fang, J. (2024). Stock transferability, the managerial learning effect and corporate innovation. *China Journal of Accounting Research*, 17(1), 100341. Advance online publication. DOI: 10.1016/j.cjar.2023.100341

Zhang, H., He, J., Zhu, J., & Chan, K. C. Used as a Tool: When Esops Meet Controlling Shareholders' Share Pledging in an Emerging Market. Available at *SSRN* 4583067. DOI: 10.2139/ssrn.4583067

Zhang, R., Aljumah, A. I., Ghardallou, W., Li, Z., Li, J., & Cifuentes-Faura, J. (2023). How does economic development promote the sustainability targets? Role of natural resources utilization. *Resources Policy*, 156, 102856.

Zhang, Y. (2023). Employee Stock Ownership Plans and Corporate Innovation. *Academic Journal of Management and Social Sciences*, 2(1), 54–59. DOI: 10.54097/ajmss.v2i1.5950

Zhong, X., Zhao, Z., Yan, B., & Xu, Q. (2024). Large Language Model for Dynamic Strategy Interchange in Financial Markets. *2024 9th International Conference on Cloud Computing and Big Data Analytics, ICCCBDA 2024*, 306–312.

Zhou, L., Wei, F., & Kong, Y. (2022). Do employee stock ownership plans affect corporate social responsibility? Evidence from China. *International Journal of Environmental Research and Public Health*, 19(3), 1055. DOI: 10.3390/ijerph19031055 PMID: 35162079

Zoghbi-Manrique-de-Lara, P. (2010). Do unfair procedures predict employees' ethical behavior by deactivating formal regulations? *Journal of Business Ethics*, 94(3), 411–425. DOI: 10.1007/s10551-009-0273-z

Zoorob, M. (2018). Does 'right to work'imperil the right to health? The effect of labour unions on workplace fatalities. *Occupational and Environmental Medicine*, 75(10), 736–738. DOI: 10.1136/oemed-2017-104747 PMID: 29898957

Zullo, R. (2011). Labor unions and charity. *Industrial & Labor Relations Review*, 64(4), 699–711. DOI: 10.1177/001979391106400404

About the Contributors

Zyed Achour is a dedicated scholar-researcher, holding a PhD in Management Science and serving as an assistant professor at the National Institute of Labor and Social Studies, University of Carthage. A research associate at the GEF2A Laboratory of the Higher Institute of Management, University of Tunis, he brings over 20 years of experience in higher education and research. His research spans broad themes, including corporate social responsibility, sustainability, labor sciences, trade unionism, gender diversity, finance, human resource management, and strategic management. As an author of numerous scientific articles and a contributor to several collective works, Dr. Achour distinguishes himself through innovative research that explores the complex interconnections between organizational, social, and managerial dynamics.

***

Wajdi Ben Rejeb is a Senior Lecturer in Business Strategy at Lincoln International Business School, University of Lincoln, UK. He specialises in teaching business strategy, strategic management, entrepreneurship, and innovation. His research focuses on corporate governance, strategic management, strategic leadership, startup strategy, and innovation. Specifically, his interests include examining and understanding board behavioural attributes – such as processes, roles, and leadership, and their impact on various strategic and organisational outcomes.

Sudhanshu Chandra Assistant Professor (Academic Coordinator) at Manuu Law School, Maulana Azad National Urdu University Hyderabad A Central University Established by an Act of Parliament in 1988, Accredited with Grade A+ by NACC, (Hyderabad Telangana) -500032. He Completed his B.A.LLB(Hons)-Dr. Ram Manohar Lohiya National Law University Lucknow(U.P) LLM-National Law

University Jodhpur (Rajasthan), Cleared UGC-NET, Ph.D. in Law from Gautam Buddha University Greater Noida(U.P.)

Nitika Malik is a esteemed research scholar in institute of Management Studies and Research, Maharshi Dayanand University, Rohtak.

Rishi Chaudhry is an esteemed professor in institute of Management Studies and Research, Maharshi Dayanand University, Rohtak

Miguel Cordova Professor and Researcher at the Department of Management and Leadership, Business School, at Tecnológico de Monterrey, Mexico. He holds a PhD in Strategic Management and Sustainability at Consorcio de Universidades in Peru, he has doctoral studies at the Copenhagen Business School, and an MBA of Centrum Católica. His research is oriented to Power and Influence in Organizations, Sustainable Supply Chain Management, Sustainability, Corporate Governance, and International Business. He is Associate Editor at the International Journal of Sustainability in Higher Education. He is Chair at the Teaching & Education SIG of the Academy of International Business (AIB).

Sara Elouadi is a Doctor of the Institute of Administration of Companies of Toulon in France, Sara Elouadi teaches finance and accounting in many establishments in France and Morocco. Currently, a professor and researcher in finance at Hassan II University in Casablanca, she is also the author of several scientific articles on employee shareholding and pluralist governance.

Houssam Errommani is a doctoral student at Hassan II University and is working on a doctoral project on the financial repercussions of employee shareholding, especially in the context of listed companies.

Telelaz Galaa Esposito obtained her PhD in Clinical and Psychopathological Psychology from the University of Tunis. She is currently Assistant Professor at the National Institute of Labour and Social Studies, University of Carthage. Dr. Galaa's research interests span a broad spectrum, including health psychology, burnout, the psychological impact of terrorism, and the rehabilitation of incarcerated individuals. Her expertise also extends to areas such as women's rights and the psychological well-being of populations during crises.

Ramya H P holds an MBA in finance and is pursuing a Ph.D. in investments from VTU. Currently, she works as an assistant professor at the Department of Management Studies at DSCE, with 15 years of experience. She has conducted workshops and seminars on topics such as financial management using Excel, financial accounting and taxation, and financial statement analysis, and has presented and published research papers in various national and international journals. Additionally, she is trained in personal finance, data processing using Python, taxation, financial modelling, trading strategies, portfolio optimization using the Markowitz model, and investment management. She is also an AICTE-nominated innovation ambassador for the Institute Innovation Council.

Herath is an Associate Professor of Accounting at Clark Atlanta University. She was a Renwick Faculty Fellow at New York University's Stern School of Business in 2022. She earned a BCOM (Hons) and an MBA, University of Colombo in Sri Lanka, and a Ph.D. and an MCOM Honors in Accounting, University of Wollongong in Australia. She has worked at the University of Lynchburg, Georgia State University, Georgia Institute of Technology, University of Wollongong, Western Sydney University, University of Ruhuna and the University of Colombo. She serves on the editorial boards of academic journals and has contributed over 70 publications. She has published 15 book chapters. Her research areas include Accounting Education, Management Control, Data Analytics, and Sustainability Accounting. She is a DTM and served as the President and Treasurer of the Georgia Institute of Technology Toastmasters International Club, the Treasurer of the Emory University Toastmasters International Club and as an Area Director from 2020 to 2021 in Georgia, United States. She earned the TESOL Professional Certificate from Arizona State University and the Professional Certificate in Google Data Analytics. She is the current Editor-In-Chief for Asian Journal of Economics and Business and the Global Journal of Accounting and Economy Research,

IJ. Krishna Charan is an Assistant Professor and Research Scholar at Vel Tech Rangarajan Dr. Sagunthala R&D Institute of Science and Technology University, located in Morai, Tamil Nadu, India. She is affiliated with the University's School of Law. With a strong academic background and research interest in law and related fields, she contributes to both teaching and scholarly activities at the institution. Her expertise includes legal theory, research methodology, and advancing knowledge in various aspects of law.

Vishal Jain is presently working as Professor at Department of Computer Science and Engineering, School of Engineering and Technology, Sharda University, Greater Noida, U. P. India. Before that, he has worked for several years as an Associate Professor at Bharati Vidyapeeth's Institute of Computer Applications and Management (BVICAM), New Delhi. He has more than 14 years of experience in the academics. He obtained Ph.D (CSE), M.Tech (CSE), MBA (HR), MCA, MCP and CCNA. He has authored more than 90 research papers in reputed conferences and journals, including Web of Science and Scopus. He has authored and edited more than 30 books with various reputed publishers, including Elsevier, Springer, Apple Academic Press, CRC, Taylor and Francis Group, Scrivener, Wiley, Emerald, NOVA Science and IGI-Global. His research areas include information retrieval, semantic web, ontology engineering, data mining, ad hoc networks, and sensor networks. He received a Young Active Member Award for the year 2012–13 from the Computer Society of India, Best Faculty Award for the year 2017 and Best Researcher Award for the year 2019 from BVICAM, New Delhi.

K.G.Hemalatha, B.Pharm., MBA., MPhil., PhD . Professor & HOD, Department of Management Studies, Dayananda Sagar College of Engineering. A dynamic personality with a fair understanding of the nuances of branding, strategic vision, industry connections, and people skills, adaptable to the changing scenarios and capable of taking the institutions to a new level. Strategist and good in execution, she revamped the curriculum, pedagogy, and placement scenario of the Department of Management studies. Believe in the industry connect & experiential learning- Strengthened the alumni network, significant industry connections, guest talks, events, student programs and case pedagogy that relate to real-life situations. Firm believer in sustainable practices. Introduced many signature events and industry connections for the MBA graduates' benefits. Guiding 4 Ph.D. scholars & have 20 national & International journal publications in her credit. Instrumental in introducing the sustainable practices by UN-PRME membership, Social Project on the AIM2Flourish website, and SDG Practices. Presented research article in various conferences at prestigious institutions like IIM-A, IIM-B, and IIM-K.

Mark Kaswan works at the intersection of political theory and social change, working to expand our understandings of politics and of democracy and to find ways to make democracy meaningful for people in their daily lives. His research has mostly been oriented toward the cooperative movement and worker ownership, bridging abstract ideas about democracy, happiness, and politics with political economics and ideas about the structure of social institutions—particularly the place where we spend so much of our waking hours, the workplace. His work crosses boundaries, drawing from political theory, sociology, philosophy, economics, public policy, feminism, history, business and management studies, organizational theory, and race and ethnic studies. Dr. Kaswan received his Ph.D. in political science from UCLA in 2010 and has been at UTRGV (formerly UT Brownsville) since 2011. He also holds a J. Robert Beyster, Michael W. Huber, and Kellogg Foundation fellowships from the Rutgers University School of Management and Labor Relations. In addition to his work as a faculty member, he is Academic Affairs Faculty Fellow for Strategic Initiatives, overseeing the implementation of the UTRGV strategic plan.

Hewa Gamage Eranga Ravihara Kulathunga is a Civil Engineer by profession. He has obtained his Master's degree in International Business with distinction from DeVry University - Keller Graduate School of Management, California, USA (2017). He has obtained his Bachelor of Science in Civil Engineering & Infrastructure Engineering with Honors from Asian Institute of Technology, Bangkok, Thailand (2014). He is a highly motivated and experienced young individual with a continuous growth mindset skilled in successfully executing business strategies. Currently he is the Managing Director of Cerebrozone Pvt Ltd, CRB Engineering Pvt. Ltd and Southern International Trade Line. He performs as a Director of Mahaweli Center Sri Lanka, Director Board Member at State Timber Corporation and Director Board Member at Land Reclamation and Development CO. LTD. He has demonstrated his excellence through international publications while gaining experience through international conferences and events such as European Conference on Construction Management in Hungary, Budapest (2016), TFWA (Tax Free World Association) Conference, Singapore (2017).

Hellen López Valladares is an Assistant Professor and researcher at the School of Management of the Pontifical Catholic University of Peru (PUCP). Master in International Development, Poverty and Inequality from the University of Manchester, United Kingdom and Social Manager from the Pontifical Catholic University of Peru—PUCP. Her research is focus on sustainable business model, social entrepreneurship, social innovation and teaching sustainability. She is part of the Group of Studies in Organizational Growth and Coordinator of the Social Mention of the School of Management.

Moustabchir Oussama is a PhD student in Management Science and conducts his research at the Center for Applied Management Studies and Research (CERAG), in France. He is a member of the International Academic Governance Association (AAIG) and the author of several communications at international conferences and articles in scientific journals. His research interests include Corporate Governance, Employee ownership Studies, Board Diversity, ESG, Sustainability and Corporate Social Responsibility, Firm Performance. He also teaches finance, corporate governance and corporate social responsibility at the University of Grenoble Alpes.

Oussama Moustabchir is a PhD student in Management Science and member in the "Centre d'Études et de Recherches Appliquées à la Gestion" (CERAG) Laboratory, University of Grenoble-Alpes, France. He is member of the International Academic Governance Association (AAIG). Among his Reserach interest are Corporate Governance, Employee ownership Studies, Board Diversity, ESG, Sustainability and Corporate Social Responsibility, Firm Performance.

Amirhossein Nozari received the master degree in Master of Business Administration (MBA in Finance) in 2014 from University of Guilan, Rasht, Iran. He joined ICN Business School, Nancy, France in 2022, as a PhD candidate. His research areas are Corporate Governance and Corporate Social Responsibility (CSR)

P. Selvakumar is currently an Associate Professor in the Department of Science and Humanities at Nehru Institute of Technology, Coimbatore, Tamil Nadu, India. Since 2023, he has served as the Department IQAC Coordinator at the institute. Prior to joining Nehru Institute of Technology, he held positions as an Assistant Professor in the Department of Science and Humanities various engineering colleges in Coimbatore, Tamil Nadu, India, spanning from 2011 to 2023. Dr.P. Selvakumar's academic and research interests lie primarily in the field of phytochemistry. He has made significant contributions to his field, with an impressive record that includes 30 journal publications, 12 patents, and 20 conference papers. Additionally, he has organized 5 seminars and conferences, further demonstrating his commitment to academic and scientific exchange. Throughout his career, Dr. P.Selvakumar has been recognized for his dedication and excellence in teaching, having been honored with several awards, including the Best Teacher Awards. He holds a prominent position in the academic community, contributing actively to research.

Amudha R. is an Associate Professor in School of Management, SASTRA Deemed to Be University, Thanjavur, Tamil Nadu, India. She is a fellow member in Institute of Cost Accountants of India, Kolkata, India and a doctorate in the area of marketing from SASTRA Deemed to Be University. She has 34 years of academic experience and 20 years of research experience. She has published 85 research papers in Scopus indexed journals and more than 30 papers in national and international indexed peer referred journals. She has also published case studies in case center organization, UK and reputed journals. Her area of specialization is marketing, accounting and finance.

Deepak R., is currently Head of the Department of Department & Associate Professor in the Department of Management Studies, at the Ramaiah Institute of Technology. He completed his Ph.D. in Finance from Manipal University. His thesis extended the existing literature on calendar anomalies by considering indices (broad and sectoral) over a longer time frame. The thesis was recognized for the Best Ph.D. Thesis award in a management paper presentation at the Prestige Institute of Management and Research, Indore, on the occasion of the thirteenth best Ph.D. thesis award in management and the Tenth International Conference on Quality Education, Entrepreneurship, and Exemplary Business Practices for Social Change. He obtained his MBA from Marshall University, West Virginia, USA. He was the recipient of the Best Student Award in Academics and Soft Skills in an MBA. He has 16+ years of teaching experience and has published/presented more than 50 papers on investments, behavioral finance, and business analytics at national and international conferences (India and abroad). He conducted more than 40 FDPs and workshops in Business Analytics, Behavioral Finance, Time Series Analytics, Machine Learning using R and Python programming, and data visualization using Excel, R, and Python. He has completed 100 hours of Artificial Intelligence (AI) foundation courses at NASSCOM Future Skills. He is currently recognized as a research guide at VTU and is a guiding research scholar in the area of behavioral finance.

S. Dinesh earned his Ph.D. in Business Administration from Madurai Kamaraj University and currently serves as an Associate Professor in the Sri Ramachandra Faculty of Management Sciences at the Sri Ramachandra Institute of Higher Education and Research. In his role, he oversees the Entrepreneurship Development Cell and Online Programmes. With a rich background of 3 years in the financial services industry and over 14 years in academia, he brings a wealth of experience to his current position. Dr. Dinesh has successfully secured grants totaling 26.31 lakhs from various funding agencies. He is actively involved in organizing diverse training programs aimed at fostering entrepreneurial traits among students and the broader public. Recognition for his work, he received best paper awards from esteemed institutions such as IIM Nagpur, NGI GIs, Universiti Putra, NIED, and RVS IM. His commitment to online education is evident in the development of five comprehensive online courses.

N. Shobhana, is an Assistant Professor at School of Management, SASTRA Deemed To Be University, Thanjavur, Tamilnadu, India. She specialises in Human Resource Management, Operations Research and Entrepreneurship. She has published 19 research papers in indexed journals and book chapters. She also presented papers in national and international conferences.

Index

F

G

I

www.ingramcontent.com/pod-product-compliance
Lightning Source LLC
LaVergne TN
LVHW080346011026
849161LV00009B/2206
* 9 7 9 8 3 6 9 3 7 0 3 1 5 *